murach's
HTML
and CSS

5TH EDITION

Zak Ruvalcaba

Anne Boehm

murach's
HTML
and CSS

5TH EDITION

Zak Ruvalcaba

Anne Boehm

MIKE MURACH & ASSOCIATES, INC.

3730 W Swift Ave. • Fresno, CA 93722

www.murach.com • murachbooks@murach.com

Editorial team

Authors:	Zak Ruvalcaba
	Anne Boehm
Editor:	Mike Murach
Production:	Juliette Baylon

Books on web development

Murach's HTML and CSS

Murach's JavaScript and jQuery

Murach's PHP and MySQL

Murach's ASP.NET Core MVC

Murach's Java Servlets and JSP

Books on programming languages

Murach's Python Programming

Murach's Java Programming

Murach's C#

Murach's C++ Programming

Books on data analysis

Murach's Python for Data Analysis

Books on SQL

Murach's MySQL

Murach's SQL Server for Developers

Murach's Oracle SQL and PL/SQL for Developers

For more on Murach books, please visit us at www.murach.com

10 9 8 7 6 5 4 3 2 1
ISBN: 978-1-943872-86-2

Contents

Expanded contents

Chapter 8   How to use media queries for Responsive Web Design

Section 2   Responsive Web Design

Chapter 9   How to use Flexible Box Layout for Responsive Web Design

Chapter 10   How to use Grid Layout for Responsive Web Design

Section 3   More HTML and CSS skills as you need them

Chapter 11   How to work with images, icons, and fonts

Section 4   Web design, deployment, and JavaScript

Introduction

This 5th edition of our best-selling book integrates all the HTML and CSS skills that a web developer needs today with the proven instructional approach that made the first four editions so popular. And now, this edition simplifies, improves, and enhances the previous edition so it works better than ever.

In short, this is the right book if you're learning HTML and CSS for the first time. But this is also the right book if you're a web developer who wants to expand and update your skills. And after you used this book to learn, it becomes the best on-the-job reference you've ever used.

What this book does

- To get you started right, the first eight chapters present a subset of HTML and CSS that shows you how to develop web pages at a professional level. In chapter 3, you'll learn how to use HTML. In chapters 4 through 6, you'll learn how to use CSS to format the HTML. And in chapter 8, you'll learn how use Responsive Web Design to build web pages that look good and work right on every device: from mobile phone to tablet to desktop computer.

- When you finish the first 8 chapters, you will have the perspective and skills you need for developing professional web pages. Then, you can add to those skills by reading any of the chapters in the next three sections... and you don't have to read those sections or chapters in sequence. In other words, you can skip to any of the chapters in the last three sections after you finish section 1.

- The chapters in section 2 show you how to use two more approaches to Responsive Web Design. Chapter 9 presents Flexible Box Layout, chapter 10 presents Grid Layout, and you can use whichever approach is right for the types of web pages that you're creating.

- The chapters in section 3 let you learn new skills whenever you need them. If, for example, you want to learn how to use the data validation features for forms, you can skip to chapter 13. To learn how to add audio and video to your pages, skip to chapter 14. To learn how to use tables in your web pages, go back to chapter 12. To learn how to add custom fonts to your pages, go to chapter 11. And to learn how to use CSS transitions, transforms, animations, and filters, go to chapter 15.

- The chapters in section 4 present related skills that you can pick up whenever you're ready for them. In chapter 16, you can learn the basic principles for designing a website. In chapter 17, you can learn how to test and deploy a website and get it into the search engines. And in chapter 18, you can see how to use JavaScript and jQuery to enhance your web pages.

Why you'll learn faster and better with this book

Like all our books, this one has features that you won't find in competing books or online tutorials. That's why we believe you'll learn faster and better with our book than with any other. Here are a few of those features.

- From the first page to the last, this book shows you how to use HTML and CSS the modern, professional way, with HTML for the structure and content of each page and CSS for the formatting and page layout. That way, your web pages and your websites will be easier to create and maintain.

- Because HTML and CSS are integrated throughout the book, you won't learn these features out of context, which is the way they're often treated in competing materials. Instead, you'll learn exactly where these features fit into the overall context of website development.

- Because section 1 presents a complete subset of HTML and CSS, you are ready for productive work much sooner than you are when you use competing materials.

- If you page through this book, you'll see that all of the information is presented in "paired pages," with the essential syntax, guidelines, and examples for each topic on the right page and the perspective and extra explanation on the left page. This helps you learn faster by reading less... and this is the ideal format when you need to refresh your memory about how to do something.

- To show you how HTML and CSS work together, this book presents all the code for complete web pages that range from the simple to the complex. To see how that works, just page through chapters 4, 5, 6, and 8 to see the web pages that they present. As we see it, studying complete examples like these is the best way to master HTML and CSS because they show the relationships between the segments of code. And yet, most training materials limit themselves to snippets of code that don't show these relationships.

- Of course, this book also presents dozens of short examples. So it's easy to find an example that shows you how to do whatever you need to do as you develop web pages. And our "paired pages" presentation method makes it much easier to find the example that you're looking for than it is with traditional presentations in which the code is embedded in the text.

What software you need

To develop web pages with HTML and CSS, you can use whichever text editor or IDE that you prefer. If you don't have a favorite, though, this book shows you how to use *Visual Studio Code* (*VS Code*). This text editor is widely popular, not only because it's free, but also because it provides many powerful features that will help you work faster and better. That's why Appendix A shows you how to install VS Code, and chapter 2 shows you how to use it.

Then, to test the web pages that you develop with this book, you should use at least two browsers. One of those should be Chrome, which is why Appendix A shows you how to install it. The other is the browser that comes with your computer: Edge for Windows or Safari for macOS.

 ## How our downloadable files can help you learn

If you go to our website at www.murach.com, you can download all the files that you need for getting the most from this book. These files include:

- the HTML and CSS files for all of the applications and examples in this book
- the HTML and CSS files that you will use as the starting points for the exercises in this book
- the HTML and CSS files for the solutions to the exercises in the book

These files let you test, review, and copy code. In addition, if you have any problems with the exercises, the solutions are there to help you over the learning blocks, which is an essential part of the learning process. Here again, appendix A shows you how to download and install these files.

Support materials for trainers and instructors

If you're a corporate trainer or a college instructor who would like to use this book for a course, we offer supporting materials that include:

- a complete set of PowerPoint slides that you can use to review and reinforce the content of the book
- instructional objectives that describe the skills a student should have upon completion of each chapter
- test banks that measure mastery of those skills
- guided case studies that provide more exercises for your students (without the solutions)
- projects that your students both design and develop

[handwritten margin note: use Chrome and Edge to test webpages]

If you're a college instructor and want to learn more about the instructor's materials, please go to our website at www.murachforinstructors.com. Or, if you're a trainer, go to www.murach.com and click on the Courseware for Trainers link. Another alternative is to call Kelly at 1-800-221-5528 or send an email to kelly@murach.com.

Please let us know how this book works for you

At long last, HTML and CSS have come of age, so there are no significant content additions in this edition of the book. Besides that, all modern browsers support all of the HTML and CSS features, so browser compatibility is no longer an issue that needs to be addressed.

That left us free to focus on simplifying and improving our figures and text so you can learn faster and better than ever from our book. And when you're through learning the HTML and CSS skills from this book, we want it to become the best on-the-job reference that you've ever used.

Now, we hope we've succeeded. We thank you for buying this book. We wish you all the best with your web development. And if you have any comments, we would appreciate hearing from you.

Zak Ruvalcaba
Author and content expert

Anne Boehm, Author
anne@murach.com

Section 1

The essential concepts and skills

The eight chapters in this section present the essential concepts and skills that you need for using HTML and CSS. These are the skills that you will use for almost every web page that you develop. And this is the minimum set of skills that every web developer should have.

When you complete this section, you'll be able to develop web pages at a professional level. Then, you can take your skills to the next level by reading the other sections and chapters in this book.

But please note that you don't have to read the chapters in the other sections in sequence. Instead, you can skip to any chapter that presents the skills that you want to learn next. In other words, the eight chapters in this section present the prerequisites for all of the other chapters in this book.

Chapter 1

Introduction to web development

This chapter introduces you to the concepts and terms that you need for working with HTML and CSS. When you finish this chapter, you'll have the background you need for learning how to build websites.

How web applications work

The *World Wide Web*, or web, consists of many components that work together to bring a web page to your desktop over the *Internet*. Before you start web pages of your own, you should have a basic understanding of how these components work together.

The components of a web application

The first diagram in figure 1-1 shows that web applications consist of *clients* and a *web server*. The clients are the computers, tablets, and mobile devices that use the web applications. They access the web pages through programs known as *web browsers*, such as Chrome, Edge, and Safari. The web server holds the files that make up a web application.

A *network* is a system that allows clients and servers to communicate. The Internet in turn is a large network that consists of many smaller networks. In a diagram like this, the "cloud" represents the network or Internet that connects the clients and servers.

In general, you don't need to know how the cloud works. But you should have a general idea of what's going on. That's why the second diagram in this figure gives you a conceptual view of the architecture of the Internet.

To start, networks can be categorized by size. A *local area network* (*LAN*) is a small network of computers that are near each other and can communicate with each other over short distances. Computers on a LAN are typically in the same building or in adjacent buildings. This type of network is often called an *intranet*, and it can be used to run web applications for use by employees only.

By contrast, a *wide area network* (*WAN*) consists of multiple LANs that have been connected together over long distances using *routers*. To pass information from one client to another, a router determines which network is closest to the destination and sends the information over that network. A WAN can be owned privately by one company or it can be shared by multiple companies.

An *Internet service provider* (*ISP*) is a company that owns a WAN that is connected to the Internet. An ISP leases access to its network to other companies that need to be connected to the Internet.

The Internet is a global network consisting of multiple WANs that have been connected together. ISPs connect their WANs at large routers called *Internet exchange points* (*IXP*). This allows anyone connected to the Internet to exchange information with anyone else.

If you study the diagram in this figure, you can get a better idea of how data is sent from the client in the top left to the server in the bottom right. First, the data leaves the client's LAN and enters the WAN owned by the client's ISP. Next, the data is routed through IXPs to the WAN owned by the server's ISP. Then, it enters the server's LAN and finally reaches the server. All of this can happen in less than $1/10^{th}$ of a second.

The components of a web application

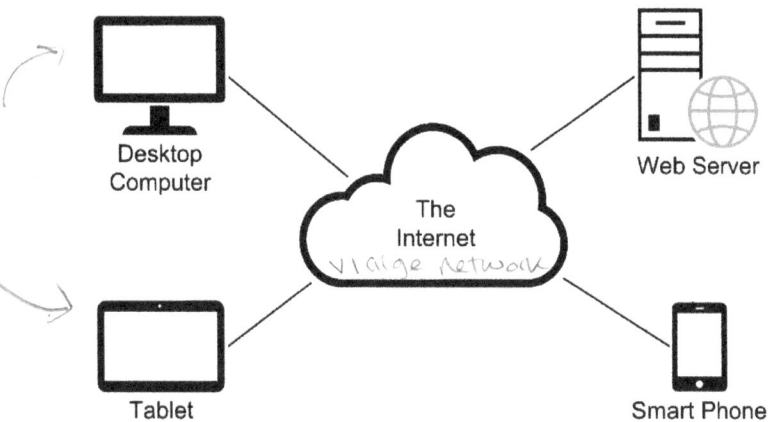

[Handwritten notes: clients]

[Handwritten notes:]
LAN: local area network
(lan intranet)

WAN: wide area network
= mult. LANs connected
thru routers

(large routers)
IXP: internet exchange
points

[Handwritten note on Internet cloud: V large network]

The architecture of the Internet

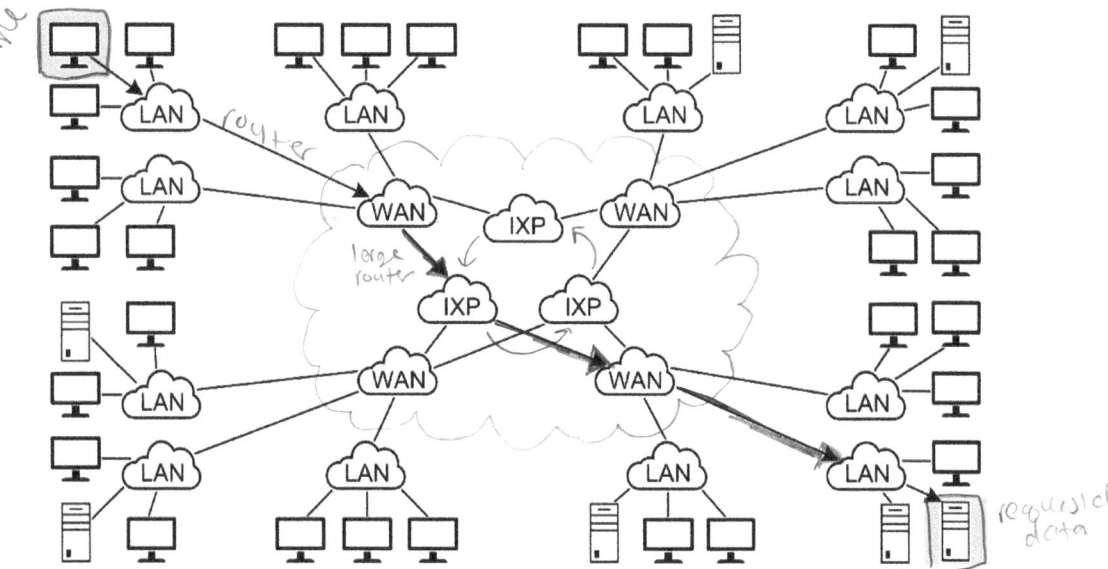

[Handwritten notes: me, router, large router, requested data]

Description

- A web application consists of clients, a web server, and a network. The *clients* use programs known as *web browsers* to request web pages from the web server. The *web server* returns the pages that are requested to the browser. *[Handwritten note: very polite process]*

- A *local area network* (LAN) directly connects computers that are near each other. This kind of network is often called an *intranet*.

- A *wide area network* (WAN) consists of two or more LANs that are connected by *routers*. The routers route information from one network to another.

- The *Internet* consists of many WANs that have been connected at *Internet exchange points* (IXPs). There are hundreds of IXPs located throughout the world.

- An *Internet service provider* (ISP) owns a WAN and leases access to its network. It connects its WAN to the rest of the Internet at one or more IXPs.

Figure 1-1   The components of a web application

How static web pages are processed

A *static web page* like the one at the top of figure 1-2 is a web page that is sent directly from the web server to the web browser when the browser requests it. This process begins when a client requests a web page using a web browser. To do that, the user can either type the address of the page into the browser's address bar or click a link in the current page that specifies the next page to load.

In either case, the web browser builds a request for the web page and sends it to the web server. This request, known as an *HTTP request*, is formatted using the *hypertext transfer protocol* (HTTP), which lets the web server know which file is being requested.

When the web server receives the HTTP request, it retrieves the requested file from the disk drive. This file contains the *HTML (HyperText Markup Language)* for the requested page. Then, the web server sends the file back to the browser as part of an *HTTP response*.

When the browser receives the HTTP response, it *renders* (translates) the HTML into a web page that is displayed in the browser. Then, the user can view the content. If the user requests another page, either by clicking a link or typing another web address into the browser's address bar, the process begins again.

HTTP: hypertext transfer protocol; request nd response

* HTML: hypertext markup language, used to define webpages

A static web page at newtonforkranch.com/attractions.html

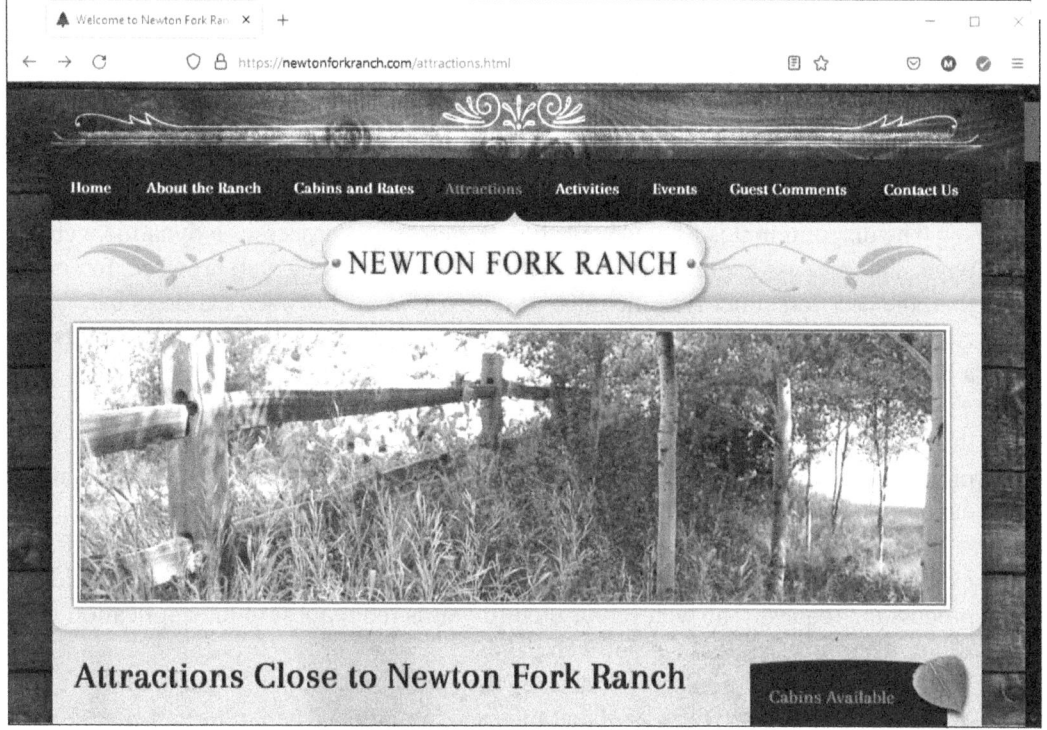

How a web server processes a static web page

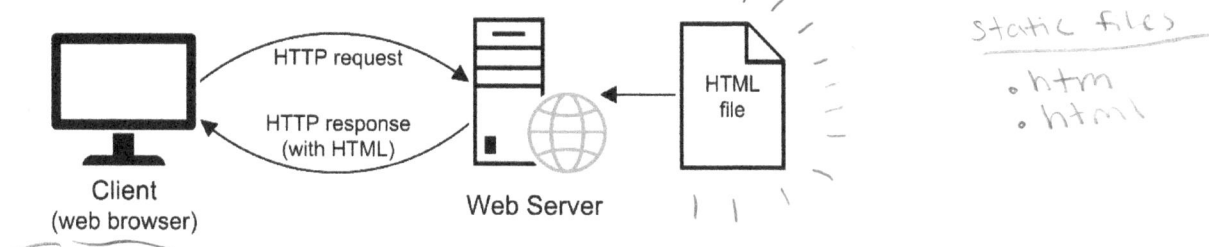

static files

. htm
. html

Description

- *Hypertext Markup Language* (*HTML*) is used to define web pages.

- A *static web page* is an HTML document that's stored on the web server and doesn't change. The filenames for static web pages have .htm or .html extensions.

- When the user requests a static web page, the *web browser* sends an *HTTP request* to the web server that includes the name of the file that's being requested.

- When the web server receives the request, it retrieves the HTML for the web page and sends it back to the browser as part of an *HTTP response*.

- When the browser receives the HTTP response, it *renders* the HTML into a web page that is displayed in the browser.

Figure 1-2   How static web pages are processed

How dynamic web pages are processed

A *dynamic web page* like the one in figure 1-3 is a page that's created by a program called a *script* that runs on the web server each time it is requested. This script is executed by an *application server* based on the data that's sent with the HTTP request. In this example, the HTTP request identifies the book that's shown. Then, the script for the requested page retrieves the image and data for that book from a *database server*.

The diagram in this figure shows how a web server processes a dynamic web page. This process begins when the user requests a page in a web browser. To do that, the user can either type the URL of the page in the browser's address bar, click a link that specifies the dynamic page to load, or click a button that submits a form that contains the data that the dynamic page should process.

In each case, the web browser builds an HTTP request and sends it to the web server. This request includes whatever data the application needs for processing the request. If, for example, the user has entered data into a form, that data will be included in the HTTP request.

When the web server receives the HTTP request, the server examines the file extension of the requested web page to identify the application server that should process the request. The web server then forwards the request to the application server that processes that type of web page.

Next, the application server retrieves the appropriate script from the hard drive. It also loads any form data that the user submitted. Then, it executes the script. As the script executes, it generates the HTML for the web page. If necessary, the script will request data from a database server and use that data as part of the web page it is generating.

When the script is finished, the application server sends the dynamically generated HTML back to the web server. Then, the web server sends the HTML back to the browser in an HTTP response.

When the web browser receives the HTTP response, it renders the HTML and displays the web page. Note, however, that the web browser has no way to tell whether the HTML in the HTTP response was for a static page or a dynamic page. It just renders the HTML.

When the page is displayed, the user can view the content. Then, when the user requests another page, the process begins again. The process that begins with the user requesting a web page and ends with the server sending a response back to the client is called a *round trip*.

Dynamic web pages let you create interactive *web applications* that do all of the types of processing that you find on the Internet, including eCommerce applications. Although you won't learn how to develop dynamic web pages in this book, you will learn how to create the HTML forms that send user data to the web server. Then, after you master HTML, you can learn how to use server-side technologies like ASP.NET or PHP to create the dynamic pages that a website needs.

A dynamic web page at amazon.com

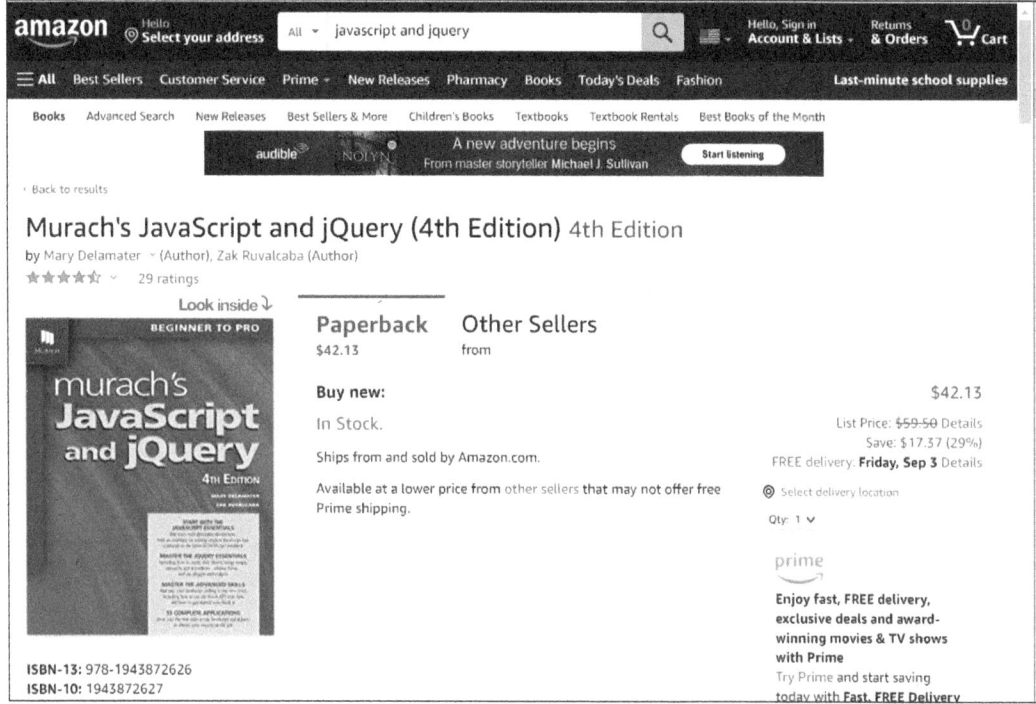

How a web server processes a dynamic web page

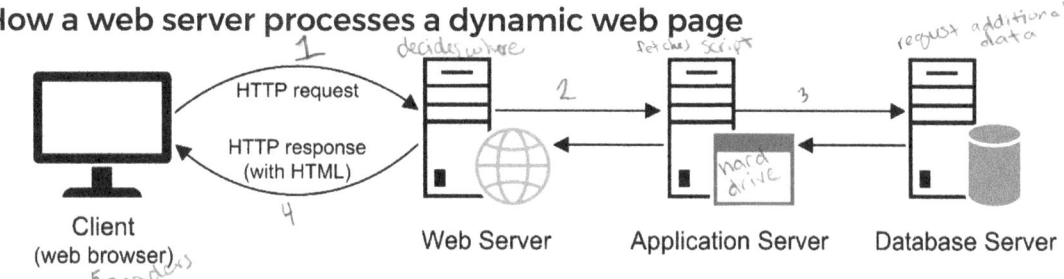

Description

- A *dynamic web page* is a web page that's generated by a program on the server that's called a *script*.

- When a web server receives a request for a dynamic web page, it looks up the extension of the requested file to find out which *application server* should process the request.

- When the application server receives a request, it runs the specified script. Often, this script uses the data that it gets from the web browser to get the appropriate data from a *database server*. This script can also store the data that it receives in the database.

- When the application server finishes processing the data, it generates the HTML for a web page and returns it to the web server. Then, the web server returns the HTML to the web browser as part of an HTTP response.

Figure 1-3   How dynamic web pages are processed

How JavaScript fits into web development

In contrast to the server-side processing that's done for dynamic web pages, *JavaScript* is a scripting language that provides for *client-side processing.* In the website in figure 1-4, for example, JavaScript is used to change the images that are shown without using server-side processing.

To make this work, all of the required images are loaded into the browser when the page is requested. Then, if the user clicks on one of the color swatches below a shirt, the shirt image is changed to the one with the right color. This is called an *image swap*. Similarly, if the user moves the mouse over a shirt, the image is replaced by the back view of the shirt. This is called an *image rollover*.

The diagram in this figure shows how JavaScript processing works. When a browser requests a web page, both the HTML and the related JavaScript are returned to the browser by the web server. Then, the JavaScript code is executed in the web browser by the browser's *JavaScript engine*. This takes some of the processing burden off the server and makes the application run faster. Often, JavaScript is used in conjunction with dynamic web pages, but it can also be used with static web pages.

Besides image swaps and rollovers, there are many other uses for JavaScript. For instance, another common use is to validate the data that the user enters into an HTML form before it is sent to the server for processing. This saves unnecessary trips to the server. Other common uses of JavaScript are to provide for carousels and accordions.

In this book, you won't learn how to code JavaScript. However, you will learn how to use existing JavaScript routines in chapter 18 of this book. There, you'll learn how to use JavaScript and a JavaScript library known as jQuery to enhance your web pages with features like image swaps, image rollovers, and data validation.

A web page with image swaps and rollovers

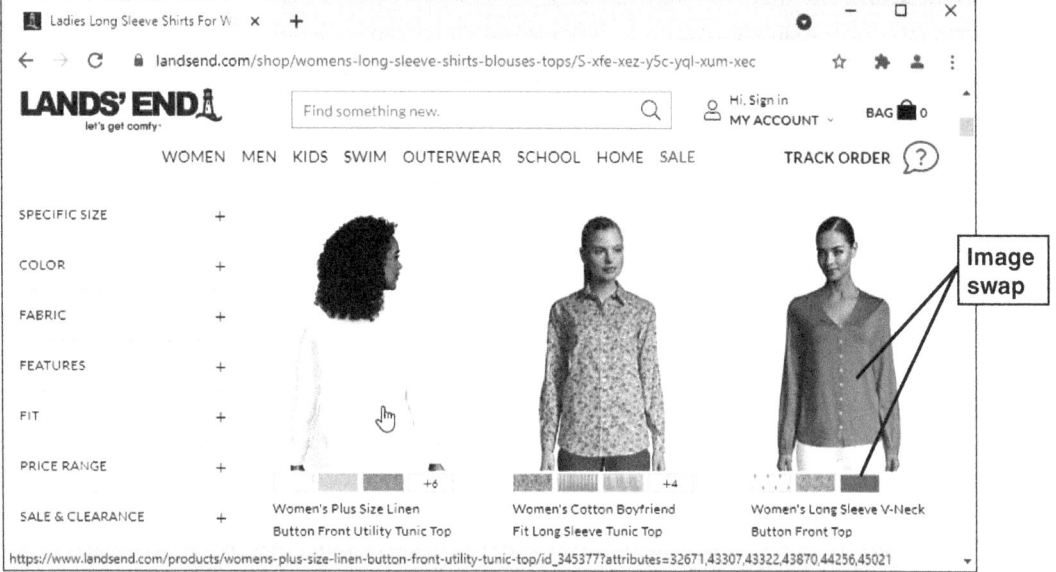

How JavaScript fits into this architecture

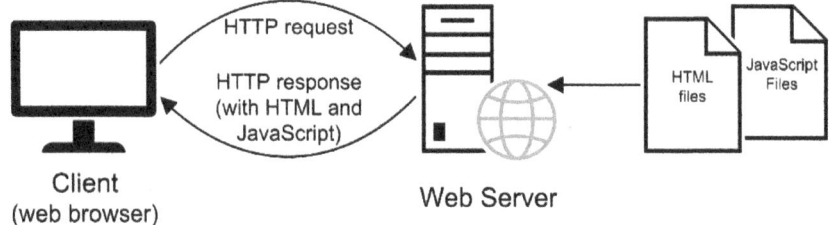

Some common uses of JavaScript

- Data validation
- Image swaps and rollovers
- Carousels and accordions
- Slide shows

Description

- *JavaScript* is a *client-side scripting language* that is run by the *JavaScript engine* of a web browser.
- When the browser requests an HTML page that contains JavaScript or a link to a JavaScript file, both the HTML and the JavaScript are loaded into the browser.
- Because JavaScript runs on the client, not the server, it provides functions that don't require a trip back to the server. This can help an application run more efficiently.

Figure 1-4 How JavaScript fits into web development

An introduction to HTML and CSS

To develop a web page, you use HTML to define the content and structure of the page. Then, you use CSS to format that content. The topics that follow introduce you to HTML and CSS.

The HTML for a web page

HyperText Markup Language (*HTML*) is used to define the content and structure of a web page. In figure 1-5, for example, you can see the HTML for a simple web page, which can be called an *HTML document*. As you've already learned, this HTML is sent from a web server to a web browser running on a client. Then, the browser renders the HTML into a web page that's displayed in the browser.

Although you're going to learn how to code HTML in chapter 3, here's a quick introduction to how the HTML works. This document starts with a *DOCTYPE declaration* that is followed by *tags* that identify the *HTML elements* within the document. The *opening tag* for each element consists of the element name surrounded by angle brackets, as in <html> And the *closing tag* consists of a left angle bracket, a forward slash, the element name, and the right angle bracket, as in </html>.

The basic structure of an HTML document consists of head and body elements that are coded within the html element. The head section contains elements that provide information about the document. The body section contains the elements that will be displayed in the web browser. For instance, the title element in the head section provides the title that's shown in the tab for the page in the web browser, while the h1 element in the body section provides the heading that's displayed in the browser window.

Many elements can be coded with *attributes* that identify the element and define the way the content in the element is displayed. These attributes are coded within the opening tag, and each attribute consists of an attribute name, an equals sign, and the attribute value. For instance, the <img> tag in this example has two attributes named src and alt. In this case, the src attribute provides the name of the image file that should be displayed, and the alt attribute provides the text that should be displayed if the image can't be found.

The code for an HTML file named javascript_jquery.html

```
<!doctype html>        DOCTYPE declaration
<html lang="en">
  <head>          < tags>            browser title
    <meta charset="utf-8">              ↓
    <title>JavaScript and jQuery book</title>
  </head>                              page title
  <body> opening tag <----->             ↓
    <h1>JavaScript and jQuery (4th Edition)</h1>
    <img src="javascript_jquery.jpg" alt="JavaScript and jQuery Book">
    <p>Today, JavaScript is used on most of the pages of a modern
       website, from small individual sites to the largest commercial
       sites. And wherever JavaScript is used, you'll also find jQuery.
       That's why every web developer should know how to use JavaScript
       for what it does best and jQuery for what it does best.</p>
    <p>Now, this one book will help you master all of the JavaScript and
       jQuery skills that every web developer should have. To find out
       how, <a href="">read more...</a></p>
  </body>  closing tag </---->
</html>
```

Handwritten annotations: Head: information about the document; Body: elements to display in browser; src= alt=)attributes; HTML elements

The HTML displayed in a web browser

Description

- *HTML (HyperText Markup Language)* is used to define the structure and content of a web page.

Figure 1-5   The HTML for a web page

The CSS for a web page

To format the contents of a web page, you use *CSS* (*Cascading Style Sheets*). To do that, you can apply a CSS *style sheet* to an HTML document by a link element in the head section, as shown at the top of figure 1-6. Here, the href attribute of the tag says that the style sheet in the file named book.css should be applied to the HTML document.

After this link element, you can see the CSS that's in the book.css file. This is followed by a browser that shows how the web page is displayed after the style sheet has been applied to it. If you compare this to the browser in the previous figure, you can see that the page is now centered with a border around it, the font for the text has been changed, there's less spacing between paragraphs, and the text is displayed to the right of the book image. This gives you a quick idea of how much you can do with CSS.

Although you're going to learn how to code CSS in chapters 4, 5, and 6, here's a brief introduction to how the CSS works. First, this CSS file consists of four *style rules*. Each of these style rules consists of a *selector* and one or more *declarations* enclosed in braces { }. The selector identifies one or more HTML elements, and the declarations specify the formatting for the elements.

For instance, the first style rule applies to the body element. Its first declaration says that the font family for the content should be Arial, Helvetica, or the default sans-serif type, in that order of preference. Then, the second declaration says that the font-size should be 100% of the browser's default font size. These declarations set the base font and font size for the elements that are coded within the body.

The third declaration for the body sets its width to 560 pixels. Then, the fourth declaration sets the top and bottom margins to zero and the left and right margins to auto, which centers the page in the browser window. Finally, the fifth declaration sets the padding within the body to 1 em (a unit that you'll learn about in chapter 4), and the sixth declaration adds a solid, navy border to the body.

Similarly, the second style rule formats the h1 element in the HTML with a larger font size and the navy color. The third style rule formats the image by floating it to the left so the <p> elements are displayed to its right. And the fourth style rule changes the spacing between <p> elements.

This should give you an idea of how HTML and CSS work together. In short, the HTML defines the content and structure of the document, and the CSS defines the formatting of the content. This separates the content from the formatting, which makes it easier to create and maintain web pages.

(handwritten: +link element)

The element in the head section of the HTML file that links it to the CSS file

```
<link rel="stylesheet" href="book.css">
```
(handwritten: filename)

(handwritten: How to apply a CSS style sheet)

The code for the CSS file named book.css

```
body {
    font-family: Arial, Helvetica, sans-serif;
    font-size: 100%;
    width: 560px;
    margin: 0 auto;
    padding: 1em;
    border: 1px solid navy;
}
h1 {
    margin: 0;
    padding: .25em;
    font-size: 200%;
    color: navy;
}
img {
    float: left;
    margin: 0 1em 1em 1em;
}
p {
    margin: 0;
    padding-bottom: .5em;
}
```

(handwritten annotations: "preference order"; "margin : ___ auto (auto = centered)"; "top bottom LR"; "page title element"; "declarations (specify format) {enclosed}"; "selector (identifies html element)"; " Style rules consist of selector declarations"; circled: <link>, h1, img; asterisks next to body, h1, img, p)*

The web page displayed in a web browser

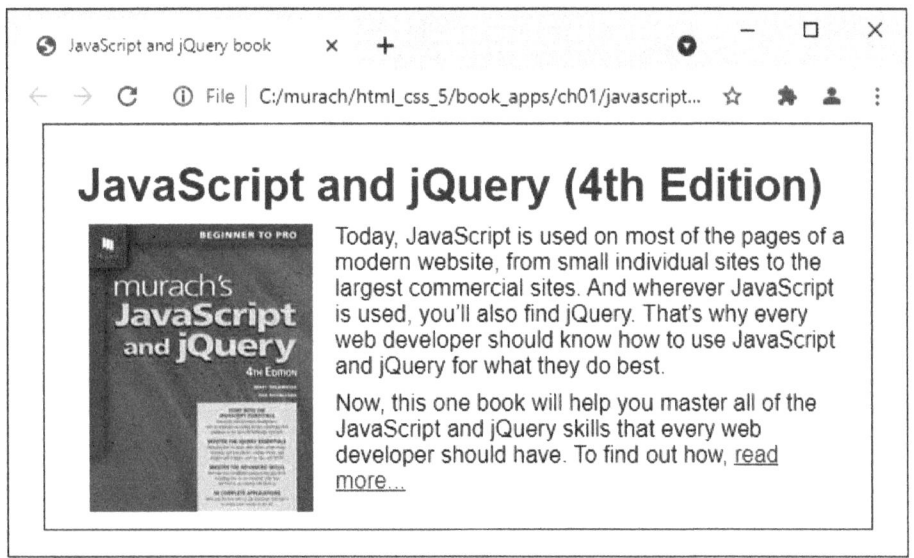

Description

- *Cascading Style Sheets* (*CSS*) are used to control how web pages are displayed by specifying the fonts, colors, borders, spacing, and layout of the pages.

Figure 1-6   The CSS for a web page

A short history of the HTML and CSS standards

In case you're interested, figure 1-7 presents a short history of the HTML and CSS standards. As you can see, HTML standards have been around since 1995, but they didn't get stabilized until version 5, which was adopted in 2014. This version is commonly referred to as HTML5.

Similarly, CSS standards have been around since 1996, but they didn't get stabilized until version 3 and that version didn't get widespread use until 2010 or later. This version is commonly referred to as CSS3.

In recent years, new features were added to HTML5 and CSS3, but without new release numbers. As a result, there's no longer any reason to include the version numbers when referring to them. So, from this point on, this book refers to HTML5 and CSS3 code as just HTML and CSS, unless there is a reason to refer to the version number.

This figure also presents two websites that you ought to become familiar with. The first is for the *World Wide Web Consortium*, which is commonly referred to as *W3C*. Until May of 2019, this was the group that developed the standards, and this site is a primary source for HTML and CSS information.

The second website is for the *Web Hypertext Application Technology Working Group* (*WHATWG*). This is a community of people interested in evolving HTML and related technologies, and this site is another primary source for HTML and CSS information. In May 2019, this group took over the development of the HTML standards, although the W3C continues to participate in the development process.

Highlights in the development of the HTML standards

Version	Description
HTML 1.0 to 4.01	HTML 2.0 was the first specification adopted as a standard by the W3C in November 1995. HTML 4.0 and 4.01 added new features and deprecated older features.
XHTML 1.0 to 1.1	XHTML 1.0 was adopted in January 2000 and reformulated HTML 4 using the syntax of XML. With XHTML 1.1, the control of the presentation of content was now done through CSS.
HTML 5 to 5.2	HTML 5 was adopted in October 2014 and replaced the current versions of both HTML and XHTML. HTML 5.1 and 5.2 were minor revisions of these standards.
HTML Living Standard	The WHATWG started developing these standards as a split from the W3C in July of 2012. In May 2019, the W3C ceded authority over the HTML standards to WHATWG.

HTML5: 2014
CSS3: 2010

Highlights in the development of the CSS standards

Version	Description
1.0	Adopted in December 1996.
2.0	Adopted in May 1998.
2.1	First released as a candidate standard in February 2004, it returned to working draft status in June 2005. It became a candidate standard again in July 2007.
3.0	A modularized version of CSS with the earliest drafts in June 1999. Some modules build on existing features of CSS 2.1, and others provide entirely new features. Each module is accepted as a standard independently.

Two websites that you should become familiar with

- The *World Wide* _____ _____ _____ nunity in which member organiz _____ _____ her to help develop Web sta _____

- The *Web Hypert* _____ *ITWG*) is a community of pe _____ chnologies, and it currently mainta _____ ttps://html.spec. whatwg.org.

Description

- The W3C ceded _____ TWG in May 2019 after determinin _____ er, the W3C still participates in the development process.

- Unlike the W3C standards, the WHATWG Living Standard is continually evolving. Because of that, it doesn't use version numbers. Today, all modern browsers support the Living Standard.

- The last version numbers for HTML and CSS were HTML5 and CSS3, but you don't need to specify the version numbers any more. As a result, they aren't used in the rest of this book.

Figure 1-7   A short history of the HTML and CSS standards

Tools for web development

To create and edit the HTML and CSS files for a website, you need either a text editor or an IDE for web development. To deploy a website on the Internet, you also need an FTP client that lets you upload files from your computer or network server to the web server. You'll learn about these tools next.

Text editors and IDEs

A *text editor* lets you enter and edit HTML and CSS, and figure 1-8 lists four of them. Of these, we recommend that you use *Visual Studio Code* (or just *VS Code*). It is a free editor that runs on both Windows and macOS systems; it has many excellent features; and it will help you work faster and better.

In this figure, for example, you can see how VS Code provides an auto-completion list that lets you select an item after you enter the first character or two. To help you get started with VS Code, appendix A shows how to install it, and chapter 2 presents a short tutorial on how to use it.

The alternative to a text editor is an *Integrated Development Environment* (*IDE*) for web development. As this figure shows, two of the most popular IDEs for web development are Adobe Dreamweaver and AWS (Amazon Web Services) Cloud9. As you would expect, an IDE provides all the features of a text editor plus other features like a built-in FTP client, which you'll learn about in the next figure.

VSCode with the auto-completion feature in progress

Four of the text editors that you can use for web development

Editor	Runs on
VS Code	Window, macOS, and Linuxs
Notepad++	Windows
TextMate	macOS
Codepen	The Web

Two of the IDEs for web development

integrated development environment

IDE	Runs on
Adobe Dreamweaver	Windows and macOS
AWS Cloud9	The Web

Description

- A *text editor* lets you enter and edit the HTML and CSS files for a web application. Some common features of a text editor are syntax highlighting and auto-completion.

- An *Integrated Development Environment* (*IDE*) goes beyond text editing to provide other features for the development of websites, like a built-in FTP program (see the next figure).

Figure 1-8   Text editors and IDEs for web development

FTP clients

If you want to *deploy* (or *publish*) your website on the Internet, you need to transfer the folders and files for your website from your computer or network to a web server with Internet access. One way to do that is to use an *FTP client* that uses *File Transfer Protocol* (or *FTP*) to transfer the folders and files. Figure 1-9, for example, shows an FTP client named FileZilla as it uploads files to a web server.

Note, however, that FileZilla is just one of many FTP clients that you can use for uploading files. Remember too that IDEs like Dreamweaver have built-in FTP clients.

deploying website

FileZilla as it is used to upload files to the web server

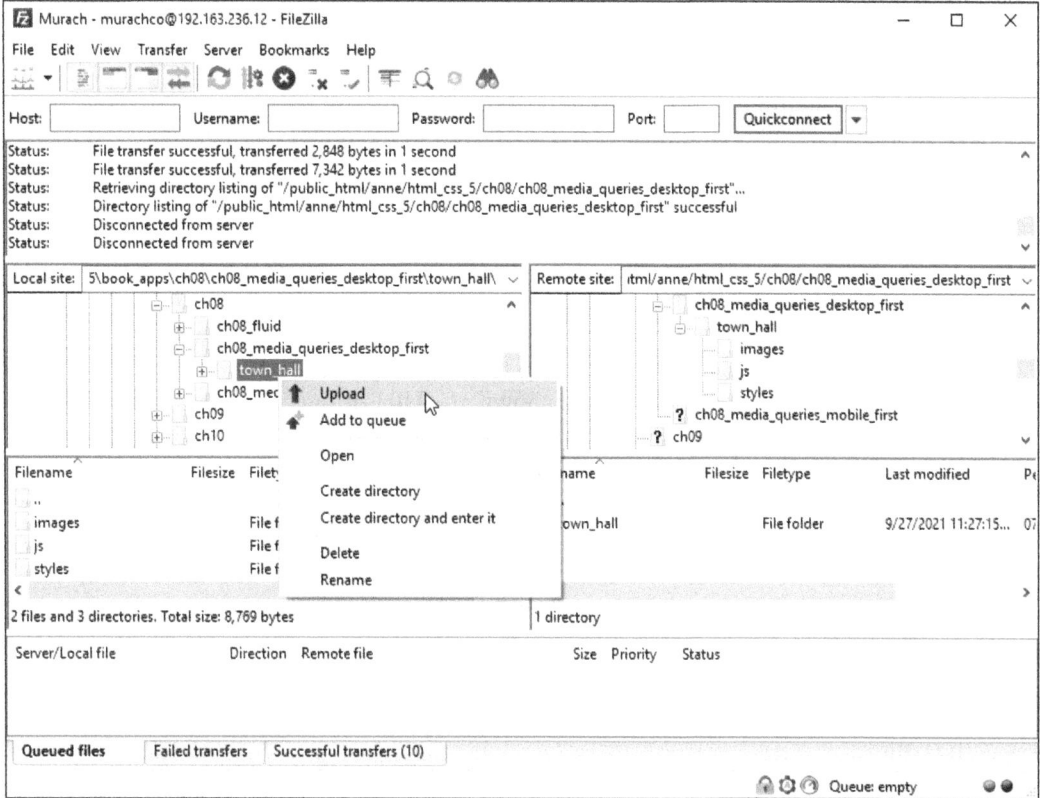

Some free FTP clients

Program	Runs on
FileZilla	Windows, macOS, and Linux
FireFTP	Windows, macOS, and Linux
Classic FTP	Windows and macOS

FTP: File transfer protocol

Description

- To *deploy* (or *publish*) a website on the Internet, you can use *File Transfer Protocol* (or *FTP*) to transfer the folders and files for the website from your computer or local network to a web server on the Internet. To do that, you can use an *FTP client*.

- If you're using a text editor, you typically have to use a separate FTP client or add a plugin FTP client to your editor. In contrast, most IDEs have built-in FTP clients.

Figure 1-9   FTP clients for uploading files to the web server

How to view a web page and its source code

Next, you'll learn how to view a web page in a web browser and how to view the source code for a web page that's displayed in the browser. These are valuable skills that you can use when you test your own web pages or study the web pages on other sites.

How to view a web page

Figure 1-10 shows you how to view a web page on the Internet by entering a a *uniform resource locator* (*URL*) into the address bar of your browser. As the diagram at the start of this figure shows, the URL for an Internet page can include four components. In most cases, the *protocol* is HTTP. But if you omit the protocol, the browser uses HTTP as the default.

The second component is the *domain name* that identifies the web server that the HTTP request will be sent to. The web browser uses this name to look up the address of the web server for the domain. Although you can't omit the domain name, you can usually omit the www and the dot that precede it.

The third component is the *path* that lists the folders on the server that contain the file. Forward slashes are used to separate the names in the path and to represent the server's top-level folder at the start of the path. In this example, the path is:

```
/courseware-for-trainers/what-our-courseware-includes
```

The last component is the name of the file. But if you omit the filename, as in this example, the web server will search for a default document in the path. Depending on the web server, this file will be named index.html, default.htm, or some variation of the two.

If you want to view an HTML page that's on your own computer or a local network, you can use one of the two techniques that are presented next. First, your text editor or IDE should provide a way that makes it easy to view a page that you're working on. Second, you can find the file in your file explorer, and then double-click on it to open it in your default browser. Or, you can right-click on it and select the browser that you want to open it with.

At the bottom of this figure, you can see our naming recommendations for your folders and files. In general, your folder and file names should only contain lowercase letters, numbers, underscores or hyphens, and the period. In the examples in this book, you'll see the author's preference, which is to use underscores instead of hyphens to separate the words in a name. But many developers use hyphens instead of underscores.

The other recommendation is to create names that clearly indicate the contents of your folders and web pages. That can improve search engine optimization (SEO), which you'll learn more about in a moment.

The components of an HTTP URL

```
protocol://domain-name/path/filename
```

A URL with an omitted filename

http://www.murach.com/courseware-for-trainers/what-our-courseware-includes

The web page at that URL

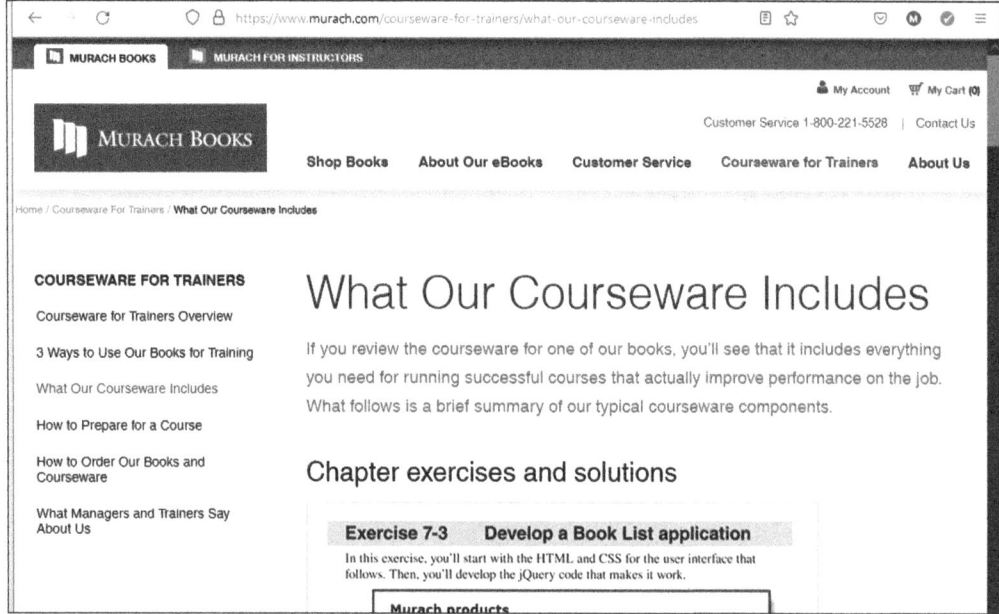

What happens if you omit parts of a URL

- If you omit the protocol, the default of http will be used.
- If you omit the filename, the default document name for the web server will be used. This is typically index.html, default.htm, or some variation.

How to access a web page on the Internet

- Enter the URL of a web page into the browser's address bar.

How to access a web page on your own server or computer

- Use the features of your text editor or IDE.
- Find the file in your file explorer. Then, double-click on it to open it in your default browser. Or, right-click on it and use the Open With command to select the browser.

Naming recommendations for your own folders and files

- Create names for folders and files that consist of lowercase letters, numbers, underscores or hyphens, and the period.
- Use filenames that clearly indicate what a page contains. This is good for search engine optimization (see figure 1-15).

Figure 1-10   How to view a web page

How to view the source code for a web page

When a web page is displayed by a browser, you can use the first technique in figure 1-11 to view the HTML for the page. You just right-click on the page and select View Page Source. Then, if you want to view the CSS for the page, you can click on the CSS file or files that the HTML page is linked to. Or, if the CSS is coded in the head element of the HTML file, you can see it there.

In this example, the source code for the web page in figure 1-6 is displayed in a new tab that was opened for it. At this point, you can click on the book.css link to open the CSS file in another new tab.

In some cases, viewing the source code can be useful when you're testing and debugging a web page. At the least, it lets you confirm that the browser is running the HTML and CSS that you've coded in your text editor or IDE. Sometimes, this helps you discover problems that you wouldn't have imagined. This is especially true when you're debugging dynamic web pages that were generated by a script.

You may also want to view the source code for the pages on other Internet sites so you can study it. That can be a good way to learn how other sites work. Although some sites use various techniques to hide their code, a lot of the code for Internet sites is available. But beware, the code for all but the simplest of sites can get complicated in a hurry. That's partly because the code is generated by a content management system.

The source code for the web page in figure 1-6

```
 1  <!doctype html>
 2  <html lang="en">
 3      <head>
 4          <meta charset="utf-8">
 5          <title>JavaScript and jQuery book</title>
 6          <link rel="stylesheet" href="book.css">
 7      </head>                                              ← to view CSS
 8      <body>
 9          <h1>JavaScript and jQuery (4th Edition)</h1>
10          <img src="javascript_jquery.jpg" alt="JavaScript and jQuery Book">
11          <p>Today, JavaScript is used on most of the pages of a modern
12              website, from small individual sites to the largest commercial
13              sites. And wherever JavaScript is used, you'll also find jQuery.
14              That's why every web developer should know how to use JavaScript
15              and jQuery for what they do best. </p>
16          <p>Now, this one book will help you master all of the JavaScript and
17              jQuery skills that every web developer should have. To find out
18              how, <a href="">read more...</a></p>
19      </body>
20  </html>
21
```

How to view the HTML for a web page

- Right-click the page and select View Page Source from the popup menu.

How to view the CSS if it's in an external CSS file

- Click on the link that refers to the CSS file.

How to view the CSS if it's in the HTML file

- You'll find it in the head element of the file.

Description

- When you're debugging your own web pages, it is sometimes useful to view the HTML and CSS for a page that's being displayed in a browser. At the least, this can confirm that the browser is displaying the page that you think it's displaying.

- This also provides a way to see how other websites are coded. In general, though, the code for large, commercial websites is extremely complicated. That's often because it's generated by a content management system like Joomla.

Figure 1-11   How to view the source code for a web page

Four critical web development issues

Whenever you develop a web application, you should be aware of the issues that are presented in the next four figures. Then, as you progress through this book, you will learn how to provide for each of them.

Responsive Web Design   RWD

Responsive Web Design, or *RWD*, just means that a website should work on all devices that access it: from desktop computers to tablets to mobile phones in landscape mode, to mobile phones in portrait mode. The statistics in figure 1-12 help explain why that's important, and you can find many other statistics along the same lines. But the need for RWD is so obvious that it shouldn't need statistical support.

This figure illustrates how a site that uses RWD adapts to the size and orientation of the screen. Here, you can see the home page of the Lands' End website in a desktop browser and also on a mobile phone in portrait mode. This shows that the look-and-feel of the page remains the same in both screen sizes. And that's the beauty of Responsive Web Design!

Because RWD is such an important subject, this book has three chapters that show you how to implement it. In chapter 8, you'll learn the essential concepts and skills. Then, chapter 9 shows you how to use Flexible Box Layout to implement RWD, and chapter 10 shows you how to use Grid Layout to implement it.

The Lands' End home page
on a desktop computer and a mobile phone

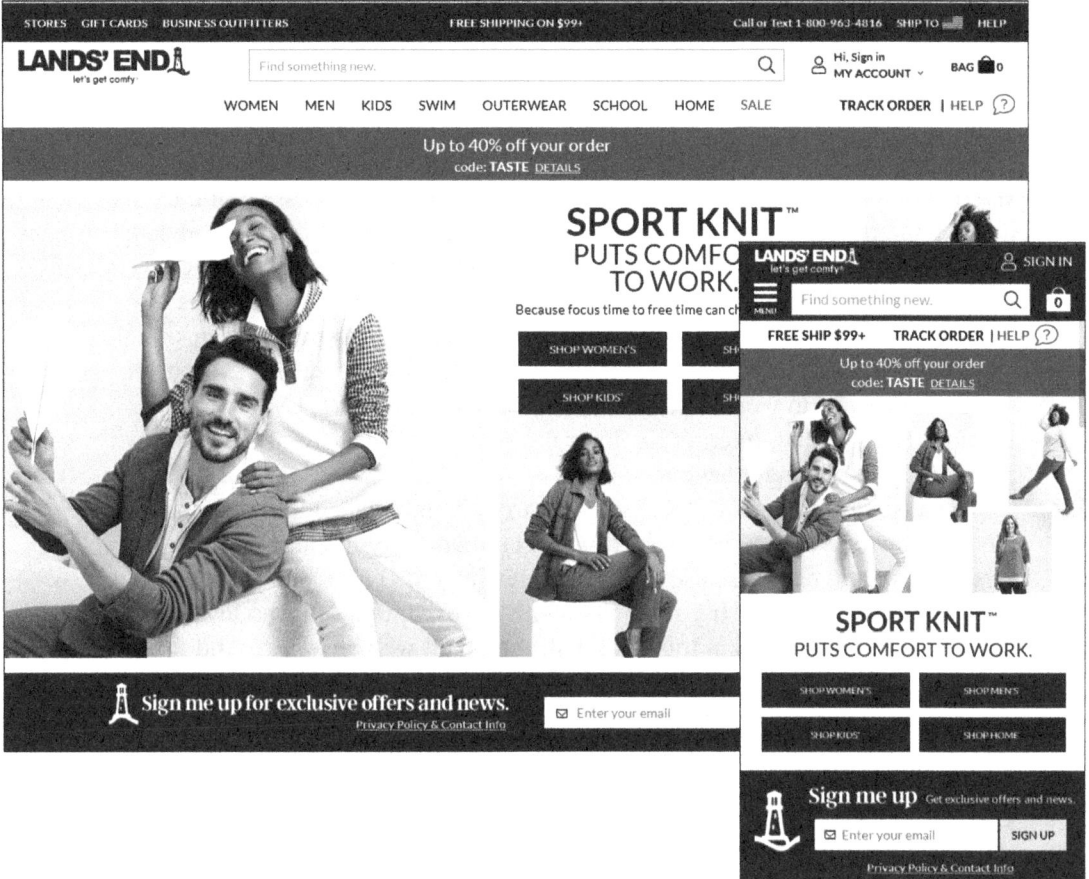

Four of the many statistics that prove the need
for Responsive Web Design

- In a global survey of 87,000 users, 95% used mobile phones to access the Internet, 93% used desktops, and 73% used tablets.
- 57% of all web traffic comes from mobile devices.
- 50% of all web shoppers in the United States buy from mobile devices.
- 40% of the mobile users will go to a different site if the first one isn't mobile friendly.

Description

- *Responsive Web Design* means that a website should adapt to the screen size of the device that's accessing it, whether it's a desktop computer, a tablet, or a mobile phone.

Figure 1-12   Responsive Web Design

Cross-browser compatibility

If you want your website to be used by as many visitors as possible, you need to make sure that your web pages are compatible with all the browsers that people may use to access your website. That's known as *cross-browser compatibility*.

Although this was a big issue just a few years back, modern browsers support almost all of the features that are provided by the latest versions of HTML and CSS. This is indicated by the table in figure 1-13 that rates the HTML compatibility of the five browsers that account for almost all of the desktop Internet activity in the US and throughout the world. To get an updated version of this information, you can go to the website at www.html5test.com.

In the past, Internet Explorer gave web developers the most problems because it was the least standard and didn't provide for automatic updates. In contrast, the five desktop browsers in this figure provide for automatic updates so you don't have to wonder whether they include the latest HTML and CSS features. Besides that, Internet Explorer has such a trivial share of the market today that you no longer have to support it.

What's new is that now you have to worry about tablet and mobile browsers too. So, how do you provide cross-browser compatibility in today's world? First, you should of course use the current versions of HTML and CSS as you develop your web pages. If you do that, with the exception of just a few features, everything that you learn in this book will run on all web browsers. And for those few features that aren't implemented yet by one or more of the browsers, this book provides an appropriate workaround.

Second, you should test your pages on desktop, tablet, and mobile browsers. The good news is that the five desktop browsers in this figure provide Developer Tools that make that easy. For instance, the example at the top of this figure shows how you can use Chrome's Developer Tools to display a working version of a web page in mobile landscape format. You'll learn more about this in chapter 8.

Eventually, you'll want to test your web pages on the actual browsers too. But since Chrome, Edge, and Opera are all Chromium-based, you only need to test on one of them. Then, you can test on Firefox and Safari just to be sure that they don't present any problems. And for good measure, you can test your web pages on tablets and mobile phones...if for no other reason than to see how well they work on those devices.

Chrome's Developer Tools with a page in mobile landscape format

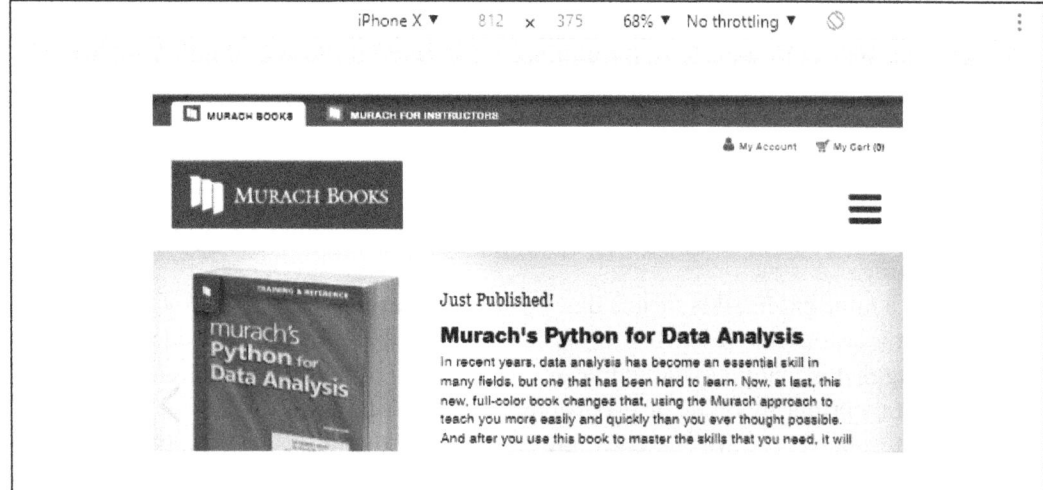

The desktop browsers and their HTML ratings (perfect score is 555)

Browser	Release	HTML5 Test Rating
Google Chrome	91	528
Opera	63	518
Edge	91	492
Mozilla Firefox	90	491
Apple Safari	11	471

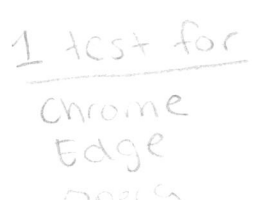

1 test for
Chrome
Edge
Opera

then test
Firefox
&
Safari

The website for these ratings

http://www.html5test.com

Coding guidelines

- Use the latest versions of HTML and CSS.
- Use the workarounds that are presented in this book for any features that aren't supported by all current browsers.

Testing guidelines

- Test your web pages on desktop browsers as well as tablet and mobile phone browsers.
- You can use Chrome's Developer Tools for the initial testing of your tablet and mobile layouts (see figure 8-2 in chapter 8).

Description

- *Cross-browser compatibility* means that your web pages will work on any browser that accesses your website, including tablet and mobile phone browsers.
- At one time, this was a major development issue. But today, with just a few exceptions, all of the current browsers support all of the features that are presented in this book.

Figure 1-13   Cross-browser compatibility

Web accessibility

Web accessibility (or just *accessibility*) is described in figure 1-14. It refers to the qualities that make a website accessible to as many users as possible, especially disabled users.

For instance, visually-impaired users may not be able to read text that's in images, so you need to provide other alternatives for them. Similarly, users with motor disabilities may not be able to use the mouse, so you need to make sure that all of the content and features of your website can be accessed through the keyboard.

To a large extent, this means that you should develop your websites so the content is still usable if images, CSS, and JavaScript are disabled. A side benefit of doing that is that your site will also be more accessible to search engines, which rely primarily on the text portions of your pages.

In this book, you will be given guidelines for providing accessibility as you learn the related HTML. And to learn more about accessibility, we recommend that you go to the sites that are identified in this figure. As the example in this figure shows, the WebAim website is a good place to start because it presents an excellent introduction to accessibility.

The WebAIM website

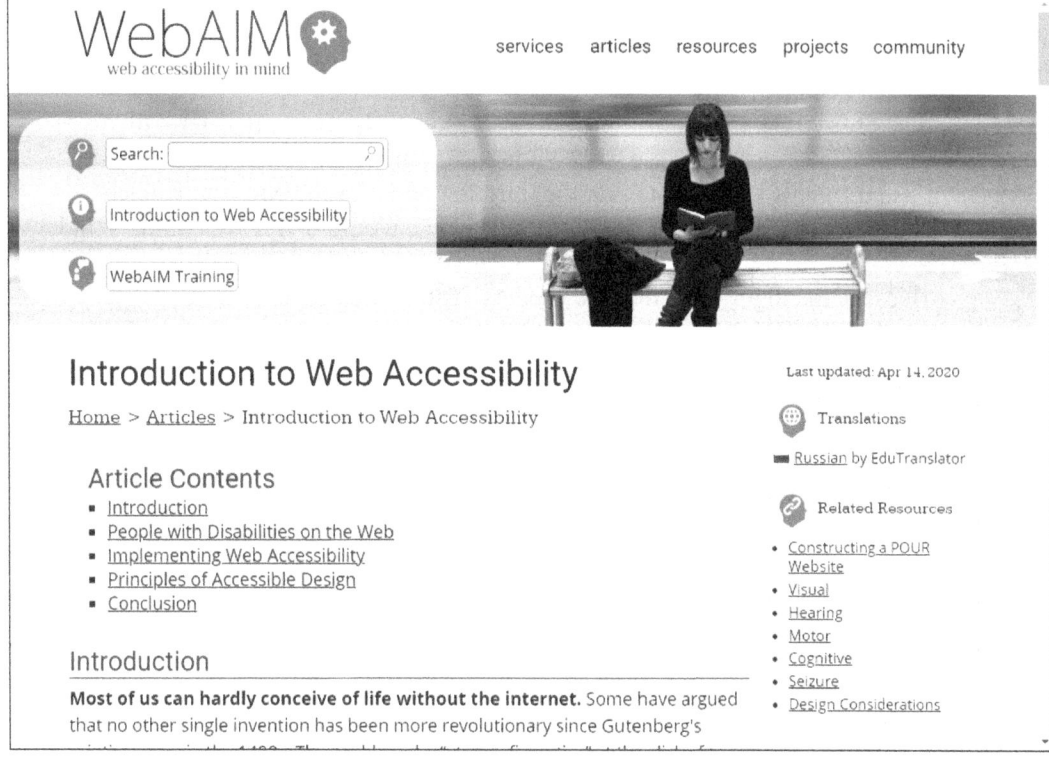

Accessibility laws that you should be aware of

- The Americans with Disabilities Act (ADA).
- Sections 504 and 508 of the federal Rehabilitation Act.
- Section 255 of the Telecommunications Act of 1996.

Types of disabilities

- Visual
- Hearing
- Motor
- Cognitive

Information sources for accessibility

- The WebAIM website: http://www.webaim.org.
- The World Wide Web Consortium (W3C): http://www.w3.org/TR/WCAG.
- W3C provides an accessibility specification called WAI-ARIA that shows how to make applications more accessible: http://www.w3.org/TR/wai-aria.

Description

- *Web accessibility* refers to the qualities that make a website accessible to users, especially disabled users.
- As you go through this book, you'll be given guidelines for coding the elements and attributes that provide web accessibility.

Figure 1-14   Web accessibility

Search engine optimization

Search engine optimization, or *SEO*, is described in figure 1-15. It refers to the goal of optimizing your website so your pages rank higher in search engines like Google and Bing.

The example in this figure shows how important SEO can be. Here, the search term is "murach" so we would hope that our website would be the first item listed...and it is. But note that the third listing is for the Amazon website, which also sells our books. Now, imagine how we would feel if we couldn't find our site on the first page of listings.

Because the algorithms that are used by search engines are changed frequently, optimizing your website and web pages requires a continual effort. That's why large development groups have SEO specialists on their staffs. To get you started right, though, this book presents the coding practices for improved SEO that don't change.

The results of a Google search for "murach"

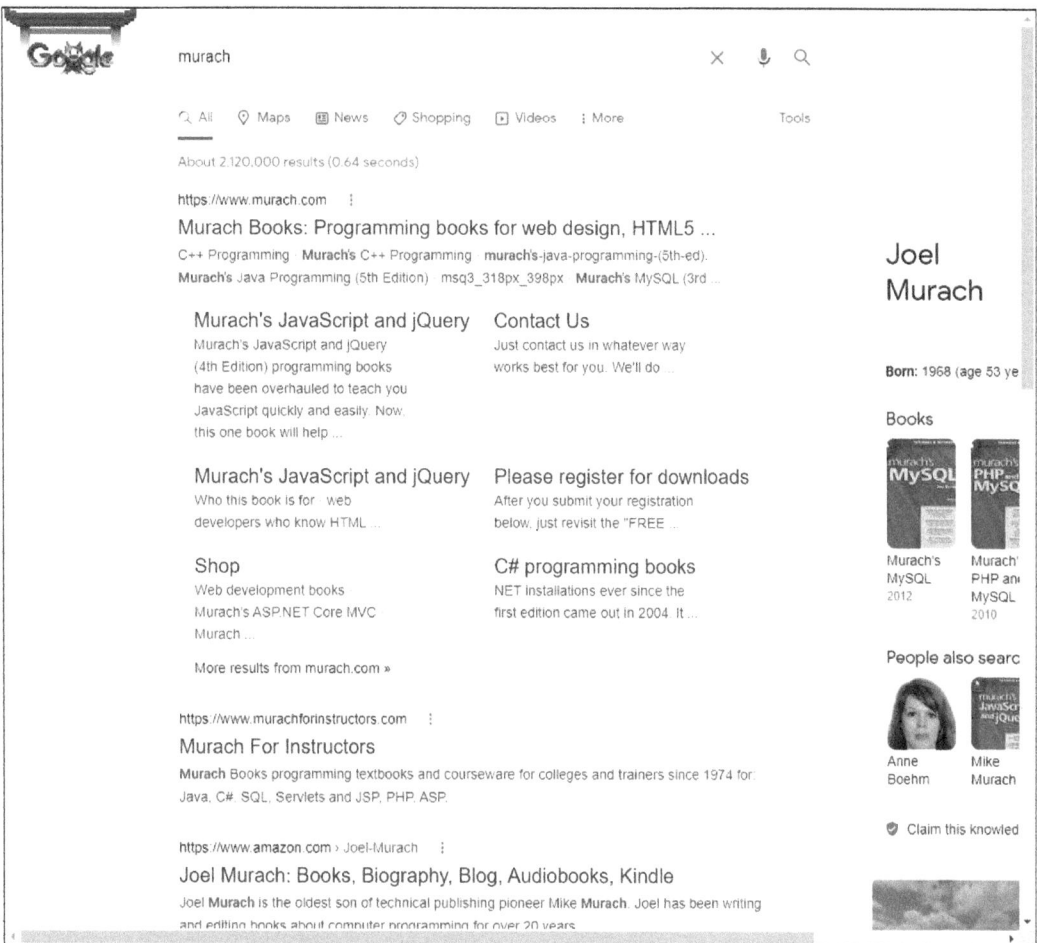

The most popular search engines

- Google
- Bing

Description

- *Search engine optimization (SEO)* refers to the goal of optimizing your website so its pages will rank high in the search engines that are used to access them.
- Although the search algorithms that are used by the search engines are changed frequently, this book presents the common coding techniques that will help your pages do better in the search engines.

Figure 1-15   Search engine optimization

Perspective

Now that you know the concepts and terms that you need for developing websites with HTML and CSS, you're ready to learn how to develop a web page. So in the next chapter, you'll learn how to create, test, and validate a web page. After that, you'll be ready to learn all the details of HTML and CSS.

Terms

client	client-side processing
web browser	JavaScript engine
web server	HyperText Markup Language
local area network (LAN)	(HTML)
intranet	HTML document
wide area network (WAN)	HTML element
Internet	CSS (Cascading Style Sheets)
HTML (HyperText Markup	style sheet
Language)	style rule
static web page	text editor
HTTP request	IDE (Integrated Development
HTTP response	Environment)
HTTP (HyperText Transfer Protocol)	deploy (publish)
render a web page	FTP (File Transfer Protocol)
dynamic web page	FTP client
script	URL (Uniform Resource Locator)
application server	Responsive Web Design (RWD)
database server	cross-browser compatibility
round trip	web accessibility
JavaScript	search engine optimization (SEO)

Summary

- A web application consists of clients, a web server, and a network. *Clients* use *web browsers* to request web pages from the web server. The *web server* returns the requested pages.

- A *local area network* (*LAN*) connects computers that are near to each other. This is often called an *intranet*. By contrast, a *wide area network* (*WAN*) uses *routers* to connect two or more LANs. The *Internet* consists of many WANs.

- To request a web page, the web browser sends an *HTTP request* to the web server. Then, the web server retrieves the HTML for the requested page and sends it back to the browser in an *HTTP response*. Last, the browser *renders* the HTML into a web page.

- A *static web page* uses the same HTML each time it is accessed. In contrast, the HTML for a *dynamic web page* is generated by a server-side *script*, so its HTML can change from one request to another.

- *JavaScript* is a *scripting language* that is run by the *JavaScript engine* of a web browser. It provides for *client-side processing*.
- *HTML* (*HyperText Markup Language*) is the language that defines the structure and content of a web page. *CSS* (*Cascading Style Sheets*) is used to control how the web pages are formatted.
- To develop web pages, you can use a *text editor* like Visual Studio Code or an *Integrated Development Environment* (*IDE*) like Dreamweaver.
- To *deploy* (or *publish*) a website on the Internet, you need to transfer the folders and files for your site from your computer to a web server with Internet access. To do that, you use an *FTP client* that uses *File Transfer Protocol* (*FTP*). to deploy
- To view a web page on the Internet, you can enter the *URL* (*Uniform Resource Locator*) into a browser's address bar.
- To view a web page that's on your own computer or server in a browser, you can use the features of your text editor or IDE. Or, you can find the file in your file explorer and double-click or right-click on it.
- To view the HTML for a web page, right-click on the page and select View Source or View Page Source. Then, to view the CSS for a page, you can click on its link in the source code.
- Four critical web development issues are *Responsive Web Design* (*RWD*), *cross-browser compatibility*, *web accessibility*, and *search engine optimization* (*SEO*).

Before you do the exercises for this book...

Before you do the exercises for this book, you should download and install the Chrome browser. You should also download and install the applications, examples, and exercises for this book. The procedures for doing both are in appendix A.

Exercise 1-1   View the example in this chapter

In this exercise, you'll visit the book page in figures 1-5 and 1-6.

1. Use File Explorer or Finder to locate this HTML file:
   `\html_css_5\book_apps\ch01\javascript_jquery.html`
   Then, double-click on the file to open it in your default browser.
2. If Chrome isn't your default browser, use your file explorer to locate the file in step 1 again. This time, right-click on it and use the Open With command to open the file in Chrome.
3. In Chrome, right-click on the page and choose View Page Source to display the source code for this page in a new tab. Then, click on book.css in the link element in the HTML code to display the CSS file for this page in a new tab.

Exercise 1-2   View book apps and examples

This exercise will introduce you to the types of examples and applications that you'll be working with in this book.

1. Use File Explorer or Finder to find and open this app in your default browser:

   `\html_css_5\book_apps\ch07\town_hall\index.html`

2. Click on the link for Scott Sampson to see that page. This is the website that's presented at the end of chapter 7, but note that the Scott Sampson link is the only one that has been implemented.

3. Open this file in the Chrome browser.

   `\html_css_5\book_examples\ch15\06_animations\index.html`

   This is the example for figure 15-6 in chapter 15.

Exercise 1-3   Visit some Internet websites

Visit a small web site and look at the source code

1. Enter www.newtonforkranch.com in the address bar of your default browser and press the Enter key. That should display the home page for this website. Here, JavaScript is used to rotate the images at the top of the page.

2. Use the technique in figure 1-11 to view the source code for the home page. Here, the link elements with a rel attribute value of "stylesheet" identify the CSS files that do the formatting for the page, and the script elements identify the JavaScript files.

3. Click on styles.css in the href attribute in the second link element. That should open the first CSS file for this page. This shows how complicated the source code can be, even for a small website.

Visit other websites

4. Go to www.landsend.com, find a page like the one in figure 1-4, and experiment with the image swaps and rollovers. Those are done by Java-Script after all the images are loaded with the page.

5. View the HTML source code for that page and see how complicated the code can be for a large, eCommerce site. Then, view the code in one of the CSS files.

6. Visit other websites on your desktop computer and also on your mobile phone to see how they handle Responsive Web Design. Then, see if the sites provide web accessibility for the motor impaired by trying to do everything with just the keyboard, no mouse.

7. When you're through experimenting, close all the browser tabs that you've opened.

Chapter 2

How to code, test, and validate a web page

In this chapter, you'll learn how to create and edit HTML and CSS files. Then, you'll learn how to test those files to make sure they work correctly. When you're through with this chapter, you'll be ready to learn all the details of HTML and CSS coding.

Although you can use any text editor or IDE for web development with this book, this chapter also shows you how to use the text editor that we recommend. It is called *Visual Studio Code* (or just *VS Code*). It runs on Windows, macOS, and Linux. And it can help you work faster and better.

The HTML syntax

When you code an HTML document, you need to adhere to the rules for creating the HTML elements. These rules are referred to as the *syntax* of the language. In the four topics that follow, you'll learn the HTML syntax.

The basic structure of an HTML document

Figure 2-1 presents the basic structure of an *HTML document*. As you can see, every HTML document consists of two parts: the DOCTYPE declaration and the document tree.

When you use HTML5, you code the *DOCTYPE declaration* exactly as it's shown in this figure. It will be the first line of code in every HTML document that you create, and it tells the browser that the document is using HTML5. If you've developed web pages with earlier versions of HTML or XHTML, you will be pleased to see how much this declaration has been simplified.

The *document tree* starts right after the DOCTYPE declaration. This tree consists of the *HTML elements* that define the web page. The first of these elements is the html element itself, which contains all of the other elements. This element can be referred to as the *root element* of the tree.

Within the html element, you should always code a head element and a body element. The head element contains elements that provide information about the page itself, while the body element contains the elements that provide the structure and content for the page. You'll learn how to code these elements in the next chapter.

You'll use the elements shown in this figure in every HTML document that you create. As a result, it's a good practice to start every HTML document from a template that contains this code or from another HTML document that's similar to the one you're going to create. Later in this chapter, you'll learn how you can use Visual Studio Code to do that.

When you use HTML, you can code elements using lowercase, uppercase, or mixed case. For consistency, though, we recommend that you use lowercase unless uppercase is required. The one exception we make is in the DOCTYPE declaration because DOCTYPE has historically been capitalized (although lowercase works too). You will see this use of capitalization in all of the examples and applications in this book.

The basic structure of an HTML document

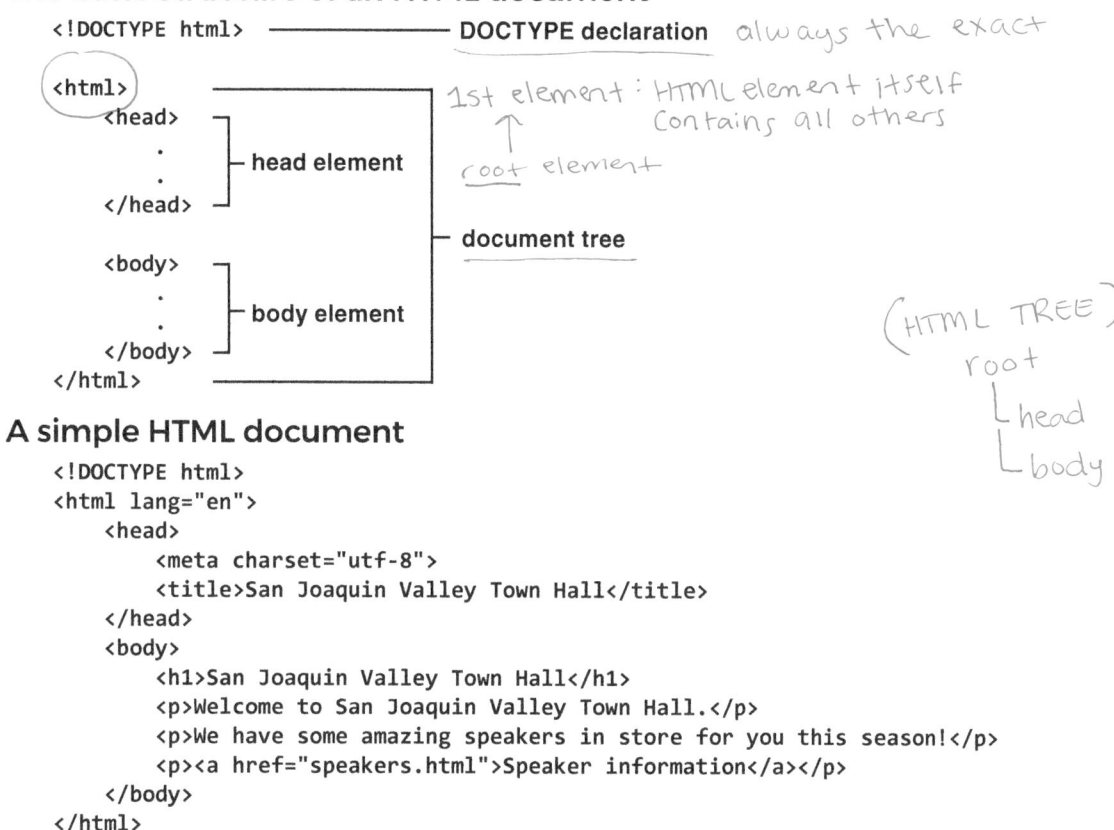

`<!DOCTYPE html>` ———————— **DOCTYPE declaration** *always the exact*

`<html>` ——————————————— *1st element: HTML element itself*
   `<head>`   *Contains all others*
      .   *↑*
      .   — **head element**   *root element*
   `</head>`

                                 — **document tree**

   `<body>`   *(HTML TREE)*
      .   *root*
      .   — **body element**   *└ head*
   `</body>`   *└ body*
`</html>`

A simple HTML document

```
<!DOCTYPE html>
<html lang="en">
    <head>
        <meta charset="utf-8">
        <title>San Joaquin Valley Town Hall</title>
    </head>
    <body>
        <h1>San Joaquin Valley Town Hall</h1>
        <p>Welcome to San Joaquin Valley Town Hall.</p>
        <p>We have some amazing speakers in store for you this season!</p>
        <p><a href="speakers.html">Speaker information</a></p>
    </body>
</html>
```

General coding recommendation for HTML

- Although you can code the HTML using lowercase, uppercase, or mixed case, we recommend that you do all coding in lowercase because it's easier to read.

Description

- An *HTML document* contains *HTML elements* that define the content and structure of a web page.

- Each HTML document consists of two parts: the DOCTYPE declaration and the document tree.

- The *DOCTYPE declaration* shown above indicates that the document is going to use HTML5. You'll code this declaration at the start of every HTML document.

- The *document tree* starts with the html element, which marks the beginning and end of the HTML code. This element can be referred to as the *root element* of the document.

- The html element always contains one head element that provides information about the document and one body element that provides the structure and content of the document.

Figure 2-1   The basic structure of an HTML document

How to code elements and tags

Figure 2-2 shows you how to code elements and tags. As you have already seen, most HTML elements start with an *opening tag* and end with a *closing tag* that is like the opening tag but has a slash within it. Thus, <h1> is the opening tag for a level-1 heading, and </h1> is the closing tag. Between those tags, you code the *content* of the element.

Some elements, however, have no content or closing tag. These tags are referred to as *empty tags*. For instance, the <br> tag is an empty tag that starts a new line, and the <img> tag is an empty tag that identifies an image that should be displayed.

The third set of examples in this figure shows the right way and the wrong way to code tags when one element is *nested* within another. In short, the tags for one element shouldn't overlap with the tags for another element. That is, you can't close the outer element before you close the inner element.

From this point on in this book, we will refer to elements by the code used in the opening tag. For instance, we will refer to head elements, h1 elements, and img elements. To prevent misreading, though, we will enclose single-letter element names in brackets. As a result, we will refer to <a> elements and <p> elements. We will also use brackets wherever else we think they will help prevent misreading.

Two elements with opening and closing tags

tag

```
<h1>San Joaquin Valley Town Hall</h1>   <open>  </close>
<p>Here is a list of links:</p>   tag
```

content

Two empty tags

```
<br> Starts a new line
<img src="logo.gif" alt="Murach Logo"> identifies image to display
```

Correct and incorrect nesting of tags

Correct nesting

```
<p>Order your copy <i>today!</i></p>   closing tag must be
                                        at end of content
```

Incorrect nesting   Nested element cannot overlap!

```
<p>Order your copy <i>today!</p></i>
```

Description

- Most HTML elements have an opening tag, content, and a closing tag. Each tag is coded within a set of brackets (<>).

- An element's *opening tag* includes the tag name. The *closing tag* includes the tag name preceded by a slash. And the *content* includes everything that appears between the opening and closing tags.

- Some HTML elements have no content. For example, the <br> element, which forces a line break, consists of just one tag. This type of tag is called an *empty tag*.

- HTML elements are commonly *nested*. To nest elements correctly, though, you must close an inner set of tags before closing the outer set of tags.

Figure 2-2   How to code elements and tags

How to code attributes

Figure 2-3 shows how to code the *attributes* for an HTML element. These attributes are coded within the opening tag of an element or within an empty tag. For each attribute, you code the attribute name, an equal sign, and the attribute value.

When you use HTML5, the attribute value doesn't have to be coded within quotation marks unless the value contains a space, but we recommend that you use quotation marks to enclose all values. Also, although you can use either double or single quotes, we recommend that you always use double quotes. That way, your code will have a consistent appearance that will help you avoid coding errors.

In the examples in this figure, you can see how one or more attributes can be coded. For instance, the second example is an opening tag with three attributes. By contrast, the third example is an empty img element that contains a src attribute that gives the name of the image file that should be displayed, plus an alt attribute that gives the text that should be displayed if the image file can't be found.

The next example illustrates the use of a *Boolean attribute*. A Boolean attribute can have just two values, which represent either on or off. To turn a Boolean attribute on, you code just the name of the attribute. In this example, the checked attribute turns that attribute on, which causes the related check box to be checked when it is rendered by the browser. If you want the attribute to be off when the page is rendered, you don't code the attribute.

The next set of examples illustrates the use of two attributes that are commonly used to identify HTML elements. The id attribute is used to uniquely identify just one element, so each id attribute must have a unique value. By contrast, the class attribute can be used to mark one or more elements, so the same value can be used for more than one class attribute. You'll see these attributes in a complete example in figure 2-6.

(handwritten, top right: 44)

How to code an opening tag with attributes

An opening tag with one attribute

```
<a href="contact.html">
```

(handwritten: attributes:)
(handwritten: < tag   name = "valu)

An opening tag with three attributes

```
<a href="contact.html" title="Click to Contact Us" class="nav_link">
```
(handwritten: 1   2   3)

How to code an empty tag with attributes

```
<img src="logo.gif" alt="Murach Logo">
```
(handwritten: text if image errors)
(handwritten: name of image file)

How to code a **Boolean** attribute

```
<input type="checkbox" name="mailList" checked>
```
(handwritten: renders this as pre-selected box in browser)
(handwritten: ☑ mail list)

Two common attributes for identifying HTML elements

An opening tag with an id attribute

```
<div id="page">
```

An opening tag with a class attribute

```
<a href="contact.html" title="Click to Contact Us" class="nav_link">
```

Coding rules

- An attribute consists of the attribute name, an equal sign (=), and the value for the attribute.
- ~~Attribute values don't have to be enclosed in quotes if they don't contain spaces.~~
- Attribute values must be enclosed ~~in single or~~ double quotes ~~if they contain one or more spaces, but you can't mix the type of quotation mark used for a single value.~~
- Boolean attributes can be coded as just the attribute name. They don't have to include the equal sign and a value that's the same as the attribute name.
- To code multiple attributes, separate each attribute with a space.

Our coding recommendation

- For consistency, enclose all attribute values in double quotes.

Description

- *Attributes* can be coded within opening or empty tags to supply optional values.
- A *Boolean attribute* represents either an on or off value.
- The id attribute is used to identify a single HTML element, so its value can be used for just one HTML element.
- A class attribute with the same value can be used for more than one HTML element.

(handwritten: id = "___" one HTML element)
(handwritten: class = "___" multiple elements)

Figure 2-3   How to code attributes

How to code comments and whitespace

Figure 2-4 shows you how to code *comments*. Here, the starting and ending characters for two comments are highlighted. Then, everything within those characters, also highlighted here, is ignored when the page is rendered.

One common use of comments is to describe or explain portions of code. That is illustrated by the first comment.

Another common use of comments is to *comment out* a portion of the code. This is illustrated by the second comment. This is useful when you're testing a web page and you want to temporarily disable a portion of code that you're having trouble with. Then, after you test the rest of the code, you can remove the comment and test that portion of the code.

This figure also illustrates the use of *whitespace*, which consists of characters like tab characters, return characters, and extra spaces. For instance, the return character after the opening body tag and all of the spaces between that tag and the next tag are whitespace.

Since whitespace is ignored when an HTML document is rendered, you can use the whitespace characters to format your HTML so it is easier to read. In this figure, for example, you can see how whitespace has been used to indent and align the HTML elements.

That of course is a good coding practice, and you'll see that in all of the examples in this book. Note, however, that the code will work the same if all of the whitespace is removed. In fact, you could code all of the HTML for a document in a single line.

Although whitespace doesn't affect the way an HTML document is rendered, it does take up space in the HTML file. As a result, you shouldn't overdo your use of it. Just use enough to make your code easy to read.

An HTML document with comments and whitespace

```
<!DOCTYPE html>
<!--
    This document displays the home page
    for the website.
-->

<html>
    <head>
        <title>San Joaquin Valley Town Hall</title>
    </head>

    <body>
        <h1>San Joaquin Valley Town Hall</h1>
        <h2>Bringing cutting-edge speakers to the valley</h2>
<!-- This comments out all of the HTML code in the unordered list
        <ul>
            <li>October: David Brancaccio</li>
            <li>November: Andrew Ross Sorkin</li>
            <li>January: Amy Chua</li>
            <li>February: Scott Sampson</li>
            <li>March: Carlos Eire</li>
            <li>April: Ronan Tynan</li>
        </ul>
The code after the end of this comment is active -->
        <p>Contact us by phone at (559) 444-2180 for ticket information.</p>
    </body>
</html>
```

explanation comment

<!-- whitespace
--> whitespace

ignored when rendered

Our coding recommendations

- Use whitespace to indent lines of code and make them easier to read.
- Don't overdo your use of whitespace, because it does add to the size of the file.

Description

- An HTML *comment* is text that appears between the <!-- and --> characters. Since web browsers ignore comments, you can use them to describe or explain portions of your HTML code that might otherwise be confusing.
- You can also use comments to *comment out* elements that you don't want the browser to display. This can be useful when you're testing a web page.
- An HTML comment can be coded on a single line or it can span two or more lines.
- *Whitespace* consists of characters like tab characters, line return characters, and extra spaces.
- Since whitespace is ignored by browsers, you can use it to indent lines of code and separate elements from one another by putting them on separate lines. This is a good coding practice because it makes your code easier to read.

Figure 2-4   How to code comments and whitespace

The CSS syntax

Like HTML, CSS has a syntax that must be adhered to when you create a CSS file. This syntax is presented next.

How to code CSS style rules and comments

A CSS file consists of *style rules*. As the diagram in figure 2-5 shows, a style rule consists of a *selector* followed by a set of braces. Within the braces are one or more *declarations*, and each declaration consists of a *property* and a *value*. Note that the property is followed by a colon and the value is followed by a semicolon.

In this diagram, the selector is h1 so it applies to all h1 elements. Then, the style rule consists of a single property named color that is set to the color navy. The result is that the content of all h1 elements will be displayed in navy blue.

In the CSS code that follows, you can see four other style rules. Three of these contain only one declaration, but the third style rule consists of two declarations: one for the font-style property, and one for the border-bottom property.

Within a CSS file, you can also code comments that describe or explain what the CSS code is doing. For each comment, you start with /* and end with */, and anything between those characters is ignored. In the example in this figure, you can see how *CSS comments* can be coded on separate lines or after the lines that make up a style rule.

You can also use comments to comment out portions of code that you want disabled. This can be useful when you're testing your CSS code just as it is when you're testing your HTML code.

The parts of a CSS style rule

```
selector
     property:
          value;
h1 {
     color: navy; ←—— declaration
}
```

A simple CSS document with comments   /* _____ */

```
/********************************************************
* Description: Primary style sheet for valleytownhall.com
* Author:      Anne Boehm
*********************************************************/
/* Adjust the styles for the body */
body {
    background-color: #FACD8A;          /* This is a shade of orange. */
}

/* Adjust the styles for the headings */
h1 {
    color: #363636;
}
h2 {
    font-style: italic;
    border-bottom: 3px solid #EF9C00;  /* Adds a line below h2 headings */
}

/* Adjust the styles for the unordered list */
ul {
    list-style-type: square;            /* Changes the bullets to squares */
}
```

Description

- A CSS *style rule* consists of a selector and zero or more declarations enclosed in braces.
- A CSS *selector* consists of the identifiers that are coded at the beginning of the style rule.
- A CSS *declaration* consists of a *property*, a colon, a *value*, and a semicolon.
- To make your code easier to read, you can use spaces, indentation, and blank lines within a style rule.
- CSS *comments* begin with the characters /* and end with the characters */. A CSS comment can be coded on a single line, or it can span multiple lines.

Figure 2-5   How to code CSS style rules and comments

How to code basic selectors

The selector of a style rule identifies the HTML element or elements that the declarations should be applied to. To give you a better idea of how this works, figure 2-6 shows how to use the three basic selectors for CSS style rules. Then, in chapter 4, you'll learn how to code all types of selectors.

The first type of selector identifies HTML elements like body, h1, or <p> elements. For instance, the selectors in the first two examples apply to the body and h1 elements. These selectors are called *type selectors*.

The second type of selector starts with the hash character (#) and applies to the single HTML element that's identified by the id attribute. For instance, #copyright applies to the HTML element that has an id attribute with a value of copyright. As you can see, that's the last <p> element in the HTML code.

The third type of selector starts with a period (.) and applies to all of the HTML elements that are identified by the class attribute with the named value. For instance, .base_color applies to all elements with class attributes that have a value of base_color. In the HTML code, this includes the h1 element and the last <p> element.

Starting with chapter 4, you'll learn all of the coding details for style rules. But to give you an idea of what's going on in this example, here's a quick review of the code.

In the style rule for the body element, the font-family is set either to Arial (if the browser has access to that font) or the sans-serif type that is the default for the browser. This font is then used for all text that's displayed within the body element, unless it's overridden later on by some other style rule. So in this example, all of the text will be Arial or sans-serif, and you can see that font in the browser display.

The style rule for the body element also sets the font-size to 100% of the default size. Although this is the default, this selector is often coded for completeness. Next, the width of the body is set to 300 pixels, and the padding between the contents and the border is set to 1 em, which is the height of the default font.

In the style rule for the h1 element, the font-size is set to 180% of the default font size for the document (the size set by the selector for the body element). Then, in the style rule for the second <p> element (#copyright), the font size is set to 75% of the default font size, and the text is right-aligned. Here again, you can see how these style rules are applied in the browser display.

Last, in the style rule for the class named base_color, the color is set to blue. This means that both of the HTML elements that have that class name (the h1 element and the second <p> element) are displayed in blue.

This example shows how easy it is to identify the elements that you want to apply CSS formatting to. This also shows how the use of CSS separates the formatting from the content and structure that is defined by the HTML.

HTML elements that can be selected by element type, id, or class

```
<body>
    <h1 class="base_color">Student materials</h1>
    <p>Here are the links for the downloads:</p>
    <ul id="links">
        <li><a href="exercises.html">Exercises</a></li>
        <li><a href="solutions.html">Solutions</a></li>
    </ul>
    <p id="copyright" class="base_color">Copyright 2022</p>
</body>
```

CSS style rules that select by element type, id, and class

Type
```
body {
    font-family: Arial, sans-serif;
    font-size: 100%;
    width: 300px;
    padding: 1em;
}
h1 {
    font-size: 180%;
}
```

ID

id elements in CSS begin with #

```
#copyright {
    font-size: 75%;
    text-align: right;
}
```

Class

class begins with .

```
.base_color {
    color: blue;
}
```

The elements in a browser

Student Materials

Here are the links for the downloads:

- Exercises
- Solutions

Copyright 2022

Description

- To code a selector for an HTML element, you simply name the element. This is referred to as a *type selector*.
- If an element is coded with an id attribute, you can code a selector for that id by coding a hash character (#) followed by the id value, as in #copyright.
- If an element is coded with a class attribute, you can code a selector for that class by coding a period followed by the class name, as in .base_color.

Figure 2-6   How to code basic selectors

How to use VS Code to develop web pages

As you learned in chapter 1, you can use a text editor or an IDE to enter and edit the HTML and CSS files for a web application. The text editor that we recommend is *Visual Studio Code* (or *VS Code*), and the topics that follow present the basic skills for using it. Of course, if you prefer to use another editor or IDE, you can skip these topics.

How to work with folders

To work with a web application in VS Code, you start by opening the top-level folder for the application. That's the one that contains all the subfolders and files for the application. The first procedure in figure 2-7 shows how.

Instead of opening the top-level folder for an application, though, this example opens the book_apps folder that contains all the applications that are presented in this book. Also, the Explorer on the left side of VS Code shows the subfolders and files for the folder that's opened by the Open Folder dialog box. In other words, the Explorer shows what happens when the book_apps folder is opened.

After you open the top-level folder for an application, you can hide or display the folders and files in the Explorer by clicking on the folder names. That makes it easy to find the folders and files that you're looking for. Then, to add, rename, or delete a folder, you can use the procedures in the third group in this figure.

The last procedure in this figure shows how to set the color theme for VS Code. This sounds like a small item, but it can make a big difference. The theme we like is Light (Visual Studio), but you can select the one that works best for you.

The dialog box for choosing a top-level folder (book_apps) in VS Code

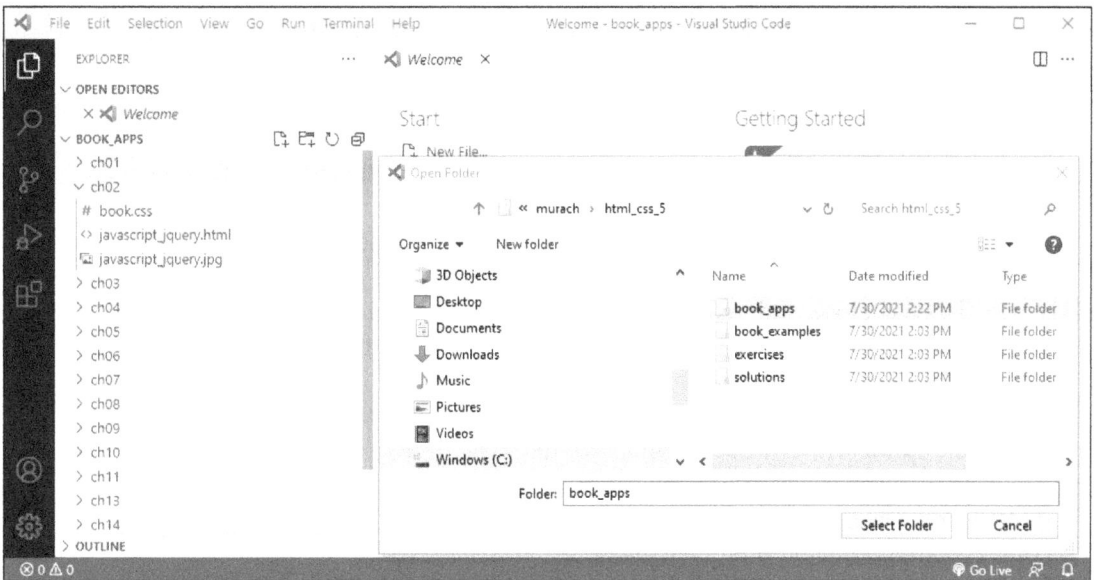

How to open the top-level folder for an application

- Select File→Open Folder from the menu system.
- Use the resulting dialog box to select the folder and click Select Folder. This sets up the folder and file tree that's shown in the Explorer.

How to hide or display the folders and files in the Explorer

- Click on the folder names.

How to add, rename, or delete a folder in the Explorer

- To add a subfolder to a folder, select the folder in the Explorer and click the New Folder icon that's displayed to the right of the top folder.
- To rename a folder, right-click on it and select Rename. Then, edit the name.
- To delete a folder, right-click on it and select Delete.

How to set the color theme for VS Code

- Select File→Preferences→Color Theme from the menu bar. (The examples in this chapter use the Light (Visual Studio) theme.)

Description

- Please refer to appendix A to learn how to install VS Code on a Windows or macOS system.

Figure 2-7   How to work with folders in VS Code

How to work with files

Figure 2-8 presents the basic skills for working with files in VS Code. To *open* a file, you find it in the Explorer and double-click on it. Then, it's displayed in a tab in the main window. This is called Standard Mode, and you use it when you're going to edit a file.

In contrast, to *preview* a file, you just click on it (no double-click). Then, the name of the file is displayed in italics on the tab, and the tab is re-used if you open or preview another file. This is called Preview Mode, and you use it when you want to take a quick look at a file or make just a few changes to it.

To save, close, add, rename, and delete files, you can use the other procedures in this figure. They work the way they do with most applications. But note that when you add a new file to a folder, you need to give it a name with either the html or css extension. Then, VS Code will know what type of file it is, and the editor will expect the syntax for that type of file.

If you've been experimenting with VS Code, you may have noticed that a Welcome page is displayed whenever you start VS Code after you've closed it with no files open or in preview mode. Now, if you want to stop this page from being displayed, you can use the last procedure in this figure.

VS Code with files in Standard and Preview mode

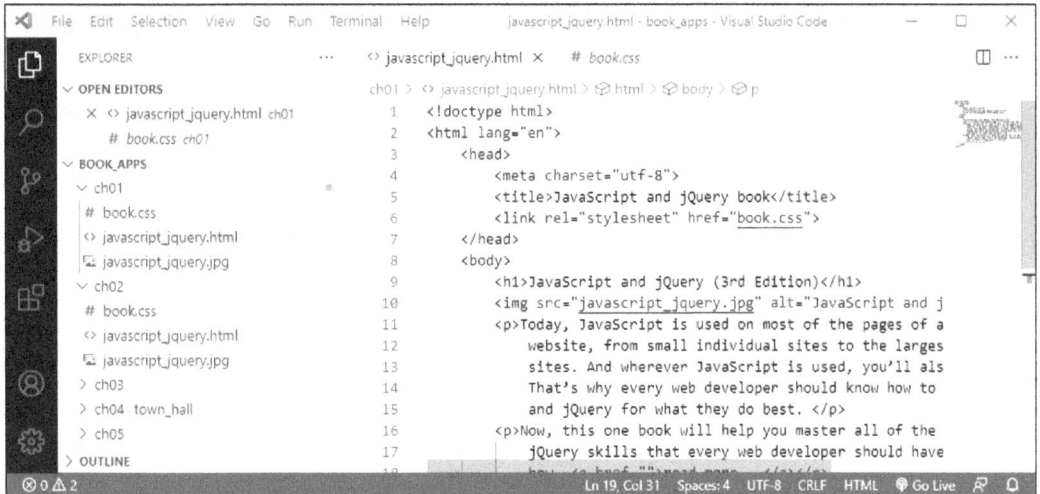

How to open or preview a file

- To *open* a file, *double-click* on it in the Explorer. This displays the file in a tab in the editor with the name of the file in normal font style, indicating that it's in Standard Mode.

- To *preview* a file, *click* on it in the Explorer. This displays the file in a tab in the editor with the name of the file in italics, indicating that it's in Preview Mode. If you open or preview another file, VS Code reuses the tab.

How to save or close a file

- If you want to save the changes to a file without closing it, select File→Save.

- To save the changes to more than one file, select File→Save All or click the Save All icon that shows when you point to Open Editors in the Explorer.

- To close a file, click the X in the upper right corner of the tab for the file, or click the X to the left of the file name in the Open Editors list.

- If you try to close a file that has been changed but not saved, you'll be asked if you want to save the changes.

How to add a new file to a folder

- Select the folder in the Explorer and click the New File icon that's displayed to the right of the top folder. Then, enter the name for the file and be sure to include the html or css extension.

How rename or delete a file

- To rename a file, right-click on it and select Rename. Then, edit the name.

- To delete a file, right-click on it and select Delete.

How to stop the Welcome page from being displayed

- Scroll down to the bottom of the page, and uncheck the check box.

Figure 2-8   How to work with files in VS Code

How to edit an HTML file

Figure 2-9 shows how to edit an HTML file with VS Code. When you open a file with an html extension, VS Code knows what type of file you're working with so it can use color to highlight the syntax components. It also uses IntelliSense to provide *completion lists* that let you select the names of elements and attributes as you type. And when you enter an opening tag, it automatically adds the closing tag.

To display the completion list for an element, you type a left bracket (<). This displays a list of all the available elements. Then, if you type one or more letters, the list is filtered to just the ones that start with those characters. In this figure, for example, I typed the letter "i" so only the elements that start with that letter are displayed.

You can use a similar technique to enter attributes within an opening tag. To start, enter a space and one or more letters after the element name. That displays a list of all the attributes that start with those letters. Then, when you select an attribute, VS Code inserts the attribute along with an equal sign and double quotes, and you can enter the value of the attribute between the quotes.

When you add a new file to a folder, you should realize that VS Code doesn't generate any code for it. However, you can generate the starting code for an HTML file by entering an exclamation mark (!) and pressing the Tab key. This is a feature of Emmet, which is a third-party plugin that's used by VS Code.

Because the Emmet starting code is minimal, another option is to copy code from another file and paste it into the new file. Or, you can open a similar file and then save it with a new name. Then, you can delete the code you don't need and add the code you do need.

As you become more familiar with HTML, you can take this to the next level by creating HTML files that contain the elements you need for different types of pages. Then, you can use those files as *templates* for creating new pages. To do that, you can open the template file and save it with a new name before you modify the file. That way, the original template file remains unchanged. What you don't want to do is to start new files from scratch.

Although this figure doesn't illustrate it, you should know that you can split the editor so you can view two or more files at once. That can be useful when you want to copy code from one file to another or compare the code in two files. The last procedure in this figure shows just one of the ways that you can split the editor. It uses View→Editor Layout to split the editor into two or more columns or rows. Then, you can open a different file in each of the rows and columns.

Although it takes some experimentation to master the use of split editors, it's worth the effort. To help you get started, exercise 2-2 guides you through the basic skills for using this feature.

The completion list for selecting an HTML element

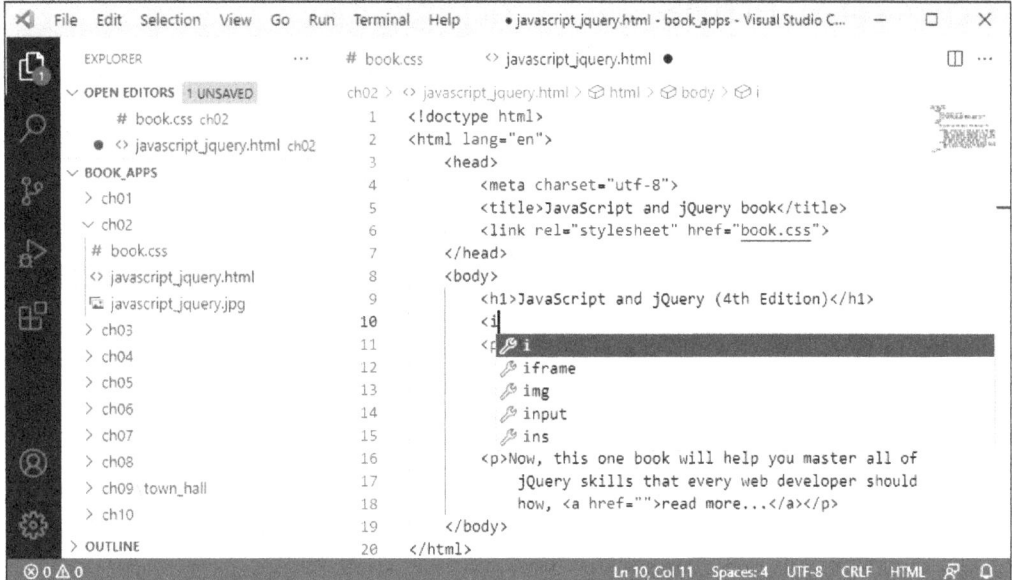

Common coding errors

- An opening tag without a closing tag.
- Misspelled element or attribute names.
- Quotation marks that aren't paired.
- Incorrect file references in link, img, or <a> elements.

How to use the IntelliSense feature

- IntelliSense displays *completion lists* for elements and attributes. To insert an item from a completion list, click on it or highlight it and press the Tab or Enter key.
- When you enter a bracket at the end of an opening tag, VS Code enters the closing tag.

How to add starting code to a new file

- Enter an exclamation mark (!) into the file and press the Tab key.

How to split the screen so you can work with two or more files at once

- After you open one file, use View→Editor Layout to split the editor into two or more columns or rows. Then, open a second file in one of the columns or rows.

Description

- VS Code provides features for editing HTML files like color coding and IntelliSense. It also makes it easy for you to add the starting code for a file.

Figure 2-9   How to edit an HTML file in VS Code

How to use the HTMLHint extension to find HTML errors

Because VS Code doesn't provide for HTML error checking out of the box, we recommend that you install an extension to VS Code that checks your HTML code as you enter it. One popular extension is the HTMLHint extension developed by Mike Kaufman, and figure 2-10 shows how to install and use it.

To start, you click the Extensions icon in the left bar. Then, the Extensions window is displayed in place of the Explorer window. This window lists any extensions that are already installed as well as any recommended extensions.

To find the HTMLHint extension, you can type "htmlhint" in the text box at the top of the Extensions window as shown in the first screen in this figure. When you do that, you'll notice that there are two extensions with that name. We recommend that you install the one developed by Mike Kaufman.

After you install the HTMLHint extension, VS Code checks your code as you enter it. Then, if it detects an error, it displays a wavy line under the error as shown in the second screen in this figure. Here, "<link" is underlined because the link tag doesn't end with a right bracket.

To display the description of an error, you can hover the mouse over the wavy underline. Alternatively, you can open the Problems window to display a list of all the errors. Then, you can click on an error to display it in the file. The Explorer also indicates whether a file contains errors by displaying the number of errors to the right of the filename.

Although HTMLHint can identify syntax errors, it has no way of knowing what the correct code should be for file references in link, img, or <a> elements. As a result, you must discover those errors when you test the web page. If, for example, the file reference for a style sheet in a link element is incorrect, the CSS won't be applied. If the file reference in an img element is incorrect, the image won't be displayed. And if the file reference for an <a> element is incorrect, the browser won't access the correct page.

VS Code as the HTMLHint extension is installed

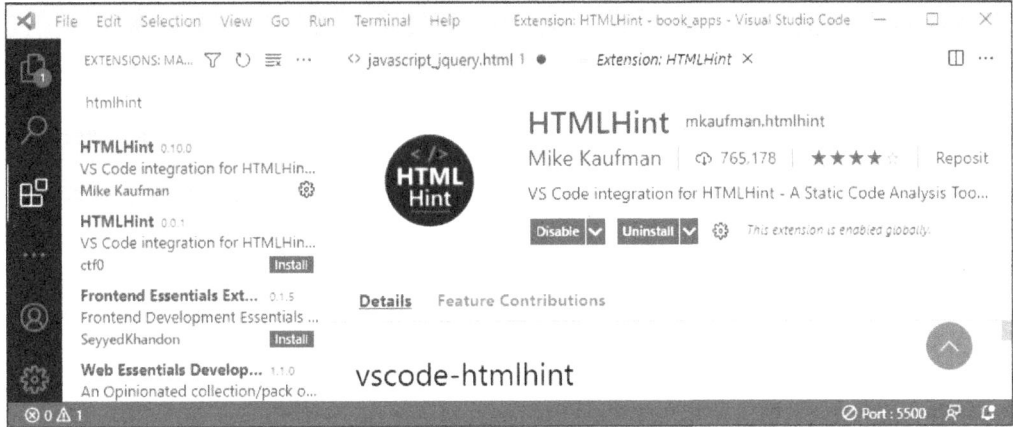

The Problems window with an error displayed

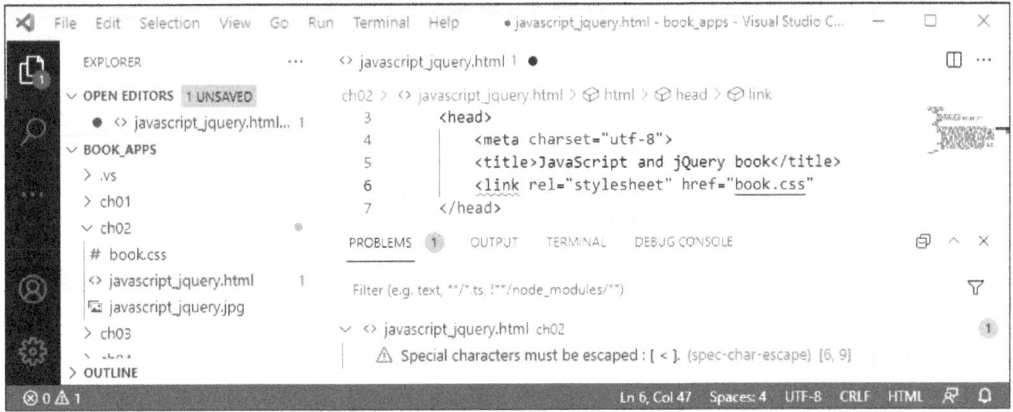

How to install the HTMLHint extension

1. Click the Extensions icon in the left bar, and enter "htmlhint" in the text box at the top of the window to filter the available extensions.
2. Click the Install button for the HTMLHint extension from Mike Kaufman.

How to identify the errors that are marked by HTMLHint

- If HTMLHint detects an HTML syntax error, it underlines it with a wavy line.
- To get the description for an error, hover the mouse over the wavy line.
- To see all the errors in a file, you can display the Problems window (View→Problems). Then, you can click on an error to take you to it in the file.

Description

- The HTMLHint extension checks your code as you enter it so you can correct your errors right away.

Figure 2-10   How to use the HTMLHint extension to find HTML errors

How to edit a CSS file

When you open a file with the css extension, VS Code knows what type of file you're working with. That way, it can use color to highlight the syntax components. It can use IntelliSense to provide *completion lists* that let you select the names of elements, properties, and values. And when you enter an opening brace, it automatically adds the closing brace.

If you start to enter the name of an element for a CSS style rule, for example, VS Code displays a list of the elements with the letters you enter. If you enter one or more letters to start a property declaration, VS Code displays a list of the properties that start with those letters. And if you start an entry for a property value, VS Code displays a list of possible values.

The example in figure 2-11 shows how completion lists work with CSS. Here, I entered a selector for the h2 element, followed by a space and a left brace, and VS Code added the right brace. Then, after I pressed Enter to start a new line and I entered the letter "b" for the first property, the completion list displayed all of the properties that start with that letter.

Similarly, when you enter the name of a property, VS Code enters the colon that follows the property as well as the semi-colon at the end of the property declaration. Then, you just need to enter the value for the property.

Unlike HTML files, VS Code provides error checking for CSS files out of the box. If it detects an error as you type, it displays a wavy line under the error. In this example, the padding property of the style rule for the h1 element is underlined because it's spelled incorrectly. To display the description of an error, you can hover the mouse over the wavy underline. And you can open the Problems window to display a list of all the errors. Then, you can click on an error to display it in the file.

The Explorer also indicates whether a file contains errors. To do that, it displays the number of errors in the file to the right of the filename. In this case, five errors have been detected.

Here again, you may want to split the editor when you work with CSS files. That can make it easier to copy code from one file to another. You can also split the editor with the HTML file in one editor and the related CSS file in another editor. That makes it easy to see the relationships between the two.

The completion list for selecting a CSS property

✳ Common coding errors ✳

- Braces that aren't paired correctly.
- Misspelled property names.
- Missing semicolons.
- Id or class names that don't match the names used in the HTML.

How to use the IntelliSense feature

- IntelliSense displays *completion lists* for elements, properties, and values. To insert an item from a completion list, click on it or highlight it and press the Tab or Enter key.
- When you select a property from a completion list, VS Code adds the colon and the semicolon for the declaration. Then, you just need to enter or select the value.
- When you enter the left brace for a style rule, VS Code adds the right brace.

How to identify the errors that are marked by VS Code

- If VS Code detects a CSS syntax error, it underlines it with a wavy line.
- To get the description for an error, hover the mouse over the wavy line.
- To see all the errors in a file, you can display the Problems window (View→Problems). Then, you can click on an error to take you to it in the file.

Description

- VS Code provides features for editing CSS files like color coding and IntelliSense. VS Code also identifies CSS syntax errors.

Figure 2-11   How to edit a CSS file in VS Code

How to use the Live Server extension to open an HTML file in a browser

As you develop web applications, you'll want to open the HTML files in a browser so you can see how they look and how they work. Unfortunately, VS Code doesn't provide an easy way to do that out of the box. Because of that, we recommend that you install an extension that does make it easy.

One popular extension for doing that is Live Server, and figure 2-12 shows how to install it. Once installed, you can click the Go Live icon at the bottom of VS Code to launch a local development server and open the active file in the default browser. In this example, the default browser is Chrome.

Once that's done, you can make changes to the HTML or CSS code for the page, save the changes, and the browser page is automatically updated. You don't have to refresh the page.

To open a different HTML file in the browser from the same development server, you can right-click on its file name in the Explorer and select Open with Live Server. That displays the new page in the same browser, but in a new tab of that browser.

While the local development server is open, the Go Live icon is replaced with an icon that has the server port number on it. Then, you can click on this icon to close the server. Note, however, that this doesn't close the browser window, so you'll eventually want to do that.

If you don't install an extension like Live Server, you should know that VS Code provides another way to open a file in a browser. Just right-click on the file you want to open in the Explorer and select Reveal in File Explorer (Windows) or Reveal in Finder (macOS). Then, the folder that contains the file will be displayed in the File Explorer or Finder, and you can double-click on the file to open it in your default browser.

Every time you open an HTML file from the File Explorer or Finder, though, a new browser or browser tab is opened. To avoid that, you can open the file in the browser just once. Then, after you use VS Code to fix the errors, you can save the changes, switch to the browser, and click on the Reload or Refresh icon to reload the file with the changes.

How install the Live Server extension

1. Click the Extensions icon in the left bar, and enter "live server ritwick dey" in the text box to find the version of Live Server that we recommend.
2. Click the Install button for the Live Server extension.

Click the Go Live icon to open an HTML file on a development server

The web page on the development server in the default Chrome browser

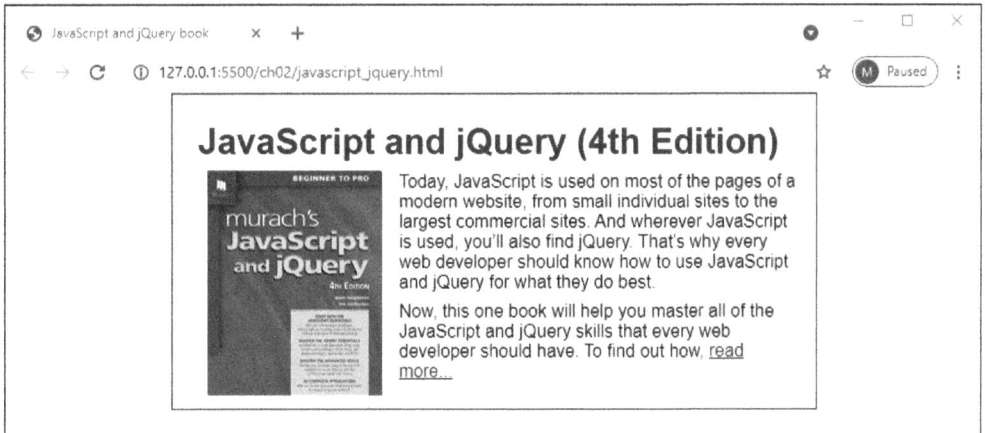

How to open an HTML file in the default browser

• To open the active editor file, click the Go Live icon.
• To open any file in the Explorer, right-click on it and select Open with Live Server.

Description

• When you open an HTML file with Live Server, the Go Live icon is replaced with the port number for the server, which you can click when you want to close the server.
• After you make changes to your HTML or CSS code, you can save them and switch to the browser to view the changes without having to click on the Refresh or Reload icon.

Figure 2-12   How to use the Live Server extension to open an HTML file in a browser

How to test and debug a web page

When you *test* a web application, your goal is to find all the errors. When you *debug* an application, your goal is to fix all the errors. The topics that follow present some ideas for testing and debugging.

How to test a web page

To test a web page, you start by running it. To do that, you can use one of the ways shown in figure 2-13. Then, to test the web page, you check its contents and appearance to make sure they're exactly the way you want them. You also check each link to make sure it goes where it's supposed to go. If you find errors, you should note them and then debug them.

When the web page works right in one browser, you'll want to test it in the other browsers that are in common use. An easy way to do that is to copy the URL from one browser, open another browser, and paste the URL into that browser.

When you test a web page in more than one browser, you will sometimes find that the page works on one browser, but doesn't work on another. That's usually because one of the browsers makes some assumptions that the other browser doesn't. If, for example, you have a slight coding error in an HTML file, one browser might make an assumption that fixes the problem, while the other doesn't.

How to debug a web page

To debug a web page, you find the causes of the errors and correct them. Often, the changes you make as you debug a web page are just minor adjustments or improvements. But sometimes, the web page doesn't look at all the way you expected it to. Often, these errors are caused by trivial coding problems like missing tags, quotation marks, and braces, but finding these problems can be hard to do when your files consist of dozens of lines of code.

To help you find the causes of your errors, you can use the Developer Tools for your browser. As figure 4-17 in chapter 4 shows, these tools make it easy to see how the HTML and CSS are related.

When you test a page for the second time, you don't need to run it again. Instead, after you save the changes, you can click on the Refresh or Reload icon in the browser's toolbar. But you don't need to do that if you're using VS Code with the Live Server extension because your changes are applied in the browser as soon as you save them.

The HTML file in the Edge browser

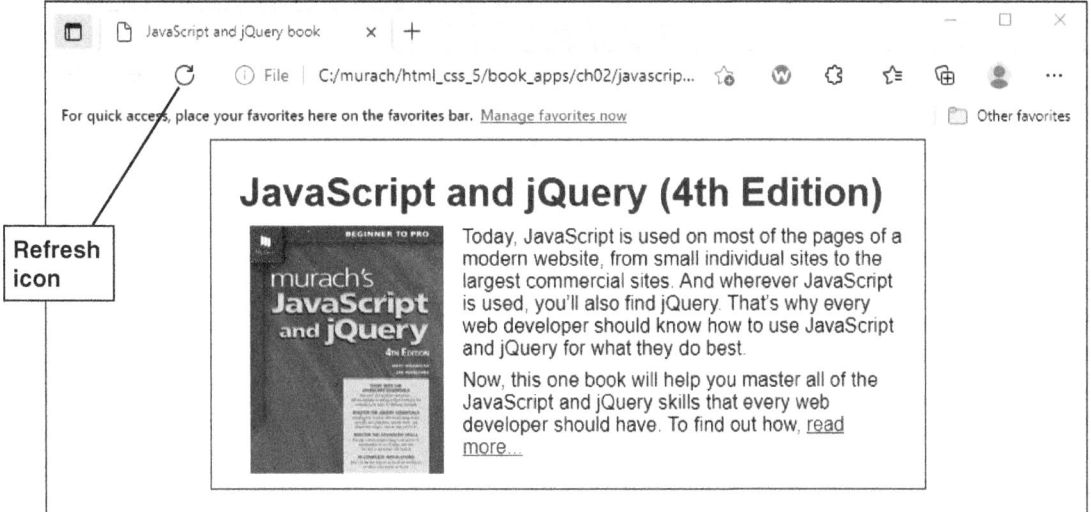

Two ways to run a web page that's on your computer or local network

- Use the features of your text editor or IDE, like Live Server with VS Code.
- Find the file in your file explorer. Then, double-click on it to open it in your default browser. Or, right-click on it and use the Open With command to select the browser.

How to test a web page

- Check the contents and appearance of each page.
- Click on all of the links on each page to make sure they work properly.
- After you've tested your web pages on one browser, test them on the other browsers that your users may be using.

How to debug a web page

- Find the causes of the errors, fix the errors, and save the changes.
- To find the causes of your errors, you can use Chrome's Developer Tools, as shown in figure 4-17 of chapter 4. This tool shows you how the CSS relates to the HTML.
- After you find the cause and fix it, you test the page again. To do that, you can switch to the browser from your text editor or IDE and then click the Refresh or Reload icon.

Description

- When you *test* a web page, you try to find all the errors.
- When you *debug* a web page, you fix the errors and test again.

Figure 2-13 How to test and debug a web page

How to validate HTML and CSS files

After you test and debug your web pages, you're pretty sure that the HTML and CSS is valid. But you can take validation to the next level by using an official validation service to *validate* your files.

These services are useful when a file is large, the HTML or CSS isn't working right, and you can't spot any errors. HTML and CSS validation may also ensure that your code will work on an infrequently-used browser that isn't one of the browsers that you're using for testing.

How to validate an HTML file

One of the most popular websites for validating HTML is the one for the W3C Markup Validation Service that's shown in figure 2-14. When you use this website, you can provide the HTML code that you want to validate in the three ways shown in this figure.

In this example, the Validate by File Upload tab is shown. Then, you click the Browse button to find the file that you want to validate. Once that's done, you click the Check button to validate the document.

If the HTML code is valid when a document is validated, the validator displays a message to that effect. However, it may also display one or more warning messages. On the other hand, if the code contains errors, the validator will display a list of the errors. Then, you can use the error messages to help you correct your code.

The home page for the W3C Markup Validation Service

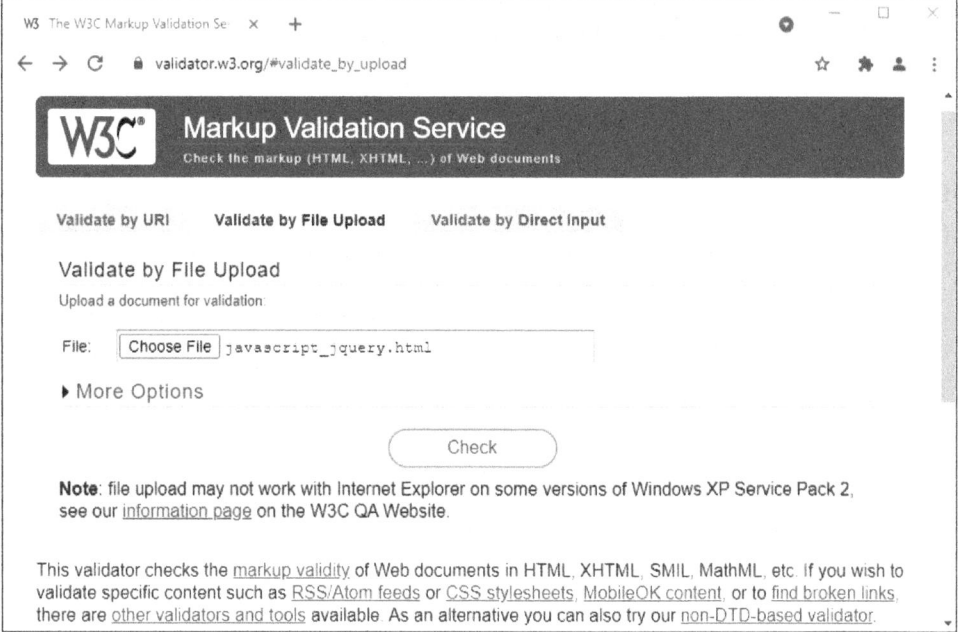

How to use the W3C Markup Validation Service

- Go to the URL that follows, identify the file to be validated, and click the Check button:

  https://validator.w3.org/

Three ways to provide the code to be validated

- If the file you want to validate has been uploaded to a web server, you can enter its URL on the Validate by URI tab.

- If the file hasn't been uploaded to a web server, you can locate it on the Validate by File Upload tab.

- You can also copy and paste the HTML code into the Validate by Direct Input tab.

Description

- To *validate* the HTML for a page, you can use a program or website for that purpose. One of the most popular websites is the W3C Markup Validation Service.

- Validation insures that your code is correct, which may improve SEO. Validation can also help you find errors in your HTML that you aren't aware of.

- If the HTML document is valid, the validator will indicate that the document passed the validation. However, one or more warnings may still be displayed.

- If the HTML document isn't valid, the validator will list and describe each error and warning. You can use the Message Filtering button above the list to display a count of the errors and warnings and to select which errors and warnings you want displayed.

Figure 2-14   How to validate an HTML file

How to validate a CSS file

You can validate a CSS file the same way you validate an HTML file. But this time, you use a website like the W3C CSS Validation Service. Just use the link in figure 2-15 to access this service. Then, you can use any one of the three tabs to validate the CSS file.

If the file contains errors when it is validated, the validation service displays a list of the errors. Then, you can use the error messages to identify and correct your coding errors.

The home page for the W3C CSS Validation Service

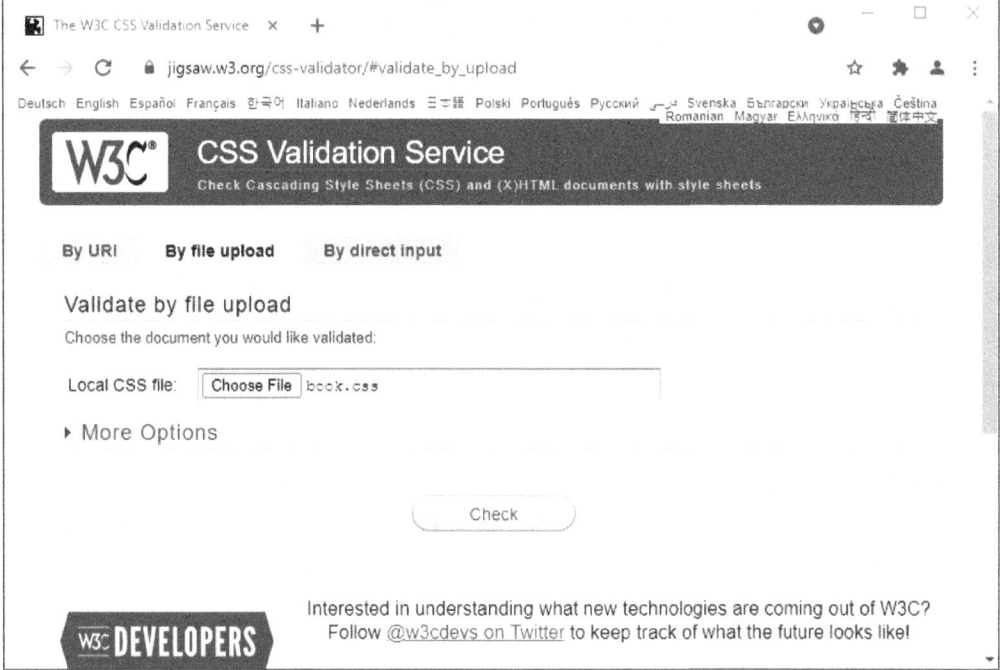

How to use the W3C CSS Validation Service

- Go to the URL that follows, identify the file to be validated, and click the Check button:

  https://jigsaw.w3.org/css-validator/

Description

- To validate the CSS for a page, you can use a program or website for that purpose. One of the most popular websites is the W3C CSS Validation Service.

- Validation not only insures that your code is correct, but it can also help you find errors in your CSS that you aren't aware of.

Figure 2-15   How to validate a CSS file

Perspective

Now that you've completed this chapter, you should be able to create and edit HTML and CSS files using Visual Studio Code. Then, you should be able to test those files by displaying their web pages in your default web browser or any of the other browsers. You should also be able to validate the HTML and CSS files for a web page whenever that's necessary.

At this point, you're ready to learn the coding details for HTML and CSS. So, in the next chapter, you'll learn the details for coding the HTML elements that define the structure and content for a web page. And in chapters 4, 5, and 6, you'll learn the details for coding the CSS style rules that format the HTML content.

Terms

syntax	whitespace
HTML document	style rule
DOCTYPE declaration	selector
document tree	declaration
HTML element	property
root element	value
opening tag	type selector
closing tag	Visual Studio Code (VS Code)
content of an element	preview a file
empty tag	completion list
nested elements	template
attribute	testing
Boolean attribute	debugging
comment	HTML validation
comment out	CSS validation

Summary

- An *HTML document* consists of a *DOCTYPE declaration* that indicates what version of HTML is being used and a *document tree* that contains the *HTML elements* that define the web page.

- The *root element* in a document tree is the html element, which always contains a head element and a body element. The head element provides information about the page, and the body element provides the structure and content for the page.

- Most HTML elements consist of an *opening tag* and a *closing tag* with *content* between these tags. When you *nest* elements with HTML, the inner set of tags must be closed before the outer set.

- *Attributes* can be coded in an opening tag to supply optional values. An attribute consists of the name of the attribute, an equal sign, and the attribute value. To code multiple attributes, you separate them with spaces.

- An *HTML comment* can be used to describe or explain a portion of code. Because comments are ignored, you can also use comments to *comment out* a portion of HTML code so it isn't rendered by the browser. This can be helpful when you're testing your HTML code.

- *Whitespace* consists of characters like tab characters, line return characters, and extra spaces that are ignored by browsers. As a result, you can use whitespace to indent and align your code.

- A *CSS style rule* consists of a selector and declarations. The *selector* identifies the HTML elements that are going to be formatted. Three of the common CSS selectors select by element (called a *type selector*), ID, and class.

- A *declaration* in a CSS style rule consists of a *property*, a colon, a *value*, and a semicolon.

- *CSS comments* work like HTML comments. However, CSS comments start with /* and end with */, and HTML comments start with <!-- and end with -->.

- *Visual Studio Code*, or just *VS Code*, is a text editor that can be used to edit HTML and CSS code. To help you enter code, VS Code provides features like color coding and Intellisense.

- Although VS code provides syntax checking for CSS code, you need to add an extension like HTMLHint to provide syntax checking for HTML code.

- To make it easy to display HTML files in a browser from VS Code, you need to install an extension like Live Server.

- To *test* an HTML file, you run it on all the browsers that your clients may use. When you discover problems, you *debug* the code and test it again.

- To *validate* an HTML or CSS file, you can use a program or website for that purpose. Sometimes, that can help solve hard-to-detect debugging problems.

Before you do the exercises for this book...

If you haven't already done it, you should install the Chrome browser and the applications, examples, and exercises for this book. If you're going to use VS Code as your text editor, you should also download and install that editor. The procedures for doing that for both Windows and macOS users are in appendix A.

Exercise 2-1   Get started right with VS Code

If you're going to be using VS Code as your text editor, this exercise will get you started right. If you aren't going to use VS Code, you can do exercise 2-2.

Start VS Code, review the Welcome page, and change the color theme

1. Start VS Code. Then, review the Welcome page that's in the editor window to see what you can do from it. You don't really need it, though, so you can close that page. And if you don't want it to be opened any more, you can uncheck the box at the bottom of the Welcome page.

2. Select File→Preferences→Color Theme if you're using Windows or Code→Preferences→Color Theme if you're using macOS. Then, review the available color themes. If you want to change the theme, do that now.

Open the folders for this book

3. Use the procedure in figure 2-7 to open the book applications that are stored in this folder:

    `murach\html_css_5\book_apps`

    After you open this folder, you should see the book_apps folder and its subfolders in the Explorer window.

4. Use the same procedure to open this exercises folder:

    `murach\html_css_5\exercises`

    When you do that, note that the exercises folder replaced the book_apps folder.

Edit the code in a book application and use Live Server to test it

5. In the Explorer window, click on the ch02 folder to display the files in that folder. Then, double-click on the file named javascript_jquery.html to open that file. Note that it is now listed under Open Editors.

6. Install the Live Server extension as shown in figure 2-12. Then, click on the Go Live icon to open the HTML file in your default browser.

7. In the javascript_jquery.html file in VS Code, start a new line after the second <p> element. Then, type <p in that line to start a new element and note how VS Code provides a completion list. Select just the p from this list, type the closing bracket for the element, and note how VS code adds the closing tag.

8. Add this text to the <p> element that you just created:

    `For customer service, call us at 1-555-555-5555.`

    Then, save this change. Now, look at the file in the browser that you opened in step 6 to see that it has been updated.

9. Double-click on the file named book.css to open that file. Then, change the color property for the h1 element to red, save the change, and look at the browser to see that the heading is now displayed in red.

Use the split editor feature

10. Close the book.css file so just the javascript_jquery.html file is open. Then, use View→Editor Layout→Two Columns to split the editor. That will open up a second editor window with nothing in it, and two groups will be shown under Open Editors.

11. Click in the right editor to put the cursor there, and double-click on the book.css file in the Explorer window. This will open the CSS file in that second editor window. Now, you can see the code for the HTML and CSS files at the same time.

12. In the CSS file, change the float property for the img element from left to right. Now, save this change, and note the change in the browser.

13. Close the CSS file, and note that the editor returns to one column. Then, close the HTML file so no files are open.

Start new HTML files

14. Use File→New File to start a new file, and use File→Save As to save it with the name testpage1.html in the ch02 folder. Then, enter an exclamation mark into the new file and press the Tab or Enter key.

    This should insert the starting code for an HTML document into the file. That's one way to start a new HTML file, but note that the starting code is minimal.

15. Open the javascript_jquery.html page in the ch02 folder, and save it as testpage2.html. This is another way to start a new file. Now, you just delete what you don't want, change what needs to be changed, and add what needs to be added.

    For example, (1) change the text in the title tag to "HTML and CSS"; (2) change the text in the H1 tag to "HTML and CSS (5th Edition)"; (3) change the code for the src attribute in the image tag to "html_css_5.jpg" and change the alt attribute to "HTML and CSS"; (4) change the text in the first <p> element to "Marketing copy goes here"; and (5) delete the second <p> element.

    Now, save the file. Then, to open this file in a browser, right-click on the file in the VS Code Explorer and select Open with Live Server.

Experiment and clean up

16. If you want to experiment, please do that. When you're through, move the cursor to a file in the Open Editors list and click the X on its left to close one file at a time.

17. When all of the files have been closed, close the browser and close VS Code.

Exercise 2-2   Edit a web page with any editor or IDE

If you aren't using VS Code, this exercise will guide you through the process of editing a web page with any text editor or IDE.

Open and test the files for the book page

1. Start your text editor. Then, open the HTML file named javascript_jquery.html that's in this folder:

   `murach\html_css_5\exercises\ch02`

2. Still in the editor, open the CSS file named book.css that's in the same folder.

3. Run the HTML file in Chrome.

Modify the HTML and CSS code and test again

4. Go to the javascript_jquery.html file, and add a <p> element at the bottom of the page that has this content:

   `For customer service, call us at 1-555-555-5555.`

   Then, save and test this change in your browser.

5. Go to your text editor and display the book.css file. Then, change the color property for the h1 element to red, save the change, and test it in your browser.

6. Still in the CSS file, change the float property for the img element from left to right. Then, save and test that change.

7. Continue to experiment on your own, and close the files when you're done.

Exercise 2-3   Validate HTML and CSS files

You can do this exercise whether or not you're using VS Code as your editor.

1. Use your editor or IDE to open the HTML file named javascript_jquery.html that's in this folder:

   `murach\html_css_5\exercises\ch02`

   Then, delete the ending > for the img tag, and save the file.

2. Go to the site in figure 2-14, and use the Validate by File Upload tab to validate the file. Then, scroll down the page to see the 3 error messages that are displayed for the one error.

3. Open the CSS file named book.css that's in the step 1 folder. Then, delete the semicolon after the font-size property in the h1 style rule, and save the file.

4. Go to the site in figure 2-15, and use the By File Upload tab to validate the file. This time, you'll see 1 error message.

5. Fix the errors, save the files, and validate the files again so there are no errors.

Chapter 3

How to use HTML to structure a web page

In chapter 2, you saw the basic structure of an HTML document, and you learned the basic techniques for coding the elements that make up a document. Now, in this chapter, you'll learn how to code the HTML elements that you'll use in most of your documents. Then, in the next three chapters, you'll learn how to use CSS to format those HTML elements.

How to code the head section

The head section of an HTML document contains elements that provide information about the web page rather than the content of the page. It requires a minimum amount of code, and figure 3-1 shows how to code it.

How to include metadata

You should use the meta element shown in this figure to provide two items of *metadata* for every web page. In the example, the first meta element specifies the character encoding used for the page, and UTF-8 is the encoding that's commonly used for the World Wide Web.

The second meta element provides a description that can be used by search engines to index the page. This description should summarize the contents of the web page. And when it's shown in the search results, it should encourage users to access your site.

How to code the title element
and link to a favicon

The head section of every web page should also include a title element that describes the content of the page. In the HTML in this figure, you can see that this element gives the name of the organization followed by the keywords *speakers* and *luncheons*. This title is used by search engines, and it appears in the search results to help the users decide whether they want to go to that page.

The content of the title element is also displayed in the browser's tab for the page. As you can see in this figure, only the portion of the title that fits on the tab is displayed. But if the user hovers the mouse over the tab, the entire title should be displayed in a tooltip.

The link element can be used in the head section to link a custom icon, called a *favicon*, to the web page. This causes the icon to be displayed to the left of the title in the tab for the page. But note that you don't need to code this element when you deploy the website to an Internet server. Instead, you can place the favicon in the root folder for the website and it will automatically appear in the tab for each page.

A browser that shows the title and favicon

A head section that sets a title, a favicon, and two items of metadata

```
<head>
    <meta charset="utf-8">
                                                    for search engines
    <meta name="description" content="A yearly lecture series with speakers
        that present new information on a wide range of subjects">
    <title>San Joaquin Valley Town Hall | speakers and luncheons</title>
    <link rel="shortcut icon" href="favicon.ico">
</head>
                                                    keywords
                                                    tags after title to help in
                          picture next to title     search engines
                            in tab
## SEO guidelines for the metadata    (favicon)
```

- Code description metadata that summarizes the contents of the page. The description should be unique for each page, and it should encourage uses to click on the link when it's displayed in search results.

SEO guidelines for the title tag

- Code a title tag in the head section of each web page. It should describe the page's content, and it should include the one or two keywords, called *focus keywords*, that you want to be used to rank the page.
- The title should entice the reader to click on it when it's shown in the search results for a search engine. It should be unique for each web page, and it should be limited to around 65 characters because most search engines don't display more than that in their results.

Description

- The meta element provides information about the HTML document that's called *metadata*. It should be used to provide the charset and description for each page.
- The title element specifies the text that's displayed in the browser's tab for the web page. It is also used as the name of a favorite or bookmark for the page.
- A *favicon* is an icon that appears to the left of the title in the browser's tab for the page. It may also appear to the left of the URL in the browser's address bar, and it may be used in a favorite or bookmark.
- To specify a favicon for a page, you use favicon.ico as the name of the favicon and you code a link element exactly like the one above. Then, the favicon will be displayed when you test the page on your computer or local server.
- Note, however, that you don't need to code the link element for the favicon when you deploy the website to an Internet server. You just need to store the favicon in the root folder.

Figure 3-1   How to code the head section of an HTML document

How to present the contents of a web page

The next three figures show how to present the contents of a web page. That includes how to structure that content for web accessibility and search engine optimization.

How to code the lang attribute

Figure 3-2 starts by showing how to code the lang attribute that should identify the language for each of your web pages. To do that, you code the lang attribute for the html element of each page just as it's shown. In this case, that attribute is set to "en" so English is the language.

How to code headings and paragraphs

Headings and paragraphs provide most of the text for a web page. They are defined by the HTML elements in the second table in figure 3-2. These elements are *block elements*, which means that they start on a new line when they are displayed.

In the example in this figure, you can see how these elements work. Here, the HTML uses the h1, h2, and <p> elements to generate the text that's shown. When these elements are displayed by a browser, each element has a default font and size that's determined by the base font of the browser. This base font is typically Times New Roman in 16 pixels.

When you use the heading elements, the most important heading on a page should be an h1 element. You should only code one h1 element on each page. And you should only go down one level at a time, not jump down two or more levels to indicate less importance. In other words, the first heading level after an h1 should be an h2, not an h3. This structure helps search engines index your site, and it makes your pages more accessible to devices like screen readers.

Incidentally, HTML provides for three more levels below h3 with tags that range from h4 through h6. However, you shouldn't need these levels for the normal structure of a web page.

An attribute that should be coded in the html element for each page

Attribute	Description
lang	Identifies the language for the page

The block elements for headings and paragraphs

Element	Description
h1	A level-1 heading with content in bold at 200% of the base font size
h2	A level-2 heading with content in bold at 150% of the base font size
h3	A level-3 heading with content in bold at 117% of the base font size
p	A paragraph of text at 100% of the base font size

HTML that uses these block elements

```html
<html lang="en">    language = english
    <h1>San Joaquin Valley Town Hall Programs</h1>
    <h2>Pre-lecture coffee at the Saroyan</h2>
    <p>Join us for a complimentary coffee hour, 9:15 to 10:15 a.m. on the
        day of each lecture. The speakers usually attend this very special
        event.</p>
    <h2>Post-lecture luncheon at the Saroyan</h2>
    <p>Extend the excitement of Town Hall by purchasing tickets to the
        luncheons.</p>
</html>
```

The block elements in a web browser

San Joaquin Valley Town Hall Programs

Pre-lecture coffee at the Saroyan

Join us for a complimentary coffee hour, 9:15 to 10:15 a.m. on the day of each lecture. The speakers usually attend this very special event.

Post-lecture luncheon at the Saroyan

Extend the excitement of Town Hall by purchasing tickets to the luncheons.

SEO guidelines

- Use the h1 tag to identify the most important information on the page, and only code one h1 tag on each page. Then, decrease one level at a time to show lower levels of importance.

Description

- *Block elements* are the building blocks of a website. They always start on a new line and take up the full space of the area that they're in.
- The base font size and the spacing above and below headings and paragraphs are determined by the browser, but you can change those values by using CSS.

Figure 3-2   How to code the lang attribute, headings, and paragraphs

How to code the structural elements

Figure 3-3 presents the structural elements that were introduced with HTML5. To illustrate, the example in this figure shows how the header, main, and footer elements can be used to divide a web page into three parts. Later, this structure makes it easy to use CSS to change the page layout and format the content.

All of these structural elements are block elements. But unlike the heading and paragraph elements, you can nest other block elements within these structural elements. In the HTML code in this figure, for example, you can see that an h1 element is nested within the header element, and a <p> element is nested within both the main and footer elements.

Although this figure only illustrates the use of three of the seven elements in the table, you'll see the nav element used in the web page at the end of this chapter. And in later chapters, you'll see how the aside element is used for a sidebar within the main element; how the section element is used for other content within the main element; and how the article element is used for an article about a speaker.

But at this point, please note that all the HTML elements that you've learned about so far in this chapter have indicated the type of content they contain. For example, an h1 element identifies the top-level heading for a page, and the main element identifies the main content for a page. Elements like these are called *semantic elements* because they give meaning to their content, and the use of these elements can be referred to as *HTML semantics*.

Semantics of course are good for both the developer and the browser. And that in turn means that they improve both web accessibility and search engine optimization.

The primary HTML structural elements

Element	Contents
header	The header for a page
main	The main content for a page
section	A generic section of a document that doesn't indicate the type of content
article	A composition like an article in the paper
nav	A section of a page that contains links to other pages or placeholders
aside	A section of a page like a sidebar that is related to the content that's near it
footer	The footer for a page

A page that's structured with header, main, and footer elements

```html
<html lang="en">
<body>
    <header>
        <h1>San Joaquin Valley Town Hall</h1>
    </header>
    <main>
        <p>Welcome to San Joaquin Valley Town Hall. We have some
            fascinating speakers for you this season!</p>
    </main>
    <footer>
        <p>Copyright 2022 San Joaquin Valley Town Hall.</p>
    </footer>
</body>
</html>
```

The page displayed in a web browser

San Joaquin Valley Town Hall

Welcome to San Joaquin Valley Town Hall. We have some fascinating speakers for you this season!

Copyright 2022, San Joaquin Valley Town Hall.

Accessibility and SEO guideline

• Use the HTML structural elements to indicate the structure of your pages.

Description

• All of the HTML structural elements are block elements that can contain other block elements.
• Since structural elements like these identify the contents of the elements, they are called *semantic elements* and the process of using them is called *HTML semantics*.

Figure 3-3 How to code the structural elements

When and how to use div elements

But what happens if you want to divide one of the structural elements into two or more parts and there isn't a semantic element for that? Then, you can use div elements as shown in figure 3-4. Here, the first example shows how two div elements can be used to divide a section element into two divisions. Then, you can use CSS to lay out and format these divisions separately.

The second example in this figure shows how div elements were used before HTML5 introduced the structural elements. Here, you can see that the div elements divide the page into header, main, and footer divisions by using id attributes to identify them. But the div elements aren't semantic and don't help web accessibility or search engine optimization. That's why you don't want to use div elements when you can use the structural elements.

The div element

Element	Description
div	A block element that can be used to divide a structural element into divisions

How to use div elements to structure the content within a section

```
<section>
    <div>
        <h1>The first priority</h1>
        <p>The elements for the first priority</p>
    </div>
    <div>
        <h1>The second priority</h1>
        <p>The elements for the second priority</p>
    </div>
</section>
```

The resulting web page

The first priority

The elements for the first priority

The second priority

The elements for the second priority

How div elements were used before HTML5

```
<body>
    <div id="header">
        <h1>San Joaquin Valley Town Hall</h1>
    </div>
    <div id="main">
        <p>Welcome to San Joaquin Valley Town Hall. We have some
            fascinating speakers for you this season!</p>
    </div>
    <div id="footer">
        <p>Copyright 2015, San Joaquin Valley Town Hall.</p>
    </div>
</body>
```

Accessibility and SEO guidelines

- Only use div tags when the HTML semantic elements don't apply.

Description

- Before HTML5, div elements were used to provide the structure for a web page. But now, div elements should only be used to provide structure within a semantic element.

Figure 3-4   When and how to use div elements

Other elements for presenting text

The next two figures show how to use inline elements, other block elements, and character entities to present the text for a web page.

How to code the inline elements for text

In contrast to a block element, an *inline element* doesn't start on a new line. Instead, an inline element is coded within a block element. In figure, 3-5, you can see how 14 inline elements can be used to provide and format the text for a web page.

The first table in this figure presents elements that you can use to identify inline content. For instance, you can use the abbr element to identify an abbreviation, the <q> element to identify a quotation, and the cite element to identify the source of a block element like a quotation.

The second table presents elements that you can use to format content. For instance, the em and strong elements can be used to provide two different levels of emphasis. And the sub and sup elements let you provide for subscripts and superscripts.

The examples illustrate a few of these elements. Note that the <q> element adds quotation marks to a quotation. The em element converts the text to italics. And the strong element converts the text to boldface.

For the record, you can also use the <i> and <b> tags to italicize and boldface text. But since they don't imply any special meaning, it's better to use the elements in the second table.

Now notice the last element in the second table. It is the span element, which is an inline element with no meaning. Although you will rarely need to use it because it's better to use elements with meaning, you will see it used by the JavaScript code in chapter 18. You can also use it to apply CSS formatting to a portion of text in a block element when that formatting doesn't fall into one of the other categories in the second table.

Inline elements that identify the content

Element	Use
abbr	An abbreviation
cite	A bibliographic citation like a book title
code	Computer code that's displayed in a monospaced font
dfn	A term that is defined elsewhere
kbd	A keyboard entry that is displayed in a monospaced font
q	A quotation that is displayed within quotation marks
samp	A sequence of characters (a sample) that has no other meaning
time	A date or a date and time in a standard format
var	A computer variable that is displayed in a monospaced font

Inline elements that format text

Element	Use
em	To indicate that the content should be emphasized with an italic font
small	To display "fine print" such as footnotes in a smaller font
strong	To indicate that the content should be strongly emphasized in a bold font
sub	To display the content as a subscript
sup	To display the content as a superscript
span	An inline element with no meaning that formatting can be applied to

HTML that uses some of the inline elements

```
<p>When the dialog box is displayed, enter <kbd>brock21</kbd>.</p>
<p>To quote Hamlet: <q>Conscience does make cowards of us all.</q></p>
<p>If you don't get 78% or more on your final, <em>you won't pass.</em></p>
<p>Save a bundle at our <strong>big yearend sale</strong>.</p>
<p>The chemical symbol for water is H<sub>2</sub>O.</p>
```

The inline elements in a web browser

When the dialog box is displayed, enter brock21.

To quote Hamlet: "Conscience does make cowards of us all."

If you don't get 78% or more on your final, *you won't pass.*

Save a bundle at our **big yearend sale**.

The chemical symbol for water is H_2O.

Description

- An *inline element* is coded within a block element and doesn't begin on a new line.
- Although you can use the <b> and <i> elements to apply bold and italics to text, it's better to use the formatting elements in this figure.

Figure 3-5   How to code the inline elements for text

How to use character entities and three block elements for text

Figure 3-6 shows how to use *character entities* and three more block elements for text. In the first table, you can see 12 of the many character entities that provide a way to include characters like ampersands (&) and degree symbols in your text. As you can see, all character entities start with an ampersand (&) and end with a semicolon (;). Then, the rest of the entity identifies the character it represents.

In the second table, you can see three more block elements for coding special types of text. For instance, the blockquote element can be used to display a quotation, and the address element can be used to present contact information. Like the structural elements, these elements are good semantically because they identify the contents.

The examples that follow illustrate how character entities and these block elements work. Here, the blockquote element is used for a quotation, but note that quotation marks aren't added to it. Then, the address element is used for contact information.

Last, two character entities are used within a <p> element. The first one provides the copyright symbol. The second one provides an ampersand.

This shows that you can't just type an ampersand in your text because the ampersand is the first character in a character entity. Similarly, because the left bracket (<) and right bracket (>) are used to identify HTML tags, you can't use those characters to represent less-than and greater-than signs. Instead, you need to use the < and > entities.

You should know, however, that in some cases the &, <, and > characters will work without coding them as character entities. If you want them to work for all purposes and pass all validation tests, though, it's best to code them as character entities.

Common HTML character entities

Entity	Character	Entity	Character
&	&	°	°
<	<	±	±
>	>	¢	¢
©	©	‘	' (opening single quote)
®	®	’	' (closing single quote or apostrophe)
™	™		non-breaking space

Block elements for special types of text

Element	Used for
blockquote	A quotation
address	Contact information for the developer or owner of a website
pre	Preformatted text with preserved whitespace and a monospaced font

HTML that uses these block elements and character entities

```
<p>Ernest Hemingway wrote:</p>
<blockquote>
    Cowardice, as distinguished from panic, is almost always simply
    a lack of ability to suspend the functioning of the imagination.
</blockquote>

<address>1-800-221-5528<br>
    <a href="emailto:murachbooks@murach.com">murachbooks@murach.com</a>
</address>

<p>&copy; 2022 Mike Murach &amp; Associates, Inc.</p>
```

The examples in a web browser

Ernest Hemingway wrote:

> Cowardice, as distinguished from panic, is almost always simply a lack of ability to suspend the functioning of the imagination.

1-800-221-5528
murachbooks@murach.com

© 2022 Mike Murach & Associates, Inc.

Description

- *Character entities* are used to display special characters in an HTML document.
- These block elements are good semantically because they identify the type of content.

Figure 3-6   How to use character entities and three block elements for text

How to code links, lists, and images

Because you'll use links, lists, and images in most of the web pages that you develop, the topics that follow introduce you to these elements. But first, you need to know how to code absolute and relative URLs so you can use them with your links and images.

How to code URLs

Figure 3-7 presents some examples of absolute and relative URLs. To help you understand how these examples work, the diagram at the top of this figure shows the folder structure for the website used in the examples. As you can see, the folders are organized into three levels. The root folder for the site contains five subfolders, including the folders that contain the images and styles for the site. Then, the books folder contains subfolders of its own.

In chapter 1, you learned the basic components of an *absolute URL*, which includes the domain name of the website. This is illustrated by the first group of examples in this figure. Here, both URLs refer to pages at www.murach.com. The first URL points to the index.html file in the root folder of this website, and the second URL points to the toc.html file in the root/books/php folder.

When used within the code for the web pages of a site, an absolute URL is used to refer to a file in another website. By contrast, a *relative URL* is used to refer to a file within the same website. And as this figure shows, there are two types of relative URLs.

In a *root-relative path*, the path is relative to the root folder of the website. This is illustrated by the second group of examples. Here, the leading slash indicates the root folder for the site. As a result, the first path refers to the login.html file in the root folder, and the second path refers to the logo.gif file in the images folder.

In a *document-relative path*, the path is relative to the current document. This is illustrated by the third group of examples. Here, the assumption is that the paths are coded in a file that is in the root folder for a website. Then, the first path refers to a file in the images subfolder of the root folder, and the second path refers to a file in the php subfolder of the books subfolder. This illustrates paths that navigate down the levels of the folder structure.

But you can also navigate up the levels with a document-relative path. This is illustrated by the fourth group of examples. Here, the assumption is that the current document is in the root/books folder. Then, the first path goes up one level for the index.html file in the root folder. The second path also goes up one level to the root folder and then down one level for the logo.gif file in the images folder.

This shows that there's more than one way to code the path for a file. If, for example, you're coding an HTML file in the root/books folder, you can use either a root-relative path or a document-relative path to get to the images subfolder. If this is confusing right now, you'll get used to it when you start coding your own pages.

A simple website folder structure

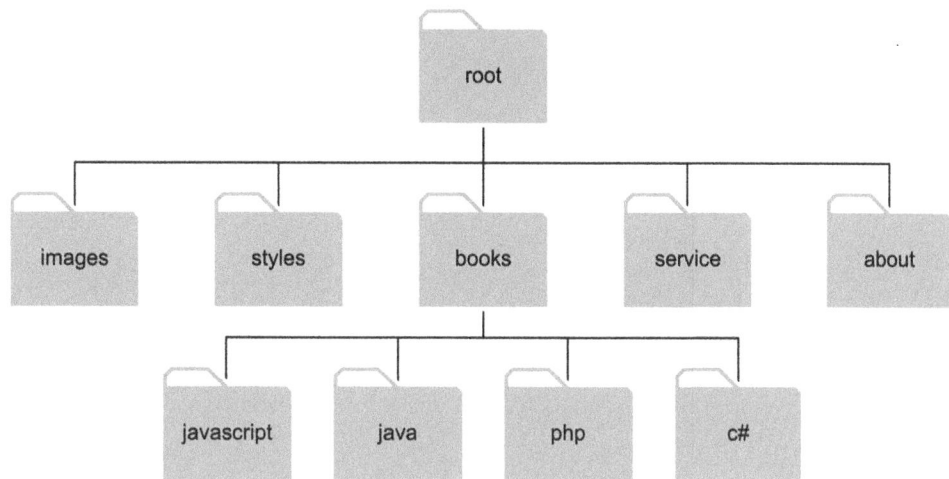

Examples of absolute and relative URLs

Absolute URLs

```
http://www.murach.com/index.html
http://www.murach.com/books/php/toc.html
```

Root-relative paths

```
/login.html              (refers to root/login.html)
/images/logo.gif         (refers to root/images/logo.gif)
```

Document-relative paths that navigate down from the root folder

```
images/logo.gif          (refers to root/images/logo.gif)
books/php/overview.html  (refers to root/books/php/overview.html)
```

Document-relative paths that navigate up from the root/books folder

```
../index.html            (refers to root/index.html)
../images/logo.gif       (refers to root/images/logo.gif)
```

Description

- When you code an *absolute URL*, you code the complete URL including the domain name for the site. Absolute URLs let you display pages at other websites.

- When you code a *relative URL*, you base it on the current folder, which is the folder that contains the current page.

- A *root-relative path* is relative to the root folder of the website. It always starts with a slash. Then, to go down one subfolder, you code the subfolder name and a slash. To go down two subfolders, you code a second subfolder name and another slash. And so on.

- A *document-relative path* is relative to the folder the current document is in. Then, to go down one subfolder, you code the subfolder name followed by a slash. To go down two subfolders, you code a second subfolder name followed by another slash. And so on.

- You can also go up in a document-relative path. To go up one level from the current folder, you code two periods and a slash. To go up two levels, you code two periods and a slash followed by two more periods and a slash. And so on.

Figure 3-7   How to code URLs

How to code links

Most web pages contain *links* that go to other web pages or web resources. To code a link, you use the <a> element (or anchor element) as shown in figure 3-8. Because this element is an inline element, you usually code it within a block element like a <p> element.

In most cases, you'll code only the href attribute for the <a> element. This attribute specifies the URL for the resource you want to link to. The examples in this figure illustrate how this works.

The first example uses a relative URL to link to a page in the same folder as the current page. The second example uses a relative URL to link to a page in a subfolder of the parent folder. The third example uses a relative URL to link to a page based on the root folder. And the last example uses an absolute URL to link to a page at another website.

By default, links are underlined when they're displayed in a browser to indicate that they're clickable. As a result, most web users have been conditioned to associate underlined text with links. Because of that, you should avoid underlining any other text.

When a link is displayed, it has a default color depending on its state. For instance, a link that hasn't been visited is displayed in blue, and a link that has been visited is displayed in purple. Note, however, that you can use CSS as described in the next chapter to change these settings.

When you create a link that contains text, the text should clearly indicate the function of the link. For example, you shouldn't use text like "click here" because it doesn't indicate what the link does. Instead, you should use text like that in the examples in this figure. In short, if you can't tell where a link goes by reading its text, you should rewrite the text. This improves the accessibility of your site, and it helps search engines index your site.

The primary attribute of the <a> element

Attribute	Description
href	Specifies a relative or absolute URL for a link.

A link to a web page in the same folder

```
<p>Go view our <a href="products.html">product list</a>.</p>
```

A link to a web page in a subfolder of the parent folder

```
<p>Read about the <a href="../company/services.html">services we
provide</a>.</p>
```

A link to a web page based on the root folder

```
<p>View your <a href="/orders/cart.html">shopping cart</a>.</p>
```

A link to a web page at another website

```
<p>To learn more about JavaScript, visit the
<a href="http://www.javascript.com/">official JavaScript web site</a>.</p>
```

The links in a web browser

Go view our product list.

Read about the services we provide.

View your shopping cart.

To learn more about JavaScript, visit the official JavaScript website.

SEO and accessibility guideline

- The content of a link should be text that clearly indicates where the link is going.

Description

- The <a> element is an inline element that creates a *link* that loads another web page. The href attribute of this element identifies the page to be loaded.
- The text content of a link is underlined by default to indicate that it's clickable.
- If a link hasn't been visited, it's displayed in blue. If it has been visited, it's displayed in purple. But you can change these values using CSS.
- If the mouse hovers over a link, the cursor is changed to a hand with the finger pointed as shown above.
- For more information on coding <a> elements, see chapter 7.

Figure 3-8   How to code links

How to code lists

Figure 3-9 shows how to code the two basic types of lists: ordered lists and unordered lists. To create an *unordered list*, you use the ul element. Then, within this element, you code one li (list item) element for each item in the list. The content of each li element is the text that's displayed in the list. By default, when a list is displayed in a browser, each item in an unordered list is preceded by a bullet. However, you can change that bullet with CSS.

To create an *ordered list*, you use the ol element, along with one li element for each item in the list. This works like the ul element, except that the items are preceded by numbers rather than bullets when they're displayed in a browser. In this case, you can change the type of numbers that are used with CSS.

The two lists shown in this figure illustrate how this works. Here, the first list displays the names of several programming languages, so these items don't need to reflect any order. By contrast, the second list identifies three steps for completing an order. Because these steps must be completed in a prescribed sequence, they're displayed in an ordered list.

When you work with the li element, you should be aware that it can contain text, inline elements, or block elements. For example, an li element can contain an <a> element that defines a link. In fact, it's a best practice to code a series of links within an unordered list. You'll see an example of that later in this chapter, and you'll learn all about it in chapter 7.

Elements that create ordered and unordered lists

Element	Description
`<ul>`	Creates an unordered list.
`<ol>`	Creates an ordered list.
`<li>`	Creates a list item for an unordered or ordered list.

HTML that creates two lists

```
<p>We have books on a variety of languages, including</p>
<ul>
    <li>JavaScript</li>
    <li>PHP</li>
    <li>Java</li>
    <li>C#</li>
</ul>

<p>You will need to complete the following steps:</p>
<ol>
    <li>Enter your billing information.</li>
    <li>Enter your shipping information.</li>
    <li>Confirm your order.</li>
</ol>
```

The lists in a web browser

We have books on a variety of languages, including

- JavaScript
- PHP
- Java
- C#

You will need to complete the following steps:

1. Enter your billing information.
2. Enter your shipping information.
3. Confirm your order.

Description

- The two basic types of lists are *unordered lists* and *ordered lists*.
- By default, an unordered list is displayed as a bulleted list, and an ordered list is displayed as a numbered list.
- For more information on coding lists, see chapter 7.

Figure 3-9   How to code lists

How to include images

Images are an important part of most web pages. To display an image, you use the img element shown in figure 3-10. This is an inline element that's coded as an empty tag. In the example in this figure, this tag is coded before an h1 element. The h1 element is displayed below it, though, because it's a block element that starts on a new line.

The src (source) attribute of an img element specifies the URL of the image that you want to display, and it is required. For instance, the src attribute for the image in this example indicates that the image named murachlogo.gif can be found in the images subfolder of the current folder.

The alt attribute should also be coded for img elements. You typically use this attribute to provide information about the image in case it can't be displayed or the page is being accessed by a screen reader. This is essential for visually-impaired users.

In this example, the image is our company's logo, so the value of the alt attribute is set to "Murach Logo". If an image doesn't provide any meaning, however, you should code the value of the alt attribute as an empty string (""). You should do that, for example, when an image is only used for decoration.

You can use the height and width attributes of an img element to tell the browser what the size of an image is. That can help the browser lay out the page as the image is being loaded. Although you can also use the height and width attributes to render an image larger (known as "stretching") or smaller than the original image, it's better to use your image editor to make the image the right size. You'll learn more about working with images in chapter 11.

Attributes of the <img> element

Attribute	Description
src	The relative URL of the image to display. It is a required attribute.
alt	Alternate text that's displayed in place of the image. This text is read aloud by screen readers for users with disabilities. It is required.
height	The height of the image in pixels.
width	The width of the image in pixels.

An img element

```
<img src="images/murachlogo.gif" alt="Murach Logo" height="75">
<h1>Mike Murach &amp; Associates, Inc.</h1>
```

The image in a web browser

Mike Murach & Associates, Inc.

Common image formats

- JPEG (Joint Photographic Experts Group)
- GIF (Graphic Interchange Format)
- PNG (Portable Network Graphics)

Accessibility guidelines

- For images with useful content, always code an alt attribute that describes the image.
- For images that are used for decoration, code the alt attribute with no value (" ").

Description

- The img element is an inline element that is used to display an image that's identified by the src attribute.
- The height and width attributes can be used to indicate the size of an image so the browser can allocate the correct amount of space on the page. These attributes can also be used to size an image, but it's usually better to use an image editor to do that.
- JPEG files have the JPG extension and are used for photographs. GIF files are used for small illustrations and logos. And PNG files combine aspects of JPEG and GIF files.
- For more information on coding img elements, see chapter 11.

Figure 3-10   How to include images

A structured web page

Now that you've seen the HTML elements for structuring a web page, figure 3-11 presents a simple web page that uses these elements.

The page layout

The purpose of the web page in this figure is to provide information about a series of lectures being presented by a non-profit organization. It shows the default formatting for the HTML that's used for this page. In the next chapter, though, you'll learn how to use CSS to improve the formatting of this page.

The HTML file

The HTML for this web page starts with the DOCTYPE declaration, the html element, and head element. They illustrate the way these items should be coded for every web page that you create.

In the html element, you can see the use of the lang attribute. In the head element, you can see the coding for the charset meta element, the title element, and a favicon. Although it isn't' shown here, you should also include a meta element for the description in most web pages.

In the body element, you can see the use of the structural elements. Here, the header element contains one h2 element. The main element contains one h1 element, a nav element, and a <p> element. And the footer element contains one <p> element.

Within the nav element is an unordered list that contains five li elements (although the HTML is shown for only two of them). Then, each li element contains an <a> element. This is a best practice because a nav element should contain a series of links. It is also a best practice to code the <a> elements within an unordered list.

You can also see the use of an <em> element that italicizes the first four words in the <p> element within the main element and a character entity that inserts the copyright symbol into the <p> element within the footer. But what's most important in this example is the use of the HTML structural elements and HTML semantics. That's good for the developer as well as for search engine optimization.

A web page that uses some of the HTML in this chapter

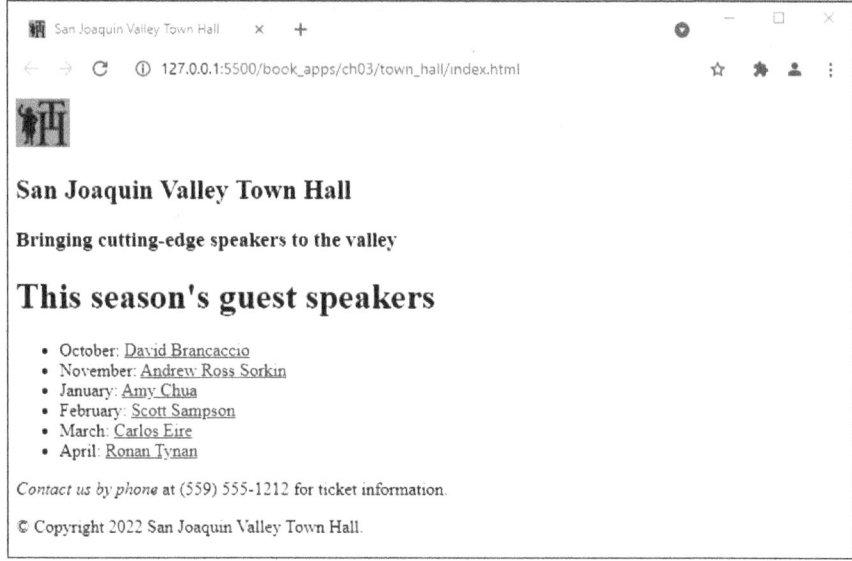

The HTML file for the web page

```html
<!DOCTYPE html>
<html lang="en">
    <head>
        <meta charset="utf-8">
        <title>San Joaquin Valley Town Hall</title>
        <link rel="shortcut icon" href="images/favicon.ico">
    </head>
    <body>
        <header>
            <img src="images/logo.jpg" alt="Town Hall Logo" width="50">
            <h2>San Joaquin Valley Town Hall</h2>
        </header>
        <main>
            <h1>This season's guest speakers</h1>
            <nav>
                <ul>
                    <li>October: <a href="speakers/brancaccio.html">
                        David Brancaccio</a></li>
                    <li>November: <a href="speakers/sorkin.html">
                        Andrew Ross Sorkin</a></li>
                    ...
                </ul>
            </nav>
            <p><em>Contact us by phone</em> at (559) 555-1212 for ticket
                information.</p>
        </main>
        <footer>
            <p>&copy; Copyright 2022 San Joaquin Valley Town Hall.</p>
        </footer>
    </body>
</html>
```

Figure 3-11   A structured web page

Perspective

This chapter has presented most of the HTML elements that you will need as you develop web pages. That includes both block and inline elements. With those skills, you can create web pages that have the default formatting of the browser. Then, in the next three chapters, you will learn how to use CSS to format your pages so they look just the way you want them.

Terms

metadata	absolute URL
favicon	relative URL
focus keywords	root-relative path
block element	document-relative path
semantic elements	link
HTML semantics	ordered list
inline element	unordered list
character entity	

Summary

- The meta elements in the head section of a document provide *metadata* that includes the character set and description for the page. This can improve search engine optimization.

- The title in the head section of an HTML document provides the text that's displayed in the browser's tab for the page. This can also improve search engine optimization.

- You can code a link element in the head section to identify a custom icon called a *favicon* that appears in the browser's tab for the page. This icon may also appear in the browser's address bar or as part of a bookmark.

- *Block elements* are the primary content elements of a website, and each block element starts on a new line when it is rendered by a browser. Headings and paragraphs are common block elements.

- The HTML structural elements are block elements that let you structure a page into components like a header, a main portion, a navigation area, a sidebar, and a footer.

- Elements like header, main, footer, h1, and <p> are called *semantic elements* because they identify their contents. These elements are good for both developer and browser, and using them is referred as *HTML semantics*.

- Div elements can be used to provide structure within the structural elements. But they should only be used when there isn't an appropriate structural element.

- *Inline elements* are coded within block elements, and they don't start on new lines when they are rendered. HTML provides many inline elements that can be used to identify and format text.

- *Character entities* are used to display special characters like the ampersand and copyright symbol in an HTML document. In code, character entities start with an ampersand and end with a semicolon as in   (a non-breaking space).

- When you code an *absolute URL*, you code the complete URL including the domain name. When you code a *relative URL*, you can use a *root-relative path* to start the path from the root folder for the website or a *document-relative path* to start the path from the current document.

- The <a> element (or anchor element) is an inline element that creates a *link* that usually loads another page. By default, the text of an <a> element is underlined. Also, an unvisited link is displayed in blue and a visited link in purple.

- Lists are block elements that can be used to display both *unordered lists* and *ordered lists*. By default, these lists are indented with bullets before the items in an unordered list and numbers before the items in an ordered list.

- The img element is used to display an image file. The three common formats for images are *JPEG* (for photographs), *GIF* (for small illustrations and logos), and *PNG*, which combines aspects of JPEG and GIF.

About the exercises

In the exercises for chapters 3 through 8, you'll develop a new version of the Town Hall website. This version will be like the one in the text, but it will have different content, different formatting, and different page layouts.

As you develop this site, you will use this folder structure:

This is a realistic structure with images in the images folder, speaker HTML pages in the speakers folder, and CSS files in the styles folder. In addition, the text folder contains text files that will provide all of the content you need for your pages. That too is realistic because a web developer often works with text that has been written by someone else.

Exercise 3-1   Enter the HTML for the home page

In this exercise, you'll code the HTML for the home page. When you're through, the page should look like the one on the facing page, but with three speakers.

Open the starting page and get the contents for it

1. Use your text editor to open this HTML file:
    `\html_css_5\exercises\town_hall_1\c3_index.html`

    Note that it contains the head section for this web page as well as a body section that contains a header element with some text, a main element, and a footer element with some text.

2. Use your text editor to open this text file:
    `\html_css_5\exercises\town_hall_1\text\c3_content.txt`

    Note that it includes all of the text for the main element.

Enter the header

3. Code the img element that gets the image at the top of the page from the images folder. To locate the image file, use this document-relative path: images/town_hall_logo.gif. Be sure to include the alt attribute, and set the height attribute of the image to 80.

4. Apply the h2 and h3 elements to the text in the header element. Then, test this page in Chrome. If necessary, correct the HTML and test again.

What the home page should look like

San Joaquin Valley Town Hall

Celebrating our 75th Year

Our Mission

San Joaquin Valley Town Hall is a non-profit organization that is run by an all-volunteer board of directors. Our mission is to bring nationally and internationally renowned, thought-provoking speakers who inform, educate, and entertain our audience! As one or our members told us:

> "Each year I give a ticket package to each of our family members. I think of it as the gift of knowledge...and that is priceless."

Our Ticket Packages

- Season Package: $95
- Patron Package: $200
- Single Speaker: $25

This season's guest speakers

October
David Brancaccio

© 2022, San Joaquin Valley Town Hall, Fresno, CA 93755

Enter the content for the main element

5. Copy all of the content for the main element from the txt file into the HTML file. Then, add an h1 tag to the heading "This season's guest speakers", and add h2 tags to these headings "Our Mission" and "Our Ticket Packages".

6. Add <p> tags to the first block of text after the "Our Mission" heading, and add blockquote tags to the second block of text as shown above.

7. Add the ul and li tags that are needed for the three items after the "Our Ticket Packages" heading. Then, test these changes and make any adjustments.

8. Format the name and month for the first speaker after the "This season's guest speakers" heading as one h3 element with a <br> in the middle that rolls the speaker's name over to a second line. Then, test and adjust. When that works, do the same for the next two speakers.

9. Enclose the name for each speaker in an <a> tag. The href attribute for each tag should refer to a file in the speakers subfolder that has the speaker's last name as the filename and html as the file extension.

10. After the h3 element for each speaker, code an img element that displays the image for the speaker, and be sure to include the alt attribute. The images are in the images subfolder, and the filename for each is the speaker's last name, followed by 75 (to indicate the image size), with jpg as the extension. Now, test and adjust.

Add character entities and the remaining formatting tags

11. Enclose the text in the footer in a <p> element. And use a character entity to add the copyright symbol to the start of the footer.

12. Add the sup tags that you need for raising the *th* in the second line of the header (as in 75th). Then, test these enhancements.

Test the links and add a link to one of the speaker pages

13. Click on the link for the first speaker page. This should display a page that gives the speaker's name and says "This page is under construction". If this doesn't work, fix the href attribute in the link and test again. To return to the first page, you can click the browser's Back button.

14. Open the sorkin.html file that's in the speakers subfolder. Then, add a link within a <p> element that says "Return to index page." To refer to the index.html file, you'll have to go up one level in the folder structure with a document-relative path like this: ../index.html. Now, test this link.

15. Test the index page in Chrome. If necessary, fix any problems and test again.

Chapter 4

How to use CSS to format the elements of a web page

After you code the HTML that defines the structure of a web page, you're ready to code the CSS that formats the page. So that's what you'll start to learn in this chapter. Then, in chapter 5, you'll learn how to use the CSS box model for spacing, borders, and backgrounds. And in chapter 6, you'll learn how to use CSS for page layout.

An introduction to CSS

Before you can code the CSS for a web page, you need to know how to provide the CSS for a web page. Then, you need to know how to apply the styles to specific HTML elements. This introduction ends by showing you how you can use a CSS style sheet to provide browser compatibility

How to provide CSS styles for a web page

The first example in figure 4-1 shows how to use an *external style sheet* to provide the styles for a web page. To do that, you code a link element that uses the href attribute to identify the file that contains the style sheet. Because using an external style separates the content from the formatting, this makes it easy to use the same styles for more than one page.

As you learned in the last chapter, href attributes are usually coded with a URL that is relative to the current file. As a result, the relative URL in the first example goes down one folder to the styles folder and locates a file named main.css.

The second example shows that you can use two or more external style sheets for the same page. In that case, the styles are applied from the first style sheet to the last. So if two different styles are applied to the same HTML element, the last one overrides the earlier one. You'll learn more about this later in this chapter.

Next, this figure shows two other ways to provide styles. First, you can code a style element in the HTML for a page that contains the styles. This is referred to as an *embedded style sheet*. Second, you can use *inline styles* by coding a style attribute for the HTML element with a value that contains all the CSS declarations that apply to the element.

Although you should be aware of these methods in case you ever encounter them, you shouldn't use them for web development. Instead, it's a best practice to use external style sheets. Note, however, that we do use embedded styles for some of the examples that you can download for this book just because that's an easy way to present them.

A head element that provides an external style sheet

```
<head>
    <title>San Joaquin Valley Town Hall</title>
    <link rel="stylesheet" href="../styles/main.css">
</head>
```

A head element that provides two external style sheets

```
<head>
    <title>San Joaquin Valley Town Hall</title>
    <link rel="stylesheet" href="../styles/main.css">
    <link rel="stylesheet" href="../styles/speaker.css">
</head>
```

The sequence in which styles are applied

- From the first external style sheet to the last

Two other ways to provide styles (not recommended)

Embed the styles in the head section

```
<style>
    body {
        font-family: Arial, Helvetica, sans-serif;
        font-size: 100%; }
    h1 { font-size: 250%; }
</style>
```

Use the style attribute to apply styles to a single element

```
<h1 style="font-size: 500%; color: red;">Valley Town Hall</h1>
```

The sequence in which styles are applied

- Styles from an external style sheet

- Embedded styles

- Inline styles

Description

- When you use *external style sheets*, you separate content (HTML) from formatting (CSS). That makes it easy to use the same styles for two or more documents.

- If you use *embedded styles*, you have to copy the styles to other documents before you can use them again. And if you use *inline styles* to apply styles, the formatting is likely to get out of control.

- If you apply more than one declaration for the same property to the same element, the last declaration overrides the earlier declarations.

- When you specify a relative URL for an external CSS file, the URL is relative to the current file.

Figure 4-1   How to provide CSS styles for a web page

How to use the basic selectors to apply CSS to HTML elements

To apply styles to HTML elements, you code *selectors* that identify the elements that you want to format. To get you started with that, figure 4-2 shows how to code and use the four types of selectors that you'll use the most.

To start, this figure shows the body of an HTML document that contains a main and a footer element. Here, the two <p> elements in the main element have class attributes with the value "blue". This means that the elements are assigned to the same *class*. By contrast, the <p> element in the footer has an id attribute of "copyright", as well as a class attribute with two values: "blue" and "right". This means that this element is assigned to two classes.

Next, this figure shows some CSS style rules that format the HTML. Here, the style rule in the first example uses the *universal selector* (*) so it applies to all HTML elements. This sets the top and bottom margins for all elements to .5em and the left and right margins to 1em (more about sizing in a moment).

The three style rules in the second group of examples select elements by type. These are referred to as *type selectors*. To code a type selector, you just code the name of the element. As a result, the first style rule in this group selects the main element, the second style rule selects the h1 element, and the third style rule selects all <p> elements. These style rules set the border and padding for the main element, the font family for the h1 element, and the left margin for all <p> elements.

The style rule in the third group of examples is an *id selector* that selects an element by its id. To do that, the selector is a hash character (#) followed by an id value that uniquely identifies an element. As a result, this style rule selects the <p> element that has an id of "copyright". Then, its declaration sets the font size for the paragraph to 80% of the font size for the page.

The two style rules in the last group of examples are *class selectors* that select HTML elements by class. To do that, the selector is a period (.) followed by the class name. As a result, the first style rule selects all elements that have been assigned to the "blue" class, which are all three <p> elements. The second style rule selects any elements that have been assigned to the "right" class. That is the paragraph in the footer. Then, the first style rule sets the color of the font to blue and the second style rule aligns the paragraph on the right.

One of the key points here is that a class attribute can have the same value for more than one element on a page. Then, if you code a selector for that class, it will be used to format all the elements in that class. By contrast, since the id for an element must be unique, an id selector can only be used to format a single element.

Incidentally, the margin-left property for the <p> elements overrides the margin setting for all elements, which of course includes all <p> elements. That's why the two paragraphs in the main element are indented. You'll learn more about that in a moment.

HTML that can be selected by element type, id, or class

```
<main>
    <h1>This Season's Speaker Lineup</h1>
    <p class="blue">October: David Brancaccio</p>
    <p class="blue">November: Andrew Ross Sorkin</p>
</main>
<footer>
    <p id="copyright" class="blue right">Copyright 2022</p>
</footer>
```

CSS style rules that select by element type, id, and class

All elements
```
* { margin: .5em 1em; }
```

Elements by type
```
main {
    border: 2px solid black;
    padding: 1em; }
h1 { font-family: Arial, sans-serif; }
p { margin-left: 3em; }
```

One element by ID
```
#copyright { font-size: 80%; }
```

Elements by class
```
.blue { color: blue; }
.right { text-align: right; }
```

The elements displayed in a browser

This Season's Speaker Lineup

October: David Brancaccio

November: Andrew Ross Sorkin

Copyright 2022

Description

- You code a selector for all elements by coding the *universal selector* (*).
- You code a selector for all elements of a specific type by naming the element. This is referred to as a *type selector*.
- You code a selector for an element with an id attribute by coding a hash character (#) followed by the id value.
- You code a selector for an element with a class attribute by coding a period followed by the class name. Then, the style rule applies to all elements with that class name.

Figure 4-2   How to use the basic selectors to apply CSS to HTML elements

When and how to use the normalize style sheet for browser compatibility

Figure 4-3 shows how to download and use the *normalize.css style sheet* to provide browser compatibility. This style sheet applies CSS style rules that make minor adjustments to a web page so what would be minor variations are rendered the same in all browsers.

For instance, the normalize style sheet applies styles to the abbr element so it's rendered the same in all browsers. This style sheet also sets the margins for the body of the document to zero so those settings are the same in all browsers.

At one time, when there were many browser variations, this style sheet provided an easy way to handle those variations. As a result, it was widely used. That's why you may see it listed as the first external style sheet for some web pages. Then, the normalize styles are applied first so the browser variations are handled before your styles are applied.

Today, however, the modern browsers render most code exactly the same, and most other code in a way that's acceptable even if it's not exactly the same. Beyond that, you can use the universal selector to set defaults for each page that will resolve minor formatting differences.

For those reasons, the normalize style sheet isn't used in any of the examples in this book. Nevertheless, it's something that you should be aware of in case your development group uses it. As you learn more about CSS, you may even want to take a look at the code in this style sheet to see exactly what it does.

The URL for downloading the normalize.css style sheet

`http://necolas.github.io/normalize.css/`

How to download normalize.css and save it to your website

- Open a browser, browse to the URL shown above, and click the Download button.
- If CSS files are associated with a program that's installed on your computer, the normalize.css file will be opened in that program. Then, you can use that program to save the file to your website.
- If CSS files aren't associated with a program on your computer, the normalize.css file will be displayed on a page within the browser. Then, you can right-click the page, choose Save As, and use the dialog box that's displayed to save the normalize.css file to your website.
- Once you save the normalize.css file to your website, you can code a link element for it in each page. This element must be coded before the link elements for other style sheets.

What the normalize.css style sheet does

- Normalize.css is a style sheet that makes minor adjustments to browser defaults so all browsers render HTML elements the same way.
- For instance, the normalize.css style sheet sets the margins for the body of the document to zero so there's no space between the body and the edge of the browser window.
- The normalize.css style sheet also sets the default font family for the document to sans-serif.

Drawbacks of using the normalize.css style sheet

- It requires a small amount of overhead.
- It is a third-party dependency.

Description

- The *normalize.css style sheet* can be used to resolves minor browser variations.
- At one time, browser variations were common, and the normalize style sheet resolved many of those problems.
- Today, browser variations are so minimal that you can resolve most of them by setting your own defaults.
- To illustrate the use of the normalize style sheet, the application for this chapter uses it. But that's the last time the normalize style sheet is used by the applications for this book.

Figure 4-3   When and how to use the normalize style sheet
for browser compatibility

How to specify measurements and colors

For some of the properties of a style rule, you will need to know how to specify measurements and colors. So let's start there.

How to specify measurements

Figure 4-4 shows the five units of measure that are commonly used with CSS. Here, the first two are *absolute units of measure*, and the next three are *relative units of measure*. Other absolute units are inches and picas, but they aren't used as often.

When you use relative units of measure like ems, rems, or a percent, the measurement will change if the user changes the browser's font size. If, for example, you set the size of a font to 80 percent of the browser's default font size, that element will change if the user changes the font size in the browser. Because this lets the users adjust the font sizes to their own preferences, we recommend that you use relative measurements for font sizes.

By contrast, when you use an absolute unit of measure like pixels or points, the measurement won't change even if the user changes the font size in the browser. If, for example, you set the width of an element in pixels and the font size in points, the width and font size won't change.

When you use pixels, though, the size will change if the screen resolution changes. That's because the screen resolution determines the number of pixels that are displayed on the monitor. For instance, the pixels on a monitor with a screen resolution of 1280 x 1024 are closer together than the pixels on the same monitor with a screen resolution of 1152 x 864. That means that a measurement of 10 pixels will be smaller on the screen with the higher resolution. By contrast, a point is $1/72^{nd}$ of an inch no matter what the screen resolution is.

The examples in this figure show how you can use pixels, percentages, and ems in your CSS. Here, the bottom border for the header is set to 3 pixels. By contrast, the font sizes are set as percentages, and the margins and padding are set as ems.

In the first style rule for the body element, a font size of 100% is applied to the body element. This means that the font will be set to 100% of the default font size for the browser, which is usually 16 pixels. Although you can get the same result by omitting the font-size property, this property is typically included to make it clear that the default font size for the browser will be used.

Unlike ems, which are relative to the current font size, rems are relative to the size of the root, or html, element. Then, if you specify a font size for the html element, you can base all other font sizes on that size. You can also let the font size for the html element default to the browser's font size and base all other font sizes on that size. Note, however, that we don't use rems in this book because our pages are structured so it's easy to determine the current font size.

Common units of measure

Symbol	Name	Type	Description
px	pixels	absolute	A pixel represents a single dot on a monitor. The number of dots per inch depends on the resolution of the monitor.
pt	points	absolute	A point is 1/72 of an inch.
em	ems	relative	One em is equal to the font size for the current font.
rem	rems	relative	One rem is equal to the font size for the root element.
%	percent	relative	A percent specifies a value relative to the current value.

The HTML for a web page

```
<body>
    <header>
        <h1>San Joaquin Valley Town Hall</h1>
    </header>
    <main>
        <p>Welcome to San Joaquin Valley Town Hall. We have some
            fascinating speakers for you this season!</p>
    </main>
</body>
```

CSS that uses relative units of measure with a fixed border

```
body {
    font-size: 100%;
    margin-left: 2em;
    margin-right: 2em; }
header {
    padding-bottom: .75em;
    border-bottom: 3px solid black;
    margin-bottom: 0; }
h1 {
    font-size: 200%;
    margin-bottom: 0; }
```

The web page in a web browser

San Joaquin Valley Town Hall

Welcome to San Joaquin Valley Town Hall. We have some fascinating speakers for you this season!

Description

- You use the units of measure to specify a variety of CSS properties, including font-size, line-height, width, height, margin, and padding.
- To specify an *absolute measurement*, you can use pixels or points.
- To specify a *relative measurement*, you can use ems, rems, or percents. This type of measurement is relative to the size of another element.

Figure 4-4   How to specify measurements

How to specify colors

Figure 4-5 shows three ways to specify colors. The easiest way is to specify a color name, and this figure lists the names for 16 basic colors. In addition to these names, though, you can use names in the CSS Color specification, which is available at the URL that's given at the top of the page.

Another way to specify a color is to use an *RGB* (red, green, blue) *value*. One way to do that is to specify the percent of red, green, and blue that make up the color. For instance, the example in this figure specifies 100% red, 40% green, and 20% blue. When you use this method, you can also use any values from 0 through 255 instead of percentages. Then, 0 is equivalent to 0% and 255 is equivalent to 100%. This gives you more precision over the resulting colors.

The third way to specify a color is to use *hexadecimal*, or *hex*, *values* for the red, green, and blue values, and this is the method that is preferred by most web designers. In hex, a value of "000000" is black, and a value of "FFFFFF" is white. The simple conversion of percentages to hex is 0% is 00, 20% is 33, 40% is 66, 60% is 99, 80% is CC, and 100% is FF. When you use this technique, the entire value must be preceded by the hash character (#).

When you use hex values for colors, you usually get the hex value that you want from a chart or palette that shows all of the colors along with their hex values. For instance, you can get a complete list of the hex values for colors by going to the website listed in this figure. Or, if you're using an IDE or a text editor like VS Code, you can choose a color from a palette and then have the hex value for that color inserted into your code.

Before you go on, you should realize that the color property determines the foreground color, which is the color of the text. In the CSS in this figure, for example, the color of the h1 element is set to blue (#00F or #0000FF), and the background color of the body is set to a light yellow (#FFFFCC or #FFC).

You should also realize that the color property for an element is *inherited* by any of its *descendants*. If, for example, you set the color property of the body element to navy, that color will be inherited by the header and main elements that it contains. However, you can override an inherited property by coding a style rule with a different value for that property. More about this in a moment.

Last, whenever you're using colors, please keep the visually-impaired in mind. For anyone, dark text on a light background is easier to read, and black on white is easiest to read. In general, if your pages are hard to read when they're displayed or printed in black and white, they aren't good for the visually-impaired.

The web page for CSS colors

www.w3.org/wiki/CSS/Properties/color/keywords

The 16 basic color names

black	silver	white	aqua	gray	fuchsia
red	lime	green	maroon	blue	navy
yellow	olive	purple	teal		

Three ways to specify colors

With a color name

```
color: silver;
```

With an RGB (red-green-blue) value

```
color: rgb(100%, 40%, 20%);
color: rgb(255, 102, 51);    /* Using multiples of 51 from 0 to 255 */
```

With an RGB value that uses hexadecimal numbers

```
color: #ffffff;          /* This color is white */
color: #000000;          /* This color is black */
color: #ff0000;          /* This color is red */
```

CSS that uses hexadecimal values to specify colors

```
body {
    font-size: 100%;
    margin-left: 2em;
    background-color: #FFFFCC; }   /* This could also be coded as #FFC */
h1 {
    font-size: 200%;
    color: #00F; }               /* This could also be coded as #0000FF */
```

The HTML in a web browser

San Joaquin Valley Town Hall

Welcome to San Joaquin Valley Town Hall. We have some fascinating speakers for you this season!

Accessibility guideline

- Remember the visually-impaired. Dark text on a light background is easier to read, and black type on a white background is easiest to read.

Description

- Most graphic designers use *hexadecimal*, or *hex*, *values* to specify an *RGB value* because that lets them choose from over 16 million colors.
- With most text editors and IDEs, you can select a color from a palette of colors and have the color codes inserted into your style rules in either RGB or hex format.

Figure 4-5   How to specify colors

How to use advanced techniques to specify colors

To provide more color options for web designers, CSS provides three more ways to code color specifications. These are summarized in figure 4-6.

First, you can use *RGBA values*. This works like RGB values, but with a fourth parameter that provides an opacity value. If, for example, you set this value to 0, the color is fully transparent so anything behind it will show through. Or, if you set this value to 1, nothing will show through.

Second, you can use *HSL values*. To do that, you provide a number from 1 through 359 that represents the hue that you want. The hue is one of the main properties of a color. Then, you can provide a number from 0 through 100 that represents the saturation percent with 100 being the full hue. Last, you can provide a number from 0 through 100 that represents the lightness percent with 50 being normal, 100 being white, and 0 being black.

Third, you can use *HSLA values*. This is just like HSL values, but with a fourth parameter that provides an opacity value between 0 and 1.

The examples in this figure give you some idea of how these values work. Note here that the second and third examples are the same hue, but the saturation and lightness percentages make them look quite different. This should give you some idea of the many color variations that CSS offers. But here again, please keep accessibility in mind whenever you're using colors.

Three more ways to code CSS colors

The syntax for RGBA colors

```
rgba(red%, green%, blue%, opacity-value)
```

The syntax for HSL and HSLA colors

```
hsl(hue-degrees, saturation%, lightness%)
hsla(hue-degrees, saturation%, lightness%, opacity-value)
```

Value	Description
opacity-value	A number from 0 to 1 with 0 being fully transparent and 1 being fully opaque.
hue-degrees	A number of degrees ranging from 0 to 359 that represents the color.
saturation%	A percentage from 0 to 100 with 0 causing the hue to be ignored and 100 being the full hue.
lightness%	A percentage from 0 to 100 with 50 being normal lightness, 0 being black, and 100 being white.

Examples

```
h1 { color: rgba(0, 0, 255, .2)        /* transparent blue */ }
h1 { color: hsl(120, 100%, 25%)        /* dark green */ }
h1 { color: hsl(120, 75%, 75%)         /* pastel green */ }
h1 { color: hsla(240, 100%, 50%, 0.5)  /* semi-transparent solid blue */ }
```

The colors in a browser

Description

- *RGBA* enhances the RGB specification by providing a fourth value for opacity.
- With *HSL* (Hue, Saturation, and Lightness) and *HSLA,* you specify the number of hue degrees for a color. Then, you can enhance the hue by providing for both saturation and lightness percentages. HLSA also offers a fourth value for opacity.
- With an IDE like Dreamweaver, you can select the type of color specification you want to use (RGBA, HSL, or HSLA). Then, you can select the color or hue, saturation, lightness, and opacity.

Figure 4-6   How to use advanced techniques to specify colors

How to work with text

Now that you know how to work with colors and sizes, the next four figures show how to work with text.

How to set the font family and font size

Figure 4-7 shows how to set the *font family* and font size for text elements. The table at the top of this figure lists the five generic font families, and the examples below that table show what typical fonts in these families look like.

When you develop a website, your primary font family should be a sans-serif font family. That's because sans-serif fonts are easier to read in a browser than the other types of fonts, including serif fonts, even though serif fonts have long been considered the best for printed text. You can also use serif and monospace fonts for special purposes, but you should avoid the use of cursive and fantasy fonts.

When you code the values for the font-family property, you code a list of the fonts that you want to use. For instance, the first example in this figure lists Arial, Helvetica, and sans-serif as the fonts, and sans-serif is a generic font name. Then, the browser will use the first font in the list that is available to it. But if none of the fonts are available, the browser will substitute its default font for the generic font that's coded last in the list.

If the name of a font family contains spaces, like "Times New Roman", you need to enclose the name in quotation marks when you code the list. This is illustrated by the second and third examples in the first group.

To set the font size for a font, you use the font-size property as illustrated by the second group of examples. For this property, you should use relative measurements so the users will be able to change the font sizes in their browsers. This is also essential for responsive web design.

When you use a relative measurement, it's relative to the parent element. For example, the second rule in the second set of examples will cause the font to be 150% larger than its parent element. So if the parent element is 16 points, this element will be 24 points. Similarly, the third rule specifies 1.5 ems so it will also be 150% of the parent font.

The next example shows how the font family and font size can be set in the body element. Here, the default font family for the browser is changed to a sans-serif font. In addition, the default font size is set to 100% of the browser's default size. Although this doesn't change the font size, it does make the size relative to the browser's default size, which is usually 16 pixels. Then, if the user changes the browser's font size, that change is reflected in the web page.

Like colors, the font properties that you set for an element are inherited by all of its descendants. Note, however, that it's not the relative value that's inherited when you use a relative measurement for the font size. Instead, it's the actual size that's calculated for the font. If, for example, the default font size is 16 pixels and you set the font-size property to 125%, the size of the element and any descendants will be 20 pixels.

The five generic font families

Name	Description
serif	Fonts with tapered, flared, or slab stroke ends.
sans-serif	Fonts with plain stroke ends.
monospace	Fonts that use the same width for each character.
cursive	Fonts with connected, flowing letters that look like handwriting.
fantasy	Fonts with decorative styling.

Examples of the five generic font families

Times New Roman is a serif font. It is the default for most web browsers.

Arial is a sans-serif font that is widely used, and sans-serif fonts are best for web pages.

Courier New is a monospace font that is used for code examples.

Segoe Script is a cursive font that is not frequently used.

Impact is a fantasy font that is rarely used.

How to specify a font family

```
font-family: Arial, Helvetica, sans-serif;
font-family: "Times New Roman", Times, serif;
font-family: "Courier New", Courier, monospace;
```

How to specify the font size

```
font-size: 12pt;       /* in points */
font-size: 150%;       /* as a percent of the parent element */
font-size: 1.5em;      /* same as 150% */
```

A font-family rule in the body element that is inherited by all descendants

```
body {
    font-family: Arial, Helvetica, sans-serif;
    font-size: 100%; }
```

A font-family rule in a descendant that overrides the inherited font family

```
p { font-family: "Times New Roman", Times, serif; }
```

Description

- The fonts specified for the font-family property are searched in the order listed. If you include a font name that contains spaces, the name must be enclosed in quotes.
- If you specify a generic font last and the web browser can't find any of the other fonts in the list, it will use its default font for the generic font that you specified.
- The font properties that you set for an element are inherited by all of its descendants.
- If you use relative font sizes, the users will be able to vary the sizes by using their browsers.

Figure 4-7   How to set the font family and font size

How to set the properties for styling and formatting fonts

The first table in figure 4-8 summarizes the properties that you can use for styling a font. Like the font-family and font-size properties, these properties are inherited by their descendants.

The first group of examples in this figure shows how you can use some of these properties. There you can see that you can set the font-style property to normal if you want to remove the style from an element. That a font-weight value of bold is the same as a value of 700. That a font-weight value of lighter is relative to the parent element. And that a line-height value of 140% is the same as a value of 1.4em or 1.4. This shows how you will normally apply the styling properties, with one property in each style rule.

But next, this figure shows how to use a *shorthand property* named font to apply up to six font properties. To illustrate, the example specifies bold and italic styling with a 14 pixel font that has 5 pixels between the lines (14/19). It also specifies that the Arial font or the default sans-serif font should be used. When you use the font property, the font family is required, but otherwise, you just specify the properties that you want to change.

The second table in this figure summarizes the properties for formatting text. For instance, you can use the text-indent property to indent the first line of text in a paragraph. You can use the text-align property to center text, align it on the right, or justify it. And you can use the vertical-align property to align text vertically within an element.

Note, however, that when you use the text-align property to justify text, the spacing between words is adjusted so the text is aligned on both the left and right sides of the element that it's in. Since that often makes the text more difficult to read, you should avoid using justified text.

Last, you can use the text-decoration property to display a line under, over, or through text. However, you'll rarely if ever want to use this property for those purposes because (1) you shouldn't underline words that aren't links, (2) you should use borders to put lines over or under text, and (3) you may never need to show that text has been crossed out.

In some cases, though, you will want to use the text-decoration property to remove any text decoration that has been applied to an element. To do that, you specify a value of "none" for this property. For example, the text-decoration property of an <a> element is set to "underline" by default. If that's not what you want, you can set this property to "none". You'll see how this works in chapter 7.

The example in this figure shows how to use the text-align property. Here, the paragraph with "copyright" as its id is right-aligned.

Properties for styling fonts

Property	Description
font-style	How the font is slanted: normal, italic, and oblique.
font-weight	The boldness of the font: normal, bold, bolder, lighter, or multiples of 100 from 100 through 900, with 400 equivalent to normal. Bolder and lighter are relative to the parent element.
font-variant	Whether small caps should be used: normal and small-caps.
line-height	The amount of vertical space for each line. The excess space is divided equally above and below the font so it sets the spacing between lines.

How to specify the properties for styling fonts

```
font-style: italic;
font-style: normal;        /* remove style */

font-weight: 700;
font-weight: bold;         /* same as 700 */
font-weight: lighter;      /* relative to the parent element */

line-height: 140%;
line-height: 1.4em;        /* same as 140% */
line-height: 1.4;          /* same as 140% and 1.4em */
```

The syntax for the shorthand font property

```
font: [style] [weight] [variant] size[/line-height] family;
```

How to use the shorthand font property

```
font: italic bold 14px/19px Arial, sans-serif;
```

Properties for indenting, aligning, and decorating text

Property	Description
text-indent	The indentation for the first line of text. This property is inherited.
text-align	The horizontal alignment of text: left, center, right, and justify. Inherited.
vertical-align	The vertical alignment of text: baseline, bottom, middle, top, text-bottom, text-top, sub, and super.
text-decoration	A decoration: underline, overline, line-through, and none.

CSS that right aligns the paragraph with "copyright" as its id

```
#copyright {
    font-size: 80%;
    text-align: right; }
```

Description

- You can set the font-style, font-weight, and font-variant properties to a value of "normal" to remove any formatting that has been applied to these properties.
- The vertical-align property is often used with tables as you'll see in chapter 12.
- The text-decoration property can be set to "none" to remove the underlines from links.

Figure 4-8   How to set the properties for styling and formatting fonts

How to add shadows to text

You can also use CSS to add shadows to text. To do that, you use the text-shadow property shown in figure 4-9. As the syntax shows, you can set four parameters for this property.

The first one specifies how much the shadow should be offset to the right (a positive value) or left (a negative value). The second one specifies how much the shadow should be offset down (a positive value) or up (a negative value). The third one specifies how big the blur radius for the shadow should be. And the fourth one specifies the color for the shadow.

The first example shows text with a shadow that is 4 pixels to the right and down, with no blur and with the shadow the same color as the text. The result is shown in the browser.

By contrast, the shadow for the heading in the second example is offset to the left and up by 2 pixels, with a blur radius of 4 pixels and with the shadow in red. Since the heading is in blue, this provides an interesting effect.

When you use this property, though, remember the visually-impaired. If the offsets or blur are too large, the shadow can make the text more difficult to read.

The syntax of the text-shadow property

```
text-shadow: horizontalOffset verticalOffset blurRadius shadowColor;
```

Two examples

The h1 element

```
<h1>San Joaquin Valley Town Hall</h1>
```

The CSS

```
h1 {
    color: #ef9c00;
    text-shadow: 4px 4px; }
```

The heading in a browser

San Joaquin Valley Town Hall

Different CSS for the same h1 element

```
h1 {
    color: blue;
    text-shadow: -2px -2px 4px red; }
```

The heading in a browser

San Joaquin Valley Town Hall

Accessibility guideline

- Remember the visually-impaired. Too much shadow or blur makes text harder to read.

Description

- Positive values offset the shadow to the right or down. Negative values offset the shadow to the left or up.
- The blur radius determines how much the shadow is blurred.

Figure 4-9   How to add shadows to text

How to float an image so text flows around it

In chapters 5 and 6, you'll learn everything you need to know about setting margins and floating an image so the text flows around it. But just to get you started with this, figure 4-10 shows how you can float the logo for a header to the left so the headings flow to its right.

In the HTML for the example, you can see an img element, an h1 element, and an h2 element. Then, in the CSS for the img element, the float property is set to left and the margin-right property is set to 1em. The result is that the two headings flow to the right of the image as shown in the first browser example.

You should know, however, that this depends on the size of the image. Because the width of the image is set to 80 pixels for the first example, both headings flow to its right. But if the width is reduced to 40 pixels as in the second example, the height is also reduced. Then, the second heading is under the image because the image is too short for the heading to flow to its right.

This shows that you're going to have to fiddle with the image size to get this to work right for the time being. But in the next two chapters, you'll learn the right ways to get this result.

If you want to stop elements from flowing to the right of a floated element, you can use the clear property that's shown in this figure. Here, the clear property is used for the main element, and it stops the flow around an element that has been floated to its left. If the main element follows a header, the flow of the text will stop before any of the elements within the main element are displayed.

An image that has been floated to the left of the headings that follow

 **San Joaquin Valley Town Hall**
Bringing cutting-edge speakers to the valley

The HTML
```
<img src="images/logo.gif" alt="Town Hall Logo" width="80">
<h1>San Joaquin Valley Town Hall</h1>
<h2>Bringing cutting-edge speakers to the valley</h2>
```

The CSS
```
img {
    float: left;
    margin-right: 1em;
}
```

The page if the width of the image is reduced to 40

 San Joaquin Valley Town Hall
Bringing cutting-edge speakers to the valley

The property that will stop the floating before a subsequent element
```
main { clear: left; }
```

Description
- To float an image, you use the float property, and to set the margins around it, you use the margin property.
- In chapters 5 and 6, you'll learn how to set margins and float elements, but this will give you an idea of how you can use an image in a header.
- When you float an image to the left, the block elements that follow it fill the space to the right of it. When the elements that follow get past the height of the image and its top and bottom margins, they flow into the space below the element.
- You can use the clear property to stop an element from flowing into the space alongside a floated element.
- For now, you can experiment with the size of the image to get the effect that you want, but in the next two chapters you'll learn the right ways to get the same results.

Figure 4-10   How to float an image so text flows around it

How to use other selectors to apply styles

So far, you've learned how to use the universal, type, id, and class selectors. But now, you'll learn how to code other types of selectors. Once you understand that, you will be able to apply CSS formatting to any elements in a web page.

How to code relational, combination, and attribute selectors

Figure 4-11 starts by showing how to code *relational selectors*. As you read about these selectors, keep in mind that terms like *parent, child, sibling,* and *descendant* are used in the same way that they are in a family tree. Child elements are at the first level below a parent element. Sibling elements are at the same level. And descendant elements include all the levels below a parent element.

That means a *descendant selector* selects all the elements that are contained within another element. For instance, all of the elements in the HTML in this figure are descendants of the main element. The li elements are also descendants of the ul element. And the <a> elements are descendants of the li, ul, and main elements. To code a descendant selector, you code a selector for the parent element, followed by a space and a selector for the descendant element.

If you want to select elements only when they're child elements of a parent element, you can code a *child selector*. To do that, you separate the parent and child selector with a greater than (>) sign.

An *adjacent sibling selector* is an element that's coded at the same level as another element and is also coded right next to it. For instance, the h1, ul, h2, and <p> elements in the HTML are all siblings, and the h1 and ul elements are adjacent siblings. To code an adjacent sibling selector, you code a selector for the first element, followed by a plus sign and a selector for the sibling element.

Unlike the adjacent sibling selector, a *general sibling selector* selects any sibling element whether or not the elements are adjacent. To code this type of selector, you separate the selector for the first element and the selector for the sibling element by a tilde (~).

The second group of selectors in this figure shows how to code combinations of selectors. To select an element type by class name, for example, you code the type name, followed by a period and the class name. So, the first style rule selects ul elements that have a class of "speakers".

You can also code multiple selectors for the same style rule. To do that, you separate the selectors with commas. So, the first style rule for multiple selectors applies its declaration to all h1, h2, and h3 elements. And the second style rule applies its declaration to all <p> elements and to li elements that are descendants of the ul elements that are assigned to the speakers class.

Last, an *attribute selector* selects elements based on an attribute or attribute value. This is illustrated by the third group of examples. Although you may never need to code attribute selectors when you apply CSS, these selectors are often used by JavaScript.

HTML that can be selected by relationships

```
<main>
    <h1>This Season's Town Hall speakers</h1>
    <ul class="speakers">
        <li>January: <a href="speakers/brancaccio.html">
            David Brancaccio</a></li>
        <li>February: <a href="speakers/fitzpatrick.html">
            Robert Fitzpatrick</a></li>
        <li>March: <a href="speakers/williams.html">
            Juan Williams</a></li>
    </ul>
    <h2>Post-lecture luncheons</h2>
    <p>Extend the excitement by going to the luncheons.</p>
    <p>A limited number of tickets are available.</p>
    <p><em>Contact us by phone</em> at (559) 555-1212.</p>
</main>
```

Relational selectors

Descendant

```
main li { font-size: 90%; }
ul a { color: green; }
```

Child

```
main>p { font-size: 80%; }
li>a { color: green; }
```

Adjacent sibling

```
h2+p { margin-top: .5em; }
```

General sibling

```
h2~p { margin-left: 2em; }
```

Combinations

A selector for a class within an element

```
ul.speakers { list-style-type: square; }
```

Multiple selectors

```
h1, h2, h3 { color: blue; }
p, ul.speakers li { font-family: "Times New Roman", serif; }
```

Attribute selectors

All elements with href attributes

```
*[href] { font-size: 95%; }
```

All <a> elements with href attributes

```
a[href] { font-family: Arial, sans-serif; }
```

All input elements with type attributes that have a value of "submit"

```
input[type="submit"] {
    border: 1px solid black;
    color: #ef9c00;
    background-color: #facd8a; }
```

Description

- When you're coding the CSS for an HTML page, you usually don't need attribute selectors. They're more useful when you're using JavaScript.

Figure 4-11   How to code relational, combination, and attribute selectors

How to code pseudo-class and pseudo-element selectors

Figure 4-12 shows how to code pseudo-class and pseudo-element selectors. To code *pseudo-class selectors*, you use the classes in the first table of this figure. These classes represent conditions that apply to the elements on a page. For example, you can use the :link pseudo-class to refer to a link that hasn't been visited, the :hover pseudo-class to refer to the element that has the mouse hovering over it, and the :focus pseudo-class to refer to the element that has the focus.

You can use the last three pseudo-classes to refer to specific relationships. For example, the :first-child class refers to the first child of an element, and the :only-child class refers to the only child for an element that has only one.

The second table in this figure presents the *pseudo-element selectors* that you can use to select portions of text. For instance, you can use the ::first-line selector to refer to the first line in a paragraph that consists of more than one line. Note that the double colons for these selectors distinguish them from pseudo-class selectors.

In the examples, the first pseudo-class selector causes all links to be displayed in green. Then, the second selector is a combination selector that applies to any link that has the mouse hovering over it or the focus on it. As the accessibility guideline in this figure indicates, you should always code the hover and focus pseudo-classes for links in combination so the formatting is the same whether the user hovers the mouse over a link or tabs to it.

The third example uses a pseudo-class selector that causes the text in the first <p> element in the main element to be boldfaced. That's the first <p> element in the HTML. You can see how this works in the browser display. Note here that the second <p> element isn't boldfaced because it isn't the first child in the main element.

The fourth example takes this one step further by combining a pseudo-class and a pseudo-element in a selector. As a result, the first letter of the first child in the main element is larger than the other letters in the paragraph. Here again, that's the first <p> element in the HTML.

Although the pseudo-class and pseudo-element selectors in this figure are the ones you'll use most often, there are others that can be useful. In chapter 7, for example, you'll learn how to use the ::after pseudo-element to format a multi-tier navigation menu. And in chapter 12, you'll be introduced to some pseudo-classes that apply to tables. For a complete list of these classes and elements, you can go to the W3C documentation on the web.

Common CSS pseudo-classes

:link	A link that hasn't been visited. By default, blue, underlined text.
:visited	A link that has been visited. By default, purple, underlined text.
:active	The active link (mouse button down but not released). By default, red, underlined text.
:hover	An element with the mouse hovering over it. Code this after :link and :visited.
:focus	An element like a link or form control that has the focus.
:first-child	The first child of an element.
:last-child	The last child of an element.
:only-child	The only child of an element.

Common CSS pseudo-elements

::first-letter	The first letter of an element.
::first-line	The first line of an element.

HTML that can be used by pseudo-class and pseudo-element selectors

```
<main>
    <p>Welcome to San Joaquin Valley Town Hall.</p>
    <p>We have some fascinating speakers for you this season!</p>
    <ul>
        <li><a href="brancaccio.html">David Brancaccio</a></li>
        <li><a href="sorkin.html">Andrew Ross Sorkin</a></li>
        <li><a href="chua.html">Amy Chua</a></li></ul>
</main>
```

The CSS for pseudo-class and pseudo-element selectors

```
a:link { color: green; }
a:hover, a:focus { color: fuchsia; }
main p:first-child { font-weight: bold; }
main p:first-child::first-letter { font-size: 150%; }
```

The pseudo-class and pseudo-element selectors in a browser

Welcome to San Joaquin Valley Town Hall.

We have some fascinating speakers for you this season!

- David Brancaccio
- Andrew Ross Sorkin
- Amy Chua

Accessibility guideline

- Apply the same formatting to the :hover and :focus pseudo-classes for an element. That way, those who can't use the mouse will have the same experience as those who can.

Description

- *Pseudo-classes* are predefined classes that apply to specific conditions. By contrast, *pseudo-elements* let you select a portion of text.

Figure 4-12   How to code pseudo-class and pseudo-element selectors

How the cascade rules work

The term *Cascading Style Sheets* (*CSS*) refers to the fact that more than one style sheet can be applied to a single web page. But that means that more than one style rule may be applied to the same element. And you've already seen that more than one style in the same style sheet can be applied to the same element.

So what happens when the styles that are applied to an element conflict? CSS applies the *cascade order* in figure 4-13 to determine which style rule takes effect. In most cases, this just means that the style rule with the highest specificity is applied. For example, the p.highlight selector is more specific than the .highlight selector so its style rules are applied. And if the specificity is the same for two or more styles, the style rule that's specified last is applied.

This works the same if you provide two or more style sheets for an HTML document. Then, the cascade rules still apply, but the style rules in each style sheet will override the style rules in the preceding style sheets. This notion also applies if you accidentally code two style rules for the same element in a single style sheet. The one that is last takes precedence.

You should also know that users can create *user style sheets* for their browsers that provide default style rules for their web pages. Because most users don't create user style sheets, this usually isn't an issue. But some users do. For example, users with poor vision can create user style sheets that provide for large font sizes. That's why you need to be aware of how user style sheets could affect your web pages.

With that as background, this figure lists the five levels of the *cascade order* from highest to lowest. As you can see, the important declarations in a user style sheet override the important declarations in the style sheets for a web page, but the normal declarations in the style sheets for a web page override the normal declarations in a user style sheet. Below these declarations are the default declarations in the web browser.

In some cases, then, you may need to identify one or more of your declarations as important so they will take precedence over other declarations. To do that, you code "!important" as part of the declaration. This is shown by the example in this figure.

What happens when more than one style is applied to an element

- The style rule with the highest specificity is applied.
- If the specificity is the same for two or more style rules in a group, the style rule that's specified last is applied.

How to determine the specificity of a selector

- An id is the most specific.
- A class, attribute selector, or pseudo-class selector is less specific.
- An element or pseudo-element selector is least specific.

The cascade order for applying style rules

Search for the style rules that apply to an element in the sequence that follows and apply the style rule from the first group in which it's found:

- !important declarations in a user style sheet
- !important declarations in the style sheet for a web page
- Normal declarations in the style sheet for a web page
- Normal declarations in a user style sheet
- Default declarations in the web browser

How to identify a declaration as important

```
.highlight {
    font-weight: bold !important;
}
```

Description

- When two or more style rules are applied to an HTML element, CSS uses the *cascade order* and rules shown above to determine which style rule to apply.
- A user can create a *user style sheet* that provides a default set of style rules for web pages. Users with poor vision often do this so the type for a page is displayed in a large font.
- Since most users don't create user style sheets, you usually can control the way the rules are applied for your websites. But you should keep in mind how your web pages could be affected by user style sheets.
- If you want to create or remove a user style sheet for a browser, you can search the Internet for the procedures that the browser requires.

Figure 4-13   How the cascade rules work

The HTML and CSS for a web page

Now that you've learned how to code selectors and how to format text, you're ready to see a web page that uses these skills.

The page layout

Figure 4-14 presents a web page that uses an external style sheet. If you study this web page, you can see that CSS has been used to change the default font to a sans-serif font, to apply colors to some of the headings and text, to center the headings in the header, to apply shadows to the text in the first heading, to add line height to the items in the unordered list, to apply boldfacing to portions of text, and to right-align the footer.

Overall, this formatting makes the page look pretty good. In terms of typography, though, this web page needs to be improved. For instance, there should be less space after "San Joaquin Valley Town Hall", less space after "This season's guest speakers", less space after "Looking for a unique gift?", and less space between the first three paragraphs. There should also be more space at the left and right sides of the page.

To make these adjustments, though, you need to know how to use the margin and padding properties that are part of the CSS box model. So that's what you'll learn first in the next chapter. Once you learn how to use those properties, you'll be able to get the typography just the way you want it.

A web page that uses some of the styles presented in this chapter

Description

- This web page uses an external style sheet to apply the styles that are illustrated.
- A sans-serif font has been applied to all of the text in this document because that's the most readable type of font for web pages. Also, relative font sizes have been applied to the elements on the page.
- Italics and boldfacing have been applied to portions of the text, the copyright information has been right-aligned, and color has been applied to the first heading.
- Colors have also been applied to the <a> tags in the unordered list. Because the first two lectures have passed, the first two links in the list have the color gray applied to them.

What's wrong with the typography in this web page

- The spacing above and below the block elements and around the body of the page should be improved. In the next chapter, you'll learn how to do that by using the margin and padding properties.

Figure 4-14   The page layout for a web page

The HTML file

Figure 4-16 presents the HTML for the web page. In the head section, you can see the link element that refers to the external style sheet for formatting this web page. It is in the styles folder.

In the body section, the header and the first part of the main element are the same as they were in the example at the end of the last chapter with one exception. That is, the <a> elements in the first and second <li> elements have class attributes that assign them to the "date_passed" class. This class name will be used to apply the color gray to those items because this example assumes that the dates for those events have already passed, and the gray color is intended to indicate that to the user.

After the nav element, this HTML includes another h2 element and three new <p> elements. And the second and third <p> elements have their class attributes set to "indent". Then, this class will be used as the CSS selector for indenting those paragraphs.

You should also notice the em element that's used within the last <p> element. You may remember from the last chapter that this is an inline element that means its contents should be emphasized, which by default means that it will be italicized. As you will see, though, CSS will be used to boldface this element too.

The HTML file for the web page

```
<!DOCTYPE HTML>

<html lang="en">
<head>
    <title>San Joaquin Valley Town Hall</title>
    <meta charset="utf-8">
    <link rel="shortcut icon" href="images/favicon.ico">
    <link rel="stylesheet" href="styles/main.css">
</head>

<body>
    <header>
        <img src="images/logo.gif" alt="Town Hall Logo" width="80">
        <h2>San Joaquin Valley Town Hall</h2>
        <h3>Bringing cutting-edge speakers to the valley</h3>
    </header>
    <main>
        <h1>This season's guest speakers</h1>
        <nav>
            <ul>
              <li>October: <a class="date_passed"
                  href="speakers/brancaccio.html">David Brancaccio</a></li>
              <li>November: <a class="date_passed"
                  href="speakers/sorkin.html">Andrew Ross Sorkin</a></li>
              <li>January: <a href="speakers/chua.html">
                  Amy Chua</a></li>
              <li>February: <a href="speakers/sampson.html">
                  Scott Sampson</a></li>
              <li>March: <a href="speakers/eire.html">
                  Carlos Eire</a></li>
              <li>April: <a href="speakers/tynan.html">
                  Ronan Tynan</a></li>
            </ul>
        </nav>

        <h2>Looking for a unique gift?</h2>
        <p>Town Hall has the answer. For only $100, you can get a book of
            tickets for all of the remaining speakers. And the bargain includes
            a second book of tickets for a companion.</p>
        <p class="indent">Or, for $50, you can give yourself the gift of our
            speakers, and still get an extra ticket for a companion, but for
            just one of the events.</p>
        <p class="indent">See you at the next show?</p>

        <p><em>Contact us by phone</em> at (559) 555-1212 for ticket
            information.</p>
    </main>
    <footer>
        <p>&copy; Copyright 2022 San Joaquin Valley Town Hall.</p>
    </footer>
</body>
</html>
```

Figure 4-15   The HTML file for the web page

The CSS file

Figure 4-16 shows the CSS file for the web page. To start, notice the way that the code in this file is structured. It starts with the style rules for specific elements. In effect, this sets the default formatting for these elements. Then, these style rules are followed by style rules that are specific to the header, main, and footer elements. The declarations in these style rules override the ones for the elements because they're more specific. For instance, the font size for the main h1 selector overrides the font size for the body selector.

You might also note that many of the style rules that contain a single declaration are coded on a single line. This of course is a valid way to code these style rules because white space is ignored. For style rules that require more than one declaration, though, each declaration is coded on a separate line to make the declarations easier to read.

In the style rule for the body element, the two properties specify the font family and font size. Because these properties are inherited, they become the defaults for the document. Also, because the font size is specified as 100 percent, the actual font size will be determined by the default font size for the browser. The font sizes for the headings are also specified as percents, so they will be based on the size that's calculated for the body element.

In the style rules for the <a> element, the hover and focus pseudo-classes are set to the same color. Then, in the style rule for the unordered list, the line-height property is specified to increase the spacing between the items. Similarly, the font weight is specified for the em element so it is boldfaced. However, this element will also be italicized because that's its normal behavior. To remove the italics, you would have to code a font-style property with normal as its value.

In the style rules for the header, you can see that the image is floated to the left so the elements that follow will appear to the right. If you look back at the web page in figure 4-14, though, you'll see that only the h2 heading flows to the right of the image. That's because the image is too short for the h3 element to flow to its right. Then, although both the h2 and h3 elements are centered, the h2 element appears centered in the the space to the right of the image but the h3 element appears centered on the page. You can also see that the h2 heading has a 2 pixel, black shadow to its right and down with 2 pixels of blur.

In the style rules for the main element, you can see that the clear property is used to stop the flow of the text around the image that has been floated left. You can also see that the elements in the "indent" class will be indented 2 ems, and the elements in the "date_passed" class will be gray.

Of course, you can code the CSS in other ways and get the same results. For instance, you could code this style rule for the h2 and h3 elements in the header:

```
header h2, header h3 { text-align: center; }
```

Then, you could drop the text-align properties from the header h2 and header h3 style rules that follow. You could also code the selectors for the date_passed and indent classes so they're less specific since they aren't used outside the main element. If you code the selectors so they're more specific, though, they're less likely to cause problems if you add style rules later on.

The CSS file for the web page

```
/* the styles for the elements */
body {
    font-family: Verdana, Arial, Helvetica, sans-serif;
    font-size: 100%;
}

a { font-weight: bold; }
a:link { color: #931420; }
a:visited { color: #f2972e;}
a:hover, a:focus { color: blue; }

ul { line-height: 1.5; }
li, p { font-size: 95%; }
em { font-weight: bold; }

/* the styles for the header */
header img { float: left; }
header h2 {
    font-size: 220%;
    color: #f2972e;
    text-align: center;
    text-shadow: 2px 2px 2px black;
}
header h3 {
    font-size: 130%;
    font-style: italic;
    text-align: center;
}

/* the styles for the main content */
main { clear: left; }
main h1 { font-size: 170%; }
main h2 { font-size: 130%; }

main p.indent { text-indent: 2em; }
main a.date_passed { color: gray; }

/* the styles for the footer */
footer p {
    font-size: 80%;
    text-align: right;
}
```

Figure 4-16   The CSS file for the web page

How to use Developer Tools and custom properties

In chapter 2, you were introduced to the Developer Tools that are provided by a browser. Now, you'll learn how they can be used to inspect the styles that have been applied to the elements in a page. After that, you'll learn one more way to apply styles to elements.

How to use Developer Tools to inspect the styles that have been applied

If you have problems with cascading styles when you test a web page, you can use the Developer Tools that are provided by your browser to find out exactly what's happening, as shown in figure 4-17. If you're using Chrome, Edge, or Firefox, you can access these tools by pressing the F12 key. If you're using Opera or Safari, you can right-click on a page and select Inspect or Inspect Element.

In this figure, the Developer Tools are displayed in a panel below the web page in a Chrome browser. This is the same page that's shown in figure 4-14. In the left pane of the tools panel, you can see all of the HTML elements of the page. Then, to expand or collapse a group of elements, you click on the symbol before the element. In this figure, the html, body, and main elements have been expanded.

To inspect the styles for an element, you can click on the element in the Elements pane. Or, you can click on the inspect icon at the left of the toolbar for the Developer Tools (the one with the arrow pointing to a square on it), and then click on the element in the web page. In this case, the user has clicked on the h1 element in the Elements pane.

When an element is selected, its styles are shown in the Styles pane at the right side of the Developer Tools panel. This pane shows all of the styles that have been applied to the element, from the first styles at the bottom of the pane to the last styles at the top.

In this example, the bottom of the pane shows the styles that are inherited from the body element. Here, the font-size style has been crossed out because it has been overridden. The next group up shows the styles that are applied by the user agent style sheet, which is the one provided by the browser. Here again, the font-size style has been overridden. Above that, you can see that the style rule for the h1 element in the main element in the main.css style sheet is the one that has overridden the lower values with a font size of 170%.

If you experiment with this feature of the Developer Tools, you'll quickly see how useful it can be. Just click on an element in the left pane to see how the styles have been applied.

How Chrome's Developer Tools show the effects of cascading styles

How to use Chrome's Developer Tools

- To display the panel for the tools, press the F12 key.
- To inspect the styles that have been applied to an element, click on the element in the Elements pane at the left side of the Developer Tools panel. Or, click on the inspect icon at the left of the toolbar for this panel, and then click on an element in the web page.
- The styles that have been applied to the selected element are displayed in the Styles pane at the right side of the Developer Tools panel.

Description

- Most modern browsers provide Developer Tools that can be accessed by pressing the F12 key or by right-clicking on the page and selecting Inspect or Inspect Element.
- To help debug your web pages, you can use a browser's Developer Tools to inspect the styles that have been applied to an element, including how the styles in one style sheet have overridden the styles in another style sheet.

Figure 4-17   How to use Developer Tools to inspect the styles
that have been applied

How to create and use custom properties

Figure 4-18 shows how to use a relatively new CSS feature called *custom properties*, or *CSS variables*. This feature lets you define a property value, or variable, that you can use throughout a CSS file.

This figure starts by showing the syntax for creating and using a custom property. Then, it gives an example that defines a custom property named "color-1" that has a hex value of #f2972e. Once that's defined, other style rules can refer to that variable as "color-1" instead of coding the hex value for the color. So, if the variable is used in several or many places, you don't have to keep entering the hex value with the chance of making an entry error. And later, if you want to change that color, you only have to change the value in the custom property.

One of the keys here is the selector that you use when you create the custom property because it determines where the variable can be used. In this first example, the selector is the :root pseudo-class, which refers to the html element, but it has a higher specificity than that element. That means that you can apply this custom property anywhere in the HTML document. And that's the way you will normally use custom properties.

But the next example shows how to create a custom property with a narrower selector, in this case, for a section element. Then, the custom property can only be applied to HTML elements within the section. This makes sense if the property value is used several times within the HTML element and you don't want the property value used outside that element.

The syntax for creating and using a custom property (or variable)

The syntax for creating a custom property

```
selector {
    --custom-property: value;
}
```

The syntax for using a custom property

```
property: var(--custom-property);
```

Code that uses a custom property that's declared in the :root pseudoclass

Code that declares the custom property

```
:root { --color-1: #f2972e; }
```

Code that uses the custom property

```
h1 { color: var(--color-1); }

nav ul li a { background-color: var(--color-1); }

h2 {
    text-shadow: 2px 2px 4px var(--color-1);
    color: blue;
}
```

Code that uses a custom property that's declared in a section

Code that declares the custom property

```
section { --color-2: #f2972e; }
```

Code that uses the custom property

```
section h1 { color: var(--color-2); }

section nav ul li a { background-color: var(--color-2); }
```

Description

- *Custom properties*, also referred to as *CSS variables*, are properties that can be used throughout an entire document or within specific parts of a document.

- To create a custom property, you code it within a style rule that has a selector just like any other style rule. Then, that selector determines where the custom property can be used.

- To create a custom property that can be used throughout a document, you can declare it on the :root pseudo-class. This is the same as coding it on the html element except that the :root pseudo-class has a higher specificity.

- When a property like a color is used in many places in a CSS file, a custom property can save coding errors and make the code easier to understand.

Figure 4-18   How to create and use custom properties

Perspective

At this point, you should know how to code all the variations of CSS selectors. You should also know how to specify measurements and colors and how to apply the CSS properties for formatting text. That gets you off to a good start with CSS, but there's still a lot to learn.

So, in the next chapter, you'll learn how to use the CSS box model to set the margins, padding, and borders for the elements in your pages. That way, you can get your typography to look just the way you want it. Then, in chapter 6, you'll learn how to use CSS for page layout.

Terms

external style sheet	HSLA value
embedded styles	font family
selector	shorthand property
universal selector	relational selector
type selector	child selector
id selector	descendant selector
class selector	adjacent sibling selector
normalize.css style sheet	general sibling selector
absolute unit of measure	attribute selector
relative unit of measure	pseudo-class selector
RGB value	pseudo-element selector
hexadecimal (hex) value	Cascading Style Sheets (CSS)
inherit a property	cascade order
descendant	user style sheet
RGBA value	custom property
HSL value	CSS variable

Summary

- If you're going to use a style sheet for more than one HTML document, it's a best practice to use an *external style sheet*.

- You can code CSS selectors for element types, ids, and classes. You can also code a *universal selector*.

- In the past, the *normalize.css style sheet* was often used to make CSS adjustments that provided for browser compatibility. But you shouldn't need to use this style sheet when you're developing pages for modern browsers

- You can use *absolute units of measure* like pixels or *relative units of measure* like ems or percents to specify the CSS properties for sizes. For font sizes, though, it's better to use relative measurements so the font sizes will change based on the browser size.

- Most graphic designers use *hex* for the *RGB values* that represent the colors that they want because that gives them the most control. Beyond that, CSS lets you use *RGBA*, *HSL*, and *HLSA* values that give the web designer more control over colors and transparency.

- Some properties, like the color and font properties, are *inherited* by the *descendants* of an HTML element. However, you can override those inherited properties with other CSS style rules.

- You should set the default *font family* for a web page to a sans-serif font because that type of font is easier to read.

- CSS can be used to indent, align, and decorate the text in a block element like a heading or paragraph. CSS also provides for adding shadows to text.

- The *shorthand property* for fonts can be used to apply all six of the font properties to an element: font-family, font-size, font-style, font-weight, font-variant, and line-height.

- You can use the float property of an image to float the image to the left or right. Then, the block elements that follow in the HTML flow to its right or left. To stop the flow, you can code the clear property for an element.

- You can code CSS selectors for relations, combinations of selectors, and attributes. You can also use *pseudo-class selectors* to apply CSS formatting when certain conditions occur, and *pseudo-element selectors* to apply CSS formatting to a portion of text.

- If more than one style rule is applied to an element, the style rule with the highest specificity is used.

- The Developer Tools for a modern browser let you inspect all the styles that have been applied to an element, including the styles that have been overridden.

- You can use a *custom property*, or *CSS variable*, to assign values to the properties of elements throughout a document or within a specific element.

Exercise 4-1   Format the Town Hall home page

In this exercise, you'll format the home page that you built in exercise 3-1 by using the skills that you've learned in this chapter. When you're through, the page should look like this.

San Joaquin Valley Town Hall

Celebrating our 75th Year

Our Mission

San Joaquin Valley Town Hall is a non-profit organization that is run by an all-volunteer board of directors. Our mission is to bring nationally and internationally renowned, thought-provoking speakers who inform, educate, and entertain our audience! As one or our members told us:

"Each year I give a ticket package to each of our family members. I think of it as the gift of knowledge...and that is priceless."

Our Ticket Packages

- Season Package: $95
- Patron Package: $200
- Single Speaker: $25

This season's guest speakers

October
David Brancaccio

November
Andrew Ross Sorkin

January
Amy Chua

© 2022, San Joaquin Valley Town Hall, Fresno, CA 93755

Open the HTML file and update the head section

1. Use your text editor to open this HTML file:
    `\html_css_5\exercises\town_hall_1\c4_index.html`

2. Use your text editor to open this HTML template file:
    `\html_css_5\exercises\town_hall_1\templates\basic.html`

    Then, copy the third link element from the head section to the clipboard, switch to the index.html file, and paste it at the end of the head section.

3. Complete the href attribute in the link element that you just copied so it refers to the c4_main.css file in the styles subfolder. Then, close the template.

Open the CSS file and format the header

4. Use your text editor to open this CSS file:

    `\html_css_5\exercises\town_hall_1\styles\c4_main.css`

    Note that this file contains some of the CSS code that you'll need, including the style rule that specifies the font family and font size for the body, the style rule that floats the image in the header, the style rule that clears the floating in the main element, and the style rules that set the font sizes for the headings in the main element.

5. Add two style rules for the header to the style sheet. The first one should be for the h2 element, and it should set the font size to 170%, set the color to #800000, and indent the heading 30 pixels. The second one should be for the h3 element, and it should set the font size to 130%, set the font style to italic, and indent the heading 30 pixels.

6. Test the HTML page in Chrome to make sure that the style sheets have been linked properly, the image has been floated, and the headings have been formatted correctly. If necessary, make corrections and test again.

Format the links and the footer

7. Add a style rule that italicizes any link that has the focus or has the mouse hovering over it.

8. Add a style rule that centers the <p> tag in the footer.

9. Test these changes to be sure they work.

Use the Developer Tools to review the styles for the page

10. Display the page in Chrome, and then press the F12 key to display the Developer Tools. Next, expand the main element in the Elements pane and click on one of the h2 elements.

11. Review the styles for the h2 element in the Styles pane, and notice how the font-size style for the body element in the main style sheet and the h2 element in the user agent style sheet are overridden by the font-size style for the main h2 element in the main style sheet.

12. Click the icon in the Developer Tools toolbar that has a square with an arrow pointing to it on it, and then click on the h2 element in the header to see that it's now selected in the Elements pane.

13. Review the styles for this h2 element to see that they're similar to the styles for the main h2 element. However, the font size for this element is larger and it has a text indent.

14. When you're done with the Developer Tools, close the panel by clicking the icon with an "X" on it in the upper right corner.

Add a text shadow to a heading

15. Add a text shadow to the *75th* in the second heading in the header. To start, enclose the *75th* in the HTML in an em element and give that element a class attribute with a value of "shadow".

16. Create a style rule that uses a class selector (.shadow) for that class, and code a declaration that adds a shadow to the text with #800000 as the color of the shadow.

17. Check that the shadow is displayed properly.

Experiment with a CSS variable

18. Create a custom property named global-color-1, and assign it a value of #800000. The selector should be for the root element.

19. Use this custom property as the value of any property with this color value, and test this change.

20. Change the custom property to this hex value: #4d0080. After you check the results, change the custom property back to its previous value.

Chapter 5

How to use the CSS box model

In the last chapter, you learned some basic CSS properties for formatting text. Now, you'll learn the properties for controlling the spacing between elements and for displaying borders and backgrounds. Specifically, you'll learn how to use the CSS box model for those purposes.

An introduction to the box model

When a browser displays a web page, it places each HTML block element in a box. That makes it easy to control the spacing, borders, and other formatting for elements like headers, sections, footers, headings, and paragraphs. Some inline elements like images are placed in a box as well. To work with boxes, you use the CSS *box model*.

How the box model works

Figure 5-1 presents a diagram that shows how the box model works. By default, the box for a block element is as wide as the block that contains it and as tall as it needs to be based on its content. However, you can explicitly specify the size of the content area for a block element by using the height and width properties. You can also use other properties to set the borders, margins, and padding for a block element.

If you look at the diagram in this figure, you can see that *padding* is the space between the content area and a border. Similarly, a *margin* is the space between the border and the outside of the box.

If you need to calculate the overall height of a box, you can use the formula in this figure. Here, you start by adding the values for the margin, border width, and padding for the top of the box. Then, you add the height of the content area. Last, you add the values for the padding, border width, and margin for the bottom of the box. The formula for calculating the overall width of a box is similar.

When you set the height and width properties for a block element, you can use any of the units that you learned about in the last chapter. For now, though, we'll use pixels so the sizes are fixed. That way, the size of the page won't change if the user changes the size of the browser window. This is referred to as a *fixed layout*.

As you'll learn in chapter 8, though, Responsive Web Design depends on fluid layouts that change based on the size of the screen. As a result, you'll use relative units for various types of sizing.

The CSS box model

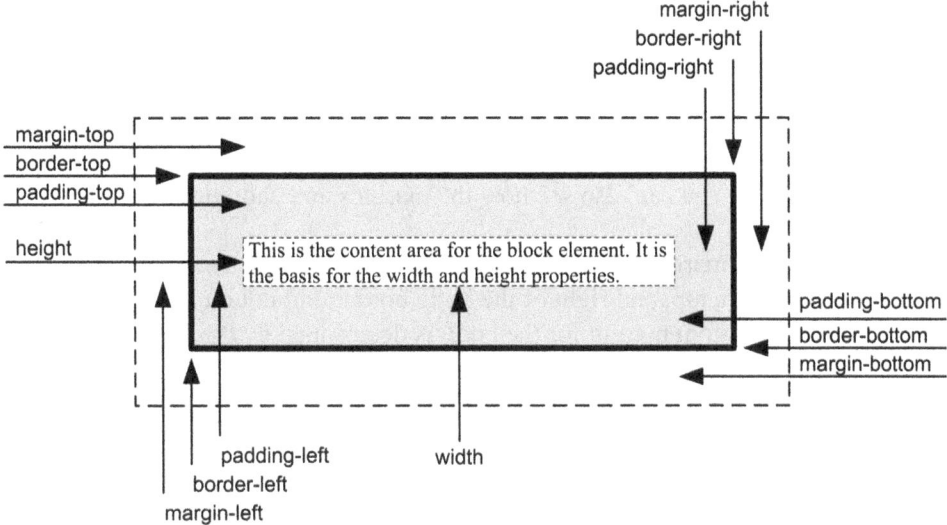

The formula for calculating the height of a box

```
top margin + top border + top padding +
height +
bottom padding + bottom border + bottom margin
```

The formula for calculating the width of a box

```
left margin + left border + left padding +
width +
right padding + right border + right margin
```

Description

- The CSS *box model* lets you work with the boxes that a browser places around each block element as well as some inline elements. This lets you add formatting such as margins, padding, and borders.

- A *margin* is the space between the border of an element and either its containing block or the element next to it.

- *Padding* is the space between an element and its border.

- By default, the box for a block element is as wide as the block that contains it and as tall as it needs to be based on its content.

- You can use the height and width properties to specify the size of the content area for a block element.

- You can use other properties to control the margins, padding, and borders for a block element. Then, these properties are added to the height and width of the content area to determine the height and width of the box.

Figure 5-1   How the box model works

A web page that illustrates the box model

To help you understand how the box model works, figure 5-2 presents the HTML for a simple web page. Then, the CSS adds borders to the four types of elements in the HTML: a dotted 3-pixel border to the body, a solid 2-pixel border to the main element, and dashed 1-pixel borders to the h1 and <p> elements. If you look at the web page in the browser, you can see how these four borders are rendered. You can also see how the margins and padding for these boxes work.

For the body, the margin on all four sides is set to 10 pixels. You can see that margin on the left, top, and right of the body border, but not on the bottom. That's because the bottom margin for the body is determined by the size of the window.

For the main element, the width is set to 500 pixels, and the margins on all four sides of the box are set to 20 pixels. You can see these margins on the left, top, and bottom of the main box, but not on the right because the width of this element is set to 500 pixels.

The next style rule sets properties for both the h1 and <p> elements. In this case, the properties set the border and the padding for these elements. Then, the next two style rules set additional properties for each of these elements.

The style rule for the h1 element sets the top margin to .5em, the right and left margins to 0, and the bottom margin to .25em. As a result, there is more space above the h1 element than below it. This style rule also sets the padding on the left side of the element to 15 pixels so space is added between the border of the box and the text.

The style rule for the <p> element starts by setting all the margins to 0. As a result, all of the space between the h1 and <p> elements is due to the bottom margin of the h1 element. In addition, the padding on the left side of the element is set to 15 pixels so the text for the h1 and <p> elements is aligned.

Please note that if I had used relative measures for the padding on the left of the h1 and <p> elements, they wouldn't be aligned because the font sizes for these elements are different. One more thing to notice is that the padding-left properties in the style rules for the h1 and <p> elements override the left padding specified by the style rule for both of these elements.

This should help you understand how the box model works. Now, it's on to the details for setting the properties for the box model.

The HTML for a page that uses the box model

```
<body>
    <main>
        <h1>San Joaquin Valley Town Hall</h1>
        <p>Welcome to San Joaquin Valley Town Hall.
        We have some fascinating speakers for you this season!</p>
    </main>
</body>
```

The CSS for the page

```
body {
    border: 3px dotted black;
    margin: 10px;
}
main {
    border:  2px solid black;
    width:   500px;
    margin:  20px;          /* all four sides */
    padding: 10px;          /* all four sides */
}
h1, p {
    border: 1px dashed black;
    padding: 10px;
}
h1 {
    margin: .5em 0 .25em;  /* .5em top, 0 right and left, .25em bottom */
    padding-left: 15px;
}
p {
    margin: 0;              /* all four sides */
    padding-left: 15px;
}
```

The web page in a browser

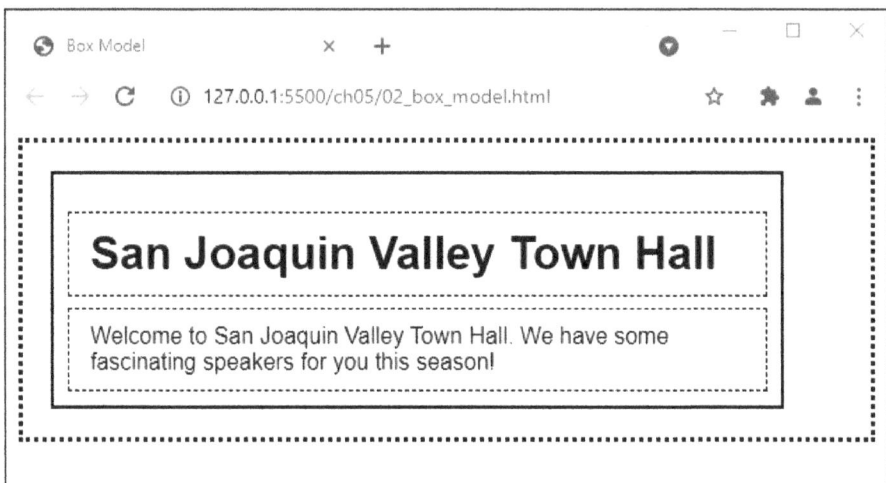

Figure 5-2   A web page that illustrates the box model

How to size and space elements

As you saw in the last figure, you can use several different properties to determine the size of an element and the spacing between the elements on a page. In the topics that follow, you'll learn the details of coding these properties.

How to set widths and heights

Figure 5-3 presents the properties for setting heights and widths. The two properties you'll use most often are width and height. By default, these properties are set to a value of "auto". As a result, the size of the content area for the element is automatically adjusted so it's as wide as the element that contains it and as tall as the content it contains. To change that, you can use the height and width properties.

The first two sets of examples in this figure illustrate how this works. Here, the first example in each set specifies an absolute value using pixels. Then, the second example specifies a relative value using percents. As a result, the width is set to 75% of the *containing block*.

Finally, the third example in each set uses the keyword "auto". That sets the width based on the size of the containing element and the height based on the content of the element. Because the default width and height is "auto", you usually won't need to use that value.

In addition to the width and height properties, you can use the min-width, max-width, min-height, and max-height properties to specify the minimum and maximum width and height of the content area. However, these properties are normally used in the context of Responsive Web Design. As a result, you won't see them used until chapter 8.

Properties for setting widths and heights

Property	Description
width	The width of the content area for a block element. Or auto (the default) if you want the width of the box calculated based on the width of its containing block.
height	The height of the content area for a block element. Or auto (the default) if you want the height of the area calculated based on its content.
min-width	The minimum width of the content area for a block element regardless of its content.
max-width	The maximum width of the content area for a block element. Or none to indicate that there is no maximum width.
min-height	The minimum height of the content area for a block element regardless of its content.
max-height	The maximum height of the content area for a block element. Or none to indicate that there is no maximum height.

How to set the width of the content area

```
width: 450px;          /* an absolute width */
width: 75%;            /* a relative width */
width: auto;           /* width based on its containing block (the default) */
```

How to set the height of the content area

```
height: 125px;
height: 50%;
height: auto;          /* height based on its content (the default) */
```

How to set the minimum and maximum width and height

```
min-width: 450px;
max-width: 600px;
min-height: 120px;
max-height: 160px;
```

Description

- The width and height properties can be set to absolute or relative values.

- If you specify a percent for the width property, the width of the content area for the block element is based on the width of the block that contains it, called the *containing block*. In that case, the width of the containing block must be specified.

- If you specify a percent for the height property, the height of the content area for the block element is based on the height of the containing block. In that case, the height of the containing block must be specified. Otherwise, "auto" is substituted for the percent.

- The min-height property can also be used to be sure that an element has the specified height even if the content doesn't fill the element.

- As you'll see in chapter 8, the min-width, max-width, min-height, and max-height properties are normally used in the context of Responsive Web Design.

Figure 5-3   How to set widths and heights

How to set margins

Figure 5-4 presents the properties for setting margins. As you can see, you can use individual properties like margin-top or margin-left to set individual margins. This is illustrated in the first set of examples in this figure.

Instead of setting individual margins, though, you can use the margin property to set the margins for all four sides of a box. When you use a *shorthand property* like this, you can specify one, two, three, or four values. If you specify all four values, they are applied to the sides of the box in a clockwise order: top, right, bottom, and left. To remember this order, you can think of the word *trouble*.

If you specify fewer than four values, this property still sets the margins for all four sides of the box. If, for example, you only specify one value, each margin is set to that value. If you specify two values, the top and bottom margins are set to the first value, and the left and right margins are set to the second value. And if you specify three values, the top margin is set to the first value, the left and right margins are set to the second value, and the bottom margin is set to the third value. This is illustrated in the second set of examples in this figure.

Although it isn't shown here, you can also specify the keyword "auto" for any margin. In most cases, you'll use this keyword to center a page in the browser window or a block element within its containing block. To do that, you specify auto for both the left and right margins. For this to work, you must also set the width of the element. You'll see an example of this in a moment.

You should also know that different browsers may have different default margins for the block elements. Because of that, it's a good practice to set the top and bottom margins of the elements that you're using. That way, you can control the space between elements like headings and paragraphs.

Finally, if you specify a bottom margin for one element and a top margin for the element that follows it, the margins are *collapsed*. That means the smaller margin is ignored, and only the larger margin is applied. One way to get around this is to set the margins to zero and use padding for the spacing.

How to set padding

The properties for setting padding are also presented in figure 5-4. These properties are similar to the properties for setting margins. As you can see, you can set the padding for the sides of a box individually, or you can set the padding for all four sides of a box at once by using the padding shorthand property.

Properties for setting margins

Property	Description
margin-top	The top margin
margin-right	The right margin
margin-bottom	The bottom margin
margin-left	The left margin
margin	One to four values that specify the margin sizes for a box. One value is applied to all four margins. Two values are applied to the top and bottom and right and left margins. Three values are applied to the top, right and left, and bottom margins. And four values are applied to the top, right, bottom, and left margins (think *trouble*).

How to set the margin on a single side of an element

```
margin-top: .5em;
margin-left: 1em;
```

How to set the margins on multiple sides of an element

```
margin: 1em;              /* all four sides */
margin: 0 1em;            /* top and bottom 0, right and left 1em */
margin: .5em 1em 2em;     /* top .5em, right and left 1em, bottom 2em */
margin: .5em 1em 2em 1em; /* top .5em, right 1em, bottom 2em, left 1em */
```

Properties for setting padding

Property	Description
padding-top	The top padding
padding-right	The right padding
padding-bottom	The bottom padding
padding-left	The left paddding
padding	Works the same as the margin property

How to set the padding on a single side of an element

```
padding-top: 0;
padding-right: 1em;
```

How to set the padding on multiple sides of an element

```
padding: 1em;             /* all four sides */
padding: 0 1em;           /* top and bottom 0, right and left 1em */
padding: 0 1em .5em;      /* top 0, right and left 1em, bottom .5em */
padding: 0 1em .5em 1em;  /* top 0, right 1em, bottom .5em, left 1em */
```

Description

- If you specify a bottom margin for one element and a top margin for the element that follows it, the margins are *collapsed*, which means that only the larger margin is applied.

- If you set the top and bottom margins for elements to zero, you can use padding to set the spacing between the elements.

Figure 5-4   How to set margins and padding

A web page that illustrates sizing and spacing

To illustrate the use of the properties for sizing and spacing, figure 5-5 presents a web page that uses these properties. This web page is similar to the one at the end of the last chapter. However, the page has been centered in the browser window, the spacing between the elements has been improved, and the second and third paragraphs aren't indented.

The HTML for the web page

The HTML for this web page is the same as in the application at the end of the last chapter, with two exceptions. First, the second and third paragraphs in the main element don't have a class attribute that's used to indent them. Second, the last paragraph in the main element has an id attribute of "contact_us".

A web page that uses widths, margins, and padding

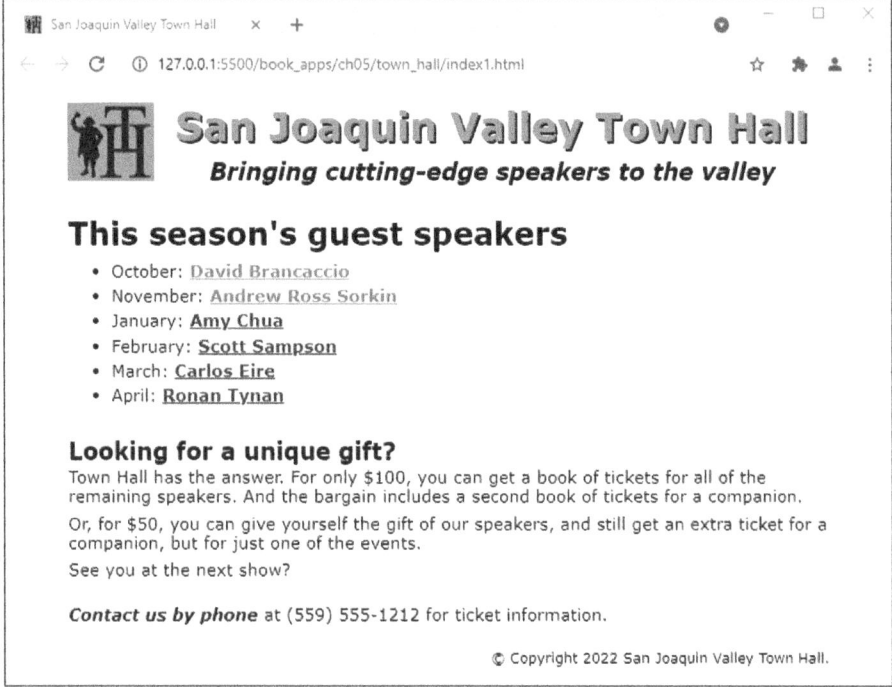

The HTML for the page

```
<header>
    <img src="images/logo.gif" alt="Town Hall Logo" width="80">
    <h2>San Joaquin Valley Town Hall</h2>
    <h3>Bringing cutting-edge speakers to the valley</h3>
</header>
<main>
    <h1>This season's guest speakers</h1>
    <nav>
        <ul>
            <li>October: <a class="date_passed"
                href="speakers/brancaccio.html">David Brancaccio</a></li>
            ...
            <li>April: <a href="speakers/tynan.html">
                Ronan Tynan</a></li>
        </ul>
    </nav>
    <h2>Looking for a unique gift?</h2>
    <p>Town Hall has the answer. For only $100, ....</p>
    <p>Or, for $50, you can give yourself the gift ....</p>
    <p>See you at the next show?</p>
    <p id="contact_us"><em>Contact us by phone</em> at (559) 555-1212 for
        ticket information.</p>
</main>
<footer>
    <p>&copy; Copyright 2022 San Joaquin Valley Town Hall.</p>
</footer>
```

Figure 5-5   A web page that illustrates the use of margins and padding

The CSS for the web page

Figure 5-6 presents the CSS for the web page. Here, I've highlighted all the style rules that affect the size and spacing of the elements on the page.

To start, the style rule for the body sets the width of the page to 700 pixels. Then, the top and bottom margins are set to 1em so there's space between the body and the top of the browser window. In addition, the left and right margins are set to "auto". That causes the left and right margins to be calculated automatically so the page is centered in the browser window.

The next highlighted style rule is for the h1, h2, h3, and <p> elements. This sets the margins and padding for these elements to 0. This prevents margin collapse when these items are next to each other. Then, the style rules that follow can provide the right margins and padding for these elements.

For instance, the style rule for the <p> element sets the top and bottom padding to .25em, which provides the spacing between the paragraphs. Also, the style rule for the h2 element in the header sets the margin bottom to .25em, and the style rule for the h1 element in the main element sets the margin top to 1em and the margin bottom to .35em. This provides the proper spacing before and after the headings.

In the style rule for the ul element, you can see that the bottom margin is set to 1.5em, and the other margins are set to zero. This reduces the space before the unordered list and increases the space after. Similarly, the bottom padding for the li elements is set to .35em. That provides the spacing after the list items.

Last, in the style rule for the element with "contact_us" as its id, you can see that the top margin is set to 1em, which provides the spacing before it. And the style rule for the footer sets the top margin to 1em, which provides more space between it and the last paragraph in the main element.

If you study this code, you can see that it avoids the problems of collapsing margins. It does that by first setting the margins for the elements to zero and then overriding those margins or using padding to provide the spacing before and after elements.

The CSS for the web page

```css
/* the styles for the elements */
body {
    font-family: Verdana, Arial, Helvetica, sans-serif;
    font-size: 100%;
    width: 700px;
    margin: 1em auto; }

h1, h2, h3, p {
    margin: 0;
    padding: 0; }

a { font-weight: bold; }
a:link { color: #931420; }
a:visited { color: #f2972e; }
a:hover, a:focus { color: blue; }

ul { margin: 0 0 1.5em; }
li {
    font-size: 95%;
    padding-bottom: .35em; }

p {
    font-size: 95%;
    padding: .25em 0; }
em { font-weight: bold; }

/* the styles for the header */
header img { float: left; }
header h2 {
    font-size: 220%;
    color: #f2972e;
    text-align: center;
    text-shadow: 2px 2px 0 black;
    margin-bottom: .25em; }
header h3 {
    font-size: 130%;
    font-style: italic;
    text-align: center; }

/* the styles for the main content */
main { clear: left; }
main h1 {
    font-size: 175%;
    margin: 1em 0 .35em;
}
main h2 { font-size: 130%; }
#contact_us { margin-top: 1em; }
a.date_passed  { color: gray; }

/* the styles for the footer */
footer { margin-top: 1em; }
footer p {
    font-size: 80%;
    text-align: right; }
```

Figure 5-6   The CSS for the web page

A version of the CSS that uses a reset selector

In figure 5-7, you can see another version of the CSS for this application. This time, the CSS uses a *reset selector*. That refers to the use of a universal selector that sets the margins and padding for all of the elements to zero. After you code the reset selector, you can get the spacing that you want by applying margins and padding to specific elements, which overrides the settings of the reset selector.

In the CSS for this figure, only the style rules that provide margins or padding are listed. This works pretty much the way the code in the previous figure works, except for the ul and li elements. Because the reset selector set the margins and padding for these elements to zero, you need to provide margins and padding for these elements.

To bring the ul element in line with the heading above it, you need to set its left margin. In this example, the left margin is set to 1.25em. You also need to provide left padding for the li elements to provide space between the bullets and the text. In this example, that space is set to .25em.

Because of these CSS differences, the formatting of the web page in this figure is slightly different than the formatting in figure 5-5. Specifically, the bulleted list isn't indented, and there's more space between the bullets and text in the list items. Of course, you could make them the same by changing the settings for the ul and li elements, but this shows the options that you have when you use a reset selector.

A slightly modified version of the page that uses a reset selector

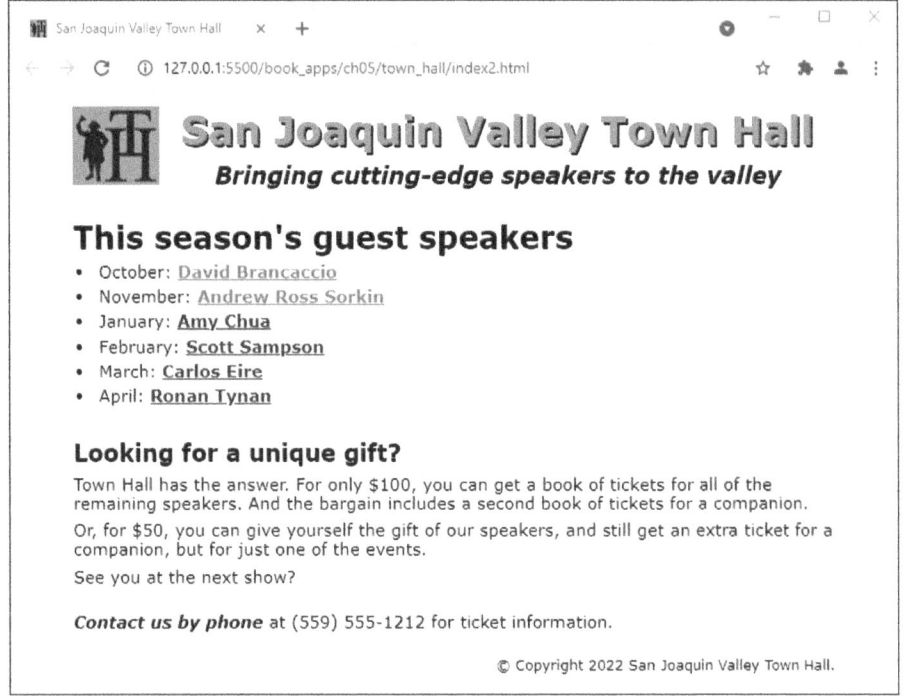

The CSS for this version of the page

```
/* the reset selector */
* {
    margin: 0;
    padding: 0; }

/* just the styles for the elements that provide margins or padding */
body {
    font-family: Verdana, Arial, Helvetica, sans-serif;
    font-size: 100%;
    width: 700px;
    margin: 15px auto; }
h1, h2, h3 { margin-bottom: .25em; }
ul { margin: 0 0 1.5em 1.25em; }
li {
    font-size: 95%;
    padding-bottom: .35em;
    padding-left: .25em; }
p {
    font-size: 95%;
    padding: .25em 0; }
main h1 { font-size: 175%; }
#contact_us { margin-top: 1em; }
footer { margin-top: 1em; }
```

Figure 5-7   A version of the CSS that uses a reset selector

How to set borders and backgrounds

Now that you know how to size and space elements using the box model, you're ready to learn how to apply other formatting to boxes. That includes adding borders and setting background colors and images.

How to set borders

Figure 5-8 presents the properties for setting *borders* and illustrates how they work. To start, if you want the same border on all four sides of a box, you can use the shorthand border property. This property lets you set the width, style, and color for the borders. This is illustrated in the first set of examples in this figure, and this is the way you will normally code borders.

Here, the first declaration creates a thin, solid, green border. But note that different browsers may interpret the thin keyword, as well as the other keywords for width, differently. Because of that, you'll typically set the width of a border to an absolute value as shown in the second and third declarations. Notice that the third declaration doesn't specify a color. In that case, the border will be the same color as the element's text.

To set the border for just one side of a box, you can use the shorthand property for a border side. This is illustrated by the second set of examples. Here, the first declaration sets the top border and the second declaration sets the right border.

Most of the time, you'll use the shorthand properties to set all four borders or just one border of a box. However, you can use the other properties in this figure to set the widths, styles, and colors for the sides of a border. This is illustrated by the last four groups of examples in this figure. You may want to use these properties to override another border setting for an element.

For instance, to set the width for each side of a border, you can use the border-width property as shown in the third set of examples. Here, you can specify one, two, three, or four values. This works just like the shorthand margin and padding properties you learned about earlier in this chapter. That means that the values are applied to the top, right, bottom, and left sides of the border.

The border-style and border-color properties are similar. You can use them to set the style and color for each side of a border by specifying one to four values. This is illustrated in the fourth and fifth sets of examples in this figure. Notice in the last example for the border-style property that the left and right borders are set to "none". That way, only top and bottom borders will be displayed.

The last set of examples shows another way to set properties for a border on just one side a box. For instance, the first example in this group sets a bottom border that's 4 pixels wide, and the second example sets a right border that has the dashed style.

Properties for setting borders

Property	Description
border	A border width, border style, and border color. The values are applied to all sides of the border.
border-*side*	Border width, style, and color values for the specified side of a border.
border-width	One to four values (excluding a percent) or keywords that specify the width for each side of a border. Possible keywords are thin, medium, and thick.
border-style	One to four keywords that specify the style for each side of a border. Possible values are dotted, dashed, solid, double, groove, ridge, inset, outset, and none. The default is none.
border-color	One to four color values or keywords that specify the color for each side of a border. The default is the color of the element.
border-*side*-width	A value (excluding a percent) or a keyword that specifies the width of the indicated side of a border.
border-*side*-style	A keyword that specifies the style for the indicated side of a border.
border-*side*-color	A color value or keyword that specifies the color of the indicated side of a border.

The syntax for the shorthand border and border-*side* properties

```
border: [width] [style] [color];
border-side: [width] [style] [color];
```

How to set border properties

```
border: thin solid green;
border: 2px dashed #808080;
border: 1px inset;              /* uses the element's color property */
```

How to set side borders

```
border-top: 2px solid black;
border-right: 4px double blue;
```

How to set the widths of borders

```
border-width: 1px;              /* all four sides */
border-width: 1px 2px;          /* top and bottom 1px, right and left 2px */
border-width: 1px 2px 2px;      /* top 1px, right and left 2px, bottom 2px */
border-width: 1px 2px 2px 3px; /* top 1px, right 2px, bottom 2px, left 3px */
```

How to set the style of borders

```
border-style: dashed;      /* dashed line all sides */
border-style: solid none; /* solid top and bottom, no border right and left */
```

How to set the color of borders

```
border-color: #808080;
border-color: black gray; /* black top and bottom, gray right and left */
```

How to set the width, style, and color of border sides

```
border-bottom-width: 4px;
border-right-style: dashed;
border-left-color: gray;
```

Figure 5-8   How to set borders

How to add rounded corners and shadows to borders

Figure 5-9 shows how to use the CSS features for adding *rounded corners* and *shadows* to borders. This lets you supply these graphic effects without using images.

To round the corners, you use the border-radius property that's summarized in this figure. If you supply one value for it, it applies to all four corners of the border. But if you supply four values as in the example, you can apply specific rounding to each corner. Here, the upper-left corner has a 10 pixel radius, the upper-right corner has a 20 pixel radius, the lower-right corner has a zero radius so it isn't rounded, and the lower-left corner has a 20 pixel radius.

To add shadows to a border, you use the box-shadow property. This works much like the text-shadow property that you learned about in the last chapter. With the first two values, you specify the offset for the shadow. With the third value, you can specify the blur radius. With the fourth value, you specify how far the blur is spread. And with the fifth value, you can specify a different color for the shadow than the one for the border. To get the effects that you want, you usually need to experiment with these values, but this is easier than using an image to get those effects.

Incidentally, there are some options for these features that aren't presented in this figure. For instance, you can use a separate property like border-top-left-radius for each corner. You can also set the curvature of a corner by supplying two values for a single corner like this:

```
border-top-left-radius: 50px 20px;
```

So, if you want to go beyond what this figure offers, please refer to the W3C documentation.

The syntax for the border-radius and box-shadow properties

```
border-radius: radius;  /* applies to all four corners */
border-radius: topLeft topRight lowerRight lowerLeft;
box-shadow: horizontalOffset verticalOffset blurRadius spread color;
```

The HTML for a section

```
<section>
    <a href="ebooks_index.html">$10 Ebooks!</a>
</section>
```

The CSS for the section

```
section {
    padding: 20px;
    width: 160px;
    border: 5px double blue;
    color: blue;
    font-size: 200%;
    text-align: center;
    font-weight: bold;
    border-radius: 10px 20px 0 20px;
    box-shadow: 3px 3px 4px 4px red;
}
```

The section in a browser

Description

- When you code the border-radius property, you can assign one rounding radius to all four corners or a different radius to each corner.

- When you code the box-shadow property, positive values offset the shadow to the right or down, and negative values offset the shadow to the left or up.

- The third value in the box-shadow property determines how much the shadow is blurred, and the fourth value determines how far the blur is spread.

- The fifth value in the box-shadow property specifies the color of the shadow. If this is omitted, it is the same color as the border.

Figure 5-9   How to add rounded corners and shadows to borders

How to set background colors and images

Figure 5-10 presents the properties you can use to set the *background* for a box. When you set a background, it's displayed behind the content, padding, and border for the box, but it isn't displayed behind the margin.

Although this figure presents all the properties for using background colors and images, please remember the need for web accessibility. In brief, that means that the background colors and images should never make the text more difficult to read, especially for the visually impaired. That's why the background colors for commercial websites are usually light colors or white, and background images are used only for special purposes. With that in mind, the only property that you may ever need is the background-color property.

If, however, you do want to provide a special background for one element on the page, this figure summarizes the information that you need. To start, you can set a background color, a background image, or both. If you set both, the browser displays the background color behind the image. As a result, you can only see the background color if the image has areas that are transparent or the image doesn't repeat.

As this figure shows, you can set all five properties of a background by using the shorthand background property. When you use this property, you don't have to specify the individual properties in a specific order, but it usually makes sense to use the order that's shown. If you omit one or more properties, the browser uses their default values.

The first set of examples illustrates how this works. Here, the first declaration sets the background color to blue, the second declaration sets the background color and specifies the URL for an image, and the third declaration specifies all five background properties. You can also code each of these properties individually.

If you add a background image to a box, it will repeat horizontally and vertically to fill the box by default. This works well for small images that are intended to be tiled across or down a box. But if you want to change this behavior, you can set the background-repeat property so the image is only repeated horizontally, only repeated vertically, or isn't repeated at all. This is illustrated by the first four declarations in the last set of examples.

If an image isn't repeated, you may need to set additional properties to determine where the image is positioned and whether it scrolls with the page. By default, an image is positioned in the top left corner of the box. But to change that, you can use the background-position property.

The next three declarations illustrate how this works. The first declaration positions the image at the top left corner of the box, which is the default. The second declaration centers the image at the top of the box. And the third declaration positions the image starting 90% of the way from the left side to the right side of the box and 90% of the way from the top to the bottom of the box.

In most cases, you'll want a background image to scroll as you scroll the box that contains it. If not, you can set the background-attachment property to "fixed". This is illustrated by the last declaration in this figure.

The properties for setting the background color and image

Property	Description
background	Background color, image, repeat, attachment, and position values.
background-color	A color value or keyword that specifies the color of an element's background. You can also specify the transparent keyword if you want elements behind the element to be visible. This is the default.
background-image	A relative or absolute URL that points to the image. You can also specify the keyword none if you don't want to display an image. This is the default.
background-repeat	A keyword that specifies if and how an image is repeated. Possible values are repeat, repeat-x, repeat-y, and no-repeat. The default is repeat, which causes the image to be repeated both horizontally and vertically to fill the background.
background-attachment	A keyword that specifies whether an image scrolls with the document or remains in a fixed position. Possible values are scroll and fixed. The default is scroll.
background-position	One or two relative or absolute values or keywords that specify the initial horizontal and vertical positions of an image. Keywords are left, center, and right; top, center, and bottom. If a vertical position isn't specified, center is the default. If no position is specified, the default is to place the image at the top-left corner of the element.

Accessibility guideline

- Don't use a background color or image that makes the text that's over it difficult to read.

The syntax for the shorthand background property

```
background: [color] [image] [repeat] [attachment] [position];
```

How to use the shorthand property

```
background: blue;
background: blue url("../images/texture.gif");
background: #808080 url("../images/header.jpg") repeat-y scroll center top;
```

How to control image repetition, position, and scrolling

```
background-repeat: repeat;        /* repeats both directions */
background-repeat: repeat-x;      /* repeats horizontally */
background-repeat: repeat-y;      /* repeats vertically */
background-repeat: no-repeat;     /* doesn't repeat */

background-position: left top;    /* 0% from left, 0% from top */
background-position: center top;  /* centered horizontally, 0% from top */
background-position: 90% 90%;     /* 90% from left, 90% from top */

background-attachment: scroll;    /* image moves as you scroll */
background-attachment: fixed;     /* image does not move as you scroll */
```

Figure 5-10   How to set background colors and images

How to set background gradients

Figure 5-11 shows the basics of how to use the CSS feature for *linear gradients*. Here again, this feature lets you provide interesting backgrounds without using images.

If you study the examples in this figure, you'll start to see how this feature works. In the first example, the color goes from left to right; the first color is white starting at the far left (0%), and the second color is red ending at the far right (100%). Then, CSS provides the gradient from left to right when the page is rendered.

In the second example, the direction is 45 degrees and there are three color groups. Red starts at the far left (0%). White is in the middle (50%). And blue is on the right (100%). Then, CSS provides the gradients when the page is rendered.

In the third example, you can see how to code solid stripes. Here, both a starting and ending point is given for each color. The result is three solid stripes of red, white, and blue at a 45 degree angle.

If you experiment with this feature, you'll see the interesting effects that you can get with it. But you can take this feature even further. For complete details, please refer to the W3C documentation.

The syntax for using a linear gradient in the background-image property

```
background-image:
    linear-gradient(direction, color %, color %, ... );
```

The HTML for three divisions

```
<div id="eg1"></div>
<div id="eg2"></div>
<div id="eg3"></div>
```

The CSS for the three divisions

```
#eg1 { background-image: linear-gradient(
        to right, white 0%, red 100%); }
#eg2 { background-image: linear-gradient(
        45deg, red 0%, white 50%, blue 100%); }
#eg3 { background-image: linear-gradient(
        45deg, red 0%, red 33%, white 33%, white 66%, blue 66%, blue 100%); }
```

The linear gradients in a browser

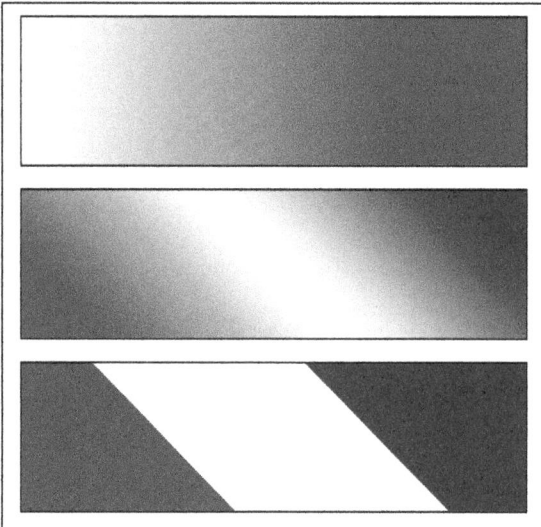

Description

- The CSS for *linear gradients* lets you create gradients for backgrounds without using images.

- The first parameter of a linear gradient indicates the direction the gradient will go: a number of degrees if the gradient should be on an angle, "to right" for left to right, "to bottom" for top to bottom, "to left" for right to left, and "to top" for bottom to top.

- The direction is followed by two or more parameters that consist of a color and a percent. The first percent indicates where the first color should start, the last percent indicates where the last color should end, and the percents in between indicate the points at which one gradient stops and the next one starts.

Figure 5-11   How to set background gradients

A web page that uses borders and backgrounds

Figure 5-12 presents a web page that's similar to the one in figure 5-5. In fact, the HTML for these two pages is identical. However, the page in this figure has some additional formatting.

First, this page uses a gradient for the background behind the body. It also uses white as the background color for the body. That way, the gradient doesn't show behind the body content.

Second, this page has a border around the body with rounded corners and shadows. Also, the header has a border below it, and the footer has a border above it.

The HTML for the web page

The HTML is the same as the HTML in figure 5-5. Only the CSS has changed.

A web page that uses borders and backgrounds

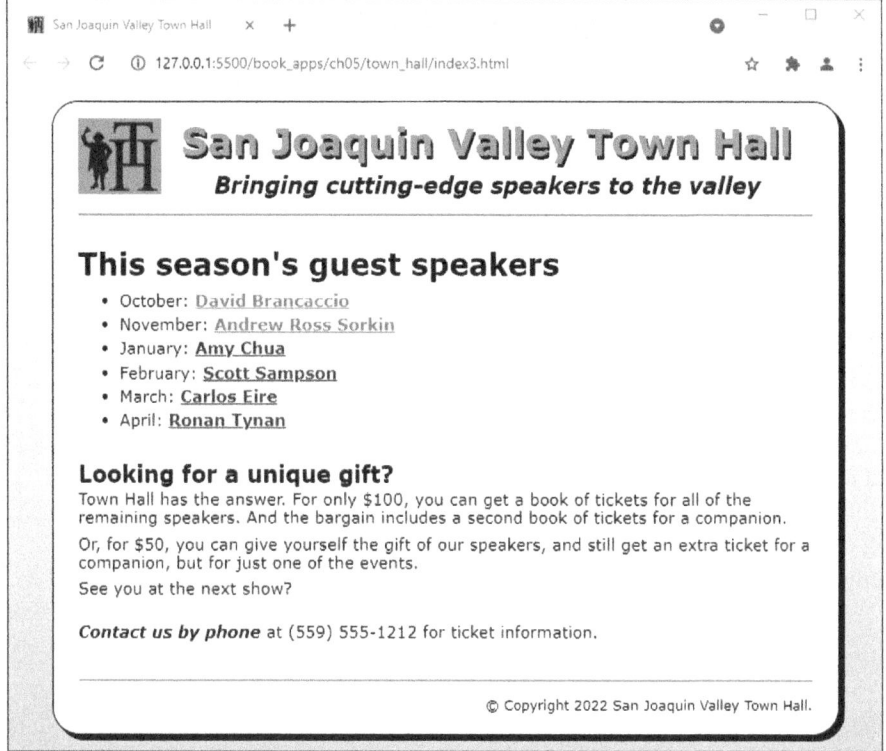

The HTML for the page

```html
<header>
    <img src="images/logo.gif" alt="Town Hall Logo" width="80">
    <h2>San Joaquin Valley Town Hall</h2>
    <h3>Bringing cutting-edge speakers to the valley</h3>
</header>
<main>
    <h1>This season's guest speakers</h1>
    <nav>
        <ul>
            <li>October: <a class="date_passed"
                href="speakers/brancaccio.html">David Brancaccio</a></li>
            ...
        </ul>
    </nav>
    <h2>Looking for a unique gift?</h2>
    <p>Town Hall has the answer. For only $100, ....</p>
    <p>Or, for $50, you can give yourself the gift ....</p>
    <p>See you at the next show?</p>
    <p id="contact_us"><em>Contact us by phone</em> at (559) 555-1212 for
        ticket information.</p>
</main>
<footer>
    <p>&copy; Copyright 2022 San Joaquin Valley Town Hall.</p>
</footer>
```

Figure 5-12   A web page that uses borders and backgrounds

The CSS for the web page

Figure 5-13 presents the CSS for the web page. In this case, I've highlighted the rules that are different from the ones in figure 5-6. Although you should be able to understand this code without any help, here are some points that you should note.

First, a gradient is used for the background image of the html element. This is the gradient that you see on the top, bottom, and sides of the body element.

Second, the background color of the body of the document is set to white. That way, the contents of the page will be displayed on a white background. Also, the top and bottom margins for the body are set to 1em, which lets the gradient show above and below the body, and the right and left margins are set to auto, which centers the body in the browser window.

Third, the top and bottom padding for the body is set to 1em and the left and right padding is set to 1.5ems. Then, a border with rounded corners and a shadow is added to the body.

Fourth, a border has been added below the header and above the footer. For the footer, the top margin is 2ems, which is the space above the border, and the top padding is .7ems, which is the space between the border and the paragraph below it.

The CSS for the web page

```css
/* the styles that provide the background behind the body */
html {
    background-image: linear-gradient(
        to bottom, white 0%, #facd8a 100%);
}
body {
    font-family: Verdana, Arial, Helvetica, sans-serif;
    font-size: 100%;
    width: 700px;
    background-color: white;
    margin: 15px auto;
    padding: 15px 1.5em;
    border: 1px solid black;
    border-radius: 25px;
    box-shadow: 5px 5px 0 0;
}

/* the styles for the other type selectors are the same as in figure 5-7 */

/* the styles for the header */
header {
    padding-bottom: 1em;
    border-bottom: 2px solid #f2972e; }
header img { float: left; }
header h2 {
    font-size: 220%;
    color: #f2972e;
    text-align: center;
    text-shadow: 2px 2px 0 black;
    margin-bottom: .25em; }
header h3 {
    font-size: 130%;
    font-style: italic;
    text-align: center; }

/* the styles for the main content */
main { clear: left; }
main h1 {
    font-size: 175%;
    margin: 1em 0 .35em; }
main h2 { font-size: 130%; }

#contact_us { margin-top: 1em; }
a.date_passed  { color: gray; }

/* the styles for the footer */
footer {
    margin-top: 2em;
    border-top: 2px solid #f2972e;
    padding-top: .7em; }
footer p {
    font-size: 80%;
    text-align: right; }
```

Figure 5-13   The CSS for the web page

Perspective

Now that you've completed this chapter, you should understand how the box model is used for margins, padding, borders, and backgrounds. As a result, you should be able to get the spacing, borders, and backgrounds for your web pages just the way you want them. Then, in the next chapter, you'll learn how to use CSS for laying out the elements on a page in two- and three-column arrangements with both headers and footers.

Terms

box model	reset selector
margin	border
padding	rounded corners
fixed layout	shadows
containing block	linear gradient
shorthand property	background
collapsed margins	

Summary

- The CSS *box model* refers to the box that a browser places around each block element as well as some inline elements. Each box includes the content of the element, plus optional margins, padding, and borders.

- To set the height and width of a content area, you can use absolute measurements like pixels or relative measurements like percents. If you use a percent, the percent applies to the block that contains the box you're formatting.

- You can set the *margins* for all four sides of a box. But if you set a bottom margin for one element and a top margin for the element that follows, the margins are *collapsed* to the size of the largest margin.

- Like margins, you can set the *padding* for all four sides of a box. One way to avoid margin collapse is to set the margins to zero and use padding for the spacing.

- A *border* can be placed on any or all sides of a box. That border goes on the outside of the padding for the box and inside any margins, and you can set the width, style, and color for the border.

- When you set the *background* for a box, it is displayed behind the content, padding, and border for the box, but not behind the margins. The background can consist of a color, an image, or both.

- You can also *round corners* and add *shadows* to borders, and you can provide *linear gradients* as backgrounds.

Exercise 5-1   Enhance the Town Hall home page

In this exercise, you'll enhance the formatting of the Town Hall home page that you formatted in exercise 4-1. To make that easier, we'll provide some of the CSS for you. When you're through, the page should look like this:

San Joaquin Valley Town Hall
Celebrating our 75th Year

Our Mission

San Joaquin Valley Town Hall is a non-profit organization that is run by an all-volunteer board of directors. Our mission is to bring nationally and internationally renowned, thought-provoking speakers who inform, educate, and entertain our audience! As one or our members told us:

> *"Each year I give a ticket package to each of our family members. I think of it as the gift of knowledge...and that is priceless."*

Our Ticket Packages

- Season Package: $95
- Patron Package: $200
- Single Speaker: $25

This season's guest speakers

October
David Brancaccio

November
Andrew Ross Sorkin

January
Amy Chua

© 2022, San Joaquin Valley Town Hall, Fresno, CA 93755

Open the HTML and CSS files and start enhancing the CSS

1. Use your text editor to open the HTML and CSS files:

    `\html_css_5\exercises\town_hall_1\c5_index.html`

    `\html_css_5\exercises\town_hall_1\styles\c5_main.css`

2. Enhance the style rule for the body by setting the width to 600 pixels, setting the top and bottom margins to 0 and the right and left margins to auto, and adding a 3-pixel, solid border with #931420 as its color. Then, test this change in Chrome. If the page isn't centered with a border, make the required corrections.

3. Add one more declaration to the style rule for the body that sets the background color to #fffded. Then, test this change, and note that the entire window is set to the background color, not just the body.

4. To fix this, code a style rule for the html element that sets the background color to white. Then, test to make sure that worked.

Add the other borders and another background color

From this point on, test each change right after you make it. If you have any problems, use the Developer Tools shown in figure 4-17 to help you debug them.

5. Add a bottom border to the header that's the same as the border around the body.

6. Add top and bottom borders to the h1 heading in the main element. Both borders should be the same as the borders for the header and footer.

7. Set the background color of the footer to the same color as the borders, and then set the font color for the paragraph in the footer to white so it's easier to read.

Get the padding right for the header, main element, and footer

At this point, you have all of the borders and colors the way they should be, so you just need to set the margins and padding. In the steps that follow, you'll start by adding a reset selector to the CSS file. Then, with one exception, you'll use padding to get the spacing right.

8. Add a reset selector like the one in figure 5-7 to the CSS file. When you test this change, the page won't look good at all because the default margins and padding for all of the elements have been removed.

9. For the header, add 1.5ems of padding at the top and 2ems of padding at the bottom. Then, delete the text-indent declarations for the h2 and h3 elements in the header, and add 30 pixels of padding to the right and left of the image in the header. When you test these changes, you'll see that the heading looks much better.

10. For the main element, add 30 pixels of padding to the right and left.

11. Test these changes. At this point, all of the spacing should look right.

Add the finishing touches

12. Italicize the blockquote element to make it stand out.

13. Add a linear gradient as the background for the header. The one that's shown uses #f6bb73 at 0%, #f6bb73 at 30%, white at 50%, #f6bb73 at 80%, and #f6bb73 at 100% as its five colors at a 30 degree angle. But experiment with this until you get it the way you want it.

14. Do one final test to make sure that the page looks like the one at the start of this exercise. Then, experiment on your own to see if you can improve the formatting.

Exercise 5-2   Add rounded corners and box shadows to the Speakers heading

Use CSS to add a double border with rounded corners and box shadows to the Speakers heading so it looks like this:

This season's guest speakers

Chapter 6

How to use CSS for page layout

In this chapter, you'll learn how to use CSS to control the layout of a page. That means that you can control where each of the HTML elements appears on the page. When you finish this chapter, you should be able to implement effective 2- and 3-column page layouts.

How to develop 2- and 3-column page layouts

To create a page layout with two or three columns, you can float the elements that make up the columns of the page. You'll learn how to do that in the topics that follow.

How to float and clear elements

By default, the block elements defined in an HTML document flow from the top of the page to the bottom of the page, and inline elements flow from the left side of the block elements that contain them to the right side. When you *float* an element, though, it's taken out of the flow of the document. Because of that, any elements that follow the floated element flow into the space that's left by the floated element.

Figure 6-1 presents the basic skills for floating an element on a web page. To do that, you use the float property to specify whether you want the element floated to the left or to the right. You also have to set the width of the floated element. In the example, the aside is 150 pixels wide, and it is floated to the right. As a result, the main element that follows flows into the space to the left of the aside.

Although you can use the float property with any block element, you can also use it with some inline elements. In chapter 4, for example, you learned how to float an image in the header of a document. When you float an img element, you don't have to set the width property because an image always has a default size.

By default, any content that follows a floated element in an HTML document will fill in the space to the side of the floated element. That includes block elements as well as inline elements. However, if you want to stop the flow of elements into the space beside a floated element, you can use the clear property.

In this example, the clear property is used to stop the footer from flowing into the space next to the aside. The value for this property can be left, right, or both, and either right or both will work if the element ahead of it is floated to the right. Similarly, left or both will work if the element ahead of it is floated to the left.

The properties for floating and clearing elements

Property	Description
float	A keyword that determines how an element is floated. Possible values are left, right, and none. None is the default.
clear	Determines whether an element is cleared from flowing into the space left by a floated element. Possible values are left, right, both, and none (the default).

The HTML for a web page with an aside

```
<body>
    <aside>
        <p>The luncheon starts 15 minutes after the lecture ends</p>
    </aside>
    <main>
        <p>Welcome to San Joaquin Valley Town Hall. We have some fascinating
            speakers for you this season!</p>
    </main>
    <footer>
        <p>Please call today at (559) 555-1212 to get your tickets!</p>
    </footer>
</body>
```

The CSS for floating the aside

```
body { width: 500px; }
main, aside, footer {
    margin: 0;
    padding: 0px 20px; }
aside {
    margin: 0 20px 10px;
    width: 150px;
    float: right;
    border: 1px solid black; }
footer { clear: both; }
```

The web page in a browser

Welcome to San Joaquin Valley Town Hall. We have some fascinating speakers for you this season!

The luncheon starts 15 minutes after the lecture ends

Please call today at (559) 555-1212 to get your tickets!

Description

- When you *float* an element to the right or left, the content that follows flows around it.
- When you use the float property for an element, you also need to set its width.
- To stop the floating before an element, use the clear property.
- In the example above, if the clear property for the footer isn't set, its content will flow into the space beside the floated element.

Figure 6-1   How to float and clear elements

How to use floating in a 2-column, fixed-width layout

Figure 6-2 shows how floating can be used to create a 2-column, fixed-width page layout. Here, the HTML consists of four elements: header, main, aside, and footer.

In the CSS, you can see that the width is set for the body, main, and aside elements. Here, the width of the body must be the sum of the widths of the main and aside elements, plus the widths of any margins, padding, or borders for the main and aside elements. Since the right border for the main element is 2 pixels and neither the main nor aside elements have margins or padding, the width of the body is 962 pixels (360 + 600 + 2).

After you set the widths for the body and columns, you create the columns by floating the main element to the left and the aside element to the right. This will work whether the main or aside element is coded first in the HTML.

An alternative is to float both the main and aside elements to the left. But then, the main element must come first in the HTML. In that case, though, the aside doesn't need to be floated at all. That's because the natural behavior of the aside is to flow into the space left by the floated main element that's ahead of it in the HTML.

A 2-column web page with fixed-width columns

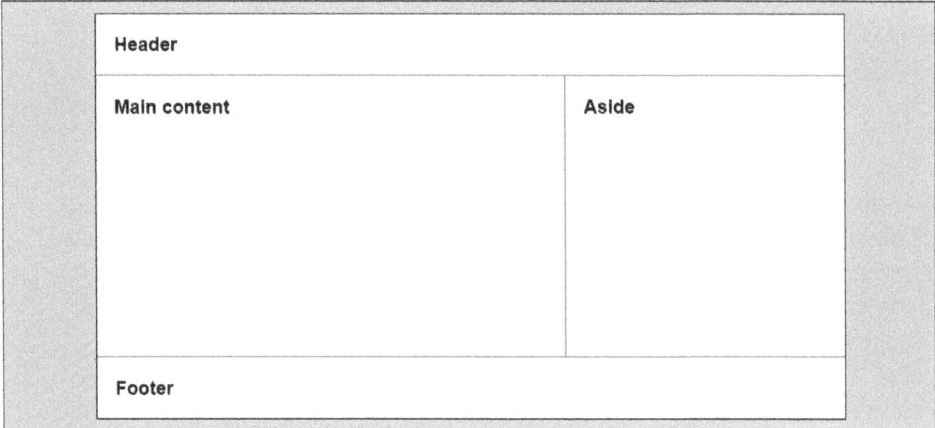

The HTML for the page

```
<body>
    <header><h2>Header</h2></header>
    <main><h2>Main content</h2></main>
    <aside><h2>Aside</h2></aside>
    <footer><h2>Footer</h2></footer>
</body>
```

The CSS for the page

```
* { margin: 0; padding: 0; }
body {
    width: 962px;
    background-color: white;
    margin: 15px auto;
    border: 1px solid black; }
h2 { padding: 1em; }

header { border-bottom: 2px solid #ef9c00; }
main {
    height: 350px;     /* to give the aside some height for its border */
    width: 600px;
    float: left;
    border-right: 2px solid #ef9c00; }
aside {
    width: 360px;
    float: right; }
footer {
    clear: both;
    border-top: 2px solid #ef9c00; }
```

Description

- The main element is floated to the left and the aside is floated to the right. So it doesn't matter whether the aside comes before or after the main element in the HTML.

- An alternative is to float both the main element and the aside to the left, but then the main element has to be coded before the aside in the HTML.

Figure 6-2   How to use floating in a 2-column, fixed-width layout

How to use floating in a 2-column, fluid layout

Instead of creating a *fixed layout* like the one in figure 6-2, you can create a *fluid layout*. With a fluid layout, the width of the page changes as the user changes the width of the browser window. Also, the width of one or more columns within the page changes.

The key to creating a fluid layout is using percents to specify the widths. This is illustrated by figure 6-3. In both of these examples, the width of the page is set to 90%. That means that the page will always occupy 90% of the browser window, no matter how wide the window is. Of course, you can omit the width property entirely if you want the page to occupy 100% of the browser window.

In the first example, the widths of the main and aside elements are set to percents. This means that the widths of both columns will change if the user changes the width of the browser window. In this case, since the main element has a 2-pixel right border, the sum of the widths of the main and aside elements is 99%, not 100%. However, if there wasn't a border, the sum could be 100%.

In the second example, the width of the aside element is set to 360 pixels and no width is specified for the main element. This means that only the width of the main element will change if the width of the browser window changes. In this case, the border is applied to the left of the aside element rather than to the right of the main element because it's the width of the aside element that's fixed.

As you will see in chapter 8, fluid layouts are one component of Responsive Web Design. That way, the layouts can adjust to the screen sizes of the devices that are used.

A 2-column web page with fluid widths for both columns

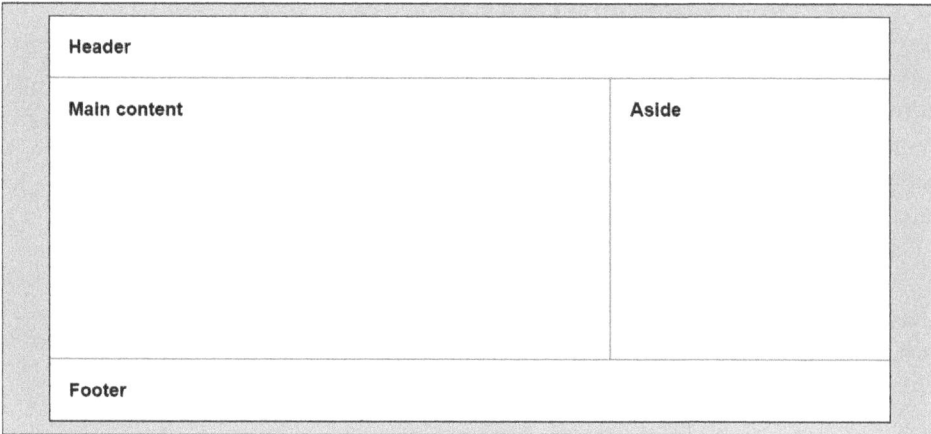

The CSS for the page when both columns are fluid

```
body {
    width: 90%;
    background-color: white;
    margin: 15px auto;
    border: 1px solid black; }
main {
    width: 66%;
    height: 350px;          /* to give the main content some height */
    border-right: 2px solid #ef9c00;
    float: left; }
aside {
    width: 33%;
    float: right; }
```

The CSS for the page when the aside is fixed and the section is fluid

```
body {
    width: 90%;
    background-color: white;
    margin: 15px auto;
    border: 1px solid black; }
main {
    float: left; }
aside {
    height: 350px;          /* to give the aside some height */
    width: 360px;
    border-left: 2px solid #ef9c00;
    float: right; }
```

Description

- The benefit of using fluid column widths is that the width of the page is adjusted based on the width of the browser.

Figure 6-3   How to use floating in a 2-column fluid layout

How to use floating in a 3-column, fixed-width layout

Figure 6-4 shows how to take floating to one more level and create a 3-column, fixed-width page layout. Here, the width of the body is 964 pixels, which is the sum of the two sidebars, the main content, and the two sidebar borders. Once those widths are set up, the first sidebar is floated to the left. The main content is floated to the left. And the second sidebar is floated to the right.

One of the keys here is getting the widths right. If, for example, you set the body width to 960 pixels instead of 964 pixels, the two sidebars and the main content won't fit into the width of the body. In that case, the right sidebar will flow beneath the main content.

A 3-column web page with fixed-width columns

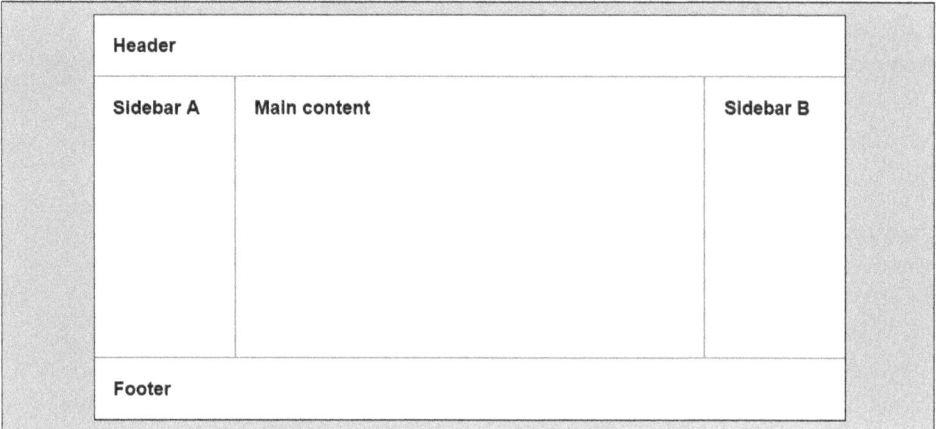

The HTML for the page

```
<body>
    <header><h2>Header</h2></header>
    <aside id="sidebarA"><h2>Sidebar A</h2></aside>
    <main><h2>Main content</h2></main>
    <aside id="sidebarB"><h2>Sidebar B</h2></aside>
    <footer><h2>Footer</h2></footer>
</body>
```

The critical CSS for the page

```
body {
    width: 964px;
    background-color: white;
    margin: 15px auto;
    border: 1px solid black; }
#sidebarA {
    width: 180px;
    height: 350px;      /* to give the sidebar some height for its border */
    float: left;
    border-right: 2px solid #ef9c00; }
main {
    width: 600px;
    float: left; }
#sidebarB {
    width: 180px;
    height: 350px;      /* to give the sidebar some height for its border */
    float: right;
    border-left: 2px solid #ef9c00; }
```

Description

- The first aside is floated to the left; the main content is floated to the left; and the second aside is floated to the right.

- You could get the same result by floating both asides and the main content to the left.

Figure 6-4   How to use floating in a 3-column, fixed-width layout

A home page
with a 2-column, fixed-width layout

To show how floating works in a more realistic application, the next figures present the HTML and CSS for a home page that has a 2-column, fixed-width layout.

The home page

Figure 6-5 shows the home page for the Town Hall website. It uses a 2-column, fixed-width layout. Except for the aside, this is the same content that you saw in the page at the end of the last chapter. It's just formatted a little differently.

Note here that instead of using a border to separate the two columns on this page, a background color is applied to the aside. This adds some visual interest to the page.

A home page with a sidebar floated to the right of a section

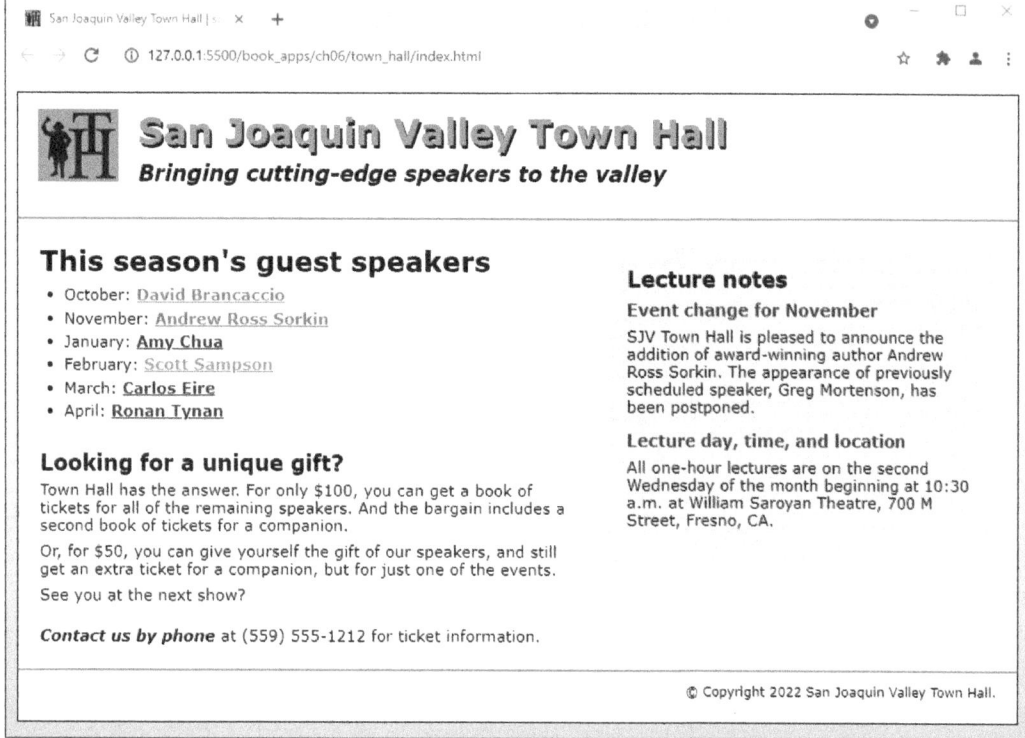

Description

- This web page illustrates a common page layout that includes a header, two columns, and a footer.
- The columns for this page are coded as a section element and an aside element within a main element.
- The columns are created by floating the aside element to the right so the section element that follows it in the HTML flows to its left.
- The image in the header is floated to the left so it appears to the left of the h2 and h3 elements that follow it.
- A bottom border is applied to the header, and a top border is applied to the footer. The page is formatted so these borders extend to the left and right borders for the body of the page.
- Instead of using a border to separate the two columns, this page uses a background color for the portion of the aside with content. That way, you don't have to worry about which column is longer like you do if you use a border.

Figure 6-5   A 2-column, fixed-width home page

The HTML for the home page

Figure 6-6 presents the HTML for this web page. Here, the only new content is the aside. But note that the aside is coded before the section. Then, if the aside is floated to the right, the section will flow beside it.

Before looking at the CSS, take a minute to note the use of the HTML semantic elements for this page. The header and footer start and end the HTML and the remaining content of the page is coded within a main element. The aside and section provide the content for the two columns. And the nav element within the section marks the navigation list. That helps make this code easy to understand.

The HTML for the home page (index.html)

```
<head>
    .
    <link rel="stylesheet" href="styles/main.css">
</head>
<body>
    <header>
        <img src="images/logo.jpg" alt="Town Hall Logo" width="80">
        <h2>San Joaquin Valley Town Hall</h2>
        <h3>Bringing cutting-edge speakers to the valley</h3>
    </header>
    <main>
        <aside>
            <h2>Lecture notes</h2>
            <h3>Event change for November</h3>
            <p>SJV Town Hall is pleased to announce the addition of award-
                winning author Andrew Ross Sorkin. The appearance of previously
                scheduled speaker, Greg Mortenson, has been postponed.</p>
            <h3>Lecture day, time, and location</h3>
            <p class="news_item">All one-hour lectures are on the second
                Wednesday of the month beginning at 10:30 a.m. at William
                Saroyan Theatre, 700 M Street, Fresno, CA.</p>
        </aside>
        <section>
            <h1>This season's guest speakers</h1>
            <nav>
                <ul>
                    <li>October: <a class="date_passed"
                        href="speakers/brancaccio.html">
                        David Brancaccio</a></li>
                    .
                    .
                    <li>March: <a href="speakers/eire.html">
                        Carlos Eire</a></li>
                    <li>April: <a href="speakers/tynan.html">
                        Ronan Tynan</a></li>
                </ul>
            </nav>
            <h2>Looking for a unique gift?</h2>
            <p>Town Hall has the answer. For only $100, you can get
                a book of tickets for all of the remaining speakers. And the
                bargain includes a second book of tickets for a companion.</p>
            <p>Or, for $50, you can give yourself the gift of our speakers,
                and still get an extra ticket for a companion, but for just one
                of the events.</p>
            <p>See you at the next show?</p>
            <p id="contact_us"><em>Contact us by phone</em> at (559) 555-1212
                for ticket information.</p>
        </section>
    </main>
    <footer>
        <p>&copy; Copyright 2021 San Joaquin Valley Town Hall.</p>
    </footer>
</body>
</html>
```

Figure 6-6   The HTML for the home page

The CSS for the home page

Figure 6-7 presents the CSS for this web page in two parts. Since you've already seen code like this in the earlier figures, you shouldn't have much trouble following it. But here are a few highlights.

First, the width of the body is set to 992 pixels, but the width of the section is set to 535 pixels and the width of the aside is set to 350 pixels, or a total of 885 pixels. The other 107 pixels come from the left and right borders for the body (2 pixels), the left margin for the section (20 pixels), the right padding for the section (25 pixels), the left and right padding for the aside (40 pixels), and the right margin for the aside (20 pixels).

Second, the left margins of the h2 and h3 elements in the header are set to 120 pixels instead of being centered as they were in previous examples. This sets them to the right of the image in the header, which has been floated to the left.

The CSS for the home page (main.css)   Page 1

```css
/* type selectors */
html {
    background-image: linear-gradient(to bottom, white 0%, #facd8a 100%); }
body {
    font-family: Verdana, Arial, Helvetica, sans-serif;
    font-size: 100%;
    width: 992px;
    background-color: white;
    margin: 15px auto;
    padding: 15px 0;
    border: 1px solid black; } /* no border radius or box shadow */
section, aside, h1, h2, h3, p {
    margin: 0;
    padding: 0; }
section, aside {
    margin-top: 1.5em;
    margin-bottom: 1em; }

a { font-weight: bold; }
a:link { color: #931420; }
a:visited { color: #f2972e; }
a:hover, a:focus { color: blue; }

ul {
    margin-top: 0;
    margin-bottom: 1.5em; }
li {
    font-size: 95%;
    padding-bottom: .35em; }
p {
    font-size: 95%;
    padding-bottom: .5em; }
em { font-weight: bold; }

/* the styles for the header */
header {
    padding-bottom: 2em;
    border-bottom: 2px solid #f2972e; }
header img {
    float: left;
    margin-left: 20px; }
header h2 {
    font-size: 220%;
    color: #f2972e;
    text-shadow: 2px 3px 0 black;
    margin-left: 120px;
    margin-bottom:.25em; }
header h3 {
    font-size: 130%;
    font-style: italic;
    margin-left: 120px; }
```

Figure 6-7   The CSS for the home page (part 1 of 2)

Third, both the aside and section are floated to the right, but you could float the section to the left. This would also work if you didn't float the section at all since the aside comes first in the HTML.

Finally, because both the aside and the section are floated, the footer is cleared so it will appear below both columns. In this case, because both the aside and section are floated to the right, you could code the clear property with a value of right. In most cases, though, you'll code this property with a value of both so it doesn't matter how the columns are floated.

You may also be interested in the left margin setting for the image in the header and the right margin settings for the aside and the footer paragraph. All three are set two 20 pixels instead of setting the padding for the body as in chapter 5. That's what allows the borders below the header and above the footer to extend to the left and right edges of the border for the body of the page.

The CSS for the home page (main.css)   **Page 2**

```css
/* the styles for the section */
section {
    width: 535px;
    margin-left: 20px;
    padding-right: 25px;
    float: right; }
section h1 {
    font-size: 170%;
    margin-bottom: .35em; }
section h2 {
    font-size: 130%;
    margin-bottom: .35em; }

#contact_us { margin-top: 1em; }
a.date_passed  { color: gray; }

/* the styles for the sidebar */
aside {
    width: 350px;
    float: right;
    padding: 20px;
    background-color: #ffebc6;
    margin-right: 20px; }
aside h2 {
    font-size: 130%;
    padding-bottom: .5em; }
aside h3 {
    font-size: 100%;
    color: #931420;
    padding-bottom: .5em; }
aside p { margin-bottom: .5em; }

/* the styles for the footer */
footer {
    clear: both;
    border-top: 2px solid #f2972e;
    padding-top: .7em; }
footer p {
    font-size: 80%;
    text-align: right;
    margin-right: 20px; }
```

Figure 6-7   The CSS for the home page (part 2 of 2)

A speaker page
with a 2-column, fixed-width layout

Next, you'll see a speaker page with a 2-column, fixed-width layout. That includes the HTML and CSS for the page.

The speaker page

Figure 6-8 shows the page that's displayed if you click on the fourth link of the home page. This page has the same header and footer as the home page, and it has a 2-column, fixed-width page layout like the one for the home page.

Unlike the home page, though, this page uses an article for the left column instead of a section. This is consistent with HTML semantics since the content is an article about the speaker. Within the article, an image of the speaker is floated to the left of the text.

A speaker page with a sidebar floated to the right of an article

Description

- The columns for this page are coded as an article element and an aside element.
- The columns are created by floating the aside element to the right so the article element that follows it in the HTML flows to its left.
- The image in the article is floated to the left. In the HTML, the image is coded after the h1 element and before the <p> elements that make up the article.
- A background color is applied to the aside to separate it visually from the article.

Figure 6-8   A 2-column, fixed-width speaker page

The HTML for the speaker page

Figure 6-9 presents just the HTML changes for the speaker page. For instance, it doesn't include the header and footer elements because they are the same for the home page and the speaker page.

To start, the link element refers to a different style sheet named speaker.css. This style sheet can be used for all of the speaker pages.

After that, you can see the contents for the aside, which includes a nav element. You can also see the contents for the article, which includes an h1 element, an img element, and several <p> elements.

The CSS for the speaker page

Figure 6-9 also presents the CSS changes for the speaker page. Otherwise, the CSS is the same as the CSS for the home page.

First, the margins and padding are set for the article and the aside, just as they were for the section and aside of the home page. Then, the article is formatted just like the section of the home page. In addition, though, the img element within the article is floated to the left.

Like the home page, both the aside and article are floated to the right, but you could float the article to the left. This would also work if you didn't float the article at all.

Because the CSS for the home page (main.css) and the CSS for the speaker pages (speaker.css) are so much alike, you could combine the CSS into a single file. Often, though, it's easier to manage the CSS if you keep it in separate files. Then, if you want to modify the CSS for the speaker pages, you don't have to worry about affecting the home page.

The HTML changes for the speaker page (sampson.html)

```
<head>
    .
    <link rel="stylesheet" href="styles/speaker.css">
</head>
<aside>
    <h2>This season's guest speakers</h2>
    <nav>
        <ul>
            <li>October: <a class="date_passed"
                href="speakers/brancaccio.html">David Brancaccio</a></li>
            .
            .
            <li>April: <a href="speakers/tynan.html">Ronan Tynan</a></li>
        </ul>
        <p><a href="index.html">Return to Home page</a></p>
    </nav>
</aside>
<article>
    <h1>Fossil Threads in the Web of Life</h1>
    <img src="images/sampson_dinosaur.jpg" alt="Scott Sampson" width="260">
    <p>What's 75 million years old and brand spanking new? A teenage
        ...</p>
    <p>Scott Sampson is a Canadian-born paleontologist who received his
        ...</p>
    <p>Following graduation in 1993, Sampson spent a year working at the
        ...</p>
    <p>In addition to his museum and laboratory-based studies, Sampson has
        ...</p>
</article>
```

The CSS changes for the speaker page (speaker.css)

```
article, aside, h1, h2, p, ul {
    margin: 0;
    padding: 0; }
article, aside {
    margin-top: 1.5em;
    margin-bottom: 1em; }

/* the styles for the article */
article {
    width: 535px;
    margin-left: 20px;
    padding-right: 25px;
    float: right; }
article h1 {
    font-size: 170%;
    margin-bottom: .35em; }
article img {
    float: left;
    margin: 0 1.5em 1em 0; }
```

Figure 6-9   The HTML and CSS for the speaker page

How to create text columns

So far, we've been talking about the columns in a page layout. But CSS also provides a feature that makes it easy to create text columns. For instance, you can easily format an article into two or more text columns within a 2- or 3-column page layout.

The properties for creating text columns

Figure 6-10 summarizes the properties for creating text columns. For instance, the column-count property formats the text within an article into the number of columns specified. The column-gap property sets the width of the gaps between columns. The column-rule property sets the vertical rules between the columns. And the column-span property causes an element like a heading that's within an article to span two or more columns.

These properties are illustrated by the example in this figure. Here, the HTML for an article includes the heading for the article followed by the paragraphs of text for the article. Then, the CSS for the article formats it into 3 columns with 35-pixel gaps and 2-pixel rules between the columns.

Next, the CSS for the h1 element sets the column-span property to all. As a result, the heading within the article spans all three columns. If this property weren't set, the heading would be in the first column of the article. And if this property were set to 2, it would span just the first two columns of the article.

As you can see, this feature can improve the readability of an article by shortening the line length. When you use this feature, though, you don't want to make the columns too narrow because that can make the text more difficult to read. And you for sure don't want to justify the text in narrow columns because that can cause large spaces between words.

The CSS properties for creating text columns

Property	Description
column-count	The number of columns that the text should be divided into.
column-gap	The width between the columns. Otherwise, this is set by default.
column-rule	Defines a border between columns.
column-span	The number of columns that a child element within the article should span. If set to all, it will span all columns. The default is 1.

The start of the HTML for an article

```
<article>
    <h1>Fossil Threads in the Web of Life</h1>
    <p>What's 75 million years old and brand spanking new? A teenage
       Utahceratops! ....
    </p>
    ...
    ...
```

The CSS for formatting the article

```
article {
    column-count: 3;
    column-gap: 35px;
    column-rule: 2px solid black; }
h1 {
    font-size: 170%;
    margin-top: 0;
    column-span: all; }
p {
    margin-top: 0;
    margin-bottom: .5em; }
```

The resulting article

Fossil Threads in the Web of Life

What's 75 million years old and brand spanking new? A teenage Utahceratops! Come to the Saroyan, armed with your best dinosaur roar, when Scott Sampson, Research Curator at the Utah Museum of Natural History, steps to the podium. Sampson's research has focused on the ecology and evolution of late Cretaceous of Montana, as well as the growth and function of certopsid horns and frills.

Following graduation in 1993, Sampson spent a year working at the American Museum of Natual History in New York City, followed by five years as assistant professor of anatomy at the New York College of Osteopathic functional morphology, and evolution of Late Cretaceous dinosaurs.

In addition to his museum and laboratory-based studies, Sampson has conducted paleontological work in Zimbabwe, South Africa, and Madagascar, as well as the United States and Canada. He was also the on-the-air host for the

Description

- In this example, the heading for the article is coded within the article, and the column-span property for the heading displays the heading over all the columns.

Figure 6-10   The properties for creating text columns

A 2-column web page with a 2-column article

Figure 6-11 shows how this feature can be used to add columns to the article in the speaker page of figure 6-8. As you can see, the article requires just one column-count property plus a column-span property for the h1 element that's in the article.

Incidentally, if you want to float the image that's coded at the start of the text to the right when you use two or more columns, it won't work the way you might think. Instead of floating the image in the rightmost column, the browser will float the image to the right in the first column. Although there are ways around this, it's usually best to float the image to the left when you use this feature.

A web page with a two-column article

The start of the HTML for the article

```
<article>
    <h1>Fossil Threads in the Web of Life</h1>
    <img src="images/sampson_dinosaur.jpg" alt="Scott Sampson" width="260" />
    <p>What's 75 million years old and brand spanking new? A teenage ...</p>
    ...
```

The CSS for formatting the article and its heading

```
article {
    column-count: 2;
}
article h1 {
    column-span: all;
}
```

Description

- If you compare this page with the one in figure 6-8, you can see that this page is easier to read because the lines are shorter, but not too short.

- In general, it's best to float an image within an article to the left so it will be in the leftmost column. If you float it to the right, the browser will float the image to the right, but in the first column, which usually isn't what you want.

Figure 6-11   A 2-column web page with a 2-column article

How to position elements

This chapter ends by presenting several positioning techniques that you may never need. However, you should at least be aware of them.

Four ways to position an element

To position the elements on a page, you use the properties shown in the first table in figure 6-12. Here, the position property determines the type of positioning that will be used. This property can have four different values as shown in the second table. The static value is the default. This causes elements to be placed in the normal flow.

The absolute value removes the element from the normal flow and positions it based on the top, bottom, right, and left properties that you specify. When you use *absolute positioning*, the element is positioned relative to the closest containing block that is positioned. If no containing block is positioned, the element is positioned relative to the browser window.

The fixed value works like the absolute value in that the position of the element is specified by using the top, bottom, left, and right properties. However, instead of being positioned relative to a containing block, an element that uses *fixed positioning* is positioned relative to the browser window. That means that the element doesn't move when you scroll through the window.

In contrast, the relative value causes an element to be positioned relative to its normal position in the flow. So when you use the top, bottom, left, and right properties with *relative positioning*, they specify the element's offset from its normal position.

One more property you can use to position elements is z-index. This property is useful if an element that you position overlaps another positioned element. In that case, you can use the z-index property to determine which element is on top. By default, the elements are stacked in the same order that they're declared in the HTML.

The example in this figure shows how an aside can be positioned with fixed positioning. In this case, the right and top properties position the aside relative to the browser window. That is, 0 pixels from the right and 170 pixels from the top.

Properties for positioning elements

Property	Description
position	A keyword that determines how an element is positioned. See the table below for possible values.
top, bottom, left, right	For absolute or fixed positioning, a relative or absolute value that specifies the top, bottom, left, or right position of an element's box.
	For relative positioning, the top, bottom, left, or right offset of an element's box.
z-index	An integer that determines the stack level of an element whose position property is set to absolute, relative, or fixed.

Possible values for the position property

Value	Description
static	The element is placed in the normal flow. This is the default.
absolute	The element is removed from the flow and is positioned relative to the closest containing block that is also positioned. The position is determined by the top, bottom, left, and right properties.
fixed	The element is positioned absolutely relative to the browser window. The position is determined by the top, bottom, left, and right properties.
relative	The element is positioned relative to its position in the normal flow. The position is determined by the top, bottom, left, and right properties.

The CSS for a positioned element

```
aside {
    width: 350px;
    padding: 20px;
    background-color: #ffebc6;
    position: fixed;
    right: 0;
    top: 170px;
}
```

Description

- By default, static positioning is used to position block elements from top to bottom and inline elements from left to right.

- To change the positioning of an element, you can code the position property. In most cases, you also code one or more of the top, bottom, left, and right properties.

- When you use absolute, relative, or fixed positioning for an element, the element can overlap other elements. Then, you can use the z-index property to specify a value that determines the level at which the element is displayed. An element with a higher z-index value is displayed on top of an element with a lower z-index value.

Figure 6-12   Four ways to position an element

How to use absolute positioning

To give you a better idea of how positioning works, figure 6-13 presents an example of absolute positioning. Here, the aside element is positioned absolutely within its containing element, which is the body of the HTML document.

For this to work, the containing element must also be positioned. However, the positioning can be either relative or absolute, and the top, bottom, left, and right properties don't have to be set. Since they aren't set in this example, the body is positioned where it is in the normal flow. In other words, nothing changes. However, because the body is positioned, the elements that it contains can be absolutely positioned within it. In this case, the aside element is positioned 30 pixels from the right side of the body and 50 pixels from the top.

When you use absolute positioning, you typically specify the top or bottom and left or right properties. You also are likely to specify the width or height of the element. However, you can also specify all four of the top, bottom, left, and right properties. Then, the height and width are determined by the difference between the top and bottom and left and right properties.

How to use fixed positioning

Fixed positioning is like absolute positioning except that its positioning is relative to the browser window. So, to change the example in figure 6-13 from absolute positioning to fixed positioning requires just two changes. First, you delete the position property for the body since fixed positioning is relative to the browser window. Second, you change the position property for the aside to fixed.

The benefit of fixed positioning is that the element that's fixed stays there when you scroll down the page. If, for example, the section in this figure was so long that it required scrolling, the aside would stay where it is while the user scrolls.

The HTML for a web page

```
<body>
    <main>
        <h1>Our speakers this season</h1>
        <ul>
            <li>October: <a href="speakers/brancaccio.html">
                David Brancaccio</a></li>
            <li>November: <a href="speakers/sorkin.html">
                Andrew Ross Sorkin</a></li>
            <li>January: <a href="speakers/chua.html">
                Amy Chua</a></li>
        </ul>
        <p>Please contact us for tickets.</p>
    </main>
    <aside>
        <p><a href="raffle.html">Enter to win a free ticket!</a></p>
    </aside>
</body>
```

The CSS for the web page with absolute positioning

```
p { margin: 0;}
body {
    width: 550px;
    margin: 0 25px 20px;
    border: 1px solid black;
    position: relative; }  /* not needed for fixed positioning */
aside {
    width: 80px;
    padding: 1em;
    border: 1px solid black;
    position: absolute;    /* change to fixed for fixed positioning */
    right: 30px;
    top: 50px; }
```

The web page with absolute positioning in a browser

Description

- When you use *absolute positioning*, the remaining elements on the page are positioned as if the element weren't there. As a result, you may need to make room for the positioned element by setting the margins or padding for other elements.

- When you use *fixed positioning* for an element, the positioning applies to the browser window and the element doesn't move even when you scroll.

Figure 6-13   How to use absolute and fixed positioning

Perspective

Now that you've completed this chapter, you should be able to develop web pages with headers, and footers, and 2- or 3-column layouts for the other components of the pages. This is the first step toward developing web pages that provide for Responsive Web Design, which you'll learn how to do in chapter 8.

Terms

float
fixed layout
fluid layout
absolute positioning
relative positioning
fixed positioning

Summary

- When you use the float property to *float* an element, any elements after the floated element will flow into the space left vacant. To make this work, the floated element has to have a width that's either specified or implied.

- To stop an element from flowing into the space left vacant by a floated element, you can use the clear property.

- In a *fixed layout*, the widths of the columns are set. In a *fluid layout*, the width of the page and the width of at least one column change as the user changes the width of the browser window.

- When you use *absolute positioning* for an element, the remaining elements on the page are positioned as if the element weren't there. When you use *relative positioning*, the remaining elements leave space for the moved element as if it were still there. And when you use *fixed positioning*, the element doesn't move in the browser window, even when you scroll.

Exercise 6-1   Enhance the Town Hall home page

In this exercise, you'll enhance the formatting of the Town Hall home page that you formatted in exercise 5-1. You'll also format the Speaker of the Month part of the page that has been added to the HTML. When you're through, the page should look like this:

San Joaquin Valley Town Hall
Celebrating our 75th Year

Guest speakers

October
David Brancaccio

November
Andrew Ross Sorkin

January
Amy Chua

February
Scott Sampson

Our Mission

San Joaquin Valley Town Hall is a non-profit organization that is run by an all-volunteer board of directors. Our mission is to bring nationally and internationally renowned, thought-provoking speakers who inform, educate, and entertain our audience! As one or our members told us:

> *"Each year I give a ticket package to each of our family members. I think of it as the gift of knowledge...and that is priceless."*

Speaker of the Month

Fossil Threads in the Web of Life

February
Scott Sampson

What's 75 million years old and brand spanking new? A teenage Utahceratops! Come to the Saroyan, armed with your best dinosaur roar, when Scott Sampson, Research Curator at the Utah Museum of Natural History, steps to the podium. Sampson's research has focused on the ecology and evolution of late Cretaceous dinosaurs and he has conducted fieldwork in a number of countries in Africa.

Read more. **Or meet us there!**

Our Ticket Packages

- Season Package: $95
- Patron Package: $200
- Single Speaker: $25

© 2022, San Joaquin Valley Town Hall, Fresno, CA 93755

Open the HTML and CSS files

1. Use your text editor to open HTML and CSS files:

    `\html_css_5\exercises\town_hall_1\c6_index.html`

    `\html_css_5\exercises\town_hall_1\styles\c6_main.css`

2. In the HTML file, note that it has all the HTML that you need for this exercise. That way, you can focus on the CSS.

Enhance the CSS file so it provides the formatting shown above

3.   In the CSS file, enhance the style rule for the body so the width is 800 pixels. Next, set the width of the section to 525 pixels and float it to the right, and set the width of the aside to 215 pixels and float it to the right. Then, use the clear property in the footer to clear the floating. Last, delete the style rule for the h1 heading. Now, test this. The columns should be starting to take shape.

4.   To make this look better, delete the left and right padding for the main element, set the left and bottom padding for the aside to 20 pixels, change the right and left padding for the section to 20 pixels, and set the bottom padding for the section to 20 pixels. You can also delete the clear property for the main element. Now, test again.

5.   To make the CSS easier to read, change the selectors for the main elements so they refer to the section or aside element as appropriate and reorganize these style rules. Be sure to include a style rule for the h2 headings in both the section and aside. Then, test again to be sure you have this right.

Add the CSS for the Speaker of the Month

6.   Add a style rule for the h1 element that sets the font size to 150%, sets the top padding to .5 ems and the bottom padding to .25 ems, and sets the margins to 0.

7.   Float the image in the article to the right, and set its top, bottom, and left margins so there's adequate space around it. Then, add a 1-pixel, black border to the image so the white in the image doesn't fade into the background.

8.   Make any final adjustments, use the Developer Tools if necessary, and test the page.

Exercise 6-2   Add one speaker page

In this exercise, you'll add the page for one speaker. This page will be like the home page, but the speaker information will be in the second column like this:

San Joaquin Valley Town Hall
Celebrating our 75ᵗʰ Year

Guest speakers

October
David Brancaccio

November
Andrew Ross Sorkin

January
Amy Chua

February
Scott Sampson

Return to Home page

Fossil Threads in the Web of Life

February
Scott Sampson

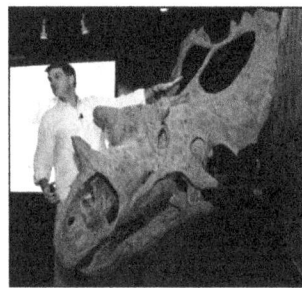

What's 75 million years old and brand spanking new? A teenage Utahceratops! Come to the Saroyan, armed with your best dinosaur roar, when Scott Sampson, Research Curator at the Utah Museum of Natural History, steps to the podium. Sampson's research has focused on the ecology and evolution of late Cretaceous dinosaurs and he has conducted fieldwork in a number of countries in Africa.

Scott Sampson is a Canadian-born paleontologist who received his Ph.D. in zoology from the University of Toronto. His doctoral work focused on two new species of ceratopsids (horned dinosaurs) from the Late Cretaceous of Montana, as well as the growth and function of certopsid horns and frills.

Following graduation in 1993, Sampson spent a year working at the American Museum of Natural History in New York City, followed by five years as assistant professor of anatomy at the New York College of Osteopathic Medicine on Long Island. He arrived at the University of Utah accepting a dual position as assistant professor in the Department of Geology and Geophysics and curator of vertebrate paleontology at the Utah Museum of Natural History. His research interests largely revolve around the phylogenetics, functional morphology, and evolution of Late Cretaceous dinosaurs.

In addition to his museum and laboratory-based studies, Sampson has conducted paleontological work in Zimbabwe, South Africa, and Madagascar, as well as the United States and Canada. He was also the on-air host for the Discovery Channel's Dinosaur Planet and recently completed a book, Dinosaur Odyssey: Fossil Threads in the Web of Life, which is one of the most comprehensive surveys of dinosaurs and their worlds to date.

Open the HTML and CSS files for the speaker

1. Use your text editor to open these HTML and CSS files:

    \html_css_5\exercises\town_hall_1\speakers\c6_sampson.html

    \html_css_5\exercises\town_hall_1\styles\c6_speaker.css

2. In the HTML file, note that it has all the HTML that you need for this exercise. That way, you can focus on the CSS.

Enhance the CSS file so it provides the formatting above

3. Test the page to see that it looks pretty good. That's because the CSS file has some starting styles for the page. As a result, you just need to adjust the styles to get the page to look like the one above.

4. For instance, you should delete the borders from the style rule for the article, switch the colors of the h1 and h2 headings in the section, adjust the space between those headings, and reduce the size of the h2 heading.

5. Test all the links to make sure they work correctly. Also, make sure the favicon and all images are displayed correctly. If necessary, make any corrections and test again.

Chapter 7

How to work with lists, links, and navigation menus

In chapter 3, you were introduced to the coding for lists and links. Now, in this chapter, you'll review those skills, and you'll learn the other skills that you may need for working with lists and links. That includes using lists and links to create navigation menus.

How to code lists

In the topics that follow, you'll learn the HTML skills that you'll need for working with lists. That includes unordered, ordered, and description lists.

How to code unordered lists

Figure 7-1 presents the two elements for coding an *unordered list*. You use the ul element to create an unordered list, and you use the li element to create each item in the list. This is illustrated by the example in this figure.

In addition to containing text, list items can contain inline elements like links and images. They can also contain block elements like headings, paragraphs, and other lists. For example, the first list item in this figure contains text and a link within a paragraph. Then, the second list item contains only text, but it's divided into two paragraphs. As you can see, the second paragraph is aligned with the first paragraph, but it doesn't have a bullet because it's part of the same list item.

Elements that create unordered lists

Element	Description
ul	Creates an unordered list.
li	Creates a list item for the list.

HTML for an unordered list with text, links, and paragraphs

```
<h1>San Joaquin Valley Town Hall Programs</h1>
<ul>
    <li>
        <p>Join us for a complimentary coffee hour at the
        <a href="saroyan.html">William Saroyan Theatre</a>, 9:15 to 10:15
        a.m. on the day of each lecture. The speakers usually attend this
        very special event.</p>
    </li>
    <li>
        <p>Extend the excitement of Town Hall by purchasing tickets to the
        post-lecture luncheons. This unique opportunity allows you to ask
        more questions of the speakers--plus spend extra time meeting new
        Town Hall friends.</p>
        <p>A limited number of tickets are available. Call (559) 555-1212
        for reservations by the Friday preceding the event.</p>
    </li>
</ul>
```

The list in a web browser

San Joaquin Valley Town Hall Programs

- Join us for a complimentary coffee hour at the William Saroyan Theatre. 9:15 to 10:15 a.m. on the day of each lecture. The speakers usually attend this very special event.

- Extend the excitement of Town Hall by purchasing tickets to the post-lecture luncheons. This unique opportunity allows you to ask more questions of the speakers--plus spend extra time meeting new Town Hall friends.

  A limited number of tickets are available. Call (559) 555-1212 for reservations by the Friday preceding the event.

Description

- By default, an *unordered list* is displayed as a bulleted list, but you can change the bullets as shown in figure 7-5.
- An li element typically contains text, but it can also contain other inline elements such as links, as well as block elements such as paragraphs and other lists.

Figure 7-1   How to code unordered lists

How to code ordered lists

If you want to indicate that the items in a list have a sequence like the steps in a procedure, you can use an *ordered list*. To create an ordered list, you use the ol and li elements. These elements are presented in figure 7-2.

The only thing new here is the start attribute of the ol element. You can use this attribute to start a list at a value other than the default. You might want to do that if one list continues from a previous list. For example, this figure shows a procedure that's divided into two parts, and each part is coded as a separate list. Because the first list consists of three items, the start attribute of the second list is set to 4.

When you use the start attribute, you need to know that it doesn't represent the actual value that's displayed. Instead, it represents the position of the item in the list. When you use decimal values to indicate the sequence of the items in a list as shown here, the position and the value are the same. Later in this chapter, though, you'll learn how to number lists using other values like alphabetic characters. In that case, a start value of 4 represents the letter "D".

Elements that create ordered lists

Element	Description
ol	Creates an ordered list. You can include the start attribute to specify the starting value for the list. The default is 1.
li	Creates a list item for the list.

HTML for an ordered list that continues from another ordered list

```
<h1>How to use the WinZip Self Extractor</h1>
<h2>Before you start the WinZip Self Extractor</h2>
<ol>
    <li>Create a text file that contains the message you want to be
        displayed when the executable starts.</li>
    <li>Create a batch file that copies the exercises, and store it
        in the main folder for the files to be zipped.</li>
    <li>Create the zip file.</li>
</ol>
<h2>How to create an executable file</h2>
<ol start="4">
    <li>Run the WinZip Self Extractor program and click through the first
        three dialog boxes.</li>
    <li>Enter the name of the zip file in the fourth dialog box.</li>
    <li>Click the Next button to test the executable.</li>
</ol>
```

The lists in a web browser

How to use the WinZip Self Extractor

Before you start the WinZip Self Extractor

1. Create a text file that contains the message you want to be displayed when the executable starts.
2. Create a batch file that copies the exercises, and store it in the main directory for the files to be zipped.
3. Create the zip file.

How to create an executable file

4. Run the WinZip Self Extractor program and click through the first three dialog boxes.
5. Enter the name of the zip file in the fourth dialog box.
6. Click the Next button to test the executable.

Description

- By default, an *ordered list* is displayed as a numbered list, but you can change that as shown in figure 7-6.
- The start attribute can be used to continue the numbering from one list to another.

Figure 7-2   How to code ordered lists

How to code nested lists

When you code a list within another list, the lists are referred to as *nested lists*. Figure 7-3 illustrates how nested lists work.

If you look at the HTML in this figure, you'll see that it consists of three lists. The outer list is an unordered list that contains two list items. The first list item defines the first subheading shown in the web browser, along with the three steps that follow it. Then, the second list item defines the second subheading and the remaining steps.

To define the steps, an ordered list is defined within each list item of the unordered list. These lists are coded just like any other ordered list. Because they're nested within other lists, though, they're indented an additional amount.

HTML for ordered lists nested within an unordered list

```
<h1>How to use the WinZip Self Extractor program</h1>
<ul>
    <li>Before you start the WinZip Self Extractor
        <ol>
            <li>Create a text file that contains the message you want
                to be displayed when the executable starts.</li>
            <li>Create a batch file that copies the exercises, and
                store it in the main folder for the files to be zipped.</li>
            <li>Create the zip file.</li>
        </ol>
    </li>
    <li>How to create an executable file
        <ol start="4">
            <li>Run the WinZip Self Extractor program and click through the
                first three dialog boxes.</li>
            <li>Enter the name of the zip file in the fourth dialog
                box.</li>
            <li>Click the Next button to test the executable.</li>
        </ol>
    </li>
</ul>
```

The lists in a web browser

How to use the WinZip Self Extractor

- Before you start the WinZip Self Extractor
    1. Create a text file that contains the message you want to be displayed when the executable starts.
    2. Create a batch file that copies the exercises, and store it in the main directory for the files to be zipped.
    3. Create the zip file.
- How to create an executable file
    4. Run the WinZip Self Extractor program and click through the first three dialog boxes.
    5. Enter the name of the zip file in the fourth dialog box.
    6. Click the Next button to test the executable.

Description

- You can nest lists by coding one list as an item for another list.
- When you nest an unordered list within another list, the default bullet is a hollow circle.

Figure 7-3   How to code nested lists

How to code description lists

HTML also provides for *description lists*. As the name implies, description lists are used to list terms and their descriptions. Figure 7-4 shows how this works.

To code a description list, you use the dl, dt, and dd elements. The dl element creates the description list, the dt element creates the term, and the dd element creates the description for the term. The example in this figure illustrates how this works. Here, the dt and dd elements are coded within the dl element that defines the list. Notice that the dt and dd elements are coded in pairs so there's a description for each term.

When you code a description list, you should know that the dt element can only contain text and inline elements. By contrast, dd elements can also contain block elements. For example, they can contain paragraphs and nested lists.

You should also know that you can code more than one dd element for each dt element. That's useful if you're creating a glossary and a term has more than one meaning. You can also code a single dd element for two or more dt elements. That's useful if you're defining terms that have the same description.

Elements that create description lists

Element	Description
dl	Creates a description list that contains pairs of dt and dd elements.
dt	Creates a term in a description list.
dd	Creates a description in a description list.

HTML for a description list

```
<h2>Components of the Internet architecture</h2>
<dl>
    <dt>client</dt>
    <dd>A computer that accesses the web pages of a web application using a
        web browser.</dd>
    <dt>web server</dt>
    <dd>A computer that holds the files for each web application.</dd>
    <dt>local area network (LAN)</dt>
    <dd>A small network of computers that are near each other and can
        communicate with each other over short distances.</dd>
    <dt>wide area network (WAN)</dt>
    <dd>A network that consists of multiple LANs that have been connected
        together over long distances using routers.</dd>
    <dt>Internet exchange point</dt>
    <dd>Large routers that connect WANs together.</dd>
</dl>
```

The list in a web browser

Components of the Internet architecture

client
    A computer that accesses the web pages of a web application using a
    web browser.
web server
    A computer that holds the files for each web application.
local area network (LAN)
    A small network of computers that are near each other and can
    communicate with each other over short distances.
wide area network (WAN)
    A network that consists of multiple LANs that have been connected
    together over long distances using routers.
Internet exchange point
    Large routers that connect WANs together.

Description

- A *description list* consists of terms and descriptions for those terms.

- The dt element that creates a term in a description list can only contain text. However, dd elements can contain block elements such as headings and paragraphs.

- You can use one or more dd elements to describe a dt element, and you can describe two or more dt elements with a single dd element.

Figure 7-4   How to code description lists

How to format lists

Once you have a list coded the way you want it, you can format it so it looks the way you want. In most cases, that just means changing the spacing above and below the list and its items. But you can also change the bullets that are used for an unordered list. You can change the numbering system that's used for an ordered list. And you can change the vertical alignment of the items in a list. You'll learn these skills in the topics that follow.

How to change the bullets for an unordered list

To change the bullets for an unordered list, you can use the list-style-type and list-style-image properties shown in the first table in figure 7-5. In most cases, you'll use the list-style-type property to specify one of the values listed in the second table.

By default, a list displays a solid round bullet, but you can specify a value of "circle" to display a circle bullet as shown in the first list in this figure. You can also specify a value of "square" to display a square bullet or "none" if you don't want to display any bullets.

If these predefined bullet types aren't adequate, you can display a custom image before each item in an unordered list. To do that, you start by getting or creating the image that you want to use. For instance, you can get many images that are appropriate for lists from the Internet, often for free or for a small charge, as shown in chapter 11.

Once you have the image that you want to use, you use the list-style-image property to specify the URL for the image file. This is illustrated by the second example in this figure.

In most cases, you'll code the list-style-type and list-style-image properties for the ul element. Then, this property is inherited by all the items in the list. Another way to do that, though, is to code these properties for the li elements.

Properties for formatting unordered lists

Property	Description
list-style-type	The type of bullet that's used for the items in the list. See the table below for possible values. The default is disc.
list-style-image	The URL for an image that's used as the bullet.

Values for the list-style-type property of an unordered list

Value	Description
disc	solid circle
circle	hollow circle
square	solid square
none	no bullet

HTML for two unordered lists

```
<h2>Popular web browsers include</h2>
<ul class="circle">
    <li>Chrome</li>
    <li>Safari</li>
    <li>Edge</li>
</ul>
<h2>Prime skills for web developers are</h2>
<ul class="star">
    <li>HTML and CSS</li>
    <li>JavaScript</li>
    <li>Python</li>
</ul>
```

CSS that changes the bullets

```
ul.circle { list-style-type: circle; }
ul.star { list-style-image: url("../images/star.png"); }
```

The lists in a web browser

Popular web browsers include

- ◦ Chrome
- ◦ Safari
- ◦ Edge

Prime skills for web developers are

- ★ HTML and CSS
- ★ JavaScript
- ★ Python

Figure 7-5   How to change the bullets for an unordered list

How to change the numbering system for an ordered list

By default, decimal values are used to number the items in an ordered list. To change that, though, you can use the list-style-type property as shown in figure 7-6. In the example, you can see that "lower-alpha" is used for the value of this property.

Common values for the list-style-type property of an ordered list

Value	Example
decimal	1, 2, 3, 4, 5 ...
decimal-leading-zero	01, 02, 03, 04, 05 ...
lower-alpha	a, b, c, d, e ...
upper-alpha	A, B, C, D, E ...
lower-roman	i, ii, iii, iv, v ...
upper-roman	I, II, III, IV, V ...

HTML for an ordered list

```
<h2>How to create an executable file</h2>
<ol>
    <li>Run the WinZip Self Extractor program and click through the first
        three dialog boxes.</li>
    <li>Enter the name of the zip file in the fourth dialog box.</li>
    <li>Click the Next button to test the executable.</li>
</ol>
```

CSS that formats the list

```
ol { list-style-type: lower-alpha; }
```

The list in a web browser

How to create an executable file

a. Run the WinZip Self Extractor program and click through the first three
    dialog boxes.
b. Enter the name of the zip file in the fourth dialog box.
c. Click the Next button to test the executable.

Description

- You can change the numbering system that's used for an ordered list by using the
  list-style-type property. The default is decimal.

Figure 7-6   How to change the numbering system for an ordered list

How to change the alignment of list items

Often, the items in a list will be aligned the way you want them. However, you will usually want to adjust the spacing before and after a list, and you will sometimes want to adjust the spacing before or after the list items. Beyond that, you may want to change the indentation of the items in a list or the amount of space between the bullets or numbers in a list.

In figure 7-7, you can see the HTML and the CSS for a formatted list. In this case, the space between the lines has been adjusted. But more important, the list items have been moved left so the bullets are aligned on the left margin instead of being indented. Also, the space between the bullets and the items has been increased. If you compare this list to the one in figure 7-5, you can see the differences.

In the CSS for the list in this figure, you can see that the margins for the unordered list and its list items have been set to 0. Then, the left padding for the ul element has been set to 1 em. This determines the left alignment of the items in the list. Often, though, you have to experiment with this setting to get the alignment the way you want it.

Similarly, the left padding for the li element is set to .25 ems. This determines the distance between the bullet and the text for an item. Here again, you may have to experiment with this value to get it the way you want it.

For ordered lists, you can use the same techniques to adjust the indentation and to adjust the space between the number and the text in an item. Remember, though, that the numbers in an ordered list are aligned on the right. So if the numbers vary in width, you have to adjust your values accordingly.

HTML for an unordered list

```
<h2>Popular web browsers</h2>
<ul>
    <li>Chrome</li>
    <li>Safari</li>
    <li>Edge</li>
    <li>Firefox</li>
    <li>Opera</li>
</ul>
```

CSS that aligns the list items

```
h2, ul, li {
    margin: 0;
    padding: 0;
}
h2 {
    padding-bottom: .25em;
}
ul {
    padding-left: 1em;       /* determines left alignment */
}
li {
    padding-left: .25em;    /* space between bullet and text */
    padding-bottom: .25em; /* space after list item */
}
```

The list in a web browser

Popular web browsers
- Chrome
- Safari
- Edge
- Firefox
- Opera

Description

- You can use margins and padding to control the indentation for the items in an ordered or unordered list, and to control the space between the bullets or numbers and the text that follows.

- You can also use margins and padding to remove the indentation from the items in a list as shown above. However, this doesn't work as well with ordered lists because the numbers or letters are aligned at the right.

- You can remove the indentation from the descriptions in a description list by setting the left margin of the descriptions to zero.

- These techniques work best if you specify the padding and margins using ems.

Figure 7-7   How to change the alignment of list items

How to code links

In section 1, you learned how to code and format simple text links that open another web page in the same window. Now, you'll learn other ways to code and use links.

How to link to another page

Figure 7-8 starts by reviewing some of the information that you learned earlier about coding <a> elements that *link* to other pages. Then, it goes on to some new skills.

To start, you code the href attribute so it identifies the page you want the link to display. Then, you code the content that you want to be displayed for the link. The content can be text, an image, or both text and an image.

The example in this figure illustrates how this works. Here, the first link displays text, and the second link displays an image. The third link shows how the title attribute can be used to improve accessibility. Here, the text for the link is just "TOC", but the title attribute says: "Review the complete table of contents". This title is displayed as a tooltip if the mouse hovers over it, and it can also be read by assistive devices. You should also code the title attribute if you include an image-only link, as shown by the second link in this example.

If the user presses the Tab key while a web page is displayed, the focus is moved from one link or form control to another based on the tab sequence. By default, this *tab order* is the sequence in which the links and controls are coded in the HTML, which is usually what you want. If you need to change that order, though, you can use the tabindex attribute of a link. In the first link in this figure, this attribute is set to zero so that link will be the first one that gets tabbed to.

To set an *access key* for a link, you can code the accesskey attribute. Then, the user can press that key in combination with one or more other keys to activate the link. For example, the accesskey attribute for the first text link in this figure is set to the letter "c". Then, the user can activate the link by pressing a control key plus the shortcut key. For instance, Alt+C (the Alt key and the C key) works in Chrome and Edge on a Windows system.

To indicate what the access key for a link or control is, you normally underline the letter in the text for the control. By default, though, the links are underlined so this won't work. However, if you remove the underlining, as shown in the next figure, you can use this technique to identify the access keys. You can learn more about tab order and access keys in chapter 13.

Four attributes of the <a> element

Attribute	Description
href	The URL that identifies the page that the link will go to.
title	The description that is displayed as a tooltip.
tabindex	The tab order for the link starting with 0. To take a link out of the tab order, code a negative value.
accesskey	The keyboard key that can be used in combination with other keys to activate the control. The key combination depends on the operating system and browser.

A text link, an image link, and a text link with a title attribute

```
<p>
    <a href="/orders/cart.html" accesskey="c" tabindex="0">Shopping cart</a>
    <a href="/orders/cart.html" title="Go to shopping cart">
        <img src="images/cart_animated.gif" alt="Shopping cart"></a>
</p>
<p><a href="/books/php_toc.html"
       title="Review the complete table of contents">TOC</a></p>
```

The text and image links in a web browser

Accessibility guidelines

- If the text for a link has to be short, code the title attribute to clarify where the link is going.
- You should also code the title attribute if a link includes an image with no text.

Description

- You use the <a> element to create a *link* that loads another web page. The content of an <a> element can be text, an image, or text and an image.
- The *tab order* is the sequence that the links will be tabbed to when the user presses the Tab key. For more on this, see chapter 13.
- An *access key* is a key stroke combination that can be used to activate a link.

Figure 7-8   How to link to another page

How to format links

Figure 7-9 reviews the formatting skills for links that were introduced in chapter 4. In particular, you can use the pseudo-code selectors to change the default styles for a link.

This figure also shows how to remove the underline for a text link. To do that, you can set the text-decoration property for a text link to "none."

In the past, text links were almost always underlined to clearly indicate that the text was a link. Today, though, you often see text links without underlines. What's most important now is that you don't underline text that isn't a link, since that can confuse users.

It's also good to avoid the use of image-only links unless it's clear where the link is going. For instance, most users recognize a shopping cart or shopping bag image because they're common to many sites, but they may not recognize images that are specific to a single site. One exception is using the logo in the header to link to the home page of a site because that's become a website convention.

Common CSS pseudo-classes for formatting links

Name	Description
:link	A link that hasn't been visited. Blue is the default color.
:visited	A link that has been visited. Purple is the default color.
:hover	An element with the mouse hovering over it. Hover has no default color.
:focus	An element like a link or form control that has the focus. It has a thick purple border by default.
:active	An element that's currently active. Red is the default color.

The property for removing underlines

Property	Description
text-decoration	To remove the underlining from a link, set this to none.

The HTML for three links

```
<ul>
    <li><a href="brancaccio.html">David Brancaccio</a></li>
    <li><a href="sorkin.html">Andrew Ross Sorkin</a></li>
    <li><a href="chua.html">Amy Chua</a></li>
</ul>
```

The CSS for pseudo-class selectors that apply to the links

```
a:link {
    color: green;
}
a:hover, a:focus {
    text-decoration: none;
    font-size: 125%;
}
```

The links in a web browser with the focus on the third link

- David Brancaccio
- Andrew Ross Sorkin
- Amy Chua

Accessibility guideline

- Apply the same formatting for the :hover and :focus selectors. That way, the formatting is the same whether you hover the mouse over a link or use the keyboard to tab to the link.

Figure 7-9   How to format links

How to use a link to open a new browser window or tab

In most cases, you'll want the page that's loaded by a link to be displayed in the same browser window as the current page. In some cases, though, you may want to open the next page in a new browser window or tab. If, for example, the link loads a page from another website, you may want to display it in a new window or tab.

To open a new browser window or tab, you set the target attribute of the <a> element to "_blank" as shown in figure 7-10. In this case, the link opens a page on another website in a new tab. But whether a browser opens a new window or a new tab depends upon the browser settings.

The HTML for a link that loads a web page into a new window or tab

```
<h1>Want to read other books like this one?</h1>
<p>Just go to
    <a href="http://www.murach.com/" target="_blank"> Murach Books.
</p>
```

The HTML in one browser tab

The murach.com home page in a new tab

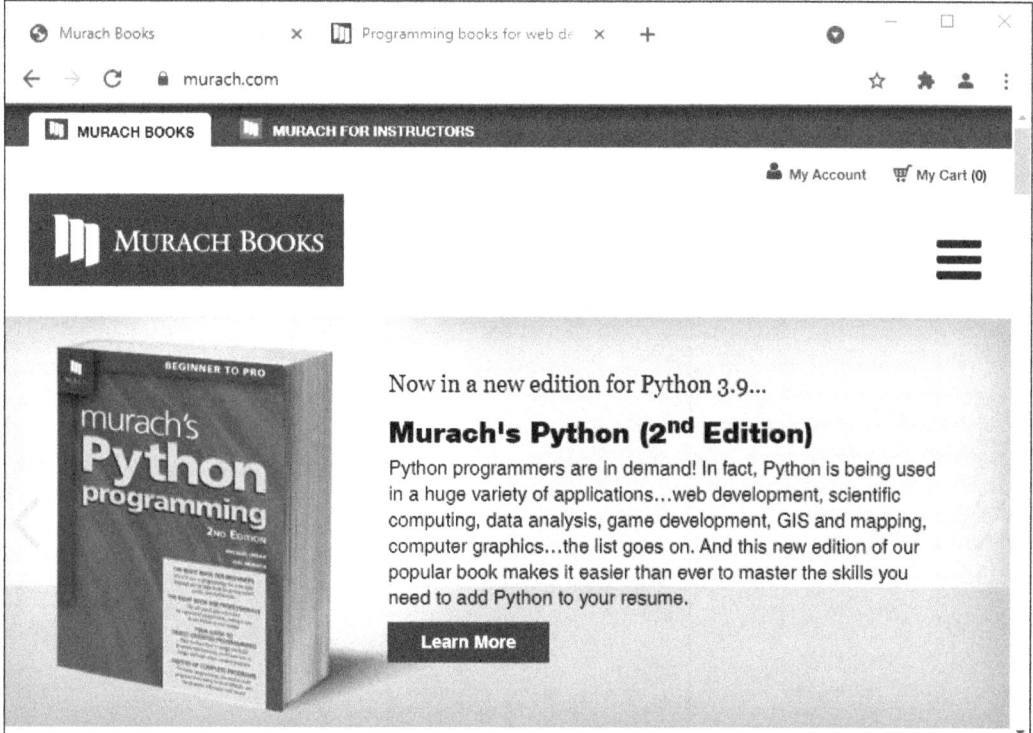

Description

- You can use the target attribute of the <a> tag to specify where the document referred to in a link should be loaded. To load the document in a new browser window or tab, specify "_blank" for this attribute.

- Whether a browser opens a new window or a new tab depends on the browser settings.

Figure 7-10   How to use a link to open a new browser window or tab

How to create and link to placeholders

Besides displaying another page, you can code links that jump to a location on the same page. To do that, you first create a *placeholder* that identifies the location you want the link to jump to. Then, you code a link that points to that placeholder. This is illustrated in figure 7-11.

To create a placeholder, you code the id attribute for the element you want to jump to. In this figure, the first example shows a placeholder with the id "reason6" that's coded for an h2 element. Then, the second example shows a link that jumps to that placeholder. To do that, the href attribute of the link uses the value of the id attribute for the placeholder, preceded by a hash character (#). When the user clicks on this link, the element that contains the id is displayed.

Although placeholders are typically used for navigating within a single page, they can also be used to go to a location on another page. The third example in this figure shows how this works. Here, the name of the page that contains the placeholder is coded before the value of the placeholder's id attribute. Then, when that page is displayed, it will be positioned at the specified placeholder.

Placeholders can make it easier for users to navigate through a long web page. For pages like these, it's common to include navigation links for each component of the page. Then, at the end of each component, it's common to include a link to return to the top of the page.

The last group of examples shows two ways to jump to the top of the page. In the first link, the value of the href attribute is set to "#top". In the second link, the value of the href attribute is set to just "#". Either way, you don't need to identify the element at the top of the page so you don't need to code an id attribute for it.

The 8reasons.html web page that provides links to topics on the same page

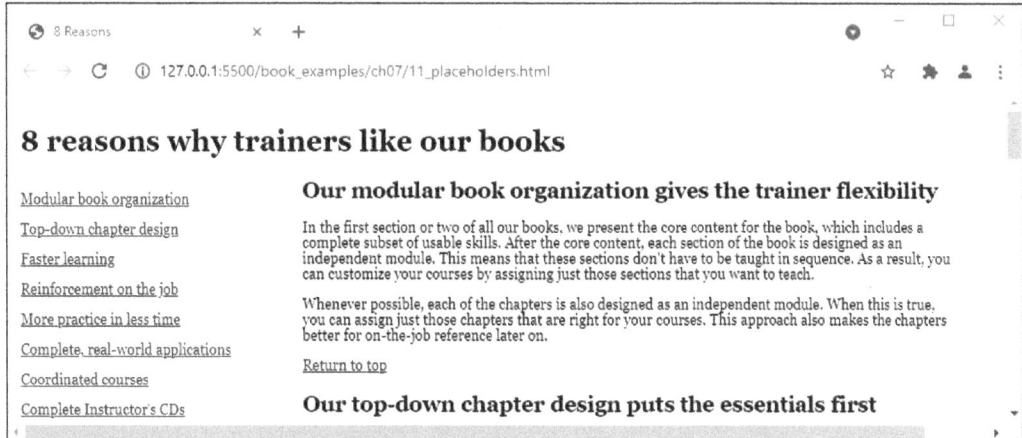

The portion of the page that's displayed when the sixth link is clicked

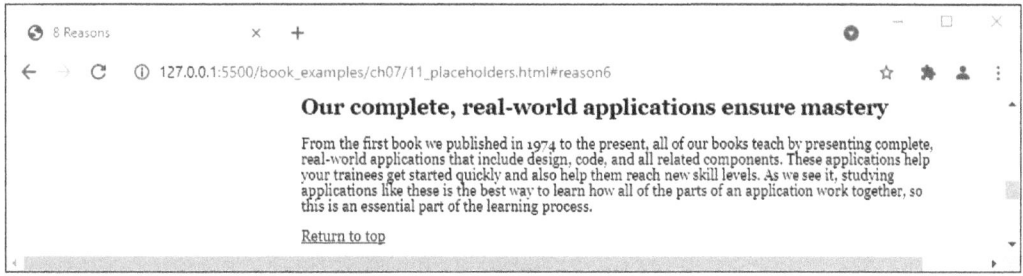

The HTML for the placeholder for reason 6

```
<h2 id="reason6">Our complete, real-world applications ensure mastery</h2>
```

A link on the same page that jumps to the placeholder

```
<p><a href="#reason6">Complete, real-world applications</a></p>
```

A link on another page that jumps to the placeholder

```
<a href="8reasons.html#reason6">Complete, real-world applications</a>
```

Two links that jump to the top of the page

```
<p><a href="#top">Return to top</a></p>
<p><a href="#">Return to top</a></p>
```

Description

- To create a *placeholder*, code an id attribute for the element you want to jump to.
- To jump to a placeholder, code a link with its href attribute set to the value of the id attribute, preceded by the hash character.
- To jump to a placeholder on another page, code the URL for the page followed by the id for the placeholder.
- To jump to the top of the page, you can code the href attribute as either #top or #.

Figure 7-11   How to create and link to placeholders

How to link to a media file

If the href attribute of an <a> element points to a media file, the normal behavior of a browser is to try to display or play it using the right program for that type of file. For instance, the first example in figure 7-12 is a link that opens a PDF file in a new browser window or tab. The second example starts a PowerPoint slide show. The third example displays an image. And the fourth example plays an MP3 audio file.

In chapter 14, you'll learn more about adding audio and video to your website. For other types of media, though, the <a> element can do a good job of getting the results that you want.

Common media types

Format	Description
PDF	Portable Document Format file
MP3	MPEG audio file
MP4	MPEG video file

A link that displays a PDF file in a new window

```
<a href="documents/instructors_summary.pdf"
    target="_blank">Read the Instructor's Summary<a>
```

The PDF file in a browser

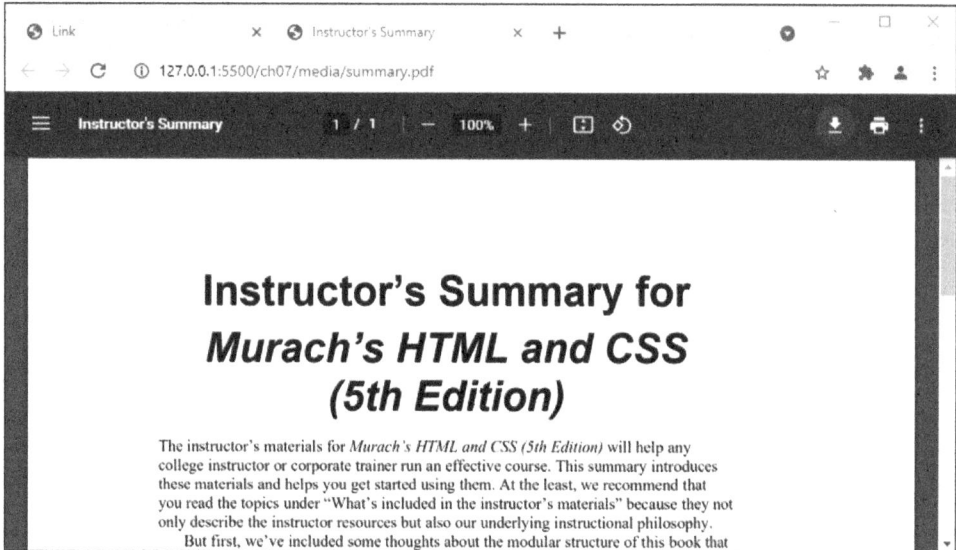

A link that plays a PowerPoint slide show

```
<a href="media/chapter_01.ppsx"
    target="_blank">Review the slides for chapter 1</a>
```

A link that displays an image

```
<a href="images/sampson_dinosaur.jpg">Image</a>
```

A link that plays an MP3 file

```
<a href="music/twist_away.mp3">MP3 file</a>
```

Description

- When you use the <a> element to display a media file, the file is typically displayed in a new browser window or tab.

Figure 7-12   How to link to a media file

How to create email and phone links

Figure 7-13 shows how to create links that start email messages and phone calls. The email links should work on any device, but the phone call links are designed for mobile phones.

You should know, however, that email links are designed to work with the user's default email program. But if that program isn't set up correctly, the email link won't work right. That's why commercial websites typically set up their own applications for user email. In general, though, the email programs for mobile phones are set up correctly so both email and phone links will work on mobile phones.

To code an email link, you use the mailto: prefix in the href attribute of the link, as shown in the first example. But you can also populate the subject, cc, bcc, or body fields, as shown by the second example, which adds a cc and a subject to the email that the link will start.

To code a phone link, you use the tel: prefix. But because this only works on mobile phones, the phone numbers aren't coded as links on other devices. Instead, the phone numbers are displayed as text so the users can enter them on their phones.

Prefixes for coding email and phone links

Link type	Prefix
Email	`mailto:`
Phone	`tel:`

A link that starts an email

```
<a href="mailto:support@murach.com">Send us an email</a>
```

A link that starts an email with a CC address and a subject

```
<a href="mailto:support@murach.com?cc=ben@murach.com&subject=Web mail">
Send us an email with a copy to Ben</a>
```

A link that calls a phone number

```
<a href="tel:555-555-5555">Call us</a>
```

A web page with the links that will start email messages and phone calls

Contact Us
- Send us an email
- Send us an email with a copy to Ben
- Call us

Description

- To provide a link that will start an email message, you code the email address after the mailto: prefix. You can also populate the subject, cc, bcc, or body fields in the email by coding a question mark after the address followed by one or more name/value pairs separated by ampersands.

- To provide a link that will start a phone call on a mobile phone, you code the phone number after the tel: prefix.

- Both email and phone links work well on mobile phones.

- Because phone links don't work on devices that don't have phone capabilities, the phone numbers aren't coded as links on those devices.

- Because email links only work when the user's default email service is set up correctly, most commercial websites develop their own applications for user emails.

Figure 7-13   How to create email and phone links

How to create navigation menus

This chapter closes by showing you how to create the navigation menus for your web pages. To do that, you code links within an unordered list.

How to create a vertical navigation menu

Figure 7-14 shows how to create a vertical *navigation menu*. This is just a vertical list of links. Here, the <a> elements are coded within an unordered list. This is the preferred way to create a navigation menu, because a list is a logical container for the links.

If you look at the CSS for the ul element, you can see that the bullets are removed by the list-style-type property. If you look at the CSS for the li element, you can see that a border is placed around each item and the width of each item is set to 200 pixels. In addition, the margin-bottom property for these elements puts space below them.

The most critical CSS, though, is for the <a> elements. First, the display property of these elements is set to "block". This makes the entire block for each link clickable, not just the text. Then, the padding sets the size of each block. Last, the text-decoration property is used to remove the underlining for the text. This formatting makes the links in the list look like buttons.

Of course, the simple formatting in this example could be improved by making the list items look even more like buttons. For instance, you could round the corners and add shadows. Or, you could add an icon, like an >> icon, to the right side of the link to indicate that it's a link.

To let the users know which page they're on, it's also a good practice to highlight the link that represents the current page. To do that, the HTML in this example uses the "current" class for the third item, and the CSS changes the background color for that class to silver.

A vertical navigation menu

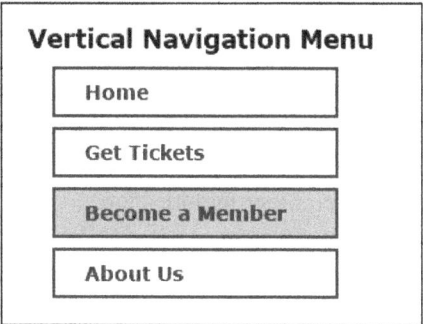

The HTML for the navigation menu

```
<nav id="nav_list">
    <ul>
        <li><a href="index.html">Home</a></li>
        <li><a href="tickets.html">Get Tickets</a></li>
        <li><a href="members.html" class="current">Become a Member</a></li>
        <li><a href="about_us.html">About Us</a></li>
    </ul>
</nav>
```

The CSS for the navigation menu

```
* { margin: 0;
    padding: 0; }
#nav_list ul {
    list-style-type: none;
    margin-left: 1.25em;
    margin-bottom: 1.5em; }
#nav_list ul li {
    width: 200px;
    margin-bottom: .5em;
    border: 2px solid blue; }
#nav_list ul li a {
    display: block;
    padding: .5em 0 .5em 1.5em;
    text-decoration: none;
    font-weight: bold;
    color: blue; }
#nav_list ul li a.current {
    background-color: silver; }
```

Description

- The HTML for a vertical *navigation menu* is best coded as a series of <a> elements within the li elements of an unordered list.

- To make the entire box for a link clickable, you can set the display property for the <a> elements to block and use padding to provide the space around the links.

- To show the users what page they're on, it's a good practice to highlight the current link. One way to do that is to apply a different background color to it.

Figure 7-14   How to create a vertical navigation menu

How to create a horizontal navigation menu

Figure 7-15 shows how to create a *horizontal navigation menu*, which is commonly referred to as a *navigation bar*. This is a horizontal list of links that often provide the primary navigation for a site. Here again, the <a> elements are coded within an unordered list because that's the preferred way to do this.

The examples in this figure use HTML that's similar to the example in the previous figure. The only difference is that the last <a> element includes the "lastitem" class. I'll explain how this class is used in just a minute.

In the CSS for the first horizontal menu, the bullets are removed from the ul element and the display of the li elements is set to "inline". That displays the links horizontally rather than vertically. In addition, the text for the links is centered in the ul element and top and bottom borders are added to that element. Finally, the link for the current page has its underline (text-decoration) removed.

The CSS for the second menu is somewhat different. Here, the links are displayed horizontally by floating each li element to the left of the previous li element. Then, the text for each <a> element is centered within that element, and the display property for those elements is set to "block" so the entire block for each link will be clickable.

To define each block, the width of the <a> elements is set to 175 pixels, padding is added to the top and bottom of the links, and a border is added at the right side of the link. In addition, the background color for each link is set to blue, the text color of the links is set to white, and the underlines are removed from the links.

In this example, the widths of the <a> elements are set so the sum of the widths of those elements plus the widths of the right borders are equal to the page width. Note, however, that you don't need to include a border to the right of the last link. Because of that, the "lastitem" class for that element is used to remove the border.

Of course, you won't always be able to divide the width of the element that contains the navigation menu equally among the links. In that case, you can adjust the width of the last link so the menu extends across the entire width of its parent element.

Two horizontal navigation menus

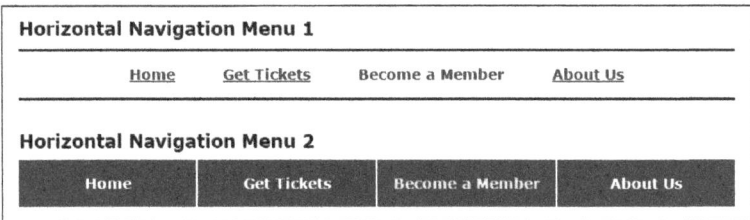

The HTML for the navigation menus

```
<nav id="nav_menu">
    <ul>
        <li><a href="index.html">Home</a></li>
        <li><a href="tickets.html">Get Tickets</a></li>
        <li><a href="members.html" class="current">Become a Member</a></li>
        <li><a href="about_us.html" class="lastitem">About Us</a></li>
    </ul>
</nav>
```

The CSS for the first navigation menu

```
#nav_menu ul {
    list-style-type: none;
    padding: 1em 0;     /* padding above and below li elements */
    text-align: center;
    border-top: 2px solid black;
    border-bottom: 2px solid black; }
#nav_menu ul li {
    display: inline;
    padding: 0 1.5em; }
#nav_menu ul li a {
    font-weight: bold;
    color: blue; }
#nav_menu ul li a.current { text-decoration: none; }
```

The CSS for the second navigation menu

```
#nav_menu ul { list-style-type: none; }
#nav_menu ul li { float: left; }
#nav_menu ul li a {
    text-align: center;
    display: block;
    width: 175px;
    padding: 1em 0;        /* padding above and below a elements */
    text-decoration: none;
    background-color: blue;
    color: white;
    font-weight: bold;
    border-right: 2px solid white; }
#nav_menu ul li a.lastitem { border-right: none; }
#nav_menu ul li a.current { color: yellow; }
```

Description

- You can code a horizontal navigation menu using an unordered list. You can do that by displaying the li elements inline or by floating the li elements.

Figure 7-15   How to create a horizontal navigation menu

How to create a 2-tier navigation menu

Figure 7-16 shows how to create a *2-tier navigation menu*. In a *multi-tier navigation menu* like this, each item in the navigation bar can contain a submenu with additional items. For example, the About Us item in the navigation bar in this figure contains a submenu with two items. Then, the submenus can drop down from the navigation bar when the user hovers the mouse over an item in the bar.

To create a 2-tier navigation menu, you nest an unordered list within a list item of another unordered list. The HTML in this figure shows how this works. Here, two of the items in the navigation bar contain unordered lists: the Speakers and the About Us items.

Next, this figure shows the CSS that makes the submenus drop down from the navigation bar when the user hovers over an item. To start, all of the ul elements in the nav element have their list-style properties set to none so the bullets are removed and their position properties set to relative so the submenus can be positioned absolutely. Then, the list items in the top-level ul element (#nav_menu ul li) are floated to the left, thus forming the navigation bar.

The third style rule is for the submenus that the HTML contains (#nav_menu ul ul). Here, the display property is set to none so a submenu isn't displayed until the user hovers the mouse over the related item in the navigation bar. In addition, the position property is set to absolute, and the top property is set to 100%. That means that the submenu will be positioned just below the navigation bar (100% from the top of the bar).

The fourth style rule sets the float property for the list items in the submenus (#nav_menu ul ul li) to none. As a result, the list items in the submenus will be displayed vertically instead of horizontally.

Then, the fifth style rule uses the child selector (>) to select the nested ul element when the user hovers the mouse over a list item in the navigation bar. This style rule sets the display property for the submenu to block to display the drop-down menu for the item.

The last style rule uses the child selector to select just the first ul element in the HTML (the child of the nav element). Then, this selector uses the ::after pseudo-element to add content after the first ul element. To do that, it sets the content property to an empty string so there is some content after the ul element. It uses the display property to make this content a block element. And it uses the clear property to stop the floating of the items in the ul element.

This last style rule is critical to the operation of this 2-tier menu system. Without it, the submenus will float up into the navigation bar, which certainly isn't what you want. So if this style rule is a little cryptic and hard to understand, just copy it into the CSS for your 2-tier menus.

Although this figure doesn't show the CSS for the other formatting of the menus, you'll see that in the next example. In particular, you'll see how the lastitem class is used by the CSS. Often, in a menu structure like this, you need to apply some special formatting to the last item in the navigation bar, so a class attribute named "lastitem" has been coded for the last item in this example.

A 2-tier navigation menu

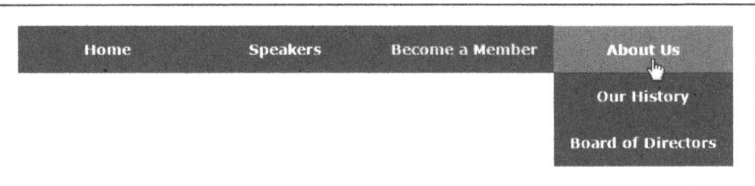

The HTML for the menus

```
<nav id="nav_menu">
    <ul>
        <li><a href="index.html">Home</a></li>
        <li><a href="speakers.html">Speakers</a>
            <ul>
                <li><a href="brancaccio.html">David Brancaccio</a></li>
                <li><a href="sorkin.html">Andrew Ross Sorkin</a></li>
                ...
            </ul>
        </li>
        <li><a href="members.html" class="current">Become a Member</a></li>
        <li class="lastitem"><a href="aboutus.html">About Us</a>
            <ul>
                <li><a href="history.html">Our History</a></li>
                <li><a href="board.html">Board of Directors</a></li>
            </ul>
        </li>
    </ul>
</nav>
```

The CSS for the operation of the menus

```
#nav_menu ul {
    list-style: none;              /* Remove bullets from all ul elements */
    position: relative; }          /* So the submenus can be positioned */
#nav_menu ul li { float: left; }   /* Display items horizontally */
#nav_menu ul ul {
    display: none;          /* Don't display submenus until hover of li */
    position: absolute;
    top: 100%;              /* Position submenu at bottom of main menu */
}
#nav_menu ul ul li { float: none; }     /* Display submenus vertically */
#nav_menu ul li:hover > ul {            /* Select ul child of li element */
    display: block; }       /* Display submenu on hover of li element */
#nav_menu > ul::after {
    content: "";            /* Add empty content to the end of the first ul */
    display: block;         /* Display that content as a block element */
    clear: both; }          /* Stop the floating of the li elements */
```

Description

- To create a *multi-tier navigation menu*, you code unordered lists within the li
  elements of another unordered list.

Figure 7-16   How to create a 2-tier navigation menu

How to create a 3-tier navigation menu

Figure 7-17 shows a *3-tier navigation menu*. Here, tier 1 is the navigation bar. Tier 2 is the menus that drop down when the user hovers over an item in the navigation bar. And tier 3 is the submenus that are displayed to the left or right of a drop-down menu when the user hovers the mouse over an item in the menu. In this example, the tier-3 menu is displayed when the user hovers over the Scott Sampson item in the Speakers menu.

The HTML for a 3-tier menu like this consists of nested unordered lists. In this figure, you can see unordered lists nested within the Speakers and About Us items in the navigation bar. You can also see nested lists in the Scott Sampson item within the Speakers item and in the Past Speakers item within the About Us item.

Note here that just as in the example for the two-tier navigation menu, a "lastitem" class has been coded for the last list item in the navigation bar. You'll see how this class is used in the CSS in the next figure.

A 3-tier navigation menu

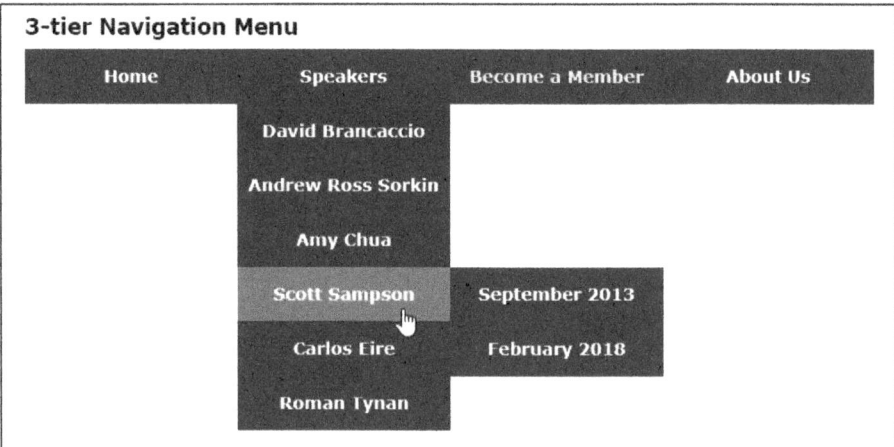

The HTML for the menus

```
<nav id="nav_menu">
    <ul>
        <li><a href="index.html">Home</a></li>
        <li><a href="speakers.html">Speakers</a>
            <ul>
                <li><a href="brancaccio.html">David Brancaccio</a></li>
                <li><a href="sorkin.html">Andrew Ross Sorkin</a></li>
                <li><a href="chua.html">Amy Chua</a></li>
                <li><a href="sampson.html">Scott Sampson</a>
                    <ul>
                        <li><a href="sampson13.html">September 2013</a></li>
                        <li><a href="sampson18.html">February 2018</a></li>
                    </ul>
                </li>
                <li><a href="eire.html">Carlos Eire</a></li>
                <li><a href="tynan.html">Roman Tynan</a></li>
            </ul>
        </li>
        <li><a href="members.html" class="current">Become a Member</a></li>
        <li class="lastitem"><a href="aboutus.html">About Us</a>
            <ul>
                <li><a href="history.html">Our History</a></li>
                <li><a href="board.html">Board of Directors</a></li>
                <li><a href="past_speakers.html">Past Speakers</a>
                    <ul>
                        <li><a href="2021.html">2021</a></li>
                        <li><a href="2020.html">2020</a></li>
                        <li><a href="2019.html">2019</a></li>
                    </ul>
                </li>
                <li><a href="contact.html">Contact Information</a></li>
            </ul>
        </li>
    </ul>
</nav>
```

Figure 7-17   How to create a 3-tier navigation menu

The CSS for a 3-tier navigation menu

Figure 7-18 presents the CSS for both the operation and formatting of the 3-tier menu. In the operational CSS, the first four style rules are the same as in the CSS for the 2-tier menu.

Then, the fifth style rule formats all tier-3 submenus so they're displayed to the right of the drop-down menus. To accomplish that, all the submenus are selected (#nav_menu ul ul li ul). Then, the submenus are positioned absolutely, and their left property is set to 100%. That causes each submenu to be displayed on the right side of the drop-down menu, or 100% from the left side. Then, the top property is set to zero, so the submenu will be displayed at the top of the list item in the drop-down menu.

It's important to note that these styles will be applied to all tier-3 submenus, including those for the last item in the navigation bar. If the submenu is displayed to the right of the last item, though, it will extend beyond the body of the page. Because of that, the sixth style rule overrides the fifth style rule so the submenu is displayed to the left of the drop-down menu. To do that, it uses the "lastitem" class to select the unordered list in the drop-down list for the last item in the navigation bar (#nav_menu ul li.lastitem ul li ul). Then, it sets the left property to minus 100% instead of 100%.

The seventh style rule is the one that displays a drop-down menu or submenu when the user hovers the mouse over a list item. Here, the child selector (>) is used so only the submenu for the list item that the mouse is hovering over is displayed. Otherwise, both the drop-down menu and its submenus would be displayed when the mouse hovered over an item in the navigation bar.

Then, the last style rule in the operational CSS is like the last style rule for the 2-tier menu in figure 7-16. It stops the floating of the items in the navigation bar. Otherwise, the items in the nested ul elements would float too.

If you look now at the CSS for formatting the menus, you should be able to understand it without much trouble. But note the highlighted properties.

First, the width of the <a> elements in the list items is set to 176 pixels. That adds up to 704 pixels, but the width of the body (not shown) is set to 706 pixels. To provide for that, the selector for the <a> element in the list item with the "lastitem" class (#nav_menu ul li.lastitem a) overrides the 176 pixels and sets the width to 178 pixels. That way, the four list items add up to 706 pixels and fill out the width of the body.

Incidentally, the CSS for the operation of this menu will also work for a 2-tier navigation menu. In that case, the style rules for the third tier will be ignored. Or, you can delete them.

The CSS for the operation of the menus

```css
#nav_menu ul {
    list-style-type: none;
    position: relative; }    /* So the submenus can be positioned */
#nav_menu ul li { float: left; }
#nav_menu ul ul {
    display: none;            /* Don't display submenu until hover of li */
    position: absolute;
    top: 100%; }
#nav_menu ul ul li {
    float: none;
    position: relative; }
#nav_menu ul ul li ul {
    position: absolute;
    left: 100%;        /* Display submenu to the right of the li element */
    top: 0; }          /* Display submenu at the top of the li element */
#nav_menu ul li.lastitem ul li ul {
    left: -100%; }     /* Display submenu to the left of the li element */
#nav_menu ul li:hover > ul {        /* Select ul child of li element */
    display: block; }               /* Display the submenu on hover over li */
#nav_menu > ul::after {
    content: "";
    clear: both;
    display: block; }
```

The CSS for formatting the menus

```css
#nav_menu ul {
    margin: 0;
    padding: 0; }
#nav_menu ul li a {
    text-align: center;
    display: block;
    width: 176px;
    padding: 1em 0;
    text-decoration: none;
    background-color: blue;
    color: white;
    font-weight: bold; }
#nav_menu ul li.lastitem a {
    width: 178px; }    /* So the navigation bar fills the 706px body width */
#nav_menu ul li a.current {
    color: yellow; }
#nav_menu ul li a:hover, #nav_menu ul li a:focus {
    background-color: gray; }
```

Description

- The CSS for the operation of this 3-tier menu will work for any 3-tier menu like this one. It will also work for a 2-tier menu.

- To add more tiers to a menu system, you continue the logic of the 3-tier menu.

Figure 7-18   The CSS for a 3-tier navigation menu

Perspective

Now that you've completed this chapter, you should have a good perspective on what you can do with lists and links. From this point on, you can use this chapter as a reference whenever you need it.

Terms

unordered list
ordered list
nested list
description list
link
tab order
access key
placeholder
media player
plugin
navigation menu
vertical navigation menu
horizontal navigation menu
navigation bar
multi-tier navigation menu

Summary

- An *unordered list* is displayed as a bulleted list, but you can change the bullets with CSS.

- An *ordered list* is displayed as a numbered list, but you can change the types of numbers that are used with CSS.

- A *description list* consists of terms and descriptions.

- You typically code an <a> element to create a *link* that loads another web page. You can use the tabindex attribute of an <a> element to change the *tab order* of a link, and you can use the accesskey attribute to provide an *access key* for activating the link.

- You can use pseudo-code selectors in CSS to change the default colors for links and to change the styles when the mouse hovers over a link.

- You can use the target attribute to load a linked page in a new browser window or tab.

- A *placeholder* is a location on a page that can be linked to. To create a placeholder, you use the id attribute of an <a> element. To go to the placeholder, you specify that id in the href attribute of another <a> element.

- If an <a> element links to a media file, the browser tries to display or play it.

- You can also use an <a> element to start an email message from any browser or call a phone number from a mobile phone.

- To create a *navigation menu*, you code a series of <a> elements within the li elements of an unordered list. Then, you can use CSS to remove the bullets and to change the display property so the list is displayed horizontally.

- To create a *multi-tier navigation menu*, you code an unordered list within an li element of another unordered list. Then, you can use CSS to position the submenu relative to the main menu, hide the submenu when the page is first displayed, and display the submenu when the mouse hovers over the list item that contains the submenu.

Exercise 7-1   Enhance the Town Hall home page

In this exercise, you'll add a two-tier navigation menu to the Town Hall home page that you worked on in chapter 6. You'll also add a link that plays a video, and you'll enhance the formatting of the list on the page. When you're through, the page should look like this:

Open the HTML and CSS files for this page

1. Use your text editor to open the these HTML and CSS files:

    `\html_css_5\exercises\town_hall_1\c7_index.html`

    `\html_css_5\exercises\town_hall_1\styles\c7_main.css`

Add the HTML for the main navigation menu
Use figure 7-16 as a guide as you complete steps 2 through 17.

2. Add a nav element with the id "nav_menu" between the header and main elements. Then, add a ul element within the nav element.

3. Add the first li element for this list. Then, add an <a> element to this list item with the href attribute set to index.html and the text set to "Home".

4. Copy the li element you just created and paste it four times to create four more list items. Then, change the text for the links in each list item as shown above and change the href attributes accordingly.

5. Set the class for the first link to "current".

Add the CSS for the main navigation menu
6. Add a style rule for the ul element of the navigation menu that removes the bullets from the list and sets the margins and padding for the list to 0.

7. Add a style rule for the li elements in the unordered list for the navigation menu that floats the elements to the left so they're displayed horizontally.

8. Add a style rule for the <a> elements within the li elements that displays these elements as block elements, sets the widths of the elements to 1/5th the width of the body element, and aligns the text for these elements in the center of the block. This style rule should also set the padding above and below the <a> elements to 1 em, remove the underline from the links, set the background color to #800000, set the text color to white, and set the font weight to bold.

9. Add a style rule for the "current" class that sets the text color for that class to yellow. Then, test these changes in Chrome and adjust the CSS until you get it right.

Create and format the submenu
10. Add a ul element within the last li element in the navigation menu. Then, add four li elements with <a> elements that contain the text shown above, but just set the value for the href attribute of these elements to the hash character (#) so they don't link anywhere.

11. Modify the style rule for the main navigation menu so it uses relative positioning.

12. Add a style rule for the submenu that uses the display property to keep the submenu from being displayed by default. This style rule should also position the submenu absolutely 100% from the top of the main menu.

13. Add a style rule for the list items in the submenu that keeps them from floating so they're displayed vertically.

14. Add a style rule that causes the submenu to be displayed as a block element when the mouse hovers over the list item that contains the submenu.

15. Test these changes in Chrome. When you point to the About Us menu item, notice that the first item in the submenu is displayed on top of the main menu.

16. Add one more style rule for the ::after pseudo-element of the navigation menu. This style rule should add empty space after the navigation menu, clear the content so it doesn't float, and display the content as a block element.

17. Test the page again. This time, the submenu should be displayed below the main menu.

Play a video

18. At the bottom of the Speaker of the Month copy, change "Or meet us there!" to a link that plays the sampson.mp4 file in the media folder in a new tab or window. This link should say: "Or play video." Then, test this change.

Change the bullets in the unordered list

19. Change the bullets in the unordered list at the bottom of the page to circles. Then, test this change.

Exercise 7-2   Add the navigation menu to the speaker's page

1. Add the navigation menu of exercise 7-1 to the speaker's page for Scott Sampson. To do that, you need to add the HTML for the menu to the file named c7_sampson.html in the speakers folder, and you need to add the CSS for the menu to the file named c7_speaker.css in the styles folder.

2. Test and adjust to get the formatting right if necessary.

3. In the HTML file, make sure the paths in the links for the navigation menu are correct. Because the c7_sampson.html page is in the speakers folder and the c7_index.html page is in the root folder, you'll need to use a document-relative path to go to this page. Also, none of the links in the navigation menu of the c7_sampson.html page should be current.

4. Test to be sure that you can use the link for the Home menu item to return to the home page from the speaker's page. When this works, delete the link at the bottom of the aside that returns to the home page.

Chapter 8

How to use media queries for Responsive Web Design

In the first seven chapters of this book, you've learned how to create and format web pages for desktop computers. That gets you off to a good start, but now it's time to learn how to develop web pages that work on any device from mobile phone to tablet to desktop. In short, your web pages need to provide for Responsive Web Design and that's what you learn how to do in this chapter.

Introduction to Responsive Web Design

In chapter 1, you learned that a website that uses *Responsive Web Design* (*RWD*) adapts to the size of the screen that's being used while maintaining the overall look-and-feel of the site. So to start, you'll learn about the three components that you use to implement a *responsive design*. Then, you'll learn about some of the ways that you can test a website that uses a responsive design.

The three components of a Responsive Web Design

Figure 8-1 describes the three components of a responsive design. To start, a responsive design uses *fluid layouts* rather than fixed layouts. That way, the web page adjusts to the size of the screen. If, for example, you were to drag the right border of the browser window on a desktop computer, the page would adapt to the various widths.

To make a fluid layout work, the web pages also need to use *scalable images*. Those are images that adjust to the size of their containing elements. In the example in this figure, the tiger image is scalable so it gets smaller as the browser window gets narrower.

Although you can use a fluid layout to adjust the widths of the structural elements on a page, you can't use them to adjust the appearance of the page. To do that, you need to use *media queries*. In this example, you can see how media queries have been used to adjust the pages in the landscape and portrait modes of a mobile phone.

A website that uses Responsive Web Design

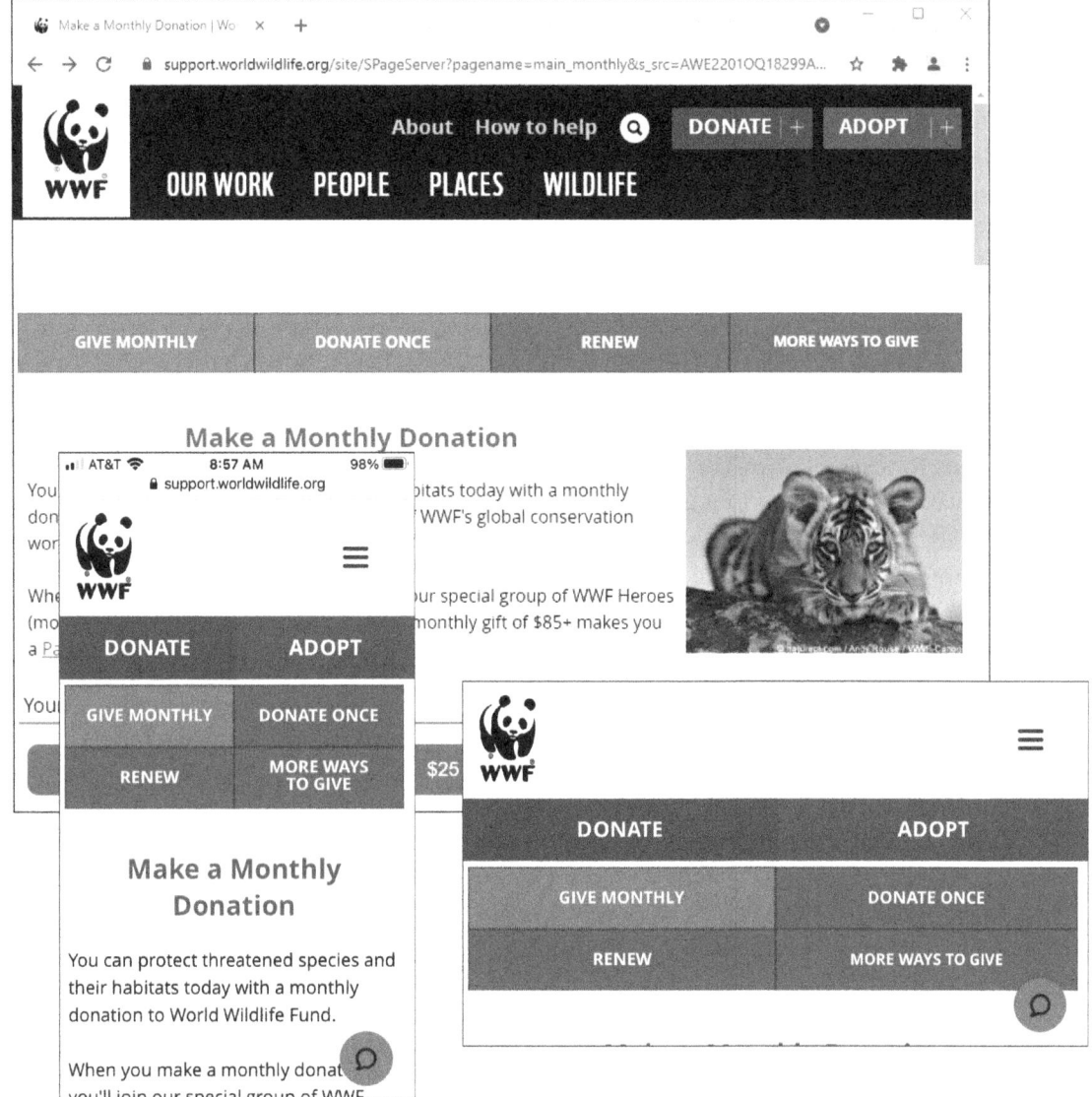

The three components of Responsive Web Design

- *Fluid layout* so the web pages adjust to the widths of the devices that access them.
- *Scalable images* so the images adjust to the sizes of the elements that contain them.
- *Media queries* that adjust the page layouts to the devices that access them.

Description

- *Responsive Web Design* (RWD) means that the web pages adapt to the devices that access them: from desktop computers...to tablets in landscape and portrait modes... to mobile phones in landscape and portrait modes.

Figure 8-1   The three components of Responsive Web Design

How to test a responsive design

As you develop a website with responsive design, you need to test it on devices of various sizes to be sure that it works as expected. Figure 8-2 describes how to do that.

To get started, you can use the Developer Tools for a browser as shown in this figure, which illustrates the Chrome browser. To access these tools, you display a page in the browser and press F12. In this example, the tools are displayed at the bottom of the web page, but to change that, you can click the menu icon near the right side of the toolbar and select a Dock Side option.

Then, to display the page in another screen size, you can you click the Toggle Device Toolbar icon in the toolbar as shown by the pointer in this figure. After that, you can select a device from the drop-down list at the top of the window to display the page for that device size.

Chrome also provides a variety of other options. After you select a specific device, for example, you can click the Rotate icon in the toolbar to change the orientation between portrait and landscape. If you select Responsive from the drop-down list instead of selecting a specific device, you can drag the edges of the screen to create a custom size. And you can select a zoom factor from the second drop-down list in the toolbar. If you experiment with the options, you'll quickly see how easy they are to use.

Once a page is displayed for a device, you can use the mouse to work with it. For mobile devices, this means clicking with a mouse instead of tapping with your finger. But otherwise, the device works the same as it would if you had the device.

After you test a responsive design with the Developer Tools, you'll want to test it on the actual devices and browsers. Before you can do that, of course, you must deploy the website to a server. The trouble is that there are so many different devices that you probably won't be able to test your site on all of them. But even then, it feels great to see your pages working on whatever devices are available to you.

A web page displayed by Chrome's Developer Tools

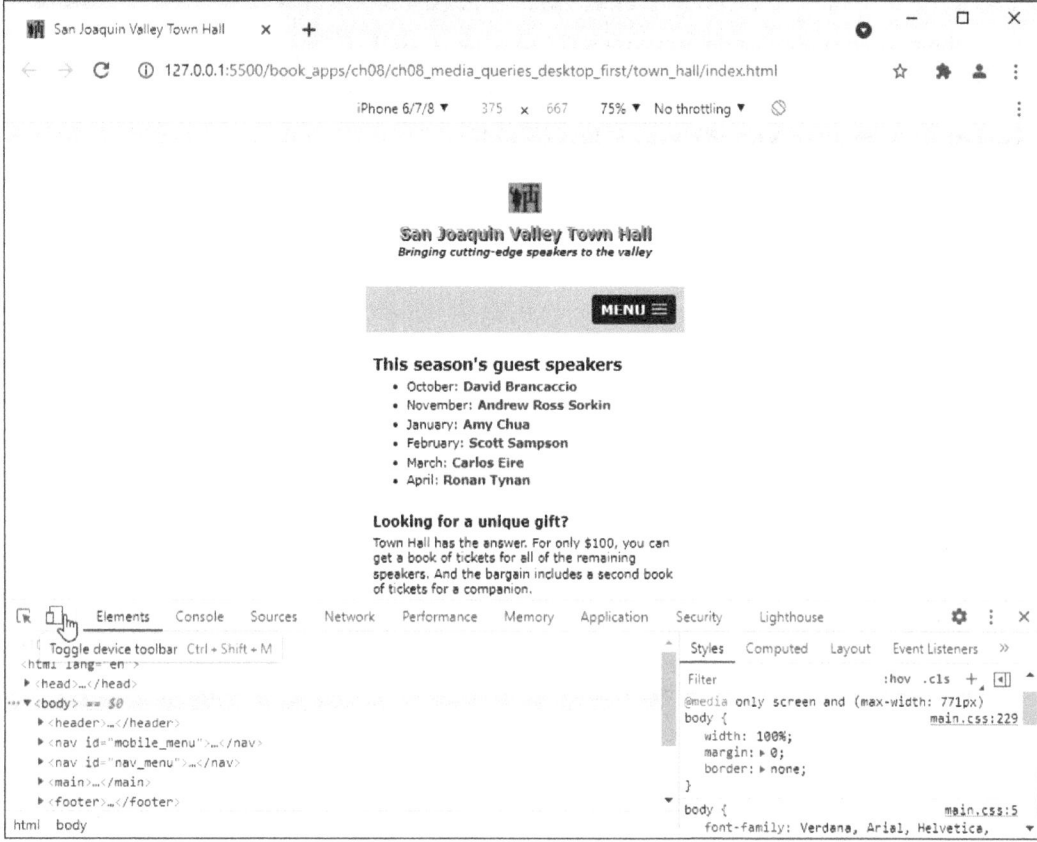

Two ways to test a responsive design

- Use the Developer Tools provided by most modern browsers.
- Deploy your website to a server and then test it on each device.

How to use Chrome's Developer Tools to test a responsive design

- Display the page in a browser and press F12.
- Click the Toggle Device Toolbar icon near the left side of the toolbar. Then, select the device you want to emulate from the drop-down list at the top and middle of the page.
- If you select Responsive from the drop-down list, you can also drag the edges of the screen to create a custom size or enter a size in the available boxes.
- When a page is displayed for a device, you can use the mouse to work with it just as if the device were there.

Figure 8-2   How to test a responsive design

How to implement a fluid design

The first step toward developing a responsive design is developing a *fluid design* that has a fluid layout, relative font sizes, and scalable images.

Fluid layouts vs. fixed layouts

To help you understand how fluid layouts work, figure 8-3 presents settings for comparable fixed and fluid layouts. This assumes that the screen width is 960 pixels wide.

For a *fixed layout*, the page has a width of 960 pixels, the same as the screen (or browser window). Then, the header and a footer for this page occupy the entire width of the page. But the main content is 600 pixels wide, and its sidebar is 360 pixels wide, which add up to 960 pixels.

In contrast, the *fluid layout* adjusts to the size of the screen. In this example, the width of the web page is 90%, which means that the page will fill just 90% of the screen. Then, the width of the element that contains the main content is 62.5% and the width of the sidebar is 37.5%, which add up to 100%.

But note that the percents for the main and sidebar elements are relative to the size of the page, not the size of the screen. So in this case, the width of the element that contains the main content is 56.25% of the screen width (62.5% of 90%), and the width of the sidebar is 33.75% of the screen width (37.5% of 90%).

Fixed and fluid widths in a two-column layout when the screen is 960 pixels wide

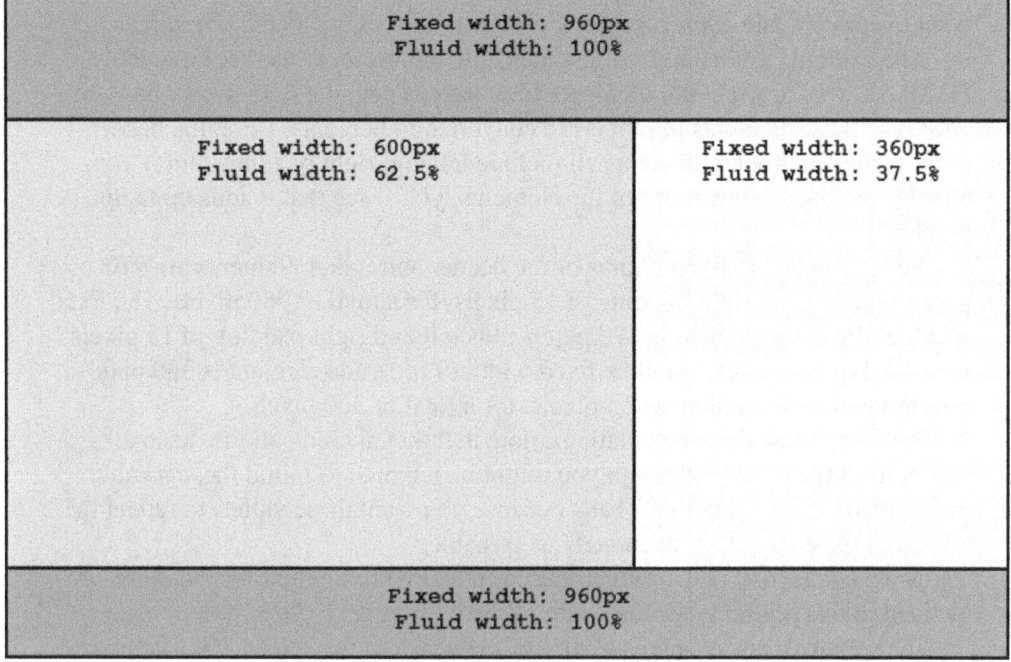

```
                          Fixed width: 960px
                          Fluid width: 90%
```

```
                     Fixed width: 960px
                     Fluid width: 100%
```

```
     Fixed width: 600px              Fixed width: 360px
     Fluid width: 62.5%              Fluid width: 37.5%
```

```
                     Fixed width: 960px
                     Fluid width: 100%
```

The benefit of using fluid layout

- The page layout automatically adjusts to the size of the screen on the device that's accessing the web page.

Description

- A *fixed layout* uses absolute measurements to specify the widths of a page and its main structural elements.

- A *fluid layout* uses percentages to specify the widths of a page and its main structural elements. That meets the challenge of a web page adapting to all screen sizes.

- In this example, the fixed layout fills the entire screen, which is 960 pixels wide. But the fluid layout fills just 90% of the screen.

Figure 8-3   Fluid layouts vs. fixed layouts

How to convert fixed widths to fluid widths

If you design a page using fixed widths like pixels, you need to know how to convert those widths to percents. To do that, you can use the formula shown at the top of figure 8-4. Here, *target* is the width of the element in pixels that you want to convert, and *context* is the width of its containing element in pixels.

The example in this figure illustrates how this formula works. First, the HTML shows the structural elements for a page. Then, the CSS shows how the widths of those elements in pixels are converted to percents. Here, the header, main, aside, and footer elements all include left and right padding. But if you add this padding to the width of the elements, you'll see that it adds up to 960 pixels.

For example, the fixed widths of the header and footer elements are 930 pixels plus left and right padding of 15 pixels, for a total of 960 pixels. The fixed width of the main element is 570 pixels plus left and right padding of 15 pixels, for a total of 600 pixels. And the fixed width of the aside element is 330 pixels plus left and right padding of 15 pixels, for a total of 360 pixels.

As you review these calculations, note that they include all the decimal places from the result. Although you might be tempted to round these results, please resist that temptation. That's because you want these values to reflect the widths of the elements as accurately as possible.

Now, take a look at the two properties that are highlighted for the body element in this figure. First, the width of the body is set to 90%, which means that the page will always take up 90% of the width of the screen. This value is typically set between 90% and 100%.

Second, the max-width property is set to a fixed width of 1024 pixels. Because of that, the page won't expand beyond this width even if the browser window can accommodate a wider page. This is useful because most fluid pages don't look good when displayed beyond a given width, and many desktop screens provide for much wider widths.

Although you can specify widths, padding, and margins as percents, you can't specify the width of a border as a percent. Because of that, you may sometimes have to adjust the widths of one or more elements within a page if the page contains left or right borders.

A formula for converting pixels to percents

```
target ÷ context x 100 = result
```

The HTML for a page with padding and borders

```html
<body>
    <header><p>This is the text for the header.</p></header>
    <main><p>This is the text for the main element.</p></main>
    <aside><p>This is the text for the aside.</p></aside>
    <footer><p>This is the text for the footer.</p></footer>
</body>
```

The CSS for a fluid layout

```css
body {
    width: 90%;                      /* changed from 960px */
    max-width: 1024px;              /* maximum width of page */
    margin: 0 auto;
    border: 2px solid black; }
header {
    width: 96.875%;                 /* 930 ÷ 960 x 100 */
    padding: 15px 1.5625%;          /* 15 ÷ 960 x 100 */
    border-bottom: 2px solid black; }
main {
    width: 59.375%;                 /* 570 ÷ 960 x 100 */
    padding: 15px 1.5625%;          /* 15 ÷ 960 x 100 */
    float: left; }
aside {
    width: 34.375%;                 /* 330 ÷ 960 x 100 */
    padding: 15px 1.5625%;          /* 15 ÷ 960 x 100 */
    float: right; }
footer {
    clear: both;
    width: 96.875%;                 /* 930 ÷ 960 x 100 */
    padding: 15px 1.5625%;          /* 15 ÷ 960 x 100 */
    border-top: 2px solid black; }
```

Description

- To convert the width of an element from pixels to a percent, you divide the width of that element (the *target*) by the width of its parent element (the *context*) and then multiply that value by 100.

- The width of the outermost element determines how much of the screen the page occupies. This width is typically set between 90% and 100%.

- Besides converting the widths of the structural elements to percents, you should convert the left and right margins and padding to percents. But note that you can't set the width of a border to a percent.

- To limit the width of an element, you can use the max-width property. This property is typically used to limit the width of the entire page.

Figure 8-4   How to convert fixed widths to fluid widths

How to use other units of measure with responsive design

Besides the units of measure that you've learned about so far, figure 8-5 presents some units that were developed especially for responsive design. These units are based on the size of the *viewport* of the device that is accessing the web page. On a desktop browser, the viewport is the visible area of the web page, but the user can change the size of the viewport by changing the size of the browser window. On a mobile device, the viewport is usually the size of the screen, but you'll learn more about that in a moment.

As you can see in the table at the top of this figure, each of these units is relative to the height or width of the viewport. For example, one vw is equal to 1/100 of the width of the viewport. That means that if the viewport is 600 pixels wide, one vw is equal to 6 pixels. Similarly, if the viewport is 800 pixels tall, one vh is equal to 8 pixels.

The vmin and vmax units are similar, but vmin corresponds to the smallest dimension of the viewport and vmax corresponds to the largest dimension of the viewport. So if the viewport is 600 pixels wide by 800 pixels tall, one vmin is equal to 6 pixels and one vmax is equal to 8 pixels.

The two examples in this figure illustrate how the vw and vmin units work. In the first example, you can see that the width of the body of the page is set to 95vw. That means that the width of the body will always be 95/100 of the viewport width. In addition, since the left and right margins are set to auto, the body will be centered in the viewport.

The two screens for this example show how the page appears when the viewport is 580 and 412 pixels wide. Here, you can see that as the width of the viewport changes, the width of the body also changes.

In the second example, the width of the body is set to 95vmin. That means its width will be determined by the smallest dimension of the viewport. In the screen for this example, the viewport is 580 pixels wide and 180 pixels tall. That means that the width of the body is based on the minimum of these two values, or 180 pixels.

Relative units of measure for responsive design

Symbol	Name	Description
vh	viewport height	One vh is equal to 1/100 of the height of the viewport.
vw	viewport width	One vw is equal to 1/100 of the width of the viewport.
vmin	viewport minimum	One vmin is equal to 1/100 of the height or width of the viewport, depending on which is smaller.
vmax	viewport maximum	One vmax is equal to 1/100 of the height or width of the viewport, depending on which is larger.

The HTML for a simple page

```
<body>
    <header>
        <h1>San Joaquin Valley Town Hall</h1>
    </header>
    <main>
        <p>Welcome to San Joaquin Valley Town Hall. We have some fascinating
        speakers for you this season!</p>
    </main>
</body>
```

CSS that sets the width of the body based on the width of the viewport

```
body { width: 95vw;
       margin: 0  auto; }
```

The page when the viewport is 580 pixels wide

San Joaquin Valley Town Hall

Welcome to San Joaquin Valley Town Hall. We have some fascinating
speakers for you this season!

The page when the viewport is 412 pixels wide

San Joaquin Valley Town Hall

Welcome to San Joaquin Valley Town Hall. We have
some fascinating speakers for you this season!

CSS that sets the width based on the minimum dimension of the viewport

```
body { width: 95vmin;
       margin: 0 auto; }
```

The page when the viewport is 580 pixels wide and 180 pixels tall

**San Joaquin
Valley Town Hall**

Welcome to San
Joaquin Valley Town
Hall. We have some
fascinating speakers for
you this season!

Figure 8-5   How to use other units of measure with responsive design

How to size fonts

In chapter 4 of this book, we recommended that you use relative measurements for your font sizes. That way, the size of the font that's used by an element is relative to the size of the font used by the parent element. So if you want to change the font size that's used by a parent element and all of its child elements, you just need to change the font size for the parent element.

To illustrate, figure 8-6 starts by presenting the HTML for a web page. Then, the CSS sets the font sizes for the elements. Here, the base font size in the body element is set to 100% rather than 1em. Although both of these values result in the same font size, the base font size is often specified as a percent.

Then, the font size for h1 elements is set to 1.75em, the size for h2 elements to 1.5em, and the size for h3 elements to 1.125em. As a result, all three of these heading types will be larger than the base font size of 1em. Last, the <p> element in the footer is set to .75em so it will be smaller than the base font.

You can also use ems for top and bottom margins and padding. That way, if the size of the font changes, the margins and padding change too.

You can see how these font sizes are displayed in the screenshot that follows the code, which has some borders added to it. Here, you can see the default font size of 1em in the text in the main and aside elements. You can also see the other font sizes in the headings and footer.

Although it isn't illustrated in this book, you should know that you can also use the vh and vw units of measure to size fonts and set line heights. If, for example, the font size of an element is set to 10vw, its height is always 1/10 the width of the viewport. That means the font size will change as the viewport width changes.

The HTML for a page with elements that use various font sizes

```
<body>
    <header><h2>San Joaquin Valley Town Hall</h2></header>
    <main>
        <h1>This season's guest speakers</h1>
        <ul>
            <li>October: <a href="speakers/brancaccio.html">
                David Brancaccio</a></li>
            <li>November: <a href="speakers/sorkin.html">
                Andrew Ross Sorkin</a></li>
            <li>January: <a href="speakers/chua.html">Amy Chua</a></li>
        </ul>
        <p>Please contact us for tickets.</p>
    </main>
    <aside>
        <h3>Lecture day, time, and location</h3>
        <p>All one-hour lectures are on the second Wednesday ...</p>
    </aside>
    <footer>
        <p>&copy; Copyright 2022 San Joaquin Valley Town Hall.</p>
    </footer>
</body>
```

CSS that specifies the font sizes in ems

```
body { font-size: 100%;
       width: 90%;
       max-width: 1024px;
       margin: 0 auto;
h1 { font-size: 1.75em; }
h2 { font-size: 1.5em; }
h3 { font-size: 1.125em; }
footer p { font-size: .75em; }
```

The headings in a browser with some borders

San Joaquin Valley Town Hall

This season's guest speakers

- October: David Brancaccio
- November: Andrew Ross Sorkin
- January: Amy Chua

Please contact us for tickets.

Lecture day, time, and location

All one-hour lectures are on the second Wednesday of the month beginning at 10:30 a.m. at William Saroyan Theatre. 700 M Street. Fresno, CA.

© Copyright 2022 San Joaquin Valley Town Hall.

Description

- When you use ems or percents to size fonts, the size you specify is relative to the size of the parent element. That makes it easy for you to change the size of an element and all of its children at the same time.

Figure 8-6   How to size fonts

How to scale images

As the width of an element in a fluid design changes, you typically want the width of any images within that element to change too. In other words, you want the image to *scale* with the element. Or, to say that another way, you want to use *scalable images*. Figure 8-7 shows how.

This figure presents part of a web page that includes a section with a scalable image. To make this image scalable, the max-width property is set to 100%. That way, the image will always be as wide as the section that contains it.

In general, when you use a scalable image, you shouldn't display it any larger than its native size. If you do, the quality of the image may be compromised. So, to limit an image to its native size, you use CSS like that shown in the second style rule in this figure.

Here, the width property is set to 100%. That way, the image will still be the same width as the containing block. But since the max-width property is set to 400 pixels, which is the native width of the image, the width will never be wider than 400 pixels.

When you use small images like logos, you may also want to include the min-width property. That way, the image won't get so small that you can't tell what it is. You'll soon see an example of that.

By the way, some developers also like to set the height property to "auto" when they scale images. That way, the aspect ratio of the height to the width will remain the same regardless of the scale of the image. But because "auto" is the default, the height property can be omitted.

Part of a web page with a fluid layout that includes a scalable image

Instructional materials

We provide instructional materials for all of our courses that make it easy for instructors to plan and teach a course and make it easy for students to practice the skills they learn in each chapter.

These materials include:

Books for web developers
- Murach's HTML and CSS
- Murach's JavaScript and jQuery
- Murach's PHP and MySQL
- Murach's Java Servlets and JSP
- Murach's ASP.NET Core MVC

The HTML for the image

```
<img src="images/students.jpg" alt="Instructor with students">
```

The CSS for the image

```
section img {
    max-width: 100%;
    margin-bottom: .5em;
}
```

CSS that limits the width of the image

```
section img {
    width: 100%;
    max-width: 400px;
    margin-bottom: .5em;
}
```

Description

- To create a *scalable image*, you remove any height and width attributes from the HTML for the image. In addition, you set the max-width property of the image to a percent of its containing block.

- If you want to limit the size of an image to its native width, you can set the width property to a percent and then set the max-width property to the native width in pixels. That way, the quality of the image will be maintained.

- You might also want to set the min-width property for small images like logos so they don't get so small that you can't tell what they are.

Figure 8-7   How to scale images

A web page with fluid design

Figure 8-8 presents a web page that has a fluid design. That means the widths of all of the structural elements are set to percents, and the images are scalable. As a result, if you open the page in a browser and then change the width of the browser window, the page will adjust to the size of the window.

When you study the CSS for this figure, you will see that the font sizes are set to ems. But keep in mind that the font sizes won't change when the width of the browser window changes on the desktop. In this figure, for example, the width of the browser window has been reduced, but the font sizes haven't changed. That's why the text in the fourth item in the navigation menu rolls over to a second line, as do the headings for the article and the sidebar.

To fix that, you need to use media queries. So that's what you'll learn after you study the HTML and CSS for this fluid design.

A page with a fluid layout that includes two scalable images

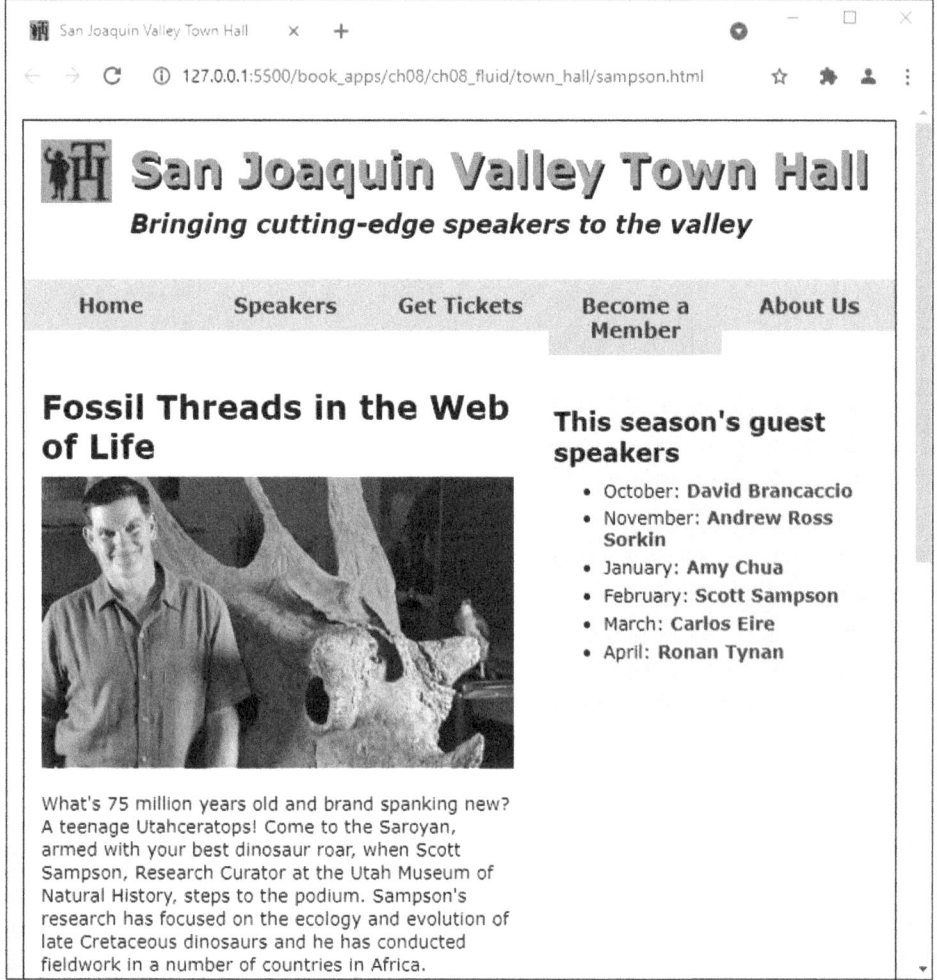

Description

- This web page uses a fluid layout so the widths of the elements change as the width of the browser window changes.

- The logo in the header is scaled so it occupies a percent of the header width, and the image in the article is scaled so it occupies the entire width of the article.

- The font sizes for this page are set in ems, but these sizes don't change as the width of the desktop browser window changes. To change them, you need to use media queries.

- When this page is displayed on a mobile device, the text may be reduced and become so small that it's hard to read. To fix that, you need to set properties that control the viewport of those devices and then use media queries to size the fonts.

- The web page above was narrowed until the fourth item in the navigation bar rolled over.

Figure 8-8   A web page with fluid design

The HTML for the web page

Now that you've seen how the web page looks, figure 8-9 shows the HTML for the page. If you were to compare this code with the code for the same page from chapter 6, you would notice two main differences other than the addition of the navigation menu.

First, the widths of the images in the header and the article have been omitted. That way, they can be scaled using CSS. Second, the sequence of the aside and article elements have been switched. You'll soon see why.

The HTML for the main structural elements

```
<body>
    <header>
        <img src="images/logo.gif" alt="Town Hall Logo">
        <h2>San Joaquin Valley Town Hall</h2>
        <h3>Bringing cutting-edge speakers to the valley</h3>
    </header>
    <nav id="nav_menu">
        <ul>
            <li><a href="index.html">Home</a></li>
            <li><a href="speakers.html">Speakers</a>
                <ul>
                    <li><a href="brancaccio.html">David Brancaccio</a></li>
                    <li><a href="sorkin.html">Andrew Ross Sorkin</a></li>
                    <li><a href="chua.html">Amy Chua</a></li>
                    <li><a href="sampson.html">Scott Sampson</a>
                        <ul>
                            <li><a href="sampson13.html">September 2013</a></li>
                            <li><a href="sampson18.html">Febuary 2018</a></li>
                        </ul>
                    </li>
                    <li><a href="eire.html">Carlos Eire</a></li>
                    <li><a href="tynan.html">Roman Tynan</a></li>
                </ul>
            </li>
            <li><a href="tickets.html">Get Tickets</a></li>
            <li><a href="members.html">Become a Member</a></li>
            <li class="lastitem" ><a href="aboutus.html">About Us</a></li>
        </ul>
    </nav>
    <main>
        <article>
            <h1>Fossil Threads in the Web of Life</h1>
            <img src="images/sampson.jpg" alt="Scott Sampson">
            <p>What's 75 million years old and brand spanking new? ... </p>
                .
                .
        </article>
        <aside>
            <h2>This season's guest speakers</h2>
            <nav>
                <ul>
                    <li>October: <a class="date_passed"
                        href="brancaccio.html">David Brancaccio</a></li>
                    .
                    .
                    <li>April: <a href="tynan.html">Ronan Tynan</a></li>
                </ul>
            </nav>
        </aside>
    </main>
    <footer>
      <p>&copy; Copyright 2022 San Joaquin Valley Town Hall.</p>
    </footer>
</body>
```

Figure 8-9   The HTML for the web page

The CSS for the web page

Figure 8-10 shows the CSS for the fluid web page. Here, the comments to the right of the width properties help explain the settings. For example, the width property for the body is 96%, so the page will occupy 96% of the screen. In addition, the max-width property for the body is set to 1200 pixels so the page won't expand beyond that on a widescreen monitor.

The comments also show the calculations for converting some of the widths to percents. Because the page was originally defined with a width of 990 pixels, and because most of the structural elements are children of an element that extends the entire width of the page, the width for each of these elements is calculated by dividing its width in pixels by 990.

There are two exceptions. First, the Speakers submenu that's displayed below the navigation menu when the mouse hovers over the Speakers list item (#nav_menu ul li:hover ul) is set to 100% of the width of the Speakers list item. This shows that you have to keep the context in mind when you specify a width as a percent. (If you need to refresh your memory about how a three-tier menu like this works, please refer back to chapter 7.)

Second, the Scott Sampson submenu that's displayed to the right of the Speakers submenu when the mouse hovers over the Scott Sampson list item (#nav_menu ul li:hover ul li:hover ul li) is set to 100% of the width of the Speakers list. Here again, the context determines the setting.

In this example, the width properties for elements that extend the entire width of the page are set to 100%. That includes the header, the navigation menu, and the footer. But note that 100% is the default if you don't specify a width. As a result, you don't need to include these properties unless you find them helpful as documentation.

To complete the fluid layout, the images are scalable. First, the max-width property of the image in the article is set to 100%. That way, the width of the image will always be the same as the width of the article.

Second, the width property of the image in the header is set to a percent and its max-width property is set to its native width in pixels. In addition, its min-width property is set to half its native width. That way, it won't become so small that you can't tell what it is.

The CSS for fluid design

```
/* the styles for the type selectors */
body { font-family: Verdana, Arial, Helvetica, sans-serif;
       font-size: 100%;
       width: 96%;
       max-width: 1200px;                    /* maximum width of page */
       ... }
article, aside, h1, h2, h3, p {
    margin: 0;
    padding: 0; }
article, aside { margin-bottom: 1em; }
p { font-size: .875em; ... }


/* the styles for the header */
header { width: 100%; ... }                  /* full width of body */
header h2 { font-size: 2.25em;
            margin-left: 12.12121%;          /* 120 ÷ 990 x 100 */
            ... }
header h3 { font-size: 1.25em;
            font-style: italic;
            margin-left: 12.12121%;          /* 120 ÷ 990 x 100 */ }
header img { width: 8.0808%;                  /* 80 ÷ 990 x 100 */
            max-width: 80px;                  /* native size */
            min-width: 40px;                  /* minimum size */
            float: left;
            margin-left: 2.0202%;             /* 20 ÷ 990 x 100 */ }


/* the styles for the navigation menu */
#nav_menu ul { width: 100%; ... }             /* width of body */
#nav_menu ul li { width: 20%; ... }           /* 198 ÷ 990 x 100 */
#nav_menu ul li:hover ul { width: 100%; }     /* width of list item */
#nav_menu ul li:hover ul li:hover ul li { width: 100%; } /* width of list */


/* the styles for the article */
article { width: 54.0404%;                    /* 535 ÷ 990 x 100 */
          float: left;
          margin-left: 2.0202%;               /* 20 ÷ 990 x 100 */
          padding: 1.5em 2.52525% 0 0;        /* 25 ÷ 990 x 100 */ }
article h1 { font-size: 1.625em; ... }
article img { max-width: 100%; ... }          /* width of article */


/* the styles for the sidebar */
aside { width: 35.35353%;                     /* 350 ÷ 990 x 100 */
        float: left;
        padding: 2.0202%;                     /* 20 ÷ 990 x 100 */
        background-color: #ffebc6;
        margin: 1.5em 2.0202% 0 0;            /* 20 ÷ 990 x 100 */ }
aside h2 { font-size: 1.25em; ... }
aside li { font-size: .875em; ... }


/* the styles for the footer */
footer { width: 100%; ... }                   /* width of body */
footer p { font-size: .75em;
           text-align: right;
           margin-right: 2.0202%;             /* 20 ÷ 990 x 100 */ }
```

Figure 8-10   The CSS for the web page with fluid design

How to use media queries

In the topics that follow, you'll learn how to use media queries to control the layout of a page at various widths. You'll also learn how to build responsive menus using a jQuery plugin called SlickNav. But first, you'll learn how to control the mobile viewport so it works in conjunction with media queries.

How to control the mobile viewport

When you develop a responsive website, you need to be sure that you configure the *viewport* appropriately for mobile devices. To do that, you can use the meta element that's presented in figure 8-11.

On a mobile device, the viewport can be larger or smaller than the visible area. In this figure, for example, you can see that the first web page is displayed so the entire width of the page is visible, and some mobile browsers reduce a page like this if no meta element is included. By contrast, other mobile browsers don't reduce the page at all, so the viewport extends beyond the visible area of the screen.

When you use media queries, you want to be sure that the web page isn't reduced. To do that, you add a meta element like the one in this figure. In fact, if you use Emmet to add the starting code for an HTML file as described in chapter 2, a meta element like this is added for you automatically. When you use this meta element, the second web page in this figure is displayed. Here, the text is displayed at its original size, so it rolls over as necessary to fit in the screen.

In the meta element, the name attribute is set to "viewport" to indicate that the element applies to the viewport. Then, the content attribute specifies the two properties for the viewport. Here, the width property sets the width of the viewport to the width of the device. And the initial-scale property sets the initial zoom factor, or *scale*, for the viewport to 1, which represents the default width for the viewport. This is what keeps the browser from scaling the page automatically.

In addition to the width and initial-scale properties, you may want to set some of the other properties that are presented in this figure. Specifically, when you use RWD, you may want to set the user-scalable property to "no" so the user can't zoom in or out of the display. Or, if you want to let the user zoom in or out, you can set the minimum-scale and maximum-scale properties to limit how much the user can zoom.

A web page on a mobile device without and with a meta viewport element

Content properties for viewport metadata

Property	Description
width	The logical width of the viewport specified in pixels. You can also use the device-width keyword to indicate that the viewport should be the width of the screen in CSS pixels at a scale of 100%.
height	The logical height of the viewport specified in pixels. You can also use the device-height keyword to indicate that the viewport should be the height of the screen in CSS pixels at a scale of 100%.
initial-scale	A number that indicates the initial zoom factor used to display the page.
minimum-scale	A number that indicates the minimum zoom factor for the page.
maximum-scale	A number that indicates the maximum zoom factor for the page.
user-scalable	Indicates whether the user can zoom in and out of the viewport. Possible values are yes and no.

A meta element that sets viewport properties

```
<meta name="viewport" content="width=device-width, initial-scale=1">
```

Description

- The *viewport* on a mobile device determines the content that's displayed on the screen. It can be larger or smaller than the actual visible area of the screen.
- You use a meta element to control the viewport settings for a device. You add this element within the head element of a page.
- When you use media queries, you should set the width property of the content attribute to "device-width", and you should set the initial-scale property to 1. You can also prevent or limit scaling with the user-scalable, minimum-scale, and maximum-scale properties.

Figure 8-11   How to control the mobile viewport

How to code media queries

Media queries are a CSS feature that lets you write conditional expressions within your CSS code. These expressions can be used to query various properties of a device, such as the screen size. Figure 8-12 shows how to code the media queries for a responsive design.

At the top of this figure, you can see the basic syntax of a media query. It starts with an *@media selector*, followed by a media type. When you're developing a responsive design, you'll set the media type to "screen" so the media query will only be used if the page is displayed on a screen.

After the media type, you code one or more conditional expressions, where each expression specifies the value of a property. The table in this figure lists some of the common properties for the screen media type.

In the first media query in this figure, the conditional expression uses the max-width property to check that the width of the viewport is 796 pixels or less. Then, the second media query includes two conditional expressions. The first one checks that the width of the viewport is 481 pixels or more, and the second one checks that the width of the viewport is 796 pixels or less.

Within each media query, you code the CSS that adjusts the appearance of the web page so it's appropriate for the screen size that's specified by the query. For instance, you can use a media query to change the font sizes or page layout for that screen size. You'll soon see how this works.

A relatively new feature of media queries is the use of the <, <=, >, and >= operators to identify a range, as shown by the third and fourth media queries in this figure. In the third media query, the conditional expression uses the <= sign with the width property to check that the viewport width is less than or equal to 796 pixels, just as in the first media query. And in the fourth media query, the conditional expression uses the <= and >= operators with the width property to check that the viewport width is greater than or equal to 481 pixels and less than or equal to 796 pixels, just as in the second media query.

The basic syntax of a media query

```
@media [only] media-type [and (expression-1)] [and (expression-2)]... {
    style rules go here
}
```

Common properties for the screen media type

Property	Description
width	The width of the viewport.
min-width	The minimum width of the viewport.
max-width	The maximum width of the viewport.
height	The height of the viewport.
min-height	The minimum height of the viewport.
max-height	The maximum height of the viewport.
orientation	Landscape or portrait.

A media query for a viewport width of 796 pixels or less

```
@media only screen and (max-width: 796px) { ... }
```

A media query for a viewport width between 481 and 796 pixels

```
@media only screen and (min-width: 481px) and (max-width: 796px) { ... }
```

How to use the range syntax in a media query

A media query for a viewport width of 796 pixels or less

```
@media only screen and (width <= 796px) { ... }
```

A media query for a viewport width between 481 and 796 pixels

```
@media only screen and (481px <= width <= 796px) { ... }
```

Description

- A *media query* is defined by a CSS @media selector. This selector specifies the media type for the query and, for the screen media type, one or more conditional expressions. If all of the conditions are true, the styles within the media query are applied to the page.

- Each conditional expression can check one of the properties listed above.

- The screen size at which a media query is used to change the appearance of a page can be referred to as a *breakpoint*.

- CSS Media Queries Level 4 introduced a new syntax that lets you use the <, <=, >, and >= operators to specify the width and height of the viewport.

Figure 8-12   How to code media queries

How to determine the breakpoints for media queries

Because so many different devices are used today, you need to determine the breakpoints for a page based on its content rather than on the screen sizes for different types of devices. To do that, you can use a browser's Developer Tools as shown in figure 8-13.

To start, you develop the web page with fluid design. Next, you open the page in a browser and display the Developer Tools. Then, you drag the right border of the browser window to the left until the design breaks, and you record the width that's shown in the upper-right corner of the page. And you continue to do that, until you have recorded all of the breakpoints.

In the example in this figure, you can see that one of the items in the navigation bar and the headings in the article and sidebar have rolled over to a second line, which probably isn't what you want. As a result, it's the first breakpoint, and the width in the upper-right corner is 848 pixels. To make sure you've got this right, you can widen the window until the elements don't roll.

Later, you can create a media query for windows that are smaller than that breakpoint. For instance, you can decrease the font sizes for the headings and menu items so they don't roll over.

But note that if the Developer Tools are docked at the bottom of the browser window in Chrome, you can only narrow the window to 500 pixels. If you need to provide for media queries that are narrower than that, you can dock the Developer Tools at the right or left side of the window. Then, you can narrow the window, and the page, as much as you need to.

Because this process isn't as exact as you might want it to be, you need to know that the breakpoints don't have to be exact. If you're going from a larger screen to a smaller screen, you just want to be sure that the breakpoint occurs before a heading or menu item rolls over or whatever else might happen that you want to prevent.

You can also have as many breakpoints as you think you need. For example, I thought about having separate breakpoints for when the heading in the article and when the heading in the sidebar rolled over. Although that would work, I thought that was overkill because the breakpoints were so close together. So I set a breakpoint before either heading rolled over.

A web page in Chrome as the headings roll over

How to determine the breakpoints

- Open the web page in your browser and press F12 to open the Developer Tools.
- To determine a breakpoint, drag the right edge of the browser window to the left, and watch for a design break. Then, record the width that's shown in the upper right corner of the window.
- Continue to narrow the window as you record other breakpoints.
- When the Developer Tools are docked at the bottom of the browser window in Chrome, the window can only be reduced to 500 pixels. To display the page at narrower widths, you can dock the Developer Tools at the right or left of the window. Then, you can narrow the window as much as you want.

Description

- Once you create a page with fluid design, you can use a browser's Developer Tools to determine where the *breakpoints* for your media queries should be. But note that they don't have to be exact.

Figure 8-13   How to determine the breakpoints for media queries

How to build responsive menus with the SlickNav plugin

When you develop a responsive design, you need to provide for menus that work on mobile devices. To illustrate, figure 8-14 shows a menu for a mobile device in landscape mode. To drop down this menu, you click on the MENU button. Then, you can click on a menu item to go to another page. Or, if a menu item has a submenu, you can click on it to display that submenu. To hide the menu, you just click the MENU button again.

One way to implement a menu like this is to use a jQuery plugin called SlickNav. To do that, you download and add the two SlickNav files to your website. Then, you code the HTML and CSS that uses it.

To start, you need to add the HTML that's shown to the head element of each page that uses the menu. Except for the two highlighted ids, this code should be the same for every page, so you don't need to understand it. But in case you're interested, the link element identifies the downloaded style sheet for using the plugin. The first script element gets the jQuery core library that's used by the plugin from the jQuery website. The second script element gets the jQuery code for the plugin. And the third script element initializes the SlickNav menu and prepends it to the menu for larger viewports.

Next, in the body of the HTML, you need to add the code for the SlickNav menu right before the menu for larger viewport sizes, which must be coded as an unordered list. This is illustrated by the second example. As you can see, you need to coordinate the ids that are used for these menus with the ids that are in the script element that contains the JavaScript code.

You can also change the appearance of a SlickNav menu by using the classes that are defined in the slicknav.css file. This is illustrated by the third example in this figure. It changes the background color of the menu to the one in this figure. Here, !important is coded so this change will override the property set in the slicknav.css file. To find out what classes are available in that style sheet, just open the slicknav.css file.

Once all of that is done, you can use media queries to hide and display the mobile menu by using the code in the last example. For instance, you'll want to display the menu for mobile devices but hide it for desktop computers. And you'll want to do the reverse for the menu for larger viewports.

A multi-tier menu that uses SlickNav

The HTML for the SlickNav plugin in the head element

```
<link rel="stylesheet" href="styles/slicknav.css">
<script src="https://code.jquery.com/jquery-3.6.0.min.js"></script>
<script src="js/jquery.slicknav.min.js"></script>
<script type="text/javascript">
    $(document).ready(function(){
        $('#nav_menu').slicknav({prependTo:"#mobile_menu"});
    });
</script>
```

The HTML for the SlickNav menu and the menu for larger viewports

```
<nav id="mobile_menu"></nav>
<nav id="nav_menu">
    <ul>
        <li><a href="index.html">Home</a></li>
        ...
    </ul>
</nav>
```

How to apply one of the styles in the slicknav.css file to the mobile menu

```
.slicknav_menu { background-color: #facd8a !important; }
```

The CSS for hiding and displaying the SlickNav menu

To hide the SlickNav menu
```
#mobile_menu { display: none; }
```

To display the SlickNav menu
```
#mobile_menu { display: block; }
```

How to implement the SlickNav plugin

- Download the SlickNav-master.zip file from: https://github.com/ComputerWolf/SlickNav.
- Unzip the file and add the slicknav.css and jquery.slicknav.min.js files to your website.
- Add the HTML for the one link element and the three script elements to the head element of any web page that uses the menu.
- Add the HTML for the SlickNav menu right before the menu for larger viewports. Then, coordinate the ids of these menus with the code for the JavaScript plugin.
- Use the CSS code to hide or display the SlickNav menu as needed by the responsive design.

Figure 8-14   How to build responsive menus with the SlickNav plugin

A web page with Responsive Web Design

Now that you know how to use media queries, the next three figures present a web page that demonstrates the use of them in a Responsive Web Design.

The design of the web page

Figure 8-15 shows a speaker page in a desktop browser as well as on a mobile phone in both landscape and portrait orientation. This is the same web page that you saw in figure 8-8 with a fluid layout, but now it uses media queries so it works for devices of all sizes.

To make this work, though, the SlickNav menu has to be implemented, as shown in the previous figure. And the nav element that's highlighted in this figure has to be added to the body of the HTML, right before the nav element that's created by the unordered list. Otherwise, the HTML for this page is the same as the HTML in figure 8-9.

If you compare the appearance of this page in the desktop browser with its appearance in the mobile phone, you'll notice some differences. First, everything is smaller on the phone, which you would expect. Second, the margin and border have been removed from the page so it can use all of the available screen. Third, the logo is displayed above the headings in the header and the logo and headings are centered. And if you scrolled down to the bottom of the page, you would see that the footer is centered too.

Beyond that, a SlickNav menu is displayed for mobile phones instead of the standard navigation menu. And the content is displayed in a single column with the article displayed before the sidebar.

You'll also notice one other difference between the page in landscape orientation and in portrait orientation. That is, the image in landscape mode is floated left, and it's sized so it takes up only a portion of the article width.

A speaker page in desktop and mobile layouts

The HTML code that provides for the SlickNav menu

```
<body>
    <header>...</header>
    <nav id="mobile_menu"></nav>
    <nav id="nav_menu">...</nav>
    ...
</body>
```

Description

- This web page has a fluid layout and scalable images like the one in figure 8-8. But it also uses media queries to change the appearance of the page depending on the size of the screen that accesses it.

- The only change to the HTML is the addition of the SlickNav menu, which requires code in the head element as well as code in the body element (see the previous figure).

Figure 8-15   The design of the web page

The CSS for the media queries

The CSS for this web page starts with the styles for fluid design that you reviewed in figure 8-10, and they're not repeated here. Those styles provide the formatting for the page in a desktop browser. Then, the CSS in figure 8-16 consists of the media queries that provide for smaller and smaller viewport sizes.

When you code the CSS in this way, the styles in each media query override the previous styles. This is the traditional way to code the CSS for Responsive Web Design. And this can be referred to as *desktop-first coding*.

So to start, the code in this figure hides the mobile menu because it won't be needed until the media queries get down to smaller viewport sizes. Then, the first media query provides for viewports from 887 pixels to 1006 pixels. This code just reduces the font sizes for the article and aside headings so they won't roll over.

The second media query is for viewports from 797 pixels to 886 pixels. Besides further decreasing the size of the headings in the article and aside, it decreases the size of the font for the <a> elements in the navigation menu and the size of the li elements in the aside so they don't roll over.

The third media query applies styles that control the page when the viewport width is from 481 to 796 pixels. This applies to most smaller tablets in portrait orientation and most mobile phones in landscape orientation. That's why this query changes the display property of the navigation menu to "none" to hide it, and it changes the display property of the mobile menu to "block" to display it. It also changes the background-color property of the SlickNav menu by using the .slicknav_menu class.

Next, this media query changes the styles for the body so it will fill the screen. To do that, it sets the width to 100%, removes the margins, and removes the border. Then, it sets the float to "none" for the header image so it's displayed above the two headings. It also aligns the text within the header so the image and headings are centered.

The CSS continues by setting the font sizes, margins, and padding for other elements. It also removes floating from both the article and the aside so the article is displayed above the aside. That's why the article element must be coded before the aside element in the HTML. And it changes the styles for the image within the article so the image floats to the left of the text.

The next two queries are for screens with a width less than or equal to 480 pixels. That applies to most mobile phones in portrait orientation. These queries further reduce the font sizes for some of the headings. And the last query formats the image in the article so it takes up the full width of the screen. To do that, it removes the float from the image, changes its width to 100%, and removes the right margin.

The CSS for the media queries when using desktop-first coding

```css
/* hide the mobile menu initially */
#mobile_menu { display: none; }
/* 887 pixels to 1006 pixels */
@media only screen and (max-width: 1006px) {
    article h1 { font-size: 1.5em; }
    aside h2 { font-size: 1.125em; } }
/* 797 pixels to 886 pixels */
@media only screen and (max-width: 886px) {
    #nav_menu ul li a { font-size: .875em; }
    article h1 { font-size: 1.25em; }
    aside h2 { font-size: 1em; }                /* base font size */
    aside li { font-size: .8125em; } }
/* 481 pixels to 796 pixels */
@media only screen and (max-width: 796px) {
    #nav_menu { display: none; }
    #mobile_menu { display: block; }            /* display mobile menu */
    .slicknav_menu { background-color: #facd8a !important; }
    body { width: 100%;                         /* full width of screen */
        margin: 0;                              /* no margins */
        border: none; }                         /* no border */
    header img { float: none; }
    header, footer p { text-align: center; }
    header h2 { font-size: 1.625em;
            margin: .4em 0 .25em 0; }
    header h3 { font-size: 1em;                 /* base font size */
            margin-left: 0; }
    footer p { margin-right: 0; }
    article { width: 95.9596%;                  /* 100 - (2 * 2.0202) for padding */
            float: none;
            margin-right: 2.0202%;        /* 20 / 990 */
            padding-right: 0; }
    article img { float: left;
            width: 50%;
            margin-right: 2%; }
    article p { font-size: .8125em; }
    aside { width: 91.9192%;        /* 100 - (4 * 2.0202) for padding and margins */
            float: none;
            margin: 0 2.0202% 2.0202% 2.0202%; } }   /* 20 / 990 */
/* 383 pixels to 480 pixels */
@media only screen and (max-width: 480px) {
    header h2 { font-size: 1.375em; }
    header h3 { font-size: .875em; }
    article h1 { font-size: 1.125em; }  }
/* 382 pixels or less */
@media only screen and (max-width: 382px) {
    header h2 { font-size: 1.125em; }
    header h3 { font-size: .75em; }
    article img { float: none;
                width: 100%;
                margin-right: 0; }
    article h1 { font-size: 1em; }              /* base font size */
    footer p { font-size: .6875em; } }
```

Figure 8-16   The CSS for the media queries when using desktop-first coding

The CSS when using mobile-first coding

Now that you've seen how to code the CSS for a web page using *desktop-first coding*, you should know that you can also start the CSS with the code for mobile phones and work your way up to the code for desktops. That can be referred to as *mobile-first coding*.

Which works better? You can decide after you review the code in the next two figures. As you will see, both approaches work. So if you're working on your own, you can use the approach that you prefer. But if you're working with a development group, you will probably have to use the approach that the group uses.

Either way, you need to plan the components and layout for each page on each range of screen sizes. You also need to code the HTML for all the components that you're going to use for a page. That's the hard work. Once that's done, either coding approach will get the results that you want.

With that as background, the next two figures present the mobile-first CSS for the speaker page in figure 8-15. It uses the same HTML as the desktop-first example. But its CSS starts with the code for the smallest viewports.

The CSS for the smallest viewports

Figure 8-17 presents the CSS for the smallest viewports, the ones under 383 pixels wide. Like the desktop-first code, the styles for the body element specify the same font-family, font-size, and padding. Then, the margins and padding for the article, aside, h1, h2, h3, and <p> elements are all set to 0. And so on.

The differences between the two coding approaches are that the article and aside are displayed in a single column to start, the image in the article occupies the entire column width, the image in the header appears above the headings, the header and footer are centered, the SlickNav menu is displayed, and the fonts are at their smallest sizes. You can of course see all of the code for this web page in the download from our website.

The CSS for the smallest viewports when using mobile-first coding

```css
/* styles for the type selectors */
body {
    font-family: Verdana, Arial, Helvetica, sans-serif;
    font-size: 100%;
    width: 100%;
    margin: 0;
    padding: 15px 0; }
article, aside, h1, h2, h3, p {
    margin: 0;
    padding: 0; }
article, aside { margin-bottom: 1em; }
p {
    font-size: .8125em;
    padding-bottom: .5em;
    line-height: 130%; }
em { font-weight: bold; }
a {
    font-weight: bold;
    text-decoration: none; }
a:link, a:visited { color: #931420; }
a:hover, a:focus { color: black; }

/* the styles for the header */
header {
    width: 100%;
    padding-bottom: 2em;
    text-align: center; }
header img {
    width: 8.0808%;
    max-width: 80px;
    min-width: 40px; }
header h2 {
    font-size: 1.125em;
    color: #f2972e;
    text-shadow: 2px 3px 0 black;
    margin-bottom: .25em; }
header h3 {
    font-size: .75em;
    font-style: italic;
    margin-left: 0; }
#mobile_menu { display: block; }
.slicknav_menu { background-color: #facd8a !important; }
#nav_menu { display: none; }              /* hide the nav menu initially */

/* the styles for the article, sidebar, and footer */
```

Figure 8-17   The CSS for the smallest viewports when using mobile-first coding

The CSS for the media queries

Once the coding for the smallest viewports is done, you use media queries for each of the other breakpoints, working from the smallest to the largest widths. These queries use the min-width property to check that the screen is greater than or equal to the specified width. For instance, the first media query in figure 8-18 is for viewports that range from 383 pixels to 480 pixels.

As you would expect, these queries work the opposite of the queries in the desktop-first coding. For example, the styles in the first query increase the font sizes of the headings in the header. They also float the image in the article to the left and set its maximum width so it can take up no more than 50% of the article width.

Here again, the majority of the changes take place when the screen reaches a minimum width of 797 pixels. After these styles are applied, the page will look similar to the desktop layout in figure 8-15. In particular, the header is reformatted so the image is floated to the left of the headings, the SlickNav menu is hidden, the navigation menu is displayed, and the article and aside are floated so they are side by side.

Besides that, the width of the body is changed to 96% of the page, a border is added around the body, a gradient is added to the page, the background of the body is changed to white so the gradient doesn't show through, and the footer is right aligned.

The next media query is applied when the screen has a minimum width of 887 pixels. This query simply increases some of the font sizes. The last media query is similar, except it also sets the body to a maximum width of 1200 pixels.

Here again, the media queries have to be coded in the sequence shown. That way, the styles in the media queries for the larger screens override the styles in the media queries for the smaller screens.

So now you can decide. Is mobile-first coding easier or better than desktop-first coding? Or is it just a different way to get the same results?

The CSS for the media queries when using mobile-first coding

```
/* 383 pixels to 480 pixels */
@media only screen and (min-width: 383px) {
    header h2 { font-size: 1.375em; }
    header h3 { font-size: .875em; }
    article img { float: left;
                  max-width: 50%;
                  margin-right: 2%; }
    article h1 { font-size: 1.125em; }
    footer p { font-size: .75em; } }
/* 481 pixels to 796 pixels */
@media only screen and (min-width: 481px) {
    header h2 { font-size: 1.625em; }
    header h3 { font-size: 1em; } }
/* 797 pixels to 886 pixels */
@media only screen and (min-width: 797px) {
    html { background-image: linear-gradient(to bottom, white 0%, #facd8a 100%); }
    body { width: 96%;
           background-color: white;
           margin: 15px auto;
           border: 1px solid black; }
    header { text-align: left; }
    header img { float: left; margin-left: 2.0202% }
    header h2 { font-size: 2.25em;
                margin-left: 12.12121%; }
    header h3 { font-size: 1.25em;
                margin-left: 12.12121%; }
    #nav_menu { display: block; }
    #mobile_menu { display: none; }

    /*  styles for  nav menu same as for desktop-first at 797px and above */

    article { width: 54.0404%;
              float: left;
              margin-left: 2.0202%;
              padding: 1.5em 0 0 0; }
    article h1 { font-size: 1.25em; }
    article img { max-width: 100%;
                  margin-right: 0;
                  float: none; }
    aside { width: 35.35353%;
            float: left;
            margin: 1.5em 2.0202% 0 0; }
    footer { clear: both;
             text-align: right;
             margin-right: 2.0202%; } }
/* 887 pixels to 1006 pixels */
@media only screen and (min-width: 887px) {
    /* further enlarge fonts in nav menu, article, and aside */
}
/* 1007 pixels or more */
@media only screen and (min-width: 1007px) {
    body { max-width: 1200px; }
    /* further enlarge fonts in nav menu, article, and aside */
}
```

Figure 8-18   The CSS for the media queries when using mobile-first coding

Perspective

Now that you've finished this chapter, you should be able to start building responsive websites of your own. That way, your users will be able to access the content of your website no matter what device they're using.

After you master the skills in this chapter, you can enhance your RWD skills by going on to chapters 9 and 10 where you'll learn how to use Flexible Box Layout and Grid Layout. These features provide two other ways to develop responsive websites that build on what you've learned in this chapter.

You should also know that a new type of query called a *container query* is currently in development. These queries let you control the content in containing elements, and you can use them in conjunction with media queries, Flexible Box Layout, and Grid Layout. Although it will be a while before all browsers support them, they should improve the code for some types of web pages.

Terms

Responsive Web Design (RWD)	viewport
responsive design	media query
fixed layout	breakpoint
fluid layout	desktop-first coding
scalable image	mobile-first coding

Summary

- *Responsive Web Design* refers to a technique that's used to create websites that adapt to any screen size. A *responsive design* includes fluid layouts, scalable images, and media queries.

- You can use the Developer Tools of your browser to test a responsive design.

- To create a web page with a *fluid layout*, you set the widths of the page and its main structural elements to percents so they increase and decrease depending on the width of the screen. You should also specify font sizes in ems or percents.

- To create a *scalable image*, you remove the height and width properties from the img element and set the max-width property to the percent of its containing block that you want it to fill.

- The *viewport* on a mobile device determines the content that's displayed on the screen. When you use media queries, the viewport should be set so the page is displayed at its full size.

- A *media query* uses conditional expressions to determine when the styles it contains are applied. You use media queries with RWD to change the appearance of a page for different screen sizes.

- The screen width at which a media query should be set can be referred to as a *breakpoint*. To determine where those breakpoints should be, you can use a browser's Developer Tools.

- SlickNav is a jQuery plugin that converts a standard navigation menu to a menu that's easier to use on smaller devices.

- When you code the CSS for a responsive web page, you can use *desktop-first coding* or *mobile-first coding*. But either way, you start by coding the HTML elements for all the components of the page at any viewport size.

Exercise 8-1   Test the fluid and RWD pages presented in this chapter

In this exercise, you'll test the two speaker pages presented in this chapter to get a feel for how a fluid design and Responsive Web Design work.

Test the page that uses a fluid design

1. Display the sampson.html file in this folder in Chrome:

   `\html_css_5\book_apps\ch08\ch08_fluid\town_hall`

2. Size the browser window so you can see the full width of the page and so none of the menu items or headings rollover.

3. Press F12 to display the Developer Tools. Then, narrow the browser window and note that the size of the window is displayed near the upper right corner.

4. Note the size of the window when the headings in the sidebar and the article roll over. Because these headings roll over at approximately the same width, you can code a single media query that changes the font size for both headings before the first one rolls over.

5. Continue to narrow the browser window to see that it has a minimum width.

6. Dock the Developer Tools on the right side of the window. Now, you'll be able to make the window as small as necessary to determine the correct breakpoints.

Test the page that uses Responsive Web Design

7. Display the sampson.html file in this folder in Chrome:

   `\html_css_5\book_apps\ch08\ch08_media_queries_desktop_first\town_hall`

8. Size the browser window so you can see the page at its maximum width. Then, narrow the window to see how the size of the text and the layout of the page change at various widths.

9. Press F12 to display the Developer Tools, and then display the Device toolbar.

10. Select different devices from the Dimensions drop-down list. For each device you choose, use the Rotate icon to see how the page looks in both portrait and landscape orientation.

Exercise 8-2   Convert the Town Hall home page to a responsive design

In this exercise, you'll convert the Town Hall home page that you worked on in exercise 7-1 to a responsive design. When you're through, the page should look something like this in portrait and landscape orientations on a mobile phone:

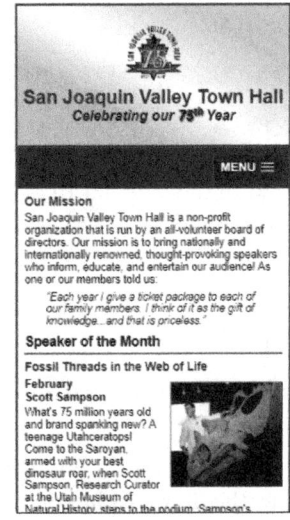
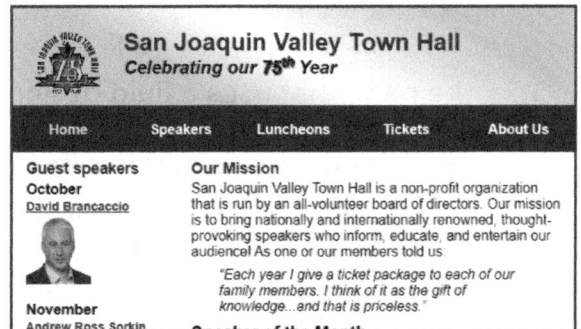

Open the HTML and CSS files for this page

1. Use your text editor to open these HTML and CSS files:

    `\html_css_5\exercises\town_hall_1\c8_index.html`

    `\html_css_5\exercises\town_hall_1\styles\c8_main.css`

Add a meta element for the viewport

2. Add a meta element like the one in figure 8-11 to the HTML for the page.

3. Display the page in Chrome. Then, size your browser window so it's just wide enough to see all of the page.

Convert the fixed widths to fluid widths

4. Display the CSS file for this page and note that the width of the body is set to 800 pixels. Then, change this width to 98% so there's room for the 3-pixel left and right borders, and change the maximum width to 960 pixels.

5. Set the width of the list in the submenu of the navigation menu to 100% so it extends the full width of the list item.

6. Change the widths of the section and aside elements and the <a> elements within the unordered list for the main navigation menu to percents by using the formula in figure 8-4. Do the same for the left and right padding for the image in the header, the left and right padding for the section, and the left padding for the aside.

7. Test these changes in Chrome. When you do, you'll notice that changing the widths of the <a> elements doesn't work.

8. Move the declaration that specifies the width of the <a> elements to the style rule for the li elements that contain the <a> elements, and then test the page again. This time, the navigation menu should look the way it did to start.

9. Notice, however, that the page now extends beyond the right side of the browser window. That's because the maximum width of the body is 160 pixels wider than the original page. Increase the width of the browser window to see that the width of the page will increase only until it reaches 960 pixels.

10. Decrease the width of the browser until the sidebar no longer fits next to the section to see that the sidebar is now displayed below the section. Although this is generally what you want to happen, this formatting can be improved.

11. Continue decreasing the width of the browser to see what happens to the article. To improve this, you'll make the image scalable.

Make the image in the article scalable

12. Display the HTML for the page, and notice that the img element for the image in the article doesn't contain width or height attributes. Because of that, the image is displayed at its native width of 250 pixels, and the text that flows into the space to its left takes up the rest of the width of the article.

13. Set the max-width property of this image to 40%. In addition, set the min-width property to 150 pixels so the image doesn't get to be too small. Then, test the page.

Identify the first breakpoint and add a media query

14. Enlarge the browser window so you can see the entire width of the page, and then press F12 to display the Developer Tools. If necessary, use the Customize menu to dock the Developer Tools at the bottom of the browser for now.

15. Start to reduce the width of the window, and notice that the screen size is displayed in the upper right corner. Continue to reduce the width of the window until the section and the aside get to be too close together, and note the width of the page.

16. Add a media query for the screen type that checks that the viewport width is the width you just noted or less. Within this media query, decrease the font size of the <a> elements within the h2 elements of the aside to 85%, decrease the font size of the h1 element in the section to 125%, and decrease the font size of the h2 elements in the section and aside to 110%.

17. Return to the browser window to see that the font sizes of the headings have been decreased.

Identify the next breakpoint and add a media query

18. Reduce the width of the window some more until the section and the aside get too close again, and note the width of the screen.

19. Code a media query for the screen type that checks that the viewport width is the width you just noted or less. Within this media query, change the image in the header so it doesn't float and center the contents of the header.

20. Return to the browser window to see that the styles you just coded have been applied. Although this looks pretty good, the line length in the section is starting to get too short.

21. Change the section and aside so they don't float. Then, set the right padding for the aside so it's the same as the left padding, and set the widths of the section and aside by subtracting the left and right padding from 100%.

22. Test the page and notice that the image in the article is too big. Fix that by changing the maximum width of the image to 30%, and then test again.

23. To improve the formatting for the aside, display the speakers in two columns. To do that, you'll need to add a div around everything in the aside except the h2 element. Then, you can set the column-count property to 2. Test this change.

Add a mobile menu using the SlickNav plugin

24. Use figure 8-14 as a guide to add a link element for the slicknav.css file in the styles folder and a script element for the jquery.slicknav.min.js file in the js folder to the head element of the page. In addition, add a script element for the jQuery core library before the script element for the SlickNav plugin.

25. Add a nav element before the nav element for the navigation menu, and give it an id of "mobile_menu".

26. Add another script element like the one in figure 8-14 that includes the jQuery for calling the slicknav method.

27. Add a style rule outside the media queries that hides the mobile menu. Then, add three style rules in the last media query you created. The first one should hide the standard navigation menu, the second one should display the mobile menu, and the third one should set the background color of the mobile menu to #800000 using the slicknav_menu class.

28. Test this code, and notice that the mobile menu still has its default background color of dark gray. To change that, add an !important declaration to the declaration for the background color and test again.

Test the page at smaller widths

29. Dock the Developer Tools at the right side of the browser window. Then, narrow the window until the p element in the footer runs over to a second line, and note the width of the screen.

30. Code one more media query for the screen type that checks that the viewport width is the more than the width you noted or less so the footer doesn't get too close to the edges of the screen. Within this media query, change the base font size to 90% to decrease all the font sizes for the page. This illustrates the advantage of using relative sizes for fonts.

Section 2

Responsive Web Design

In chapter 8, you learned how to use media queries for Responsive Web Design. Now, the two chapters in this section show you how to use two other approaches to responsive design. Because these chapters are independent modules, you can read either one first. But you should eventually read both chapters, because both of them present useful skills.

In chapter 9, you'll learn how to use Flexible Box Layout for developing simple page layouts or for laying out portions of pages, like menus. In chapter 10, you'll learn how to use Grid Layout to develop complex pages by laying out elements in rows and columns.

Chapter 9

How to use Flexible Box Layout for Responsive Web Design

In this chapter, you'll learn how to lay out pages using a feature called Flexible Box Layout. As you'll see, this feature makes it easy to lay out content in either columns or rows as part of a Responsive Web Design.

An introduction to Flexible Box Layout

Although the CSS box model and floating work well for laying out simple web pages, that approach can be cumbersome. It can also make it difficult to code the media queries that are needed for Responsive Web Design.

That's where *Flexible Box Layout*, or *flexbox*, comes in. As you'll see, it provides a more efficient way to lay out, align, and distribute space among the elements within a container, especially when the size of the container has to adapt to different screen sizes.

The basic flexbox concepts

Figure 9-1 introduces the basic concepts you need to know to use flexbox. Here, you can see that a *flex container* can contain one or more *flex items*. These items are laid out along the *main axis*, which can have either horizontal or vertical orientation depending on the *flex direction*. In this diagram, the flex direction is set so the flex items are laid out horizontally.

In addition to the main axis, a flex container has a *cross axis* that's perpendicular to the main axis. The flex items within a container can be aligned along either of these axes.

This diagram also shows that the start of the main axis is called the *main start*, and the end of the main axis is called the *main end*. Similarly, the start of the cross axis is called the *cross start*, and the end of the cross axis is called the *cross end*. Last, the width of the container from the main start to the main end is called the *main size*, and the height of the container from the cross start to the cross end is called the *cross size*.

When you use flexbox, you can still use traditional box model properties like width, height, margin, padding, and border. These can be either fixed or relative sizes. If you don't specify a width or height, the width defaults to 100% of the parent element and the height is determined by the content of the flex item unless the height of the parent element is fixed.

What flexbox does best is to simplify how elements on a page are laid out side by side without using floats. It also makes it easy to change a layout from horizontal to vertical orientation when you're developing a responsive design.

Flexbox is most appropriate for laying out components like navigation menus and small-scale page layouts. In this figure, for example, you can see a navigation menu that's laid out using flexbox. Here, the menu items are flex items within a flex container. You'll see the code for implementing menus like this throughout this chapter.

The flexible box layout

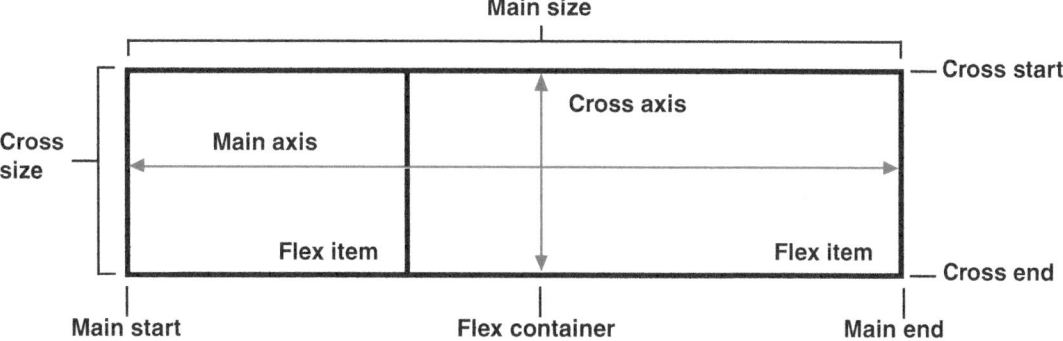

A navigation menu created using flexbox

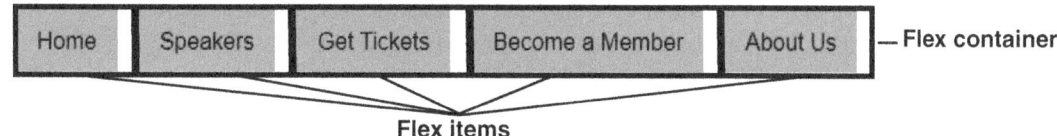

Description

- *Flexible Box Layout*, or *flexbox*, is a CSS module that can be used to develop page layouts for varying screen sizes. But unlike the box model, it doesn't require floating.

- A *flexbox* is a container that contains one or more *flex items*.

- Flex items are laid out within a flex container along the *main axis* depending on the *flex direction*. Flex items can also be aligned along the *cross axis*.

- Width and height properties are used to set the dimensions of the flex container.

- If the width for a flex container isn't set, the container will default to 100% of the parent element.

Figure 9-1   The basic flexbox concepts

How to create your first flexible box

Figure 9-2 shows how to create a navigation menu using flexbox. To start, you set the display property for a block element to either flex or flex-inline. In most cases, you'll set this property to flex. Then, the block element will become a flex container, and any block-level child elements within the container will become flex items.

By default, the items in a flex container are displayed horizontally from left to right. But you can use the flex-direction property to change that. If you want to display the flex items in a column, for example, you can specify column for this property. This changes the direction of the flex container's main and cross axes.

To illustrate how these properties work, this figure shows the code for a navigation menu that's displayed vertically. Here, the HTML consists of a nav element that contains an unordered list that defines the items in the menu.

Now, take a look at the CSS for this menu. Here, the display property for the ul element is set to flex, so all of the li elements within that element become flex items. Then, because the flex-direction property is set to column, the list items are displayed vertically.

Note in this example that the CSS includes traditional box model properties, including width, margin, and padding. Also note that these properties all specify fixed measurements. When you use responsive web design, though, you'll use relative measurements for at least some of the flex items. You'll see how that works later in this chapter.

Properties for creating a flexbox and setting the direction of the flex items

Property	Description
display	The type of box. Possible values include flex (rendered as a block) or flex-inline (rendered as inline content).
flex-direction	The direction of the flex items within the flex container. Possible values include row and column. The default is row.

The HTML for a navigation menu

```
<nav>
    <ul>
        <li id="home"><a href="index.html">Home</a></li>
        <li><a href="speakers.html">Speakers</a></li>
        <li><a href="tickets.html">Get Tickets</a></li>
        <li><a href="member.html">Become a Member</a></li>
        <li><a href="aboutus.html">About Us</a></li>
    </ul>
</nav>
```

CSS that uses flexbox to display the menu vertically

```
ul {
    display: flex;
    flex-direction: column;
    list-style-type: none;
    padding: 0;
    margin: 0; }
li {
    background: #C8DFEE;
    width: 150px;
    margin: 0 15px 15px 0;
    padding: 5px;
    text-align: center; }
a {
    text-decoration: none;
    color: #000; }
```

The layout of the navigation menu

Home

Speakers

Get Tickets

Become a Member

About Us

Description

- To display an element as a flex container, you set the display property to flex or flex-inline.

Figure 9-2   How to create your first flexible box

How to set flexbox properties

Now that you understand how to create a flexbox container and set the direction of the items within the container, you're ready to learn about other flexbox properties that let you align and wrap flex items, set the dimensions of flex items, and change the order of flex items within the container.

How to align flex items along the main axis

Figure 9-3 shows how you can align flex items along the main axis of a flexbox container. By default, the items are aligned at the beginning of the container. But you can use the justify-content property to change that alignment.

The CSS in this figure shows how to align the items in a horizontal navigation menu so there's an equal amount of space between them. To do that, you specify space-between for the justify-content property. You can see the result in the first menu in this figure.

The next two menus in this figure show other ways that you can space out flex items. The first of these examples sets the justify-content property to space-around. This is the same as space-between except that there is space before the first item and after the last item that's equal to half the space between the items. The second example sets the justify-content property to space-evenly. This is the same as space-around except that the space before the first item and after the last item is equal to the space between the items.

The last example in this figure shows the result of setting the justify-content property to flex-end. In this case, the flex items are aligned at the end of the container. You can also specify center for the justify-content property to center the flex items in the middle of the container.

Note that the CSS for a navigation menu like this needs to vary depending on how it's aligned. For instance, when you align the menu items at the right as shown in the last example in this figure, a left margin needs to be set so there's no space to the right of the menu item. By contrast, if you align the menu items at the left, you'll want to set a right margin so there's no space to the left of the first menu item. And if you want to center the menu items, you'll want to set equal left and right margins so there's an equal amount of space to the left of the first item and the right of the last item.

Finally, if you use any of the space values for the justify-content property, you'll want to set the margins of the li elements to 0. That way, the menu items can be spaced as shown in the first three examples in this figure.

You should also note that the justify-content property can be used when the flex direction of a container is set to column. In that case, though, the main axis extends from the top of the container to the bottom of the container. Because of that, the justify-content property will align items vertically rather than horizontally.

The property for aligning flex items along the main axis

Property	Description
justify-content	Aligns flex items within a flex container along the main axis.

Common values for the justify-content property

Value	Description
flex-start	Aligns items at the beginning of the flex container. This is the default.
flex-end	Aligns items at the end of the flex container.
center	Aligns items in the center of the flex container.
space-between	Allocates space evenly between flex items.
space-around	Allocates space evenly between flex items with half-size spaces before the first item and after the last item.
space-evenly	Allocates space evenly between flex items with full-size spaces before the first item and after the last item.

The CSS for a navigation menu with equal spacing between flex items

```
ul {
    display: flex;
    justify-content: space-between;
    list-style-type: none;
    background-color: #C8DFEE; }
li {
    background: #6FABCF;
    padding: 15px;
    text-align: center; }
a {
    text-decoration: none;
    color: #000; }
```

A menu with the justify-content property set to space-between

A menu with the justify-content property set to space-around

A menu with the justify-content property set to space-evenly

A menu with the justify-content property set to flex-end

Description

- The HTML for these examples is the same as the HTML in the previous figure.

Figure 9-3   How to align flex items along the main axis

How to align flex items along the cross axis

In addition to aligning the flex items along the main axis, you can align them along the cross axis. To do that, you use the align-items and align-self properties shown in figure 9-4.

The center, flex-start, and flex-end values that you can code for the align-items property work like they do for the justify-content property. In this case, though, the flex items are aligned at the start, center, and end of the cross axis instead of the main axis.

To illustrate, the CSS in this figure shows how to align a horizontal navigation menu along the cross axis so the flex items are centered in the container. To do that, the align-items property is set to center.

This example also shows how you can override the alignment of individual flex items by setting the align-self property of that item. In this case, the align-self property of the li element with the id "home" is set to flex-start, which causes this item to be aligned at the top of the container, or the start of the cross axis. You can see the result in the first navigation menu in this figure. This assumes, of course, that the id of the first li element has been set to "home".

The default value for the align-items property is stretch. This value causes the flex items to extend from the start of the cross axis to the end of the cross axis, as illustrated by the second example in this figure. Here, you can assume that the height of the ul element is set to 90px as shown in the CSS in this figure. Because no margins are added above or below the li items, these items are also 90 pixels high.

Although it isn't shown here, you can also align the content of each flex item at the bottom of the flex items. To do that, you code baseline for the align-items property. This is useful when the contents of the flex items vary in height.

Like the justify-content property that you learned about in the last figure, you can also use the align-items and align-self properties when the flex direction of a container is set to column. Then, these properties align flex items horizontally within the container. You'll see an example of that in the application at the end of this chapter.

Properties for aligning flex items along the cross-axis

Property	Description
align-items	Aligns flex items within a flex container along the cross axis.
align-self	Overrides the container's cross-axis alignment for an individual flex item.

Common values for the align-items and align-self properties

Value	Description
stretch	The flex items extend from the start of the flex container to the end of the flex container. This is the default for a flex container.
center	The flex items are centered in the flex container.
flex-start	The flex items are aligned at the start of the flex container.
flex-end	The flex items are aligned at the end of the flex container.
baseline	The content within each flex item is aligned at the bottom.
auto	For align-self items only: The item is aligned as specified by the align-items property of the flex container. This is the default.

The CSS for a navigation menu that's centered vertically in a container

```
ul {
    display: flex;
    align-items: center;
    list-style-type: none;
    background: #C8DFEE;
    height: 90px; }
li {
    background: #6FABCF';
    width: 125px;
    margin: 0 15px 0 0;
    padding: 5px;
    text-align: center; }
a {
    text-decoration: none;
    color: #000; }
#home { align-self: flex-start; }   /* for the li item with home as its id */
```

A navigation menu with the align-items property set to center

A navigation menu with the align-items property set to stretch

Description

- The align-items property determines how flex items are aligned along the cross axis for a container, and the align-self property overrides this alignment for specific items.

Figure 9-4   How to align flex items along the cross axis

How to wrap and align wrapped flex items

If the flex items within a flex container are too wide to fit within the container, the flex items don't wrap to multiple lines within the container by default. Instead, the sizes of the flex items are reduced as much as possible and the content is wrapped within the flex items. At some point, this can cause flex items to be wrapped or cut off, as shown by the first menu in figure 9-5.

To avoid this problem, you can set the flex-wrap property of the flex container to wrap. Then, when the flex container is too small for all of the flex items to fit at the specified size, the flex items will wrap within the container. This is illustrated by the second navigation menu in this figure.

The second navigation menu also shows how flex items are aligned by default when they're wrapped. Here, the flex items extend from the top of the container to the bottom of the container. In this case, though, the height of the li items has been set to 20 pixels, and the bottom margin of the li items has been set to 15 pixels. That way, the flex items on each line don't run together.

To change the alignment of wrapped flex items, you can use the align-content property. For instance, the third example in this figure shows the same navigation menu as in the second example, but with center alignment. Just as in the second example, a 15-pixel margin has been added to the bottom of the li elements.

Incidentally, the flex-flow property in the table in this figure is a shorthand property that you can use to set the flex-direction property and the flex-wrap property at the same time. For instance, this CSS declaration

```
flex-flow: column wrap;
```

sets the flex-direction property to column and the flex-wrap property to wrap.

Properties for wrapping and aligning flex items

Property	Description
flex-wrap	Determines how flex items wrap if there isn't enough room for them within the flex container. Possible values are nowrap, wrap, and wrap-reverse. The default is nowrap.
align-content	Determines how lines of flex items are aligned within the flex container. Possible values include stretch, center, flex-start, flex-end, space-between, and space-around. The default is stretch.
flex-flow	The shorthand property for setting the flex-direction and flex-wrap properties.

A navigation menu at a narrow width with no wrapping

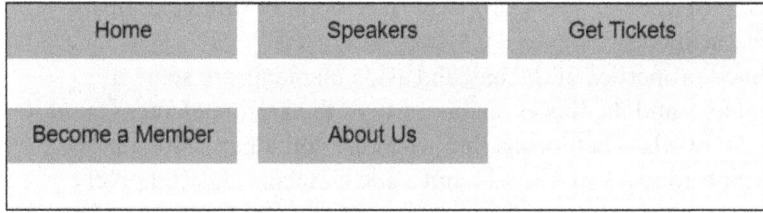

A navigation menu at a narrow width with wrapping and default alignment

```
ul { flex-wrap: wrap; }
```

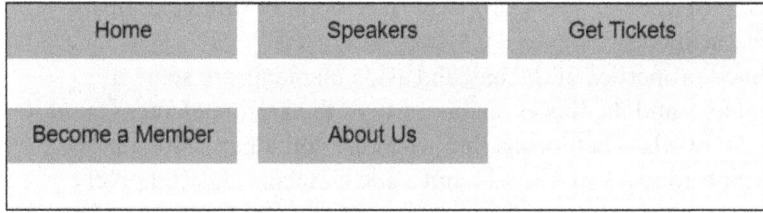

A navigation menu with wrapping and center alignment

```
ul { flex-wrap: wrap;
     align-content: center; }
```

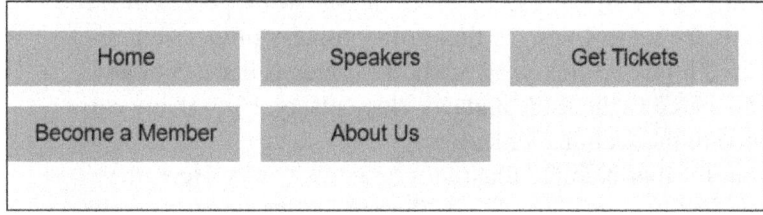

Description

- By default, flex items are not wrapped within a flex container. This causes the contents of flex items that are set to specific widths to wrap within the item or to get cut off.

- By default, wrapped flex items extend from the top to the bottom of the flex container. But you can change this vertical alignment by using the align-content property.

- The ul element in these examples is set to a fixed height of 150 pixels.

Figure 9-5   How to wrap and align wrapped flex items

How to allocate space to flex items

When you use flexbox, you can determine how space is allocated to the flex items within a container as the size of the container changes. This of course is useful when you're developing responsive websites. This is illustrated by the two parts of figure 9-6.

The first part of this figure shows how you can use the flex-basis and flex-grow properties. The two examples in this figure use the HTML shown below the table consisting of a main element that contains nav, section, and aside elements.

The first example illustrates how you can use the flex-basis property so the nav, section, and aside elements are always the same size relative to each other. To do that, the flex-basis properties are set to percents. In this case, the nav and aside elements will always occupy 25% of the available space within the container, and the section element will occupy 50% of the available space.

This is illustrated by the two layouts in this example. Here, the first layout shows the container at 400 pixels wide. That means that the aside and nav elements are 100 pixels wide (400 x 25%) and the section element is 200 pixels wide (400 x 50%). Similarly, when the container is 800 pixels wide as shown in the second layout, the nav and aside elements are 200 pixels wide and the section element is 400 pixels wide.

To specify the exact proportion that you want flex items to grow relative to each other, you can use the flex-grow property. The second example in this figure shows how this works.

Here, the flex-basis properties of the nav and aside elements are set to a fixed width of 100 pixels, and the flex-basis property of the section element is set to a fixed width of 200 pixels. That means that when the container is 400 pixels wide, 100 pixels will be allocated to the nav and aside elements and 200 pixels will be allocated to the section element. This is illustrated by the first layout for this example.

Then, as the size of the container grows, the extra space is allocated to each flex item based on the ratio of its flex-grow value to the total of the flex-grow values for all of the flex items. In this example, the flex-grow properties of the nav and aside elements are set to 1 and the flex-grow property of the section element is set to 3, for a total of 5 flex-grow units. That means that 1/5 of any extra space will be allocated to the aside and nav elements, and 3/5 of any extra space will be allocated to the section element.

The second layout for this example illustrates how this works. Here, the width of the container is 800 pixels, which is 400 pixels wider than the widths specified by the flex-basis properties of the nav, section, and aside elements. Then, the widths of the nav and aside elements are determined by multiplying 400 pixels by 1/5 and adding that to the flex-basis of 100 pixels for a total of 180 pixels. Similarly, the width of the section is determined by multiplying 400 pixels by 3/5 and adding that to the flex-basis of 200 pixels for a total of 440 pixels. As you can see, this causes the size of the section to increase more quickly than the sizes of the navigation menu and sidebar.

The flex-basis and flex-grow properties

Property	Description
flex-basis	The initial length of the flex item. Possible values include auto and units of measure such as pixels, ems, or percents. The default is auto, which means that the length is the same as the width of the item if the width is set or is determined by the content if the width isn't set.
flex-grow	A number that indicates how much a flex item will grow relative to other flex items in the container. The default is 0, which means the item won't grow.

The HTML for a simple page layout

```
<main>
    <nav>Navigation</nav>
    <section>Content</section>
    <aside>Sidebar</aside>
</main>
```

CSS that uses the flex-basis property

```
main { display: flex; }
nav, aside { flex-basis: 25%; }
section { flex-basis: 50%; }
```

The layout at 400 pixels wide

Navigation	Content	Sidebar

The layout at 800 pixels wide

Navigation	Content	Sidebar

CSS that uses the flex-basis and flex-grow properties

```
nav, aside {
    flex-basis: 100px;
    flex-grow: 1; }
section {
    flex-basis: 200px;
    flex-grow: 3; }
```

The layout at 400 pixels wide

Navigation	Content	Sidebar

The layout at 800 pixels wide

Navigation	Content	Sidebar

Description

- To set the length of the flex items so their size is the same relative to each other as the size of the screen changes, set the flex-basis properties of the items to a relative unit of measure like percents.
- The flex-grow property is used when there's more space available within a container than what's specified by the flex-basis properties for all flex items.

Figure 9-6   How to allocate space to flex items (part 1 of 2)

Part 2 of this figure shows that you can use the flex-shrink property to determine how the size of flex items change when the width of a container is less than the widths of the flex items. This is illustrated by the first example, which uses the same HTML as before.

Here, the flex-basis property of the nav, section, and aside elements are all set to 250 pixels, for a total of 750 pixels. Then, the first layout for this example shows that if the container is 750 pixels, the width of all three elements will be the same as their flex-basis properties. As the container gets narrower, though, the size of the aside and section change based on their flex-shrink values.

In this example, there are two flex-shrink units: one for the section and one for the aside. That means that as the container shrinks, 1/2 of the negative space will be subtracted from the flex-basis of the section and aside. Because the flex-shrink property of the nav element is set to 0, though, that element won't shrink.

You can see how this works in the second layout for this example. Here, the container is 500 pixels wide, which is 250 pixels less than the width specified by the flex-basis properties. So 1/2 of that space, or 125 pixels, will be subtracted from the flex-basis of the section element, and 1/2 of that space will be subtracted from the flex-basis of the aside element. That means that the width of each of these elements will be 125 pixels, and the width of the nav element will remain at 250 pixels.

The last example in this figure shows how to use the shorthand flex property. This property specifies the flex-grow, flex-shrink, and flex-basis values in that order, and W3C recommends that you use the flex property rather than the individual properties. If you review the three layouts for this example, you shouldn't have any trouble understanding how this property works.

Although it isn't shown here, you should realize that you can use relative units for the flex-basis property when you use flex-grow and flex-shrink. Then, the relative lengths are converted to absolute lengths before the widths of the flex items are calculated. You can also use a combination of relative and fixed units for the flex items.

The flex-shrink and flex properties

Property	Description
flex-shrink	A number that indicates how much a flex item will shrink relative to other flex items in the flex container. A value of 0 means that the item won't shrink. The default is 1.
flex	The shorthand property for setting the flex-grow, flex-shrink, and flex-basis properties.

The HTML for a simple page layout

```
<main>
    <nav>Navigation</nav>
    <section>Content</section>
    <aside>Sidebar</aside>
</main>
```

CSS that uses the flex-basis and flex-shrink properties

```
nav, section, aside { flex-basis: 250px; }
nav { flex-shrink: 0; }
section, aside { flex-shrink: 1; }
```

The layout at 750 pixels wide

Navigation	Content	Sidebar

The layout at 500 pixels wide

Navigation	Content	Sidebar

CSS that uses the shorthand flex property

```
nav, aside { flex: 1 1 100px; }
section { flex: 2 2 300px; }
```

The layout at 500 pixels wide

Navigation	Content	Sidebar

The layout at 750 pixels wide

Navigation	Content	Sidebar

The layout at 250 pixels wide

Navigation	Content	Sidebar

Description

- The flex-shrink property works like the flex-grow property, but it's used when the flex items occupy more space than what's available within a container.

Figure 9-6   How to allocate space to flex items (part 2 of 2)

How to change the order of flex items

By default, the flex items within a container are displayed in the order that they appear in the HTML. If the flex-direction property is set to row, that means that the items are displayed from left to right. If the flex-direction property is set to column, the items are displayed from top to bottom.

To change that order, though, you can use the order property, as shown in figure 9-7. Here, you can see the HTML for a simple page that consists of a header element, a main element that contains aside and section elements, and a footer element. Then, if you set the display property of the main element to flex, the aside and section elements will be displayed side-by-side with the aside element on the left and the section element on the right. This assumes that the flex-direction property has the default value of row.

When the page is displayed at a narrow width, though, you may want to display the flex items in a column instead of a row. You may also want to change the order of the flex items. To do that, you can use a media query like the one in this figure.

In this example, the style rules are applied when the screen width is less than or equal to 760 pixels. Then, the flex direction of the main element is changed so the section and aside are displayed in a column. Also, since the order property for the section is set to 1 and the order property for the aside is set to 2, the section is displayed before the aside.

The property for changing the order of flex items

Property	Description
order	Sets the order of a flex item relative to other flex items within a flex container.

The HTML for a page

```
<body>
    <header><h3>Header</h3></header>
    <main>
        <aside><h3>Sidebar</h3></aside>
        <section><h3>Section</h3></section>
    </main>
    <footer><h3>Footer</h3></footer>
</body>
```

A media query that changes the flex direction and reorders flex items

```
@media screen and (max-width: 760px) {
    main { flex-direction: column; }
    section { order: 1; }
    aside { order: 2; }
}
```

The page at a narrow width with the section and aside reordered

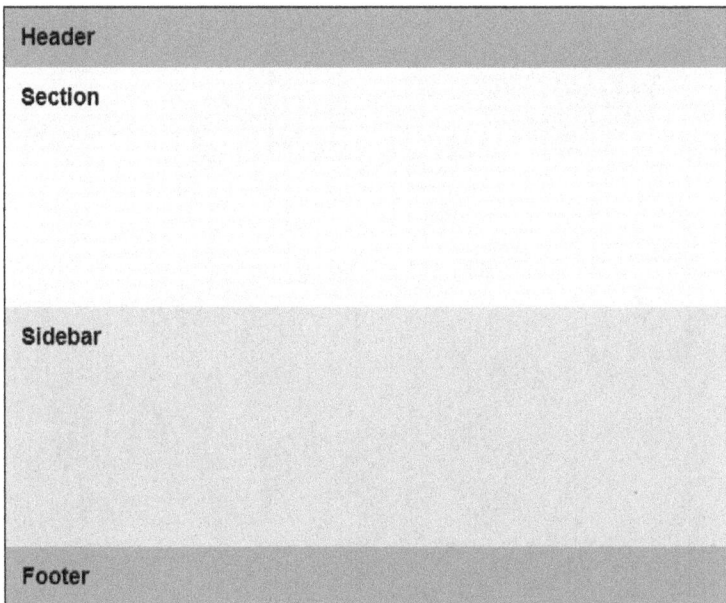

Description

- By default, the items within a flex container are displayed in the order in which they appear in the HTML. But you can use the order property to change that.

Figure 9-7   How to change the order of flex items

A responsive web page that uses flexbox

Now that you've learned the basic skills for using flexbox, you're ready to see a page that uses it for page layout and responsive web design.

The design of the web page

Figure 9-8 shows a Town Hall speaker page that uses flexbox for page layout. If you compare the desktop layout of this page to the one in figure 8-12 of chapter 8, you'll see that they're almost identical. In smaller layouts, however, the order of the article and the sidebar are changed so the sidebar is displayed before the article.

As you will see, flexbox is used for the navigation bar and the main content of this page. For smaller screens, flexbox is also used for the header.

A speaker page in desktop and mobile layouts

Description

- When this page is displayed on larger screens like a desktop, Flexible Box Layout is used for the navigation bar, the article, and the sidebar. When the page is displayed on smaller screens like a tablet or mobile phone, Flexible Box Layout is also used for the header.

- When the screen gets too narrow to display the article and sidebar side-by-side, media queries are used to change the flex direction from row to column and to change the order of the article and sidebar so the sidebar is displayed first.

Figure 9-8   The design of the web page

The HTML for the main structural elements

Figure 9-9 presents the HTML for the body of the speaker page. This code is almost identical to the code in chapter 8. To keep the focus on the use of flexbox, though, submenus aren't used for this page. As a result, the ul element for the menu bar consists of just five li elements.

The HTML for the main structural elements

```
<body>
    <header>
        <img src="images/logo.gif" alt="Town Hall Logo">
        <h2>San Joaquin Valley Town Hall</h2>
        <h3>Bringing cutting-edge speakers to the valley</h3>
    </header>
    <nav id="mobile_menu"></nav>
    <nav id="nav_menu">
        <ul>
            <li><a href="index.html">Home</a></li>
            <li><a href="speakers.html">Speakers</a></li>
            <li><a href="tickets.html">Get Tickets</a></li>
            <li><a href="members.html">Become a Member</a></li>
            <li class="lastitem" ><a href="aboutus.html">About Us</a></li>
        </ul>
    </nav>
    <main>
        <article>
            <h1>Fossil Threads in the Web of Life</h1>
            <img src="images/sampson.jpg" alt="Scott Sampson">
            <p>What's 75 million years old and brand spanking new? ... </p>
                .
                .
        </article>
        <aside>
            <h2>This season's guest speakers</h2>
            <nav>
                <ul>
                    <li>October: <a class="date_passed"
                        href="speakers/brancaccio.html">David Brancaccio</a></li>
                        .
                        .
                    <li>April: <a href="speakers/tynan.html">
                        Ronan Tynan</a></li>
                </ul>
            </nav>
        </aside>
    </main>
    <footer>
        <p>&copy; Copyright 2022 San Joaquin Valley Town Hall.</p>
    </footer>
</body>
```

Description

- The ul element for the menu bar will be implemented as a flexbox that contains the li elements as flex items.
- The main element will be implemented as a flexbox that contains the article and aside elements as flex items.
- In the media queries for smaller devices, the aside and article elements will be displayed in a column, and the aside element will be displayed before the article element.

Figure 9-9   The HTML for the main structural elements

The CSS for larger screens

Figure 9-10 shows the changes that were made to the CSS for the speaker page in chapter 8 so it now uses Flexible Box Layout. Here, the flexbox properties are highlighted so they're easy to identify.

But before you review this code, you should know that the header doesn't use flexbox for layout. Instead, it still floats the image to the left so the two headings are aligned to the right of it, but now the image isn't scalable. Beyond that, all float, width, and clear properties that are related to the navigation bar, article, and aside have been deleted. Otherwise, any properties that aren't shown here are the same as for the speaker page in chapter 8.

For the navigation menu, though, the display property of the ul element is set to flex. The flex-basis property is set to 100% so the menu occupies the full width of the screen. And the justify-content property is set to space-around so space is allocated evenly around the flex items. In addition, the flex-basis property of each li element is set to 20% so each of the five elements occupies the same amount of space.

For the main element, the display property is also set to flex. Then, the flex-basis properties of the article and aside elements that the main element contains are set to 60% and 40%. That way, their widths will remain the same relative to each other as the width of the screen changes.

Notice here that the max-height and min-height properties are also set for the aside element. If a maximum height isn't set, the background for the sidebar would extend the full height of the column. And if a minimum height isn't set, the content would extend beyond the bottom of the box when the page is displayed at narrow screen widths.

The CSS for larger screens

```
* the styles for the image in the header
header img {                              /* image isn't scaled */
    float: left;
    margin-left: 2.0202%;
}

* the styles for the navigation menu
#nav_menu ul {
    display: flex;                        /* make the unordered list a flexbox */
    flex-basis: 100%;                     /* full width of page */
    justify-content: space-around;        /* allocate space evenly */
    list-style-type: none;
    margin: 0;
    padding: 0;
}
#nav_menu ul li {
    flex-basis: 20%;                      /* each item occupies 20% of flexbox */
}

/* the styles for the main element */
main {
    display: flex;                        /* make the main element a flexbox */
}

/* the styles for the article */
article {
    flex-basis: 60%;                      /* 60% of the available width */
    margin: 2.0202% 0 2.0202%;
    padding: 1.5em 2.52525% 0 0;
}
article img {
    margin-bottom: 1em;
    max-width: 100%;                      /* full width of article */
}

/* the styles for the sidebar */
aside {
    flex-basis: 40%;                      /* 40% of the available width */
    max-height: 200px;
    min-height: 180px;
    padding: 2.0202%;
    background-color: #ffebc6;
    margin: 1.5em 2.0202% 0 0;

}
```

How this CSS differs from the CSS in chapter 8

- The image in the header isn't scalable.
- Floating and clearing aren't used for the nav, article, and aside elements.
- The article and aside elements, as well as the <a> elements in the navigation menu, don't have width properties.

Figure 9-10   The CSS for larger screens

The CSS for smaller screens

Figure 9-11 shows the media query that's applied to this page when its width is 796 pixels or less. This is the width at which the layout is changed to a single column. The other media queries are identical to the ones shown in chapter 8 for a desktop-first design.

First, notice how the properties for the main, article, and aside elements have been changed. To display the article and sidebar in a single column for smaller screen widths, the flex-direction property of the main element has been set to column. Then, to display the sidebar before the article on the page, the order property of the aside element is set to 1, and the order property of the article element is set to 2. In short, flexbox makes it much easier to adjust a page for smaller screens.

Now, look at the changes for the header. Here, the display property of the header element is set to flex, and the flex direction is set to column. That means that the three flex items in the header (the image and the two headings) will be displayed vertically. Then the align-items property is used to center the three items. This is an easy way to vertically align and center the items.

Note too that the width of the image in the header is changed to 60 pixels. That means that the image will be displayed at less than its native size on smaller screens. When you don't scale an image, you can use media queries like this one to change its size.

The media query that changes the display to a single column

```
@media only screen and (max-width: 796px) {
    header {
        display: flex;                /* make the header a flexbox */
        flex-direction: column;       /* display flex items in a column */
        align-items: center;          /* center each item within the column */
    }
    header h2, header h3, header img {
        margin-left: 0;
    }
    header img {
        float: none;
        margin-left: 0;
        width: 60px;
    }
    main {
        flex-direction: column;
    }
    article {
        order: 2;                     /* display article after aside */
    }
    aside {
        order: 1;                     /* display aside before article */
        width: 95.9596%;
        margin: 0;
        padding: 1em 2.0202% 0;
    }
}
```

How the CSS for smaller screens differs from the CSS in chapter 8

- A flexbox is used for the header, and the three flex items that it contains are centered in a column. The width of the header is also reduced.
- The article and aside are displayed in a column, and their HTML order is reversed.

Figure 9-11   The CSS for smaller screens

Perspective

In this chapter, you have seen how Flexible Box Layout lets you lay out the elements of a page without using floats. However, because you can only use flexbox to lay out elements in rows or columns, its use is limited to pages with simple layouts and to simple components within a page such as navigation menus. To develop more complex layouts, though, you can use Grid Layout, as shown in the next chapter.

Terms

Flexible Box Layout	main start
flexbox	main end
flex container	cross start
flex item	cross end
main axis	main size
flex direction	cross size
cross axis	

Summary

- *Flexible Box Layout*, or *flexbox*, can be used to lay out page elements in columns or rows.

- A *flex container* contains one or more *flex items* that are laid out along the *main axis*. The *flex direction* determines the orientation of the main axis, and the *cross axis* is perpendicular to the main axis.

- You set the display property of an element to flex or flex-inline to make that element a flex container. Then, all block-level child elements become flex items.

- You set the flex-direction property of a flex container to row or column to determine whether the items in the container are laid out horizontally or vertically.

- You can use the justify-content property to align the flex items along the main axis of a flex container, and you can use the align-items and align-self properties to align the flex items along the cross axis.

- You can use the flex-wrap property to wrap the flex items within a container when there's not enough room for them within the flex container, and you can use the align-content property to change the vertical alignment of wrapped items.

- You can use the flex-grow, flex-shrink, and flex-basis properties to determine the space that's allocated to each flex item. You can also use the shorthand flex property in place of these three properties.

- By default, the flex items in a container are displayed in the order in which they appear in the HTML. To change that order, though, you can use the order property.

Exercise 9-1   Convert the Town Hall home page to Flexible Box Layout

In this exercise, you'll convert the Town Hall home page that you worked on in exercise 8-1 so it uses Flexible Box Layout. When this page is displayed on larger screens like a desktop, the navigation bar should be a flexbox that contains the menu items, and the main element should be a flexbox that contains the aside and section elements. When the page is displayed on smaller screens like a phone in portrait orientation, the aside should be below the section.

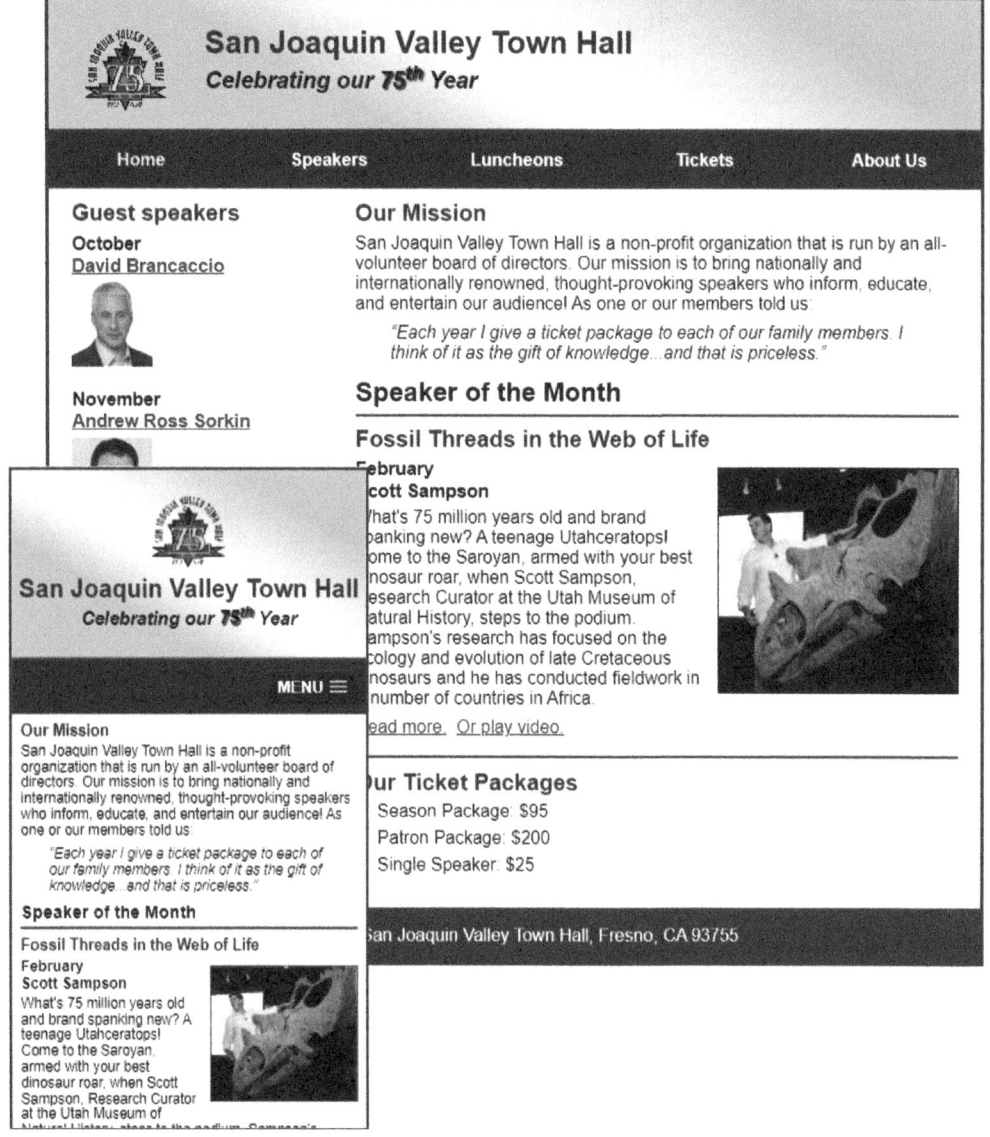

Open the HTML and CSS files for this page

1. Use your text editor to open and review these HTML and CSS files:

   \html_css_5\exercises\town_hall_2\c9_index.html

   \html_css_5\exercises\town_hall_2\c9_main.css

2.   Test the index page to see how it looks, and adjust the width of the browser window to see how it works for responsive web design.

3.   In the CSS file, delete any float or clear properties...except for the float properties for the images in the header and article. Now, test the page to see how the page layout has been disrupted.

Change the navigation menu so it uses flex

4.   In the CSS file, set the display property for the ul element in the navigation menu so the li elements are displayed as block elements within a flex container. Then, set the flex-basis property so the flex container occupies 100% of the page width. And set the justify-content property so space is allocated evenly between the flex items. Then, test this change, which should work.

5.   Change the width property for the li items to the flex-basis property and set it to 20%. Then, test this change to see that both the width and the flex-basis properties get the same result.

Change the main element so it uses flex

6.   In the CSS file, set the display property for the main element so the section and aside child elements are displayed in a flex container.

7.   Set the flex-basis properties of the section and aside elements to 70% and 30%, and delete their width properties. Then, set the order properties of these elements so the aside element is displayed before the section element.

8.   Test these changes to be sure that the aside and section elements are laid out properly when the page is displayed at its maximum width. Then, reduce the width of the browser to see that the widths of these elements change based on the values of their flex-basis properties.

Change the media query for smaller devices

9.   In the CSS file, locate the media query that checks that the viewport width is 648 pixels or less. Within this query, change the main element so the section and aside elements that it contains are displayed in a column and so the section is displayed before the aside.

10.   Test this page to be sure that it's displayed properly at all widths, and make any final adjustments that are needed.

Chapter 10

How to use Grid Layout for Responsive Web Design

If you read chapter 9, you know how to use Flexible Box Layout to lay out simple pages and the components within a page. Now, in this chapter, you'll learn how to use another CSS module called Grid Layout. As you'll see, you can use Grid Layout to develop complex page layouts more easily than you can with Flexible Box Layout or floats.

Getting started with Grid Layout

Grid Layout, or *grid*, lets you lay out content in both rows and columns. This chapter starts by presenting the basic skills that you need for doing that.

An introduction to Grid Layout

The diagram in figure 10-1 illustrates the basic components of a grid layout. Here, the *grid container* consists of four rows and four columns. These rows and columns are referred to as *grid tracks*. The lines on either side of a grid track are referred to as *grid lines*. Two adjacent row and column grid lines form a *grid cell*. And two or more grid cells that form a rectangle can be combined into a *grid area*.

In simple layouts like the ones you'll see in the next few figures, each cell contains a *grid item*, which is a structural element like a nav or div element. In more complex layouts, though, you define the grid areas that contain the grid items.

Although it's not shown here, grid tracks can also have space between them. These spaces are called *gutters* or *alleys*, and you'll learn more about them in the next figure.

The components of a grid layout

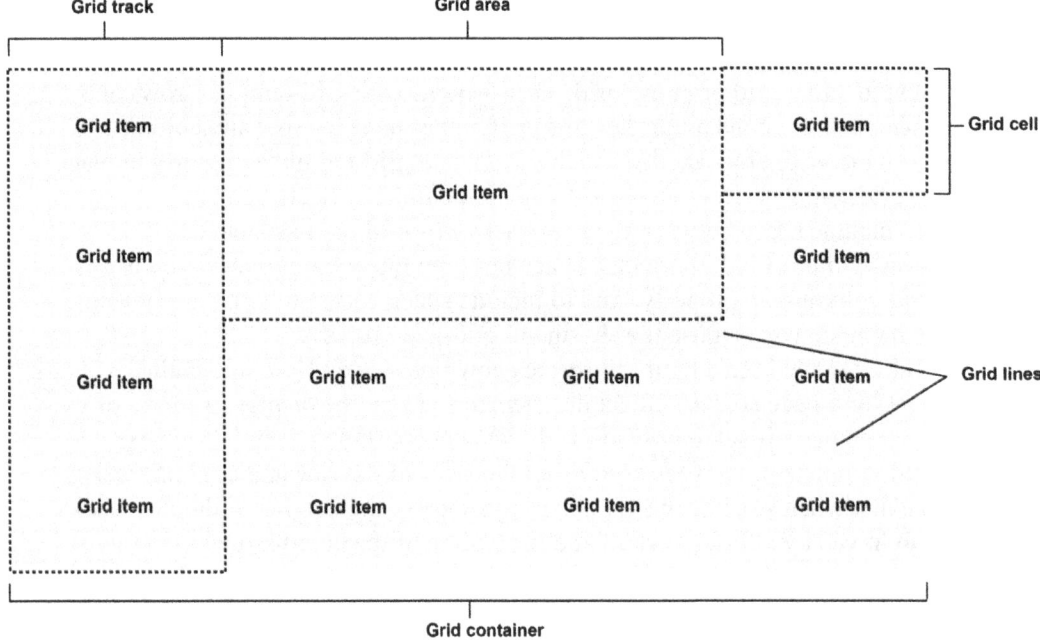

Grid layout terms

- A *grid* consists of a *grid container* with one or more columns and rows.
- A *grid track* is a column or row within the grid container.
- The lines on each side of the grid tracks are called *grid lines*.
- A *grid cell* is the space made up by two adjacent row and column grid lines.
- A *grid area* is a rectangular area that consists of one or more grid cells.

Description

- *Grid Layout*, or *grid*, is a 2-dimensional layout module in CSS that allows you to lay out web pages in a more efficient and familiar way.
- In a simple layout, each cell of a grid can contain a *grid item*. In a more complex layout, you define *grid areas* that contain the grid items.

Figure 10-1   An introduction to Grid Layout

How to create a basic grid

To create a basic grid, you use the properties presented in figure 10-2. To start, you create a grid container by setting the display property of a block element to either grid or inline-grid. Then, you use the grid-template-rows and grid-template-columns properties to specify the size of the row and column tracks in the grid. You can also use the shorthand grid-template property in place of the grid-template-rows and grid-template-columns properties.

To include space between the row tracks in a grid, you use the grid-row-gap property. To include space between the column tracks, you use the grid-column-gap property. And to include space between both the row and column tracks, you can use the shorthand grid-gap property.

The example in this figure illustrates how this works. Here, the main element for a page consists of six div elements. Then, the display property of the main element is set to grid so the div elements become grid items. Next, the grid-template property is used to set the sizes of the row and column tracks. Notice that when you use this property, you specify the heights of the row tracks first, followed by a forward slash and the widths of the column tracks. In this case, two row tracks are created, each with a height of 100 pixels, and three column tracks are created, each with a width of 150 pixels.

Finally, the grid-gap property is used to set the space between the row tracks to 15 pixels and the space between the column tracks to 20 pixels. If you wanted the row and column tracks to have the same space between them, you could code a single value that represents the space between the row tracks. Then, the space between the column tracks will default to this same value.

The layout in this figure shows the result of these values, which is a grid with two rows and three columns for a total of six cells. Then, the six div elements are placed in these cells. The important thing to notice here is the order in which the div elements are displayed. Specifically, they're displayed from left to right and from top to bottom according to the order that they appear in the HTML.

Properties for creating a grid

Property	Description
display	The type of grid used for an HTML element: grid (rendered as a block) or inline-grid (rendered as inline content).
grid-template-rows	The size of the row tracks in a grid.
grid-template-columns	The size of the column tracks in a grid.
grid-template	The shorthand property for setting the grid-template-rows and grid-template-columns properties.
grid-row-gap	The space between row tracks.
grid-column-gap	The space between column tracks.
grid-gap	The shorthand property for setting the grid-row-gap and grid-column-gap properties.

The HTML for a 2 row x 3 column grid

```
<main>
    <div>Div 1</div> <div>Div 2</div> <div>Div 3</div>
    <div>Div 4</div> <div>Div 5</div> <div>Div 6</div>
</main>
```

The CSS for laying out the grid

```
div { background-color: #C8DFEE; }
main {
    display: grid;
    grid-template: 100px 100px / 150px 150px 150px;
    grid-gap: 15px 20px;
}
```

The resulting layout

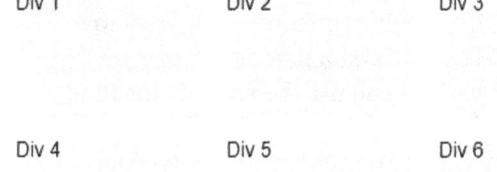

Div 1   Div 2   Div 3

Div 4   Div 5   Div 6

Description

- To define the rows and columns in a grid, you code one value for each row or column, and you separate the values with spaces. If you use the grid-template property, you code a forward slash (/) between the row and column values.
- If you use the grid-gap property to specify the gutters, you can omit the column gutter if it's the same as the row gutter.
- By default, the grid items are laid out from left to right and top to bottom.

Figure 10-2 How to create a basic grid

How to set the size of grid tracks

To set the size of the row and column tracks in a grid, you can use any of the fixed or relative units of measure that you learned about in chapter 4. In the previous figure, for example, you saw how to use pixels to set the size of row and column tracks.

When you use Grid Layout, though, you can also use the fr unit of measure to specify the size of grid tracks. This unit of measure represents a fraction of the space that's available within a container, and it's particularly useful for allocating space for fluid layouts.

In addition to the fr unit, you can use the repeat() function to repeat one or more track sizes the specified number of times. And you use the minmax() function to specify the minimum and maximum sizes for a grid track.

The first example in figure 10-3 shows how the repeat() function and the fr unit of measure work. This example, as well as the others in this figure, use the same HTML that you saw in figure 10-2. They also set the background color of the div elements as shown in that figure.

In this first example, the first repeat() function on the grid-template property indicates that the grid should contain two row tracks, each with a height of 50 pixels. Then, the second repeat() function indicates that the grid should contain three column tracks, each with a width of 1fr. That means that each of the columns will occupy 1/3 of the available space within the container.

If, for example, the width of the container is 640 pixels, 600 pixels are left after the two 20-pixel column gaps are subtracted from 640. Then, the 600 is divided by 3, which makes each column track 200 pixels wide.

The second example in this figure shows that you can combine fixed, relative, and fractional track sizes. Here, the first column track is fixed at 100 pixels. Then, the second column track is set to 30% of the container width, or 192 pixels using a 640-pixel container. Finally, the third column track is set to 1fr, which represents the remaining space within the container, or 308 pixels.

The third example in this figure shows that you can use the repeat() function to repeat more than one column track. Specifically, this repeat() function repeats two column tracks that are 50 pixels and 1fr wide two times. This creates four column tracks. The first and third column tracks are 50 pixels wide, and the second and fourth column tracks are 240 pixels wide using a 640-pixel container.

A unit of measure for specifying the size of grid tracks

Unit	Description
fr	Represents a fraction of the available space in a grid container. Use this unit when building fluid grid layouts or layouts with a combination of fixed and fluid tracks.

Functions for specifying the size of one or more grid tracks

Function	Description
repeat(*repeat, track-list*)	Repeats one or more track sizes in the track list. The repeat value can be a positive integer or the keywords auto-fill or auto-fit.
minmax(*min, max*)	The minimum and maximum size for a grid track.

CSS that uses the repeat() function with integers and fractional widths

```
main { display: grid;
       grid-template: repeat(2, 50px) / repeat(3, 1fr);
       grid-gap: 20px; }
```

The resulting layout

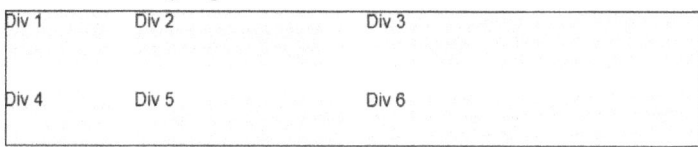

CSS that uses mixed units

```
main { display: grid;
       grid-template: repeat(2, 50px) / 100px 30% 1fr;
       grid-gap: 20px; }
```

The resulting layout

CSS that repeats two columns

```
main { display: grid;
       grid-template: repeat(2, 50px) / repeat(2, 50px 1fr);
       grid-gap: 20px; }
```

The resulting layout

Description

- You can define the size of a grid track using any unit of measure, including the fr unit.

Figure 10-3   How to set the size of grid tracks (part 1 of 2)

Instead of specifying the number of times that tracks will be repeated by a repeat() function, you can use the auto-fit or auto-fill keywords to determine how many tracks are created. The two examples in part 2 of this figure show how these keywords work in conjunction with the minmax() function.

Here, the minmax() function causes the column tracks to be a minimum of 75 pixels wide and a maximum of 1fr wide. That means that when the container becomes narrower than 550 pixels (6 column tracks at 75 pixels plus 5 column gaps at 20 pixels), the grid items will roll over to the next row track.

For instance, since the container in the first layout in each example is just 360 pixels wide, two of the grid items have rolled over to the second row track. In this case, the auto-fit and auto-fill keywords work the same way.

When the width of the container can hold more than the number of minimum-width columns, though, both the auto-fit and the auto-fill keywords display all of the columns in one row. However, these keywords don't display them the same way. Instead, the auto-fit keyword expands the width of the columns to fit the width of the container. This is shown by the second layout in the auto-fit example.

By contrast, the auto-fill keyword expands the columns until the width of the container is large enough to hold another minimum-width column, and then provides the space for that column. This is shown by the second layout in the auto-fill example.

If this is hard to visualize, and it is, you can experiment with the examples for this chapter. That will help you decide which of these keywords you need to use. In most cases, though, the auto-fit keyword will probably give you the result that you're looking for.

CSS that uses auto-fit and the minmax() function with the repeat() function

```
main {
    display: grid;
    grid-template: repeat(2, 50px) / repeat(auto-fit, minmax(75px, 1fr));
    grid-gap: 20px; }
```

The layout when the container is 360 pixels wide

Div 1	Div 2	Div 3	Div 4
Div 5	Div 6		

The layout when the container is 720 pixels wide

Div 1	Div 2	Div 3	Div 4	Div 5	Div 6

CSS that uses auto-fill and the minmax() function with the repeat() function

```
main {
    display: grid;
    grid-template: repeat(2, 50px) / repeat(auto-fill, minmax(75px, 1fr));
    grid-gap: 20px; }
```

The layout when the container is 360 pixels wide

Div 1	Div 2	Div 3	Div 4
Div 5	Div 6		

The layout when the container is 720 pixels wide

Div 1	Div 2	Div 3	Div 4	Div 5	Div 6	

Description

- The minmax() function is typically used within the track list of the repeat() function to specify the minimum and maximum sizes of one or more tracks.

- When you use the auto-fit keyword on the repeat() function, as many grid items as will fit in the available space will be placed in the container and they will be expanded when necessary to fit the available space.

- The auto-fill keyword works like the auto-fit keyword until the available space is large enough to provide for additional minimum-sized grid items. Then, this keyword provides enough space for those items.

Figure 10-3   How to set the size of grid tracks (part 2 of 2)

The properties for aligning grid items and tracks

When you create a grid, you can align the column tracks it contains horizontally if the tracks are less than the width of the container, and you can align the row tracks vertically if the tracks are less than the height of the container. You can also align the grid items within a grid area both horizontally and vertically.

The first two tables in figure 10-4 present the properties that you'll use for horizontal and vertical alignment. To align grid tracks, you can use the justify-content and align-content properties. These properties can have any of the values shown in the third table in this figure.

If you read chapter 9, you should already understand how these values work. Otherwise, you'll see these properties in action in the next figure. Or, if you want more information now, here's a quick summary.

First, the start, end, and center values work just the way you would expect. For horizontal alignment, start aligns the grid tracks at the left side of the container, end aligns the grid tracks at the right side of the container, and center aligns the grid tracks in the center of the container. Similarly, for vertical alignment, start aligns the grid tracks at the top of the container, end aligns the grid tracks at the bottom of the container, and center aligns the grid tracks in the center of the container. The default for both horizontal and vertical alignment of grid tracks is start.

If you specify stretch for the justify-content property, the grid tracks are stretched so they extend from the left side of the container to the right side of the container. If you specify stretch for the align-content property, the grid tracks are stretched so they extend from the top of the container to the bottom of the container.

The last three values provide for spacing out the grid tracks within a grid container. If you use space-between, any unused space is allocated evenly between the grid tracks. Space is also allocated evenly between the grid tracks when you use space-around, but half-size spaces are added before the first grid track and after the last grid track. And with space-evenly, full-size spaces are added before the first grid track and after the last grid track. Note that when you use these values, you won't typically include a gap between the grid tracks.

To align the grid items within a grid area, you can use the justify-items, justify-self, align-items, and align-self properties. These properties can have the values start, end, center, and stretch. The justify-items and align-items properties align all the grid items within a grid area, and the justify-self and align-self properties override the alignment of specific grid items within a grid area.

Properties for horizontal alignment

Property	Description
justify-content	Horizontally aligns grid tracks within a container when the tracks are less than the overall width of the container. The default is start.
justify-items	Horizontally aligns grid items within a grid area. The default is stretch.
justify-self	Overrides the grid area's horizontal alignment for an individual grid item.

Properties for vertical alignment

Property	Description
align-content	Vertically aligns grid tracks within a container when the tracks are less than the overall height of the container. The default is start.
align-items	Vertically aligns grid items within a grid area. The default is stretch.
align-self	Overrides the grid area's vertical alignment for an individual grid item.

Common values for these properties

Value	Description
start	Aligns grid items or grid tracks at the beginning of the container.
end	Aligns grid items or grid tracks at the end of the container.
center	Aligns grid items or grid tracks in the center of the container.
stretch	The grid items or grid tracks extend from the start of the container to the end of the container.
space-between	Allocates space evenly between grid tracks.
space-around	Allocates space evenly between grid tracks with half-size spaces before the first grid track and after the last grid track.
space-evenly	Allocates space evenly between grid tracks with full-size spaces before the first grid track and after the last grid track.

Description

- You can align the column tracks within a container horizontally, and you can align the row tracks vertically.
- You can also align the grid items within a grid area horizontally and vertically, and you can override a grid area's horizontal and vertical alignment for individual grid items.

Figure 10-4   The properties for aligning grid items and grid tracks

A page layout that uses alignment

To illustrate how alignment works, figure 10-5 presents a page layout that uses both horizontal and vertical alignment. Here, the HTML for the page shows that the body contains four structural elements: a nav element that displays a logo and a navigation menu, a section element that displays an image, a main element that displays three products, and a footer with a copyright notice.

The CSS for this page shows that all four of these structural elements are grid containers and all four of them occupy 100% of the width of the screen. Although it isn't shown here, the background color of these elements is set so you can see them against the white background of the page. In addition, the background color of the div elements within the first three structural elements is set so you can see where they appear within the structural elements.

The style rule for the nav element specifies that its container consists of one row track that is 80 pixels high and two column tracks. The first column track is 120 pixels wide and will display the company logo. The second column track occupies the remainder of the container's width (1fr), except for the 20-pixel gap between the two tracks.

The next style rule uses this selector to set the height of the second div element within the nav element to 40 pixels:

```
nav div:nth-of-type(2)
```

This is the div element for the navigation menu. Then, it uses the align-self property to align the menu vertically within the row track.

The style rule for the main element starts by setting the height of the element to 160 pixels. Then, it creates a grid with one row track that has a height of 120 pixels and three column tracks each with a width of 180 pixels. Because the height of the container is greater than the height of the row track, the align-content property is used to center the row track vertically in the container. In addition, the justify-content property is set to space-evenly so when the page is displayed at a width that's greater than the widths of the three column tracks, the column tracks will be spaced evenly.

Finally, the style rule for the footer element sets its height to 40 pixels. Then, the align-items and justify-items properties are used to center the grid item—in this case, the <p> element that contains the copyright—within the grid area for the footer. Note that I could have accomplished the same thing using the align-content and justify-content properties. That's because the size of the row and grid tracks aren't specified, which means that they're set so they can accommodate the content for the footer.

A page layout that uses alignment

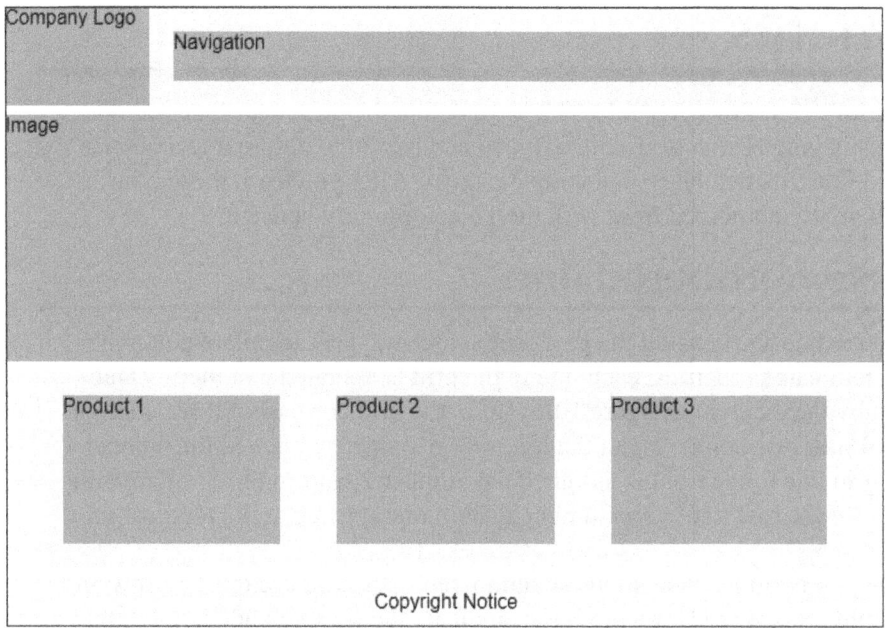

The HTML for the body of the page

```
<body>
    <nav><div>Company Logo</div><div>Navigation</div></nav>
    <section><div>Image</div></section>
    <main><div>Product 1</div><div>Product 2</div><div>Product 3</div></main>
    <footer><p>Copyright Notice</p></footer>
</body>
```

Some of the CSS for the page

```
nav, section, main, footer {
    display: grid;
    width: 100%;
    margin-bottom: 7px; }
nav {
    grid-template: 80px / 120px 1fr;
    grid-gap: 20px;
}
nav div:nth-of-type(2) {
    height: 40px;
    align-self: center; }
section { grid-template-rows: 200px; }
main {
    height: 160px;
    grid-template: 120px / repeat(3, 180px);
    align-content: center;
    justify-content: space-evenly; }
footer {
    height: 40px;
    align-items: center;
    justify-items: center; }
```

Figure 10-5   A page layout that uses alignment

How to define the grid areas for elements

In the topics that follow, you'll learn how to define the grid areas that you will use for displaying elements. To do that, you can use three different techniques: numbered lines, named lines, and template areas. After you learn those, you'll learn how to use numbered lines with the 12-column grid concept.

How to use numbered lines

When you define a grid using the grid-template-rows, grid-template-columns, and grid-template properties, each line in the grid is assigned a numeric value as shown by the diagram in figure 10-6. Here, the grid consists of three column tracks and four row tracks. Then, the leftmost grid line is assigned the number 1, the next grid line to the right is assigned the number 2, and so on. Similarly, the grid lines for the row tracks are numbered from one starting at the topmost grid line.

To position grid items using these numbered lines, you use the grid-row and grid-column properties. These properties indicate the starting and ending line numbers for the rows and columns that an element occupies. This is illustrated by the example in this figure. Although the HTML isn't shown, you should be able to determine its basic structure based on the positioning of the elements in the diagram. In this case, the body element consists of a header element, a nav element, three section elements, and a footer element.

In the CSS for this example, you can see that the style rule for the body element contains the properties that create this grid. In addition, it sets the height of the body to 600px and the width of the body to 100%. Although you won't typically set the height of a grid, it's set here because the body doesn't contain any content. And the width of the body is set to 100% so the grid will occupy the entire width of the browser window.

The CSS for the elements within the body each contain grid-row and grid-column properties. For example, the grid-row property for the header element indicates that the header occupies the first row track (grid row line 1 to grid row line 2), and the grid-column property indicates that the header occupies all three column tracks (grid column line 1 to grid column line 4). Similarly, the nav element occupies the second and third row tracks (grid row line 2 to grid row line 4) within the first column track (grid column line 1 to grid column line 2).

If you look at the definition of the grid in the style rule for the body element, you can see that grid-gap property is set to 16px. As you can see in the diagram, though, the grid-gap is only added between the grid areas that are defined by the grid-row and grid-column properties. In other words, grid gaps aren't added between cells within the same grid area.

Properties for using numbered lines to define grid areas

Property	Description
grid-row	The starting and ending line numbers for the rows of a grid area.
grid-column	The starting and ending line numbers for the columns of a grid area.

The numbered grid lines and HTML tags for a grid container

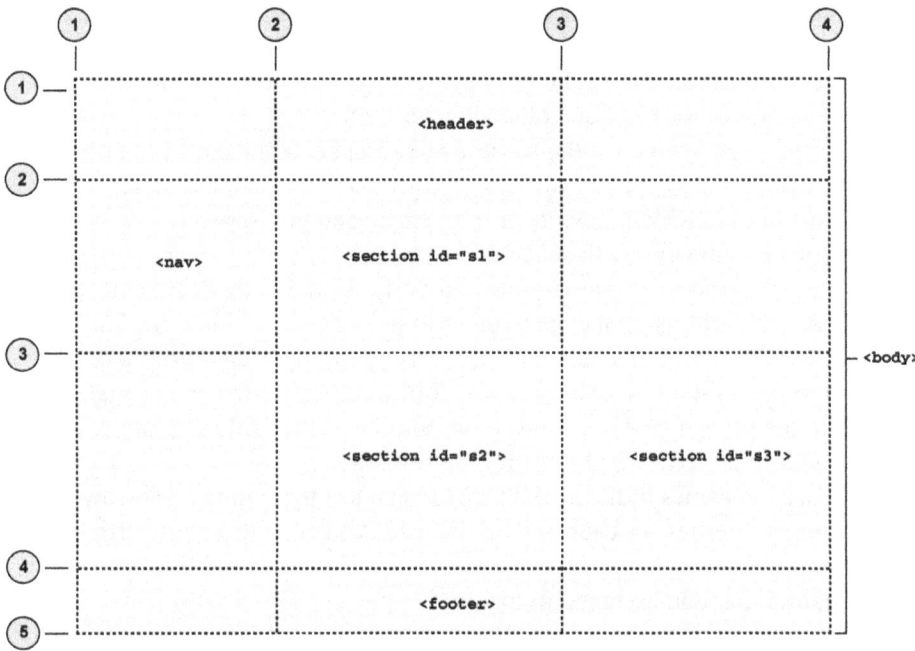

CSS that uses numbered grid lines to define the grid areas

```
body {
    margin: 0;
    height: 600px;
    width: 100%;
    display: grid;
    grid-template-columns: 200px 1fr 1fr;
    grid-template-rows: 80px 1fr 1fr 60px;
    grid-gap: 16px; }
header { grid-row: 1 / 2; grid-column: 1 / 4; }
nav    { grid-row: 2 / 4; grid-column: 1 / 2; }
#s1    { grid-row: 2 / 3; grid-column: 2 / 4; }
#s2    { grid-row: 3 / 4; grid-column: 2 / 3; }
#s3    { grid-row: 3 / 4; grid-column: 3 / 4; }
footer { grid-row: 4 / 5; grid-column: 1 / 4; }
```

Description

- When you define a grid, each grid line is assigned a numeric value. You can use those numbers to identify the rows and columns for a grid area that an element occupies.

Figure 10-6   How to use numbered lines to define the grid areas

How to use named lines

Figure 10-7 shows how to get similar results by using named lines. Here, the diagram shows the names that have been assigned to each line in the grid. But note that some of the lines have more than one name.

For example, the names "body-start" and "nav-start" are assigned to the line at the left side of the first column track to indicate that it's at the start of the body and nav elements. Similarly, the names "nav-end" and "sec-start" are assigned to the line between the first and second column tracks to indicate that it's at the end of the nav element and the start of the section element. This can make it easier to remember the names of the lines as you code your CSS.

To name a grid line, you code the name within brackets on the grid-template-columns, grid-template-rows, and grid-template properties. You code these names in the position in which they occur in the grid, and you separate two or more names for the same line with spaces.

To illustrate, the grid-template-columns property for the body element in this figure shows how to assign names to the grid lines for the column tracks. This property starts with the two names that are assigned to the first grid line, followed by the size of the first column track, followed by the two names that are assigned to the second grid line, and so on. Similarly, the grid-template-rows property assigns names to the grid lines for the row tracks.

After you assign names to the grid lines, you can use them in the grid-row and grid-column properties for each area in the grid. You code these properties the same way you do when you position grid items using numbered lines, except you use the names that you assigned to the lines.

In the example in this figure, the grid-row property for the header indicates that it occupies the row that starts at the grid line named "row1-start" and ends at the grid line named "row2-start". Then, the grid-column property indicates that it occupies the columns that start at the grid line named "body-start" and end at the grid line named "body-end". If you review the rest of the grid-row and grid-column properties, you should be able to figure out how they define the grid areas shown in this figure.

The named lines for a grid container

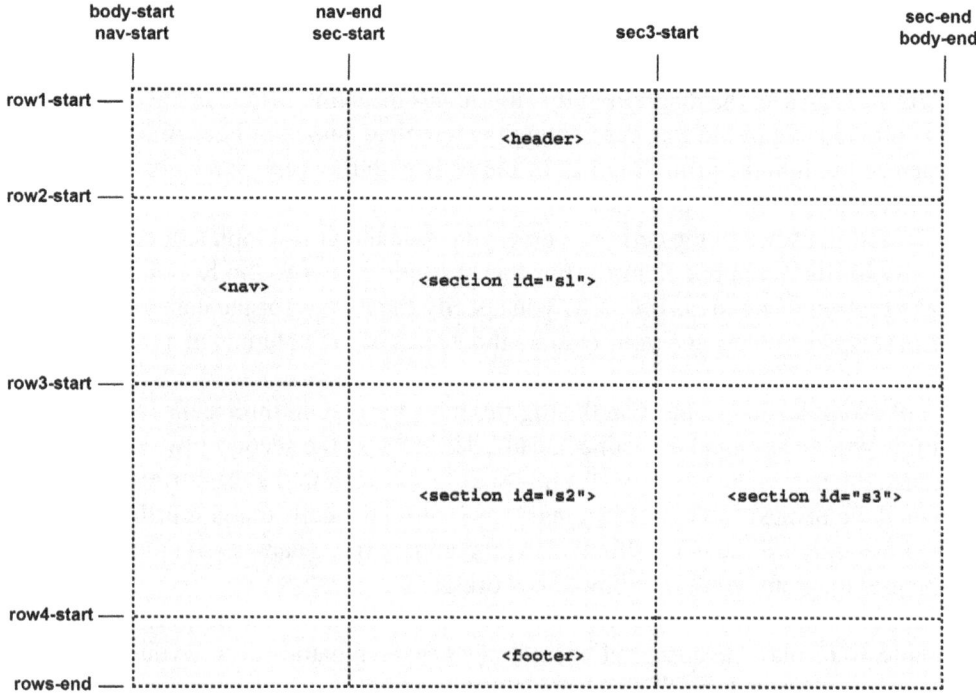

CSS that uses named lines to define the grid areas

```
body {
    display: grid;
    ...
    grid-template-columns: [body-start nav-start] 200px [nav-end sec-start]
        1fr [sec3-start] 1fr [sec-end body-end];
    grid-template-rows: [row1-start] 80px [row2-start] 1fr
        [row3-start] 1fr [row4-start] 60px [rows-end];
    grid-gap: 16px; }
header { grid-row: row1-start/row2-start; grid-column: body-start/body-end; }
nav    { grid-row: row2-start/row4-start; grid-column: nav-start/nav-end; }
#s1    { grid-row: row2-start/row3-start; grid-column: sec-start/sec-end; }
#s2    { grid-row: row3-start/row4-start; grid-column: sec-start/sec3-start; }
#s3    { grid-row: row3-start/row4-start;
           grid-column: sec3-start/sec-end; }
footer { grid-row: row4-start/rows-end; grid-column: body-start/body-end; }
```

Description

- To name the lines in a grid, you code the name or names of each line in brackets on the grid-template-columns and grid-template-rows properties in the position they appear in the grid.

- To identify the rows and columns for a grid area that an element occupies, you code the line names on the grid-row and grid-column properties.

Figure 10-7   How to use named lines to define the grid areas

How to use template areas

Because numbered and named lines can be tedious to use, it's often easier to use template areas to position grid items. Figure 10-8 shows how this works.

As you can see, the diagram in this figure has the same layout as the diagram in the previous figure. In this case, though, a template name has been assigned to each cell within the grid. Then, all of the cells with the same name are considered part of the same grid area.

To assign names to the cells in a grid, you code the grid-template-areas property for the container element. For this example, that's the body element. On the grid-template-areas property, you specify the names for the cells in each row as separate values, and you separate the names of the columns in a row with spaces.

For example, the property in this figure indicates that all three cells in the first row will be assigned the name "head". The cells in the second row will be assigned the names "navi", "sec1", and "sec1". The cells in the third row will be assigned the names "navi", "sec2", and "sec3". And the cells in the fourth row will all be assigned the name "foot". If you compare these names with the ones in the grid diagram, you'll see how this works.

To place an element within a grid area, you use the grid-area property. For example, to display the header element in the grid area name "head", you set its grid-area property to "head". Similarly, to display the nav element in the grid area named "navi", you set its grid area property to "navi". As you can see, this makes it easier to tell where an element is going to be positioned than when you use numbered lines.

When you use template areas, you should know that you don't have to assign a name to every cell in the grid. However, you do have to indicate the position of unnamed cells on the grid-template-areas property. To do that, you code a period as a placeholder for the cell. For example, if you didn't need to place a grid item in the cell in this figure named "sec3", you could code the grid-template-areas property like this:

```
grid-template-areas:
    "head head head"
    "navi sec1 sec1"
    "navi sec2 ."
    "foot foot foot";
```

Properties for using template areas to define grid areas

Property	Description
grid-template-areas	Names the grid areas for the elements. A row is created for each string, and a column is created for each named cell in a string.
grid-area	Identifies the named grid area that an element occupies.

The template names for each cell within a grid container

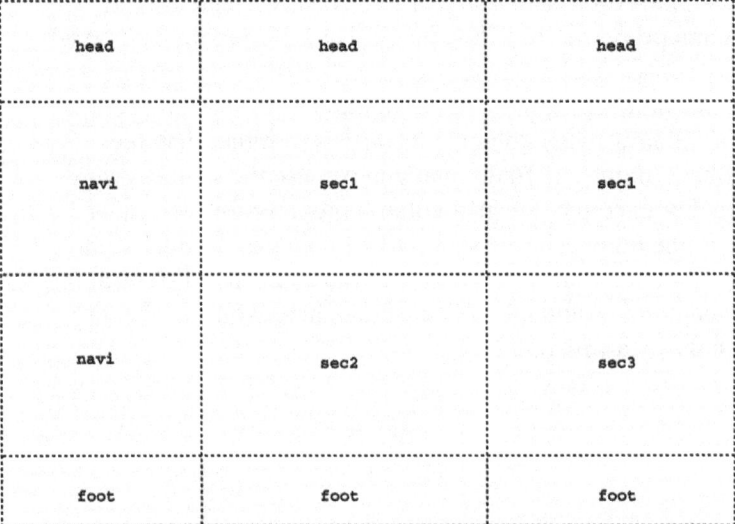

CSS that uses template names to define the grid areas

```
body {
    display: grid;
    grid-template-columns: 200px 1fr 1fr;
    grid-template-rows: 80px 1fr 1fr 60px;
    grid-gap: 16px;
    grid-template-areas:
        "head head head"
        "navi sec1 sec1"
        "navi sec2 sec3"
        "foot foot foot"; }
header { grid-area: head; }
nav     { grid-area: navi; }
#s1     { grid-area: sec1; }
#s2     { grid-area: sec2; }
#s3     { grid-area: sec3; }
footer { grid-area: foot; }
```

Description

- All of the cells with the same name form a grid area that spans those cells.
- If you don't want to include a cell in a grid area, you can code a period in place of a template name.

Figure 10-8   How to use template areas to define the grid areas

How to use the 12-column grid concept

In figure 10-6, you learned how to position grid items using numbered lines. Now, figure 10-9 shows you how to use this technique to implement the 12-column grid concept. This is a popular layout concept that's used frequently with Responsive Web Design.

As you can see, a grid container that uses this concept consists of 12 proportionally-sized columns. To create these columns, you can use the repeat() function to create 12 columns each with a size of 1fr. Then, you can use the grid-row and grid-column properties to define the grid areas using the numbered lines.

When you use this technique, it can be easier to indicate the starting column number for a grid area and how many columns it consists of rather than the starting and ending column numbers. To do that, you can use the span keyword as shown in this figure. For example, the grid-column property for the header indicates that it starts at line number 1 and spans all 12 columns. Similarly, the grid-column property for the section with the id "s1" indicates that it starts at column 5 and spans 8 columns. Although it's not shown here, you can also use the span keyword with the grid-row property.

The 12-column grid for a grid container

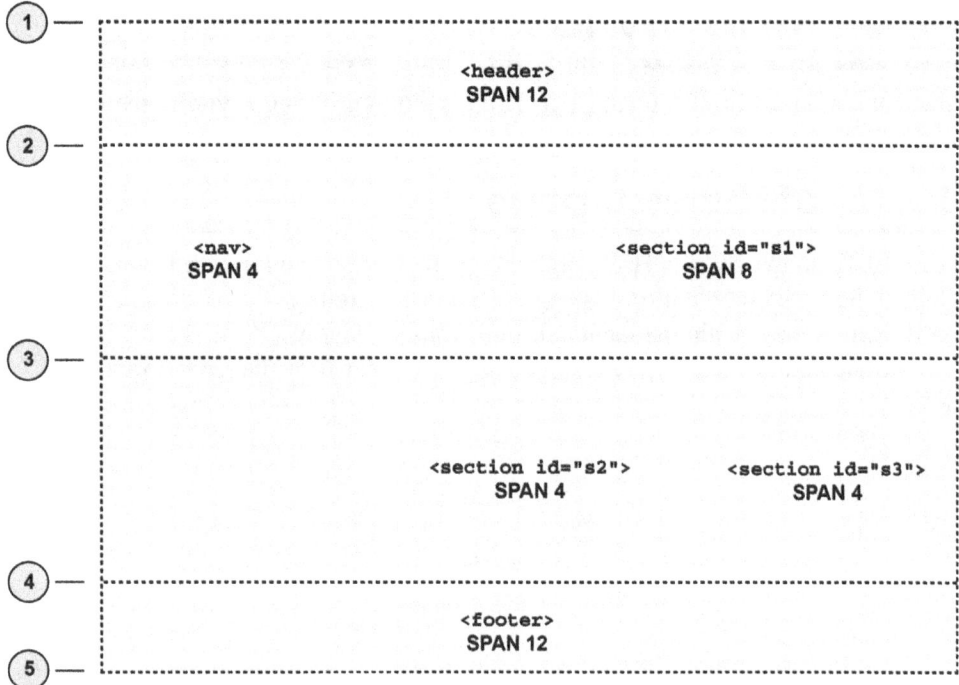

CSS that uses a 12-column grid to define the grid areas

```
body {
    display: grid;
    grid-template-columns: repeat(12, 1fr);
    grid-template-rows: 80px 1fr 1fr 60px;
    grid-gap: 16px; }
header { grid-row: 1 / 2; grid-column: 1 / span 12; }
nav    { grid-row: 2 / 4; grid-column: 1 / span 4; }
#s1    { grid-row: 2 / 3; grid-column: 5 / span 8; }
#s2    { grid-row: 3 / 4; grid-column: 5 / span 4; }
#s3    { grid-row: 3 / 4; grid-column: 9 / span 4; }
footer { grid-row: 4 / 5; grid-column: 1 / span 12; }
```

Description

- The 12-column grid concept is a popular layout concept that you can apply in grid layout using numbered lines. To create a 12-column grid, you use the repeat() function to define 12 proportional columns.

- To identify the columns that an element occupies, you can use numbered lines as shown in figure 10-5. Instead of specifying the ending line number, you can use the span keyword to indicate how many columns an element spans.

Figure 10-9   How to use the 12-column grid concept

A responsive web page that uses grid layout

Now that you know how to create a grid and position grid items, you're ready to see a page that uses Grid Layout.

The design of the web page

Figure 10-10 shows a Town Hall speaker page that uses Grid Layout. If you compare the desktop layout of this page to the one in figure 8-15 of chapter 8, you'll see that they're almost identical. In the mobile layouts, however, the order of the article and the sidebar are changed so the sidebar is displayed before the article.

A speaker page in desktop and mobile layouts

Description

- This web page uses Grid Layout to lay out all of the structural elements on the page.

- The widths of all of the structural elements are specified in fractional units or percents so they are fluid.

- Media queries are used to redefine the template areas when the screen gets too narrow to display the article and sidebar side-by-side. Then, the logo is displayed above the two headings in the header, the contents of the header and footer are centered, and the sidebar is displayed before the article.

Figure 10-10   The design of the web page

The HTML for the structural elements

Figure 10-11 presents the HTML for the body of the speaker page. This code is almost identical to the code for this page in chapter 8. To keep the focus on the use of grid, though, submenus aren't used for this page. As a result, the ul element for the navigation menu consists of just five li elements.

The HTML for the structural elements

```
<body>
    <header>
        <img src="images/logo.gif" alt="Town Hall Logo">
        <h2>San Joaquin Valley Town Hall</h2>
        <h3>Bringing cutting-edge speakers to the valley</h3>
    </header>
    <nav id="mobile_menu"></nav>
    <nav id="nav_menu">
        <ul>
            <li><a href="index.html">Home</a></li>
            <li><a href="speakers.html">Speakers</a></li>
            <li><a href="tickets.html">Get Tickets</a></li>
            <li><a href="members.html">Become a Member</a></li>
            <li class="lastitem" ><a href="aboutus.html">About Us</a></li>
        </ul>
    </nav>
    <main>
        <article>
            <h1>Fossil Threads in the Web of Life</h1>
            <img src="images/sampson.jpg" alt="Scott Sampson">
            <p>What's 75 million years old and brand spanking new? ... </p>
            .
            .
        </article>
        <aside>
            <h2>This season's guest speakers</h2>
            <nav>
                <ul>
                    <li>October: <a class="date_passed"
                        href="speakers/brancaccio.html">David Brancaccio</a></li>
                    .
                    .
                    <li>April: <a href="speakers/tynan.html">
                        Ronan Tynan</a></li>
                </ul>
            </nav>
        </aside>
    </main>
    <footer>
      <p>&copy; Copyright 2022 San Joaquin Valley Town Hall.</p>
    </footer>
</body>
```

Figure 10-11   The HTML for the structural elements

The CSS for the template areas

Figure 10-12 shows the CSS for the template areas on the speaker page. Here, the grid properties are highlighted so they're easy to identify.

When compared to the CSS for the speaker page in chapter 8, all float, width, and clear properties that are related to the navigation bar, article, or aside have been deleted. In addition, the values of the margin and padding properties have been simplified. Otherwise, any properties that aren't shown here are the same as for the speaker page in chapter 8.

To start, the style rule for the body includes the properties needed to lay out the main structural elements of the page using grid. That includes a display property that's set to grid and a grid-template property that defines a grid with four rows and one column. Notice that the heights of all four rows are specified as auto so they will always be tall enough for their content. Then, the width of the column is specified as 1fr so it will take up the full width of the body.

The style rule for the body also includes a grid-template-areas property. This property assigns a name to each of the cells defined by the grid-template property. Here, the column in the first row is named "head", the column in the second row is named "navi", and so on.

In the style rule for the header, the grid-area property places the header in the grid area that's defined by the cell named "head". Similarly, the grid-area property for the nav element with the id of nav_menu places the navigation menu in the grid-area named "navi".

Now, if you look at the style rule for the ul element within the navigation menu, you'll see that its display property is set to grid. This creates a grid within the grid area named "navi". Then, the grid-template property defines the grid with one row that will accommodate the height of its contents and five proportionally-sized columns. Finally, the align-content property centers the row vertically.

Similarly, the display property is used to make the main element a grid, and the grid-template property defines one row and two columns within the grid. Here, the columns are given the widths 1fr and 40%. That means that the size of the first column will be what's left over after 40% of the page width is allocated to the second column, minus any column gaps.

Next, the grid-template-areas property of the main element defines template areas for the two columns named "arti" and "side". Then, grid-area properties for the article and aside elements place these elements in the grid areas with these names.

Notice here that left and right margins are set for the main element. This simplifies the calculation of the margins, since it's based on the width of the body. By contrast, the margin or padding for an element in a grid is based on the width of the grid area. This is illustrated by the padding for the aside element, which is set to 5% of the width of the grid area that contains the aside.

CSS that uses template areas   **Page 1**

```css
/* the styles for the body */
body {
    ...
    display: grid;                      /* make the body a grid */
    grid-template: repeat(4, auto) / 1fr;
                                        /* define 4 rows and 1 column */
    grid-gap: 1.5em;                    /* define the gap between grid areas */
    grid-template-areas:                /* define the template areas */
        "head"
        "navi"
        "main"
        "foot";
}


/* the styles for the header */
header { grid-area: head; }             /* place the header in a grid area */


/* the styles for the navigation menu */
#nav_menu { grid-area: navi; }          /* place the navigation menu in a grid area*/
#nav_menu ul {
    ...
    display: grid;                      /* make the list a grid */
    grid-template: auto / repeat(5, 1fr); /* define 1 row and 5 columns */
    align-content: center;             /* center the row track vertically */
}


/* the styles for the main element */
main {
    margin: 0 2%;
    grid-area: main;                    /* place the main element in a grid area */
    display: grid;                      /* make the main element a grid */
    grid-template: auto / 1fr 40%;      /* define one row and two columns */
    grid-gap: 2%;                       /* define the gap between grid areas */
    grid-template-areas:                /* define the template areas */
        "arti side";
}


/* the styles for the article and sidebar */
article {
    grid-area: arti;  }                 /* place the article in a grid area */
article img {
    max-width: 100%;
    margin: 0 1.5em 1em 0; }
aside {
    max-height: 200px;                  /* to limit background */
    min-height: 180px;                  /* to limit background */
    padding: 5%;                        /* based on width of the grid area */
    background-color: #ffebc6;
    grid-area: side;                    /* place the aside in a grid area */
}
/* the styles for the footer */
footer { grid-area: foot; }             /* place the footer in a grid area */
```

Figure 10-12   The CSS for the template areas

The media query for smaller screens

Figure 10-13 shows the media query for screens that are 796 pixels or less. It starts by changing the grid gap for the body element to 0 so there's no space between the navigation menu and the main element. If you look back to the mobile layouts in figure 10-10, you'll see why that's necessary.

Next, a grid is defined for the header. This grid contains three rows for the logo, the h2 heading, and the h3 heading, and it uses a grid gap of .3 ems. It also specifies bottom padding, since no gap was specified for the grid for the body. Finally, the justify-items property is used to center the grid items in the header. Because of that, it isn't necessary to use the text-align property to center the content in the header.

Because the mobile navigation menu is displayed by this media query, this menu is placed in the grid area named "navi" that's defined by the grid-template-areas property for the body. You can see the grid-area property that accomplishes that in the style rule for the nav element with the id of mobile_menu.

Next, the grid for the main element is redefined. The new grid contains two rows and one column and a grid gap of .5 ems. In addition, the template areas are defined so the sidebar is displayed before the article.

The style rule for the article adds left and right margins of 2%. These margins are based on a grid area that's the full width of the screen. The spacing is also changed for the sidebar. In this case, the left and right padding is changed so it's based on a grid area that's the full width of the screen.

The media query for smaller screens

```
@media only screen and (max-width: 796px) {
    body {
        ...
        grid-gap: 0;                      /* no space between the menu and main */
    }
    header {
        padding-bottom: 1.5em;        /* because there's no row gap */
        display: grid;                           /* make the header a grid */
        grid-template: repeat(3, auto) / 1fr;     /* 3 rows and 1 column */
        grid-gap: .3em;                          /* gap between rows */
        justify-items: center;        /* center grid items horizontally */
    }
    #mobile_menu {
        display: block;
        grid-area: navi;              /* place the mobile menu in a grid area */
    }
    main {
        margin: 0;
        grid-template: auto auto / 1fr;        /* 2 rows and 1 column */
        grid-gap: .5em;                        /* gap between rows */
        grid-template-areas:                   /* template areas */
            "side"
            "arti";
    }
    article {
        margin: 1.2em 2%;
    }
    aside {
        padding: 1em 2% 0;
    }
}
```

Figure 10-13   The media query for smaller screens

The CSS for the page with a 12-column grid

Figure 10-14 shows the CSS for the speaker page when it uses a 12-column layout. This CSS uses the same HTML as in figure 10-11, except that the main element has been omitted. That way, all of the main structural elements—in this case, the header, navigation menu, article, sidebar, and footer—are at the same level and can be included in the same grid.

Here, you can see that the grid-template property for the body is defined so the grid has four auto-sized rows just as it did in the previous example. However, it's defined so it has 12 proportionally-sized columns. Then, the style rules for the main structural elements use the grid-row and grid-column properties to identify the grid areas for the elements.

For example, the grid area for the header occupies all 12 columns in the first row, and the navigation menu occupies all 12 columns in the second row. Then, the article occupies the first seven columns in the third row, and the sidebar occupies the last five columns in the third row. Finally, the footer occupies all 12 columns in the fourth row.

Additional changes are needed in the media query for screens that are 796 pixels or less. Here, because the article and sidebar are included in the main grid, the grid will have five rows when it's displayed in a single column instead of four rows. Then, the grid-row and grid-column properties are set for the mobile menu so it's displayed in the second row and first column. The grid-row property is set for the article so it's displayed in the fourth row below the sidebar. The grid-row property is set for the sidebar so it's displayed in the third row above the article. And the grid-row property is set for the footer so it's displayed in the fifth row. Finally, the grid-column property is set for the header, article, aside, and footer so they occupy just the one column in the grid.

In addition to the grid properties, you may notice that some of the margins are different than they are in the CSS that uses template areas. That's because the HTML for this page doesn't contain a main element.

So, instead of adding left and right margins to the main element, a left margin is added to the article and a right margin is added to the aside. These margins are based on the widths of the grid areas. Then, in the media query, the right margin for the sidebar is changed to 0 so there's no space between the right side of the sidebar and the right side of the browser window.

The CSS for a 12-column grid

```css
body { ...
    display: grid;
    grid-template: repeat(4, auto) / repeat(12, 1fr);    /* 12 columns */
    grid-gap: 1.5em;
}
header {
    grid-row: 1 / 2;                        /* row 1 of the grid area */
    grid-column: 1 / span 12;               /* all 12 columns */
}
#nav_menu {
    grid-row: 2 / 3;                        /* row 2 of the grid area */
    grid-column: 1 / span 12;               /* all 12 columns */
}
article {
    margin-left: 3.4%;
    grid-row: 3 / 4;                        /* row 3 of the grid area */
    grid-column: 1 / span 7;                /* first 7 columns */
}
aside { ...
    margin-right: 5%;
    grid-row: 3 / 4;                        /* row 3 of the grid area */
    grid-column: 8 / span 5;                /* last 5 columns */
}
footer {
    ...
    grid-row: 4 / 5;                        /* row 4 of grid area */
    grid-column: 1 / span 12;               /* all 12 columns */
}

/* the media query for smaller screens */
@media only screen and (max-width: 796px) {
    body { ...
        grid-template: repeat(5, auto) / 1fr;    /* 5 rows and 1 column */
        grid-gap: 0;        }
    header {
        grid-column: 1 / 2;                 /* 1 column */
        ... }
    #mobile_menu {
        display: block;
        grid-row: 2 / 3;                    /* row 2 of the grid area */
        grid-column 1 / 2;   }              /* 1 column */
    article { ...
        grid-row: 4 / 5;                    /* row 4 of the grid area */
        grid-column: 1 / 2; }               /* 1 column */
    aside {
        margin-right: 0;
        padding: 1em 2% 0;
        grid-row: 3 / 4;                    /* row 3 of the grid area */
        grid-column: 1 / 2; }               /* column 1 */
    footer {
        grid-row: 5 / 6;                    /* row 5 of the grid area */
        grid-column: 1 / 2; }               /* 1 column */
}
```

Figure 10-14   The CSS for the page with a 12-column grid

Common page layouts that use grid

In figure 10-5, you saw a common page layout that uses grid. Now, to complete this chapter, you'll see three more common layouts that you can implement using grid. Although the code for these layouts isn't presented here, you'll find these layouts as well as two more in the download for this book.

The headline and gallery layout

Part 1 of figure 10-15 presents a page layout called the *headline and gallery layout*. Like most layouts, it includes a company logo and navigation menu at the top of the page and a footer at the bottom of the page. In addition, it includes a headline and some text that describe the gallery of items that follows.

The entire body of this page is implemented as a grid with four rows and four columns. The first row includes the company logo and navigation menu, the second row includes the headline and text, the third row includes the gallery of items, and the fourth row includes the footer.

The first column is for the company logo, the second column is for the space between the company logo and the navigation menu, and the third and fourth columns are for the navigation menu. Four columns are used here so the width of the logo plus the space that follows are the same width as the navigation menu. Additional grids are used for the navigation menu and for the items within the gallery.

This type of layout can be used for any page that displays a series of items. For example, it can be used to display a gallery of images on a photographer's or museum's website. Or, it can be used on an ecommerce website where each item depicts a product or service offered by the company.

The fixed sidebar layout

Part 1 of figure 10-15 also presents a layout called the *fixed sidebar layout*. Here, the sidebar contains a company logo and a navigation menu that is fixed at the left side of the window. Because of that, the sidebar is always visible even when the user scrolls down the page.

Unlike the headline and gallery layout, the body of a page that uses the fixed sidebar layout can't be implemented as a grid. That's because the sidebar uses fixed positioning and the rest of the page doesn't. Instead, the contents of the sidebar and the rest of the page are implemented as two separate grids.

In this case, the grid for the sidebar includes two rows and one column. The first row contains the company logo, and the second row contains the navigation menu. Then, the navigation menu itself is implemented as a grid with four rows and one column.

You can use the fixed sidebar layout for any page that requires a fixed sidebar. Then, you can simply swap in the page layout you want to use on the right side of the page. In this case, the layout is for a page that includes a title, a main image, three products, and a footer.

The headline and gallery layout

The fixed sidebar layout

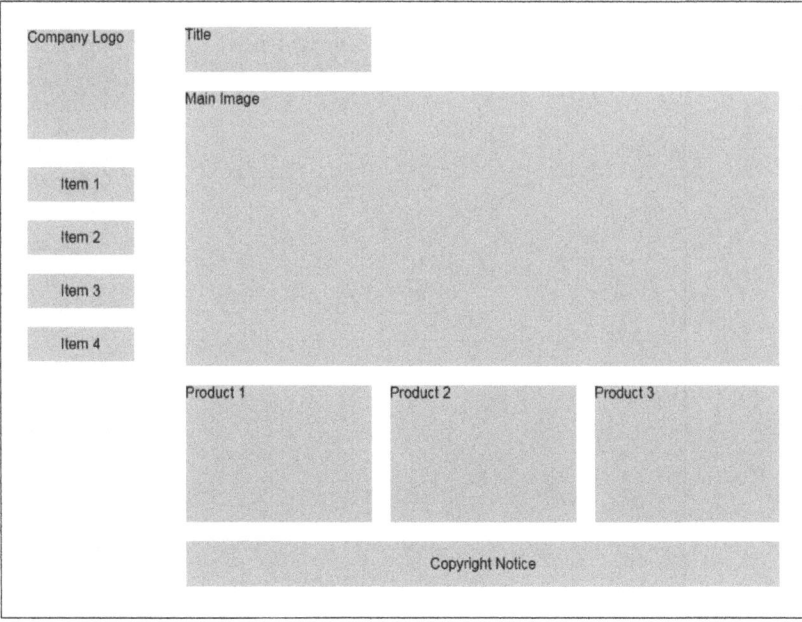

Figure 10-15   Common page layouts that use grid (part 1 of 2)

The advanced grid layout

Part 2 of figure 10-15 presents a layout called the *advanced grid layout*. As you can see, this layout is more complex than the layouts you saw in part 1 of this figure. Although you can use grid to develop layouts that are much more complex than what's shown here, this begins to illustrate the power of grid.

Like the headline and gallery layout, the advanced grid layout includes a company logo and a navigation menu at the top of the page, a headline and some text below that, and a footer at the bottom of the page. In addition, it includes two titles that identify two more areas of the page. The first area is for blog posts, and the second area is for featured products. Of course, you could use a layout like this for any content that you wanted to display in two areas.

Note that because all of the main structural elements for this page are at the same level, it uses only two grids. The first one is for all the elements that are children of the body element, and the second one is for the navigation menu.

Another way to implement this page would be to code the main content for this page—in this case, the titles, blog posts, and featured products—within a main element. Then, you could use another grid to lay out this content. This just shows that there's usually more than one way to lay out a page.

The advanced grid layout

Description

- The headline and gallery layout is frequently used to display a series of images.
- The sidebar in the fixed sidebar layout is displayed vertically and is fixed to the side of the window. That way, it's accessible even when you scroll through the page.
- Because the sidebar in the fixed sidebar layout uses fixed positioning, it's implemented as a grid that's separate from the grid for the rest of the page.
- The advanced grid layout can be used for many purposes. In the page shown above, it's used to display blog posts and featured products.

Figure 10-15   Common page layouts that use grid (part 2 of 2)

Perspective

In this chapter, you learned how to use Grid Layout to lay out the structural elements of a page in rows and columns, and you've seen how valuable it can be for complex page layouts. But keep in mind that it can also be used in conjunction with Flexible Box Layout. With those skills, you should be able to lay out your web pages just the way you want them.

Terms

Grid Layout	grid area
grid	gutter
grid container	alley
grid item	headline and gallery layout
grid track	fixed sidebar layout
grid line	advanced grid layout
grid cell	

Summary

- *Grid Layout* is a CSS layout module that lets you lay out web pages in rows and columns.

- A *grid* is a *grid container* that consists of columns and rows. These columns and rows are called *grid tracks*. The lines on each side of a grid track are called *grid lines*. And two adjacent row and column grid lines form a *grid cell*.

- A *grid area* consists of one or more grid cells that form a rectangle, and a grid item is an element that's stored in a grid area.

- When you create a grid, you set the sizes of the row and column tracks. You can add space called *gutters* or *alleys* between the grid tracks in a grid container.

- When you define the grid areas for the elements of a page, you can use numbered lines, named lines, and template areas.

- You can also use numbered lines to implement the 12-column grid concept, which is a popular approach for Responsive Web Design.

- When you use Grid Layout for page layout, you can embed smaller grids within the grid areas of the grid for an entire page.

- Although Grid Layout can be used for simple page layouts, it's especially useful for more complex layouts.

Exercise 10-1   Use template areas with the Town Hall home page

In this exercise, you'll lay out the Town Hall home page using template areas. On larger screens, the sidebar should be displayed to the left of the section. On smaller screens, the sidebar should be displayed below the section.

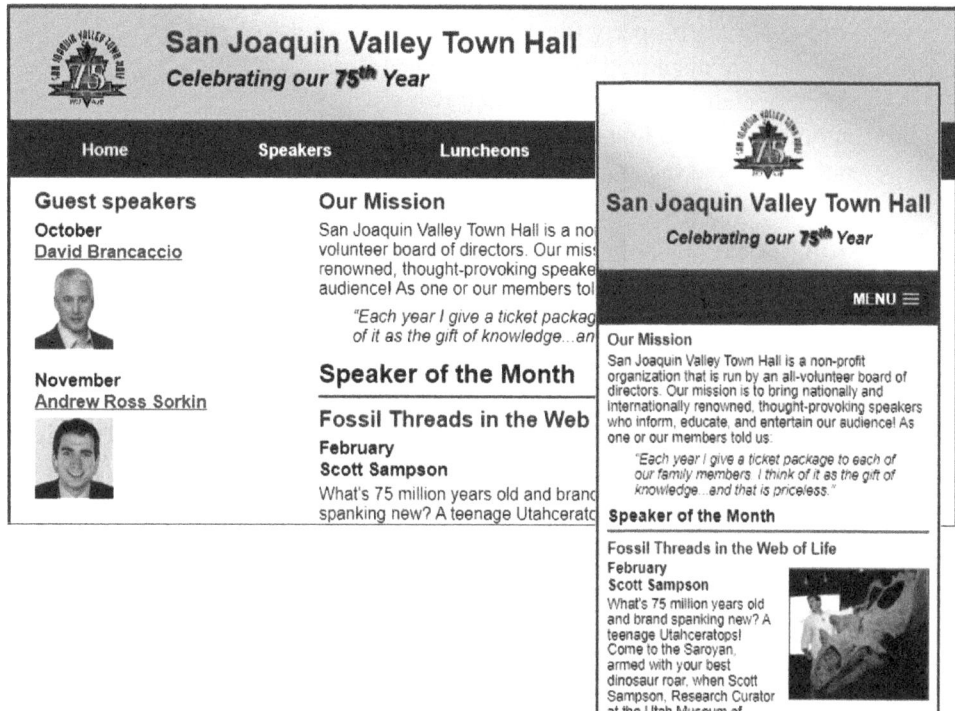

Open the HTML and CSS files for this page

1. Use your text editor to open these HTML and CSS files:

   `\html_css_5\exercises\town_hall_2\c10_index.html`

   `\html_css_5\exercises\town_hall_2\styles\c10_main.css`

2. Test the page to see that except for the two images, which are floated, everything is displayed in a single column. But in mobile layout in portrait orientation, everything looks okay.

Change the body so it uses template areas

3. In the CSS file, set the display property for the body so it uses grid. Then, define the template for the body so it has four rows and one column. All four rows should be sized automatically, and the column should be sized so it takes up the full width of the body. No gaps are required.

4. Define grid areas in the body for the header, navigation bar, main element, and footer. Then, code grid-area properties for each of these elements that place them in the right grid areas. Now test, these changes.

Change the navigation menu so it uses grid

5. Set the display property for the ul element in the navigation menu so the li elements are displayed within a grid. Then, define the template for the ul element so it has one row that's sized automatically and five columns that each occupy 1/5 the width of the menu. Center the row vertically within the grid, and test these changes.

Change the main element so it uses grid

6. Set the display property for the main element so the section and aside child elements are displayed in a grid container. Then, define the template for the main element with one row and two columns. The row should be sized automatically, the first column should occupy 30% of the available space in the grid, and the second column should occupy the rest of the remaining space after adding a column gap of 2.5%.

7. Define the grid areas for the section and aside using numbered lines. Then, test these changes.

Adjust the margins and padding

8. Adjust the top and bottom padding for the header, remembering that the padding is now based on the height of the grid area that contains the header. In this case, the height is 80 pixels, which is the same as the height of the image.

9. Adjust the left padding for the aside so it's based on the width of the aside.

10. Adjust the right padding for the section so it's based on the width of the section. Also, change the left padding for the section to 0 since a column gap is now being used.

Change the media query for smaller screens

11. Locate the media query that checks that the viewport width is 648 pixels or less. Then, within this query, create a grid for the header that has three rows and one column and a grid gap of .5 ems. All three rows should be sized automatically. Adjust the padding above and below the header based on the new height of the grid area. Then, test this change.

12. Place the mobile menu in the grid area for the navigation menu, and test this change.

13. Change the template for the main element so it contains two rows and one column. Both rows should be sized automatically, and the column should be the full width of the body. Then, redefine the positions of the section and aside in the grid using the numbered lines for the grid, and test these changes.

14. Change the left and right margins for the section and the left and right padding for the aside to 2.5%, since they're now based on the full width of the body. Also, remove the right padding from the section. Then, test these changes.

Section 3

More HTML and CSS skills as you need them

In section 1, you learned a subset of HTML and CSS skills that you can use for building most web pages. Now, in this section, you can add to those skills by learning new skills whenever you need them. To make that possible, each chapter in this section is an independent training module. As a result, you can read these chapters in whatever sequence you prefer. You can also read any of the chapters in this section without reading section 2.

In chapter 11, you'll build on the skills you learned in section 1 for working with images, and you'll learn how to work with embedded fonts. In chapter 12, you'll learn how to create tables that present tabular data. In chapter 13, you'll learn how to create forms by using the HTML controls and validation features. In chapter 14, you'll learn how to add audio and video to your web pages. And in chapter 15, you'll learn how to use CSS transitions, transforms, filters, and animations.

Chapter 11

How to work with images, icons, and fonts

In this chapter, you'll first learn how to work with images. That will take what you learned in chapter 3 to a new level. Then, you'll learn how to work with icons.

Last, you'll learn how to get new fonts and embed them within your pages. That way, the fonts are available to every browser. For graphic designers, these font features open up a whole new range of typographical options.

Basic skills for working with images

In the topics that follow, you'll learn the basic skills for working with images. This information will review and expand upon the skills you learned in chapter 3.

Types of images for the Web

Figure 11-1 presents the five types of images you can use on a web page. To start, *JPEG files* are commonly used for photographs and scanned images, because these files can represent millions of colors and they use a type of compression that can display complex images with a small file size.

Although JPEG files lose information when they're compressed, they typically contain high quality images to begin with so this loss of information isn't noticeable on a web page. Similarly, although JPEG files don't support transparency, you usually don't need it for any of the colors in a photograph.

In contrast, *GIF files* are typically used for simple illustrations or logos that require a limited number of colors. Two advantages of storing images in this format are (1) they can be compressed without losing any information, and (2) one of the colors in the image can be transparent.

A GIF file can also contain an *animated image*. An animated image consists of a series of images called *frames*. When you display an animated image, each frame is displayed for a preset amount of time, usually fractions of a second. Because of that, the image appears to be moving. For example, the two globes in this figure are actually two of 30 frames that are stored in the same GIF file. When this file is displayed, the globe appears to be rotating.

Unlike the GIF and JPEG formats, which have been used for years in print materials, *PNG files* were developed specifically for the Web. In particular, this format was developed as a replacement for the GIF format. The PNG advantages over the GIF format include better compression, support for millions of colors, and support for variable transparency.

WebP is a newer image type for the web. It is an open-source format that was developed by Google based on technology acquired from On2 Technologies. The main goal of WebP is to provide smaller, better quality images that can be displayed more quickly. WebP files are typically used to replace PNG and JPEG files.

The newest image type for the web is *AVIF (AV1 image format)*. It was developed by the Alliance for open Media, of which Mozilla is a founding member. Like WebP, it is an open-source format, and its main goal is to provide smaller, better quality images. Currently, AVIF files are only supported by the Chrome, Firefox, and Opera browsers.

Image types

Type	Description
JPEG	A JPEG file uses a type of compression that can display complex images with a small file size. It can represent millions of colors, loses information when compressed, and doesn't support transparency.
GIF	A GIF file can represent up to 256 colors, doesn't lose information when compressed, and supports transparency on a single color.
PNG	A PNG file can represent millions of colors and supports transparency on multiple colors. Compressed PNG files are typically smaller than compressed GIF files, although no information is lost.
WebP	A newer format developed by Google. When compressed with no loss of information, WebP files are 26% smaller than PNG files. When compressed with loss of information, WebP files are 25 to 34% smaller than JPEG files. Both lossless and lossy formats support transparency.
AVIF	A leading edge format developed by Alliance for Open Media. An AVIF file supports up to 68 billion colors, both lossless and lossy formats, and transparency. On average, AVIF files are 50% smaller than JPEG files and 20% smaller than WebP files.

Typical JPEG images

Typical GIF images

Description

- *JPEG* (Joint Photographic Experts Group) images are commonly used for the photographs and images of a web page. Although information is lost when you compress a JPEG file, the reduced quality of the image usually isn't noticeable.

- *GIF* (Graphic Interchange Format) images are commonly used for logos and small illustrations. They can also be used for *animated images* that contain *frames*.

- The *PNG* (Portable Network Graphics) format was developed specifically for the web as a replacement for GIF files.

- The *WebP* format was developed by Google for the web as a replacement for JPEG and PNG files.

- The *AVIF* format, or *AV1 image format*, was developed by Alliance for Open Media (AOMedia) as a replacement for JPEG, PNG, and WebP files.

Figure 11-1   Types of images for the Web

How to include an image on a page

To include an image on a web page, you use the img element. Figure 11-2 presents the most common attributes of this element. Because you were introduced to these attributes in chapter 3, you shouldn't have any trouble understanding how they work.

The HTML in this figure contains two img elements. Although they both display the same image, the first element includes height and width attributes. These attributes should be used to indicate the actual size of the image in pixels, so you shouldn't include any unit of measure when you code them.

When you code them so they represent the actual size of the image, the browser can reserve the correct amount of space for the image as the page is loaded. Then, the browser can continue rendering the page as the image is loaded. This can improve the user experience if a page contains many images.

How to resize an image

If you need to resize an image, figure 11-2 shows how to do that with CSS. Here, the CSS resizes the second image so it's half of its original size. In this example, both the height and width are specified, but if you specify either one, you'll get the same result. That's because the other value will be calculated automatically based on the original proportions of the image.

The trouble with using this technique to resize an image is that the image is still downloaded at its full size before it's reduced. The best way to resize an image, then, is to use an image editor to create an image that's the right size. You'll learn more about that later in this chapter.

Before you continue, you should remember that you can also resize an image by making it scalable. You typically do that when you create a web page with a fluid layout, as you learned in chapter 8. Then, the size of the image changes automatically along with the size of the element that contains it.

Attributes of the \<img\> tag

Attribute	Description
src	The relative or absolute URL of the image to display. It is required.
alt	Alternate text to display in place of the image. It is required.
height	The height of the image in pixels.
width	The width of the image in pixels.

CSS properties for sizing an image

Property	Description
height	A relative or absolute value that specifies the height of the image if the height is different from its original size.
width	A relative or absolute value that specifies the width of the image if the width is different from its original size.

The HTML for two images

```
<p><img src="images/students.jpg" alt="teacher and students"
     height="300" width="400">  
  <img id="small" src="images/students.jpg" alt="teacher and students"></p>
```

CSS for resizing the second image

```
#small {
    height: 150px;
    width: 200px; }
```

The images in a web browser

Accessibility guidelines

- For images with useful content, always code an alt attribute that describes the content.
- For images that are used for decoration, code the alt attribute as an empty string.

Description

- Use the height and width attributes of the \<img\> tag only to specify the size of the existing image. Then, the browser can reserve the right amount of space for the image and continue rendering the page while the image is being loaded.
- To display an image at a size other than its full size, you can use the CSS height and width properties. It's better, though, to use an image editor to correctly size the image.

Figure 11-2   How to include and resize an image

How to align an image vertically

When you include an image on a web page, you may want to align it with the inline elements that surround it. If an image is preceded or followed by text, for example, you may want to align the image with the top, middle, or bottom of the text. To do that, you use the vertical-align property shown in figure 11-3.

To indicate the alignment you want to use, you typically specify one of the keywords listed in this figure. If you specify text-bottom, for example, the image is aligned with the bottom of the adjacent text. In contrast, if you specify bottom, the image is aligned with the bottom of the box that contains the adjacent text.

In most cases, the bottom of the text and the bottom of the box are the same. The exception is if a line height is specified for the box. In that case, the text is centered in the box. Then, if you specify bottom for the image alignment, the image will be aligned at the bottom of the box, which is below the bottom of the text. The top and text-top keywords work the same way.

The middle keyword is useful because it lets you center an image with the surrounding text. This is illustrated in the example in this figure. Here, the HTML includes three paragraphs, each with an image followed by some text. When I didn't specify the vertical alignment for the images, the bottom of each image was aligned with the bottom of the text. When I specified middle for the vertical alignment, the center of each image was aligned with the center of the text.

Note that I specified a right margin for the images for both the aligned and unaligned examples to create space between the images and the text. You can also use padding and borders with images. This works just like it does for block elements.

The property for aligning images vertically

Property	Description
vertical-align	A relative or absolute value or a keyword that determines the vertical alignment of an image. See the table below for common keywords.

Common keywords for the vertical-align property

Keyword	Description
bottom	Aligns the bottom of the image box with the bottom of the box that contains the adjacent inline elements.
middle	Aligns the midpoint of the image box with the midpoint of the containing block.
top	Aligns the top of the image box with the top of the box that contains the adjacent in-line elements.
text-bottom	Aligns the bottom of the image box with the bottom of the text in the containing block.
text-top	Aligns the top of the image box with the top of the text in the containing block.

The HTML for a web page with three images

```
<h2>We want to hear from you</h2>
<p><img src="images/computer.gif" alt="web address">
    <strong>Web:</strong> www.murach.com</p>
<p><img src="images/telephone.gif" alt="phone">
    <strong>Phone:</strong> 1-800-221-5528</p>
<p><img src="images/email.gif" alt="email">
    <strong>Email:</strong> murachbooks@murach.com</p>
```

CSS that aligns the images in the middle of the text

```
img {
    vertical-align: middle;
    margin-right: 10px; }
```

The images in a web browser before and after they're aligned

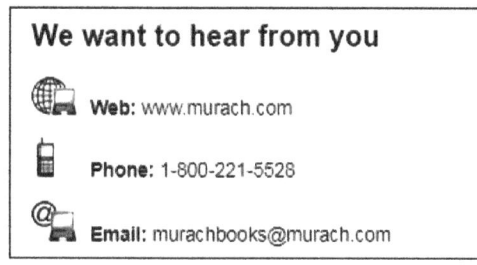 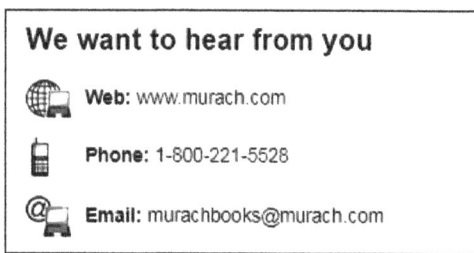

Description

- If you use pixels, points, or ems to specify the value for the vertical-align property, the image is raised if the value is positive and lowered if it's negative. If you specify a percent, the image is raised or lowered based on the percentage of the line height.

- You can use margins, padding, and borders with images just as you can with block elements.

Figure 11-3   How to align an image vertically

How to float an image

In section 1, you learned how to float a logo in a heading and how to float block elements for page layout. Now, figure 11-4 reinforces what you've learned.

At the top of this figure, you can see the two properties for floating images: float and clear. These properties work just like they do for block elements. You use the float property to determine whether the image should be floated to the right or to the left. And you use the clear property to stop an element from floating to the right or left of a floated image.

In the HTML in this figure, you can see that the first element defines an image. This image is followed by an unordered list and a paragraph. In the CSS that follows, you can see that the image is floated to the left. In addition, top and bottom margins are specified for the image to create space between the image and the text that precedes and follows it. In this case, you don't need to specify a right margin for the image because the items in the list are indented by default. Also note that you don't have to specify a width when you float an image. That's because the width can be determined from the actual width of the image.

Finally, notice that the clear property with a value of "left" is specified for the paragraph that follows the list. Because of that, this paragraph won't flow into the space to the right of the image. Instead, the text starts below the image.

The properties for floating images

Property	Description
float	A keyword that determines how an image is floated. Possible values are left, right, and none. None is the default.
clear	A keyword that determines if an element that follows a floated element flows into the space left by the floated element. Possible values are left, right, both, and none. None is the default.

Some of the HTML for a web page

```
<img src="images/students.jpg" alt="teacher and students">
<ul>
    <li>in college and university MIS programs that focus on providing
        students with practical, real-world experience</li>
    <li>by technical institutes and community colleges that focus on the
        skills that employers are looking for</li>
    <li>in Continuing Ed and Extension programs where the students are
        professionals who are expanding their skills</li>
</ul>
<p id="last">So if your program fits one of those profiles, please take
a look at our books. I&rsquo;m confident you&rsquo;ll discover a new level
of structure, clarity, and relevance that will benefit both you and your
students.</p>
```

CSS that floats the image and clears the last paragraph

```
img {
    float: left;
    margin-top: 15px;
    margin-bottom: 10px; }
#last { clear: left; }
```

The HTML in a web browser

Teach your students using the books the professionals use

Although our books are written for professional programmers who need to master new job skills, there have always been instructors teaching job-oriented curricula who've adopted our books. For example, our books are used:

- in college and university MIS programs that focus on providing students with practical, real-world experience
- by technical institutes and community colleges that focus on the skills that employers are looking for
- in Continuing Ed and Extension programs where the students are professionals who are expanding their skills

So if your program fits one of those profiles, please take a look at our books. I'm confident you'll discover a new level of structure, clarity, and relevance that will benefit both you and your students.

Description

- You can use the same techniques to float an image that you use to float a block element.

Figure 11-4   How to float an image

Other skills for working with images

The topics that follow present some additional skills for working with images. One or more of these may come in handy as you develop web pages that use images.

How to use the HTML figure and figcaption elements

The HTML figure and figcaption elements can be used with anything that is used as a figure, like an image or table. Because an image is often used as a figure, though, we're presenting these elements in this chapter.

Figure 11-5 shows how to use these elements for an image that's used as a figure. Here, the figure contains one img element plus one figcaption element that provides a caption below the image. Then, the figure is floated within an article, and the image and caption float along with it.

By default, a figcaption element is an inline element, not a block element. As a result, you will usually want to use the CSS display property to change it to a block element. That makes it easier to format the caption. In this example, the figcaption element comes after the image in the HTML so the caption is displayed below the image. But you can change that by coding the figcaption element before the image in the HTML.

Although you can get the same results without using these HTML elements, it's better to use them because they're semantic. That way, it's easy to tell that the image is used as a figure and that the caption applies to the image.

A web page that uses figure and figcaption elements

Fossil Threads in the Web of Life

What's 75 million years old and brand spanking new? A teenage Utahceratops! Come to the Saroyan, armed with your best dinosaur roar, when Scott Sampson, Research Curator at the Utah Museum of Natural History, steps to the podium. Sampson's research has focused on the ecology and evolution of late Cretaceous dinosaurs and he has conducted fieldwork in a number of countries in Africa.

Scott Sampson and friend

Scott Sampson is a Canadian-born paleontologist who received his Ph.D. in zoology from the University of Toronto. His doctoral work focused on two new species of ceratopsids (horned dinosaurs) from the Late Cretaceous of Montana, as well as the growth and function of certopsid horns and frills.

The HTML for the figure and figcaption elements

```
<article>
    <h1>Fossil Threads in the Web of Life</h1>
    <figure>
        <img src="images/sampson_dinosaur.jpg" alt="Scott Sampson">
        <figcaption>Scott Sampson and friend</figcaption>
    </figure>
    <p>What's 75 million years old and brand spanking new? A teenage
    ...
    </p>
</article>
```

The CSS for the figure and figcaption elements

```
figure {
    float: left;
    margin-right: 1.5em; }
figcaption {
    display: block;
    font-weight: bold;
    padding-top: .25em;
    margin-bottom: 1em;
    border-bottom: 1px solid black; }
```

Description

- The figure element can be used as a container for anything that is used as a figure, like an image or a table.

- The figcaption element can be used within a figure to provide a caption that describes the figure, but it is optional. When coded, it can be anywhere within the figure element.

- By default, the figcaption element is an inline element so you usually need to change that.

Figure 11-5   How to use the HTML figure and figcaption elements

How to do image rollovers

You may remember from chapter 1 that an image rollover occurs when the mouse hovers over an image and the image is replaced by another image. Although JavaScript is often used for image rollovers, you can do them without JavaScript as shown in figure 11-6.

The HTML in this figure consists of just an h1 and a <p> element within the body clement. Also, the <p> element is given an id so CSS can be applied to it. But note that the <p> element is empty. So where is the image for this page?

In the CSS for the <p> element, the first style rule specifies a background image. That displays the image within the element. Then, the second style rule specifies a different background image when the mouse is hovering over the <p> element. That accomplishes the image rollover.

This is a relatively simple technique that you can use for a limited number of image rollovers. But if coding these style rules gets cumbersome, you can use JavaScript to simplify the process.

This image has been rolled over because the mouse is hovering over it

The HTML for the page

```
<body>
    <h1>Ram Tap Combined Test</h1>
    <p id="image1"></p>
</body>
```

The CSS for the image rollover

```
#image1 {
    background-image: url("h1.jpg");
    width: 434px;
    height: 312px;
}
#image1:hover {
    background-image: url("h2.jpg");
}
```

Description

- An *image rollover* is an image that gets changed when the mouse hovers over it.
- One way to do image rollovers is to use background images and the :hover pseudo-class selector.
- When you use this method, the first background image is applied to a block element like a <p> element. Then, the second background image is displayed when the mouse hovers over it.

Figure 11-6   How to do image rollovers

How to create image maps

You've probably seen web pages that display an image and go to other pages depending on where you click in the image. For example, you might be able to click on a state within a United States map to go to a page with information about that state.

To make this work, you use an *image map* as shown in figure 11-7. Here, the image in the browser consists of pictures of two books. Then, when the PHP and MySQL book is clicked, one page is displayed. When the JavaScript and jQuery book is clicked, another page is displayed. Within the image map, each clickable area is called a *hotspot*.

To define an image map, you use the img, map, and area elements. In the usemap attribute of the img element, you code the name of the map element that will be used. In the map element, you code the name that the img element refers to. Then, within the map element, you code one or more area elements that define the hotspots of the map.

The key to defining an area map is coding the area elements. Here, you code the href attribute to specify what page you want to display when the area is clicked. Then, you code the shape attribute to identify the type of shape you want to use for the region. In this example, I used two polygons.

To identify the actual shape and location of an area, you code the coords attribute. The values for this attribute depend on the shape of the area. For rectangular areas, which assumes that the rectangle is vertical, not at an angle, four values are specified. The first two identify the x, y coordinates in pixels of the upper left corner of the area relative to the upper left corner of the image. The second two identify the x, y coordinates in pixels of the lower right corner of the area.

To define a circular region, you specify "circle" for the value of the shape attribute. Then, you specify three values for the coords attribute. The first two values are x, y coordinates for the center of the circle. The third value is the radius of the circle in pixels.

If you want to define a more complex shape than a rectangle or circle, you can specify "poly" for the value of the shape attribute. Then, the coords attribute will consist of a series of x, y coordinates that start in the upper-left corner and travel clockwise around the shape. To identify the shape for the PHP and MySQL book, for example, I included five sets of x, y coordinates because part of the book is hidden. To identify the shape for the JavaScript and jQuery book, I only used four sets of coordinates.

To get the coordinates that you need for an image map, you can use an image editor. Then, you just point to the locations in the image and record the coordinates that are shown.

The attribute of the img element that identifies the related map element

Attribute	Description
usemap	The related map element. The value of this attribute is the value of the name attribute of the map element, preceded by a pound sign (#).

The attribute of the map element that gives it a name

Attribute	Description
name	A name for the map.

The attributes of the area elements that create the image maps

Attribute	Description
href	A relative or absolute URL that identifies the page that will be displayed when the area is clicked.
shape	A keyword that indicates the type of shape the area represents. Possible keywords are rect, circle, poly, and default, which is the same as rect.
coords	Values that indicate the shape and location of the area. Two sets of x, y coordinates are required for a rectangle to identify the upper left and lower right corners. Three values are required for a circle to identify the x, y coordinates of the center and the radius. Polygonal shapes require a series of x, y coordinates.
alt	Text that's displayed in place of the area if the image can't be displayed.

An image in a web browser with hotspots created by an image map

The HTML for the image and image map

```
<img src="images/web_books.jpg" alt="PHP/MySQL and JavaScript/jQuery books"
    usemap="#books">
<map name="books">
    <area href="php_mysql.html" shape="poly" alt="PHP/MySQL book"
        title="PHP/MySQL" coords="0,30,115,0,133,67,109,156,39,174">
    <area href="javascript_jquery.html" shape="poly"
        alt="JavaScript/jQuery book" title="JavaScript/jQuery"
        coords="145,21,261,52,222,195,107,165">
</map>
```

Description

- You can use the map and area elements to define an *image map* that provides clickable areas for the image called *hotspots*.
- The coordinates for an area are relative to the upper left corner of the image and are measured in pixels.

Figure 11-7 How to create image maps

How to provide images for varying viewport sizes

When you use Responsive Web Design, you want the images that you use to be the right sizes for the varying viewport sizes. For example, you may want to use large, high-resolution images for larger viewports, but not for devices with smaller viewports. That's why the next two figures show how to provide the right images for varying viewport sizes.

How to use the img and picture elements

If you want to use the same image in various viewport sizes but you want to reduce the image file size for smaller viewports, you can do that by using the img element as shown in the first part of figure 11-8. To do that, you use the srcset attribute to specify the images to be displayed and the sizes attribute to specify when each image should be used.

In the example, three images with widths of 800, 600, and 400 pixels are identified by the srcset attribute. Then, the sizes attribute indicates that if the viewport has a minimum width of 1200 pixels, 800 pixels will be allocated to the image. And if the viewport has a minimum width of 800 pixels, 600 pixels will be allocated to the image. But note that the last item on the sizes attribute doesn't specify a condition. That means that the specified width is used if none of the other conditions are met. In this case, the image will be equal to the width of the viewport if the viewport is less than 800 pixels.

In this example, the image widths in the srcset attribute are the same as the widths of the images for the first two conditions on the sizes attribute. However, that doesn't have to be the case. If, for example, the sizes attribute had a width of 1000 pixels for viewports with a minimum width of 1200 pixels, the image that's 800 pixels wide would still be displayed because it's the largest image that's less than or equal to 1000 pixels.

The second part of this figure shows how you can use different images for different viewport sizes. That lets you use images with fewer details and smaller file sizes for smaller viewports. To do that, you use the picture element as shown in the second example in this figure. As you can see, this element contains three source elements followed by an img element.

Then, the media attributes for each source element provide the minimum width for a viewport, and the srcset attribute identifies the image to be displayed at that width. But if none of the source elements contains a media attribute that refers to the viewport size that's being used, the image that's identified by the img element is displayed.

The third example shows that the picture element can also be used to display an image in an alternative format if the other formats aren't supported by the browser. Here, the source element displays an image in AVIF format. But since that format is currently supported only by the Chrome, Firefox, and Opera, an img element provides a PNG file as an alternative.

How to use different size images for different viewport sizes

Attributes of the img element for adding multiple image resources

Attribute	Description
srcset	The URL of one or more images, each followed optionally by a space and the image width. Multiple images must be separated by commas.
sizes	A media condition, followed by a space and the size of the image. Multiple conditions must be separated by commas, and the media condition must be omitted for the last item in the list.

An img element that displays different image sizes based on viewport size

```
<img src="images/mountains_medium.png" alt="mountains"
    srcset="images/mountains_large.png 800w,
            images/mountains_medium.png 600w,
            images/mountains_small.png 400w"
    sizes="(min-width: 1200px) 800px, (min-width: 800px) 600px, 100vw">
```

How to use different images for different viewport sizes

Elements for adding multiple image resources

Element	Descrption
picture	The picture element contains one or more source elements and an img element.
source	Each source element refers to an image for a particular window size or format.
img	The image that's used if none of the images on the source elements can be used.

Attributes of the source element

Attribute	Description
media	A query that determines when the image should be loaded by the browser.
srcset	The URL of the image to be loaded. Required.
type	The MIME type for the image to be loaded.

A picture element that displays different images based on viewport size

```
<picture>
    <source media="(min-width: 960px)" srcset="images/mountains_far.png">
    <source media="(min-width: 768px)" srcset="images/mountains_mid.png">
    <source media="(min-width: 460px)" srcset="images/mountains_close.png">
    <img src="images/mountains_mid.png" alt="">
</picture>
```

How to display an image in an alternative format

```
<picture>
    <source type="image.avif" srcset="images/mountains_small.avif">
    <img src="images/mountains_small.png" alt="">
</picture>
```

Description

- The img element provides for using an image in different sizes depending on the viewport size without the need for media queries.

- The picture element provides for using different images depending on the viewport size without the need for media queries. It also provides for displaying an image in an alternative format if other formats aren't supported by a browser.

Figure 11-8   How to use the img and picture elements

How to use Scalable Vector Graphics

Scalable Vector Graphics (*SVG*) is an XML-based markup language that can be used to create scalable images within a web page. That usually means that the web page will load faster, which will improve the user experience. Besides that, the SVG images are scalable so they will work well for Responsive Web Design.

To illustrate, figure 11-9 shows the code for creating our simple logo. That's the code that's in an svg element in the HTML for the web page. To create code like this, you normally use a graphics editor and then export the code into the HTML for a web page.

One drawback of using SVG is that SVG images are hard to create unless you have a background in graphics design. In addition, SVG isn't suitable for complex images like photographs because the code gets so extensive that you lose the benefit of faster loading. As a result, SVG is normally used for relatively simple images.

The Murach logo as a Scalable Vector Graphic

The code for the logo exported from Adobe Illustrator

```
<svg viewBox="0 0 247.83 76.96">
    <rect class="cls-1" width="80" height="76.96"/>
    <path class="cls-2" d="M28.19,18.36H18.13s3.29.09,3.29,4.33V52l10.53-
    3.33V22.47C31.95,19.88,30.58,18.37,28.19,18.36Z"/>
    <path class="cls-2" d="M40.33,21.9H30.26s3.29.08,3.29,4.32V55.52l10.53-
    3.33V26C44.09,23.43,42.72,21.91,40.33,21.9Z"/>
    <path class="cls-2" d="M52.42,25.53H42.36s3.29.08,3.29,4.32V59.14l10.53-
    3.33V29.64C56.18,27.05,54.81,25.54,52.42,25.53Z"/>
</svg>
```

The benefits of SVG

- SVG code loads faster than image files so your web pages will load faster and improve the user experience.
- SVG images are scalable so they work well for Responsive Web Design.
- SVG images are recognized by Google just as other images are so they won't affect SEO.

Drawbacks of SVG

- Without a background in graphics design, SVG images can be hard to create.
- SVG isn't suitable for complex images like photographs.

Description

- *SVG*, which stands for *Scalable Vector Graphics*, is an XML-based markup language for creating two-dimensional vector graphics.
- SVG is an open standard developed by the World Wide Web consortium.
- Although you could create SVG files in HTML by coding the svg element along with its child elements, you usually create SVG files by using a graphics editor like Method Draw, Inkscape, Adobe Illustrator, or Adobe Photoshop. Then, the SVG file can be exported as an svg element and used in your HTML code.

Figure 11-9   How to work with Scalable Vector Graphics

How to get the images and icons that you need

At this point, you've learned the HTML and CSS skills that you need for working with images. If someone else is responsible for getting and sizing the images that you use, that may be all you need to know. But if you need to get and size your own images, here are some other skills that you'll need.

When to use an image editor

When you use images on a web page, you want them to be the right size and format. If they aren't that way, you can use an image editor like the one in figure 11-10 to make the adjustments.

Today, one of the most popular editors is Adobe Photoshop CC, which is currently available as a monthly subscription for as little as $9.99 per month. Adobe also offers a product called Photoshop Elements that you can purchase for a moderate price. Beyond that, there are many other image editors that range from free to hundreds of dollars.

The primary use of an image editor is to size the images and save them in the right format so they will load as quickly as possible. In this figure, you can see some of the controls for doing that. Usually, you save an image for the web with a resolution of 72 dpi (dots per inch) because that's the optimal resolution for most monitors. If you increase the dpi, it won't make the image any clearer, but it will increase the size of the file, which means it will load more slowly.

You can also use an image editor to work with an *animated image* like a GIF file that contains *frames*. For instance, you can specify whether the frames are shown only once or repeated. You can also set the timing between the frames.

If an image has a transparent color, you can save it as a GIF or PNG file with *transparency*. To understand how this works, you need to know that an image is always rectangular. This is illustrated by the first starburst example in this figure. Here, the area that's outside the starburst is white, and it isn't transparent. As a result, you can see the white when the image is displayed over a colored background. In contrast, the area outside the second starburst image is also white, but it is transparent. Because of that, you can see the background color behind it.

The second image in this example also uses a *matte*. A matte is useful when a GIF or PNG image with a transparent color is displayed against a colored background. Without a matte, the edges of the image can appear jagged. But if you add a matte that's the same color as the background, it will help the image blend into the background and minimize the jagged edges.

You can also use a matte with a JPEG image. Then, all of the transparent area in the original image is filled with the color you choose. Later, when the image is displayed against a background that's the same color as the matte, the matte area appears to be transparent.

An image editor as it is used to change the size of an image

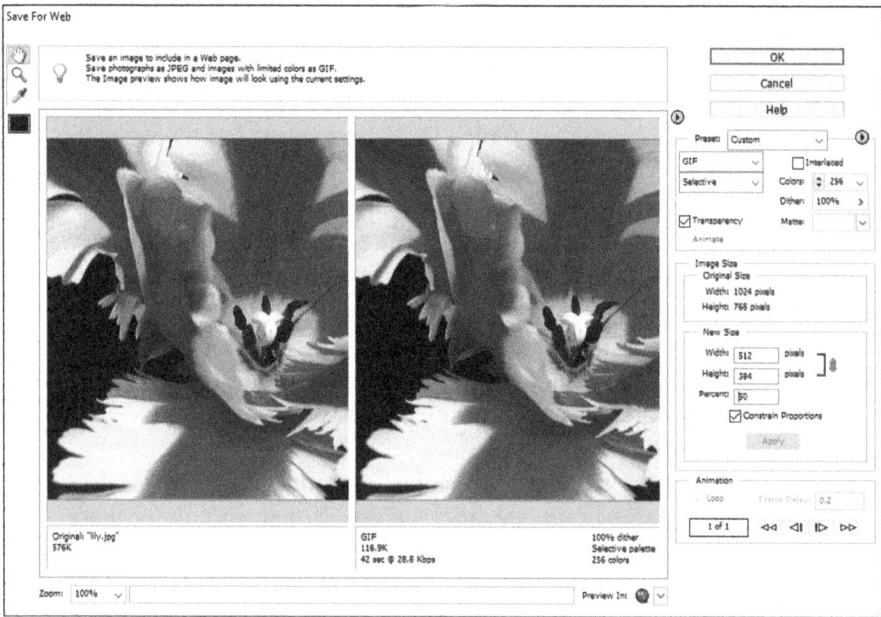

Typical editing operations

- Change the size, image type, or quality of an image.
- Control the animation of an animated GIF file.
- Save an image with transparency or a matte.
- Get the coordinates for an image map.

Three popular image editors

- Adobe Photoshop CC (the industry standard for graphic artists)
- Adobe Photoshop Elements (an inexpensive editor)
- GIMP (a free editor)

An image without transparency and with transparency and a matte

Description

- If an image with *transparency* is displayed over a colored background, the background color will show through the transparent portion of the image.
- If an image with a transparent color is displayed over a colored background, a *matte* of the same color will help the image blend into the background.

Figure 11-10   When to use an image editor

How to get images

For many websites, you'll use your own photos and create most of the graphic images that you use. But sometimes, you may need to get images or icons from another source. The easiest way to do that is to copy or download them from another website. To help you with that, figure 11-11 lists several of the websites you can use to get images.

Although many of the images that you find on the web are available for free, most require a Creative Commons license. The types of licenses that are available and the conditions required by these licenses are summarized in this figure. As you can see, all of the licenses require attribution, which means that you must give credit to the author of the image or the website that provided the image. The other license conditions determine how an image can be shared, whether it can be used for commercial purposes, and whether you can derive new images from the existing image.

Stock photos are special images that are typically produced in a studio. For example, the two images in this figure are stock photos. You must pay for these types of images, and they can be expensive.

Incidentally, you can also get an image or the link to an image from another site by right-clicking on the image and selecting the appropriate command from the shortcut menu. Then, if you save the link to the image in the href attribute of an img element, your web page will display the image that's actually stored on the other site. This is known as "hot linking" and it is highly discouraged unless you have an agreement with the other site. If, for example, you agree to provide a link to another site and that site agrees to provide a link to your site, this is a quick way to get the images and URLs that you need.

Creative Commons license conditions

Conditions	Description
Attribution	You can use the image and images derived from it as long as you give credit as requested by the author or website providing the image.
Share Alike	You can distribute the image based on the license that governs the original work.
Non-Commercial	You can use the image and images derived from it for non-commercial purposes only.
No Derivative Works	You can use only the original image and not images derived from it.

Two stock photos

Popular websites for images

- www.freeimages.com
- www.freefoto.com
- www.openphoto.net
- www.google.com/imghp

Popular websites for stock photos

- www.istockphoto.com
- www.gettyimages.com

A popular search engine for stock photos

- www.everystockphoto.com

Description

- Many of the images that are available from the Web are licensed under a Creative Commons license. The license can restrict the use of an image to one or more of the conditions listed above. The most common condition is attribution.
- Stock photos are typically produced in studios and can be purchased for a one-time fee of one dollar to several hundred dollars.
- You can also search for specific images from a generic search engine such as Google.

Figure 11-11   How to get images

How to get and work with icons and favicons

You can also get icons for commonly used symbols from the web. To help with that, figure 11-12 presents four of the popular websites for icons.

This figure also shows how to work with icons in the Font Awesome library, one of the most popular icon libraries. To do that, you add a script element like the one in the first example to get the Font Awesome library from a CDN. Then, you use classes in your HTML to identify the icon you want to use.

The second example uses three of the icons in the Font Awesome library. All of these icons are identified by the class named "fas". Then, the second class for each icon identifies the specific icon. And the third class indicates the size of the icon. If you refer to the documentation on the Font Awesome website, you'll see that other classes are also available for controlling the appearance of an icon.

Notice here that the icon classes are coded on <i> tags. As mentioned in chapter 3, the <i> element should no longer be used to italicize text, and it doesn't affect the icons here. Instead, it just indicates that the classes are for icons. You should know, however, that you can also code the classes on other inline elements.

Next, this figure shows how to work with *favicons*, which were introduced in chapter 3. These are just special-purpose icons. Like other icons, a favicon should always be stored in a file with the ico extension.

To create an icon from scratch, you can purchase a program like Axialis Icon Workshop. Or, if you're using Photoshop, you can get the plugin that lets you save files with the ico extension. You can also download a free image converter such as IrfanView from the Internet, or you can use an online image converter such as FavIcon from Pics.

Although they can be larger, most favicons are 16 pixels wide and tall. In fact, some image converters will automatically convert an image to 16x16 pixels. Then, to provide the favicon for a web page, you code a link element like the one in this figure. That will cause the favicon to be displayed in the tab for the page, and it may also be displayed in the address bar and bookmarks for the page.

Popular websites for icons

- https://fontawesome.io
- www.glyphicons.com
- www.glyphish.com
- www.flaticon.com

How to include the Font Awesome library from a CDN

```
<script src="https://use.fontawesome.com/releases/v5.0.1/js/all.js">
</script>
```

HTML that uses 3 Font Awesome icons

```
<h2>We want to hear from you</h2>
<ul>
    <li><i class="fas fa-globe fa-lg"></i>
    <strong>Web:</strong> www.murach.com</li>
    <li><i class="fas fa-phone-square fa-lg"></i>
    <strong>Phone:</strong> 1-800-221-5528</li>
    <li><i class="fas fa-envelope-square fa-lg"></i>
    <strong>Email:</strong> sales@murach.com</li>
</ul>
```

The icons in a web browser

We want to hear from you

🌐 **Web:** www.murach.com

📱 **Phone:** 1-800-221-5528

✉ **Email:** murachbooks@murach.com

Two of the tools for creating favicons

- Axialis Icon Workshop
- Photoshop plugin

A link element in the head section that adds a favicon to the browser tab

```
<link rel="shortcut icon" href="images/favicon.ico">
```

Description

- Like images, you get many of the available icons under a Creative Commons license.
- To add a Font Awesome icon to the HTML for a web page, you code a class that identifies the library and a class that identifies the icon. You can also include classes that control the size of the icon, its style, and more.
- A *favicon* is typically 16 pixels wide and tall and has the extension ico.

Figure 11-12   How to get and work with icons and favicons

How to work with fonts

For years, web designers were frustrated by the limited number of fonts that were available for a website. In fact, web pages had been limited to the fonts that were available to each browser. That's why the font families throughout this book have been set to a series of fonts like Arial, Helvetica, and sans-serif. Then, each browser uses the first font in the series that's available to it.

But now, you can use a CSS feature to *embed fonts* within your web pages. That way, you know the fonts are available to the browser. You can also use third-party services like Google and Adobe Web Fonts to embed fonts within your pages.

How to embed fonts in a web page

Figure 11-13 shows how to use the CSS @font-face selector to embed fonts in your web pages. To start, you look in the folders that are listed in this figure, where you'll see that you already have access to many fonts that most browsers don't have access to. Then, you find the font that you want and copy it into one of the folders for your website. In this example, the Windows True Type Font named HARNGTON.TTF has been copied to the root folder of the website.

Once you've copied the font to a folder, you code a CSS style rule for the @font-face selector that names and locates the font. In this example, the font-family property gives the name "Murach" to the font, and the src property points to the file, which is in the same folder as the web page.

After the font has been imported, you can code CSS style rules that apply the new font to HTML elements. In this example, the second style rule applies the font to h1 elements. To do that, the font-family property is set to the name of the embedded font.

Where to find the fonts on your computer

On a Windows system

```
C:\Windows\Fonts
```

On a macOS system

```
System\Library\Fonts
```

A heading that uses a font imported with CSS

Murach Books

The CSS for embedding a font

```
@font-face {
    font-family: Murach;
    src: url("HARNGTON.TTF"); }
```

The CSS for applying the font to an HTML element

```
h1 {
    font-family: Murach; }
```

The HTML for the element that the font is applied to

```
<h1>Murach Books</h1>
```

How to import a font

- Copy the file for the font family into a folder for your website.
- In the CSS for the page, code a style rule for the @font-face selector. Then, use the font-family property to provide a name for the imported font family, and use the src property to locate the font file.

How to apply an imported font to an HTML element

- In the style rule for the HTML element, use the name that you gave the font as the value for the font-family property.

Description

- CSS provides an @font-face selector that can be used to import a font family.
- In this example, the file for a True Type Font (TTF) named HARNGTON has been stored in the same folder as the web page.

Figure 11-13   How to embed fonts in a web page

How to use Google and Adobe Web Fonts

Figure 11-14 shows how you can use Google and Adobe Web Fonts to import fonts into your web pages. Both Google and Adobe Web Fonts are free services that let you select fonts from hundreds of different font families. Because the exact procedures for getting these fonts change often, they aren't included here.

To start, however, you can search for Google Fonts or Adobe Fonts and go to the resulting websites. There, you can follow the instructions for using one or more of the fonts.

When you select a Google font, you will be provided with a link element that points to the file for the font, as shown by the first example in this figure. Then, you can include that element in your web page, and you can use the font-family property to apply the font to an HTML element in the page. In this example, the "Sorts Mill Goudy" font is imported and applied to the h1 element. But note that the font list also includes the generic serif font in case something goes wrong and the Google font isn't available.

The technique for using an Adobe font is similar. But instead of including a link element, you include a script element that imports the font. This is shown in the second example in this figure. Here, a font called Alex Brush is imported and used in the font-family property for an h1 element. This time, the cursive font is added to the font list in case something goes wrong.

A heading that uses a Google Web Font

Murach Books

The link element that imports the font

```
<link
  href="https://fonts.googleapis.com/css2?family=Sorts+Mill+Goudy&display=swap"
  rel="stylesheet">
```

The CSS for applying the font to an HTML element

```
h1 { font-family: "Sorts Mill Goudy", serif; }
```

The HTML for the element that the font is applied to

```
<h1>Murach Books</h1>
```

A heading that uses an Adobe Web Font

The script element that imports the font

```
<script src="//use.edgefonts.net/alex-brush.js"></script>
```

The CSS that applies the font to an element

```
h1 { font-family: alex-brush, cursive; }
```

The HTML for the element that the font is applied to

```
<h1>Murach Books</h1>
```

Description

- Google Web Fonts is a free Google service that lets you select and use any of the fonts in their current collection of more than 1000 font families.

- Adobe Web Fonts is a free Adobe service that lets you use any of the fonts in their current collection of more than 300 font families. Over 2000 additional font families are available if you subscribe to Adobe Creative Cloud.

- You can locate the websites for Google and Adobe Web Fonts by searching for Google Fonts and Adobe Fonts.

- When you use Google or Adobe Web Fonts, you should list one or more other font families for the font-family attribute in case something has changed and the Google or Adobe font isn't available.

Figure 11-14   How to use Google and Adobe Web Fonts

Perspective

Now that you've finished this chapter, you should have all the HTML and CSS skills that you need for developing web pages with images. But if you're going to do your own image editing, you'll also need to get an image editor and learn how to use it.

Terms

JPEG file	image map
GIF file	hotspot
animated image	Scalable Vector Graphics (SVG)
frame	transparency
PNG file	matte
WebP file	icon
AVIF file	favicon
image rollover	embedded font

Summary

- The five common formats for images are *JPEG*, *GIF* (for small illustrations, logos, and animated images), *PNG*, *WebP* (for smaller, better quality images than JPEG and PNG files), and *AVIF* (for smaller, better quality images than JPEG, PNG, and WebP files).

- You should use the height and width attributes of an <img> tag only to specify the size of the image, not to resize it. Then, the browser can reserve the right amount of space for the image and continue rendering the page, even if the image is still being loaded.

- You can use CSS to vertically align an image within the block element that contains it. You can also use CSS to float an image.

- The HTML figure element can be used as a container for anything that represents a figure, such as an image. The HTML figcaption element can be used to provide a caption for the figure.

- An *image rollover* occurs when the mouse hovers over an image and the image is replaced by another image.

- An *image map* defines the clickable *hotspots* for an image. To define these hotspots, you code map and area elements in the HTML.

- The img element can be used to display an image with different file sizes for different viewport sizes without using media queries.

- The picture and source elements can be used to display different images for different viewport sizes without using media queries. These elements also provide for displaying an image in another format if the preferred format isn't supported by a browser.

- Scalable Vector Graphics (SVG) are two-dimensional graphics defined by an XML-based markup language. You typically use a graphics editor to create SVGs and then export them to svg elements that you include in your HTML.

- To resize an image so it's the right size for a web page, you can use an image editor like Photoshop CC or Photoshop Elements.

- You can also use an image editor to create GIF files for *animated images* that consist of two or more *frames*; to provide *transparency* for GIF and PNG files; and to specify a *matte* for an image.

- A *favicon* is a small image that appears to the left of the title in the browser's tab for the page. It is typically 16 pixels wide and tall and has ico as its extension.

- CSS provides a @font-face selector that you can use to *embed fonts* from your libraries into a web page. You can also embed fonts in your web pages by using Google or Adobe Web Fonts.

Exercise 11-1   Use a figure and the picture element on the speaker's page

In this exercise, you'll be working with a version of the website that you developed for the first seven chapters of this book. In this exercise, you'll enhance the speaker page by adding figure, figcaption, and picture elements so the page looks like this:

1. Use your text editor to open these HTML and CSS files:

    `html_css_5\exercises\town_hall_3\speakers\c11_sampson.html`

    `html_css_5\exercises\town_hall_3\styles\speaker.css`

2. In the HTML file, enclose the img element at the top of the article in a figure element. Then, add a figcaption element below the img element with the text shown above.

3. In the CSS file, add the style rules for formatting the figure and figcaption elements. Then, test this enhancement.

4. In the HTML file, change the img element so it displays the file named sampson_dinosaur.avif instead of the file named sampson_dinosaur.jpg.

5. Test this change in Chrome to be sure the image is displayed. Then, test it in Edge or Safari and notice that the image isn't displayed.

6. Change the img element back so it displays the JPEG file again. Then, enclose the img element in a picture element.

7. Add a source element before the img element that displays the image named sampson_dinosaur.avif. Test the page one more time in Chrome and in Edge or Safari to be sure the image is displayed.

Exercise 11-2   Size a picture for different viewports

In this exercise, you'll use the img element to display an image with different file sizes in different viewport sizes:

> **Teach your students using the books the professionals use**
>
> Although our books are written for professional programmers who need to master new job skills, there have always been instructors teaching job-oriented curricula who've adopted our books. For example, our books are used:
>
> - in college and university MIS programs that focus on providing students with practical, real-world experience
> - by technical institutes and community colleges that focus on the skills that employers are looking for
> - in Continuing Ed and Extension programs where the students are professionals who are expanding their skills
>
> So if your program fits one of those profiles, please take a look at our books. I'm confident you'll discover a new level of structure, clarity, and relevance that will benefit both you and your students.

1. Use your text editor to open this file:
   `html_CSS_5\exercises\ch11\students.html`

2. Display this page in your browser to see what it looks like.

3. Narrow the browser window to see that when the body of the page becomes less than its maximum width, the text will roll over to additional lines but the image will be cut off.

4. Add a srcset attribute to the img element so it provides for three images named students_750.png, students_550.png, and students_400.png. (The numbers on these names indicate the widths of the images.) Then, change the src attribute so the default image is the one named students_550.png.

5. Add a sizes attribute to the img element. If the minimum viewport width is 800 pixels, the image with a width of 750 pixels should be displayed. If the minimum viewport width is 600 pixels, the image with a width of 550 pixels should be displayed. And if neither of these conditions is met, the image with a width of 400 pixels should be displayed.

6. Test the page in your browser to see that the image that's displayed depends on the width of the browser window.

Exercise 11-3   Use a web font

In this exercise, you'll enhance the header of a page with a web font:

1. Use your text editor to open these files:
    `html_CSS_5\exercises\town_hall_3\speakers\c11_sampson.html`
    `html_CSS_5\exercises\town_hall_3\styles\speaker.css`

2. Test this page in your browser to see what it looks like.

3. Using figure 11-13 as a guide, choose a web font on your system and copy it into the styles folder.

4. Use CSS to apply the font to the h2 element in the header. Then, test to make sure the font has been changed.

Chapter 12

How to work with tables

At one time, tables were used to lay out pages. But now, the right way to do that is to use CSS. As a result, you should only use tables to display tabular data. In this chapter, you'll learn how to do that.

Basic HTML skills for coding tables

In the topics that follow, you'll learn the basic skills for coding tables. But first, you'll be introduced to the HTML structure of a table.

An introduction to tables

Figure 12-1 presents a simple table and points out its various components. To start, a table consists of one or more *rows* and *columns*. As you'll see in the next figure, you define a table by defining its rows. Then, within each row, you define a *cell* for each column.

Within each row, a table can contain two different kinds of cells. *Header cells* identify what's in the columns and rows of a table, and *data cells* contain the actual data of the table. For example, the three cells in the first row of the table in this figure are header cells that identify the contents of the columns. In contrast, the cells in the next four rows are data cells. The last row starts with a header cell that identifies the contents of the cells in that row.

In broad terms, a table starts with a *header* that can consist of one or more rows. Then, the *body* of the table presents the data for the table. Last, the *footer* provides summary data that can consist of one or more rows. For accessibility, a table should also have a caption above or below it that summarizes what's in the table.

A simple table with basic formatting

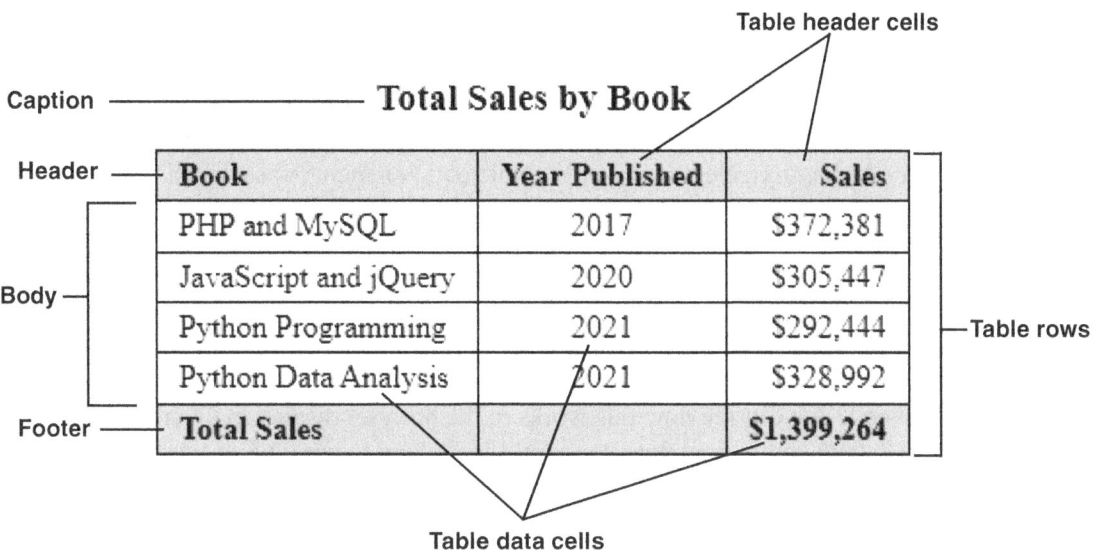

Description

- A *table* consists of *rows* and *columns* that intersect at *cells*.
- Cells that contain the data of the table are called *data cells*.
- Cells that identify the data in a column or row are called *header cells*.
- The *header* for a table can consist of more than one row, and the *footer* for a table can consist of more than one row.
- The *body* of a table, which contains the data, usually consists of two or more rows.

Figure 12-1   An introduction to tables

How to create a table

Figure 12-2 presents four of the HTML elements for coding tables. The table element defines the table itself. Then, you code the other elements within the table element.

To define each row in a table, you use the tr (table row) element. Within each row, you code one th (table header) or td (table data) element for each cell in the row. You can see how this works in the table in this figure. This is the same table that's in figure 12-1, but without the formatting. In the last row, note that the first cell is coded as a th element. That's because it identifies the data in the last row.

By default, the content of a header cell is boldfaced and centered in the cell, and the content of a data cell is left-aligned. Also, the width of the cells is determined by the data they contain, with each cell in a column being as wide as the widest cell. You can see how this works in the browser display in this figure. That's the default formatting, but soon you'll learn how to use CSS to format a table.

Common elements for coding tables

Element	Description
table	Defines a table. The other elements for the table are coded within this element.
tr	Defines a row.
th	Defines a header cell within a row.
td	Defines a data cell within a row.

The HTML for the table in figure 12-1 before it's formatted

```
<table>
    <tr>
        <th class="left">Book</th>
        <th>Year Published</th>
        <th>Sales</th>
    </tr>
    <tr>
        <td class="left">PHP and MySQL</td>
        <td>2017</td>
        <td>$372,381</td>
    </tr>
    <tr>
            .
            .
            .
    </tr>
    <tr>
        <th class="left">Total Sales</th>
        <td></td>
        <td>$1,399,264</td>
    </tr>
</table>
```

The table in a web browser with no CSS formatting

Book	Year Published	Sales
PHP and MySQL	2017	$372,381
JavaScript and jQuery	2020	$305,447
Python Programming	2021	$292,444
Python Data Analysis	2021	$328,992
Total Sales		$1,399,264

Description

- By default, the width of each column in a table is determined automatically based on its content.
- By default, the content of a th element is boldfaced and centered, and the content of a td element is left-aligned.

Figure 12-2   How to create a table

How to add a header and footer

Figure 12-3 presents the elements for grouping rows into headers and footers. It also presents the element for grouping rows in the table body, which you'll typically do when you use a header and footer. As you will see, these elements make it easier to format a table with CSS.

To code a header, you simply code the rows that make up the header between the opening and closing tags of the thead element. Similarly, you code a footer by coding rows within a tfoot element. And you code a body by coding rows within a tbody element.

The example in this figure illustrates how this works. Here, the first row of the table is coded within a thead element, the last row of the table is coded within a tfoot element, and the remaining rows are coded within a tbody element. If you compare the browser display for this table to the one in the previous figure, you'll see that they're identical.

The elements for coding the header, body, and footer

Element	Description
thead	Groups one or more rows into a table header.
tbody	Groups the rows between the header and footer into a table body.
tfoot	Groups one or more rows into a table footer.

The HTML for a table with a header, body, and footer

```
<table>
    <thead>
        <tr>
            <th class="left">Book</th>
            <th>Year published</th>
            <th>Total sales</th>
        </tr>
    </thead>
    <tbody>
        <tr>
            <td class="left">PHP and MySQL</td>
            <td>2017</td>
            <td>$372,381</td>
        </tr>
        .
        .
        .
    </tbody>
    <tfoot>
        <tr>
            <th class="left">Total Sales</th>
            <td></td>
            <td>$1,399,264</td>
        </tr>
    </tfoot>
</table>
```

The table in a web browser (same as in previous figure)

Book	Year Published	Sales
PHP and MySQL	2017	$372,381
JavaScript and jQuery	2020	$305,447
Python Programming	2021	$292,444
Python Data Analysis	2021	$328,992
Total Sales		$1,399,264

Description

- The thead, tbody, and tfoot elements make it easier to style a table with CSS.
- You can code the thead, tbody, and tfoot elements in any sequence, and the header will always be displayed first and the footer last.

Figure 12-3   How to add a header and footer

Basic CSS skills for formatting tables

Now that you know the basic skills for coding tables, you're ready to learn the basic skills for formatting tables using CSS.

How to use CSS to format a table

Figure 12-4 presents some of the common CSS properties for formatting tables. However, you can also use many of the other CSS properties that you've already learned to format a table.

As you saw in the last two figures, a table doesn't include borders by default (the border around those tables were added by the program that we use for capturing screens). In many cases, though, you'll want to add a border around a table to make it stand out on the page. You may also want to add borders around the cells or rows in a table to help identify the columns and rows.

To do that, you can use any of the border properties you learned about in chapter 5. In the CSS in this figure, for example, the shorthand border property adds a solid black border around the table and around each cell in the table.

By default, a small amount of space is included between the cells of a table. To remove that space, you can set the border-collapse property to a value of "collapse". Then, the borders between adjacent cells will be collapsed to a single border as shown in the first table in this figure. But note that if two adjacent cells have different borders, the most dominant border will be displayed. If one border is wider than the other, for example, the wider border will be displayed.

When you use the padding property with tables, it works similarly to the way it works with the box model. That is, it specifies the amount of space between the contents of a cell and the outer edge of the cell. In this figure, for example, you can see that .2 ems of space has been added above and below the contents of each cell, and .7 ems of space to the left and right of the contents.

To complete the formatting, the CSS right aligns all the th and td elements and then left aligns those elements that are in the "left" class. Then, it applies a background color to the header and footer using a selector that includes the thead and tfoot element. And it changes the font weight for the footer to bold. As you will see in the next figure, though, you can use CSS to get the same result without using classes or ids to identify the elements you want to format.

Common properties for formatting table, tr, th, and td elements

Property	Description
border-collapse	A keyword that determines whether space exists between the borders of adjacent cells or the borders are collapsed to a single border between cells. Possible values are collapse and separate. The default is separate.
border-spacing	A relative or absolute value that specifies the space between cells when the borders aren't collapsed.
padding	The space between the cell contents and the outer edge of the cell.
text-align	The horizontal alignment of text.
vertical-align	The vertical alignment of text.

The CSS for the table in figure 12-3

```
table {
    border: 1px solid black;
    border-collapse: collapse; }
th, td {
    border: 1px solid black;
    padding: .2em .7em;
    text-align: right; }
th.left, td.left { text-align: left; }
thead, tfoot { background-color: lightgreen; }
tfoot { font-weight: bold; }
```

The table in a web browser

Book	Year Published	Sales
PHP and MySQL	2017	$372,381
JavaScript and jQuery	2020	$305,447
Python Programming	2021	$292,444
Python Data Analysis	2021	$328,992
Total Sales		$1,399,264

The table without collapsed borders

Book	Year Published	Sales
PHP and MySQL	2017	$372,381
JavaScript and jQuery	2020	$305,447
Python Programming	2021	$292,444
Python Data Analysis	2021	$328,992
Total Sales		$1,399,264

Figure 12-4   How to use CSS to format a table

How to use the CSS structural pseudo-classes for formatting tables

In chapter 4, you were introduced to a few of the CSS pseudo-classes. Now, figure 12-5 presents some of the ones that you can use to format tables. These classes can be referred to as the *structural pseudo-classes*, because they let you select elements by their structural location. By using these pseudo-classes in your selectors, you can avoid the use of id and class selectors, which simplifies your HTML.

To illustrate, the first example in this figure uses the first-child pseudo-class to select the first th and the first td element in each row. This is a structural pseudo-class that you were introduced in chapter 4. Then, the style rule left aligns the data in these cells. This means that you don't need to use the "left" class that was used in figure 12-4 for formatting.

The second example uses the nth-child selector to select the second th and td element in each row. Then, the style rule centers the heading and data in those cells. The result is that the contents of the cells in the second column of the table are centered.

The last example uses the nth-child selector to select all even rows in the body of the table. Then, it applies lightyellow as the background color for these rows. If you look at the table of n values in this figure, you can see that the n value could also be coded as 2n to select all even rows or 2n+1 to select all odd rows. If you want to apply a different color to every third row, you can use other combinations of n values to get that result.

The syntax for the CSS structural pseudo-class selectors

Syntax	Description
:nth-child(n)	nth child of parent
:nth-last-child(n)	nth child of parent counting backwards
:nth-of-type(n)	nth element of its type within the parent
:nth-last-of-type(n)	nth element of its type counting backwards

Typical n values

Value	Meaning
odd	Every odd child or element
even	Every even child or element
n	The nth child or element
2n	Same as even
3n	Every third child or element (3, 6, 9, …)
2n+1	Same as odd
3n+1	Every third child or element starting with 1 (1, 4, 7, …)

The CSS code for formatting a table without using classes

```
th:first-child, td:first-child {
    text-align: left; }
th:nth-child(2), td:nth-child(2) {
    text-align: center; }
tbody tr:nth-child(even) {
    background-color: lightyellow; }
```

The table in a browser

Book	Year Published	Sales
PHP and MySQL	2017	$372,381
JavaScript and jQuery	2020	$305,447
Python Programming	2021	$292,444
Python Data Analysis	2021	$328,992
MySql	2019	$351,200
SQL Server 2019	2020	$404,332
Total Sales		**$2,054,786**

Description

- The CSS *structural pseudo-classes* let you format a table without using classes or ids.

Figure 12-5   How to use the CSS structural pseudo-classes for formatting tables

Other skills for working with tables

Besides the skills you've just learned for working with tables, you may need to use some of the skills that follow.

How to use the HTML figure and figcaption elements with tables

If you read chapter 11, you already know how to treat an image as a figure by using the HTML figure and figcaption elements. Now, figure 12-6 shows how to use these elements for a table that's used as a figure. Here, the figure element contains a figcaption element followed by a table element.

By default, a figcaption element is an inline element, not a block element. As a result, you will usually want to use the CSS display property to change it to a block element. That makes it easier to format the caption. In this example, the figcaption element comes before the table in the HTML so the caption is displayed above the table. But you can change that by coding the figcaption element after the table in the HTML.

In the CSS for the table element, you can see that the top and bottom margins are set to 10 pixels, and the right and left margins are set to "auto". As a result, the table is centered within the figure element.

In figure 12-8, you'll see that you can also use the caption element within a table element to provide a caption for a table. In general, though, it's better to use the figure and figcaption elements to present a table. That way, it's easier for a screen reader to tell that the table is used as a figure and that the caption applies to the table.

A table within a figure

Total Sales by Book

Book	Year Published	Sales
PHP and MySQL	2017	$372,381
JavaScript and jQuery	2020	$305,447
Python Programming	2021	$292,444
Python Data Analysis	2021	$328,992
Total Sales		**$2,054,786**

The HTML for the figure and figcaption elements

```
<figure>
    <figcaption>Total Sales by Book</figcaption>
    <table>

        .
        .

    </table>
</figure>
```

The CSS for the figure and figcaption elements

```
figure, figcaption {
    margin: 0;
    padding: 0; }
figure {
    border: 1px solid black;
    width: 450px;
    padding: 15px; }
figcaption {
    display: block;
    font-weight: bold;
    text-align: center;
    font-size: 120%;
    padding-bottom: .25em; }
table {
    border-collapse: collapse;
    border: 1px solid black;
    margin: 10px auto; }
```

Description

- The figure element can be used as a container for anything that is used as a figure. The figcaption element can be used within a figure to provide a caption that describes the figure, but it is optional. When coded, it can be anywhere within the figure element.
- By default, the figcaption element is an inline element.
- Although you can use the HTML caption element to provide a caption for a table, it's better semantically to use the figure and figcaption elements.

Figure 12-6   How to use the HTML figure and figcaption elements with tables

How to merge cells in a column or row

To make a table easier to read, it often makes sense to *merge* some of the cells. This is illustrated in figure 12-7. Here, four cells are merged in the first row so "Sales" spans the last four columns of the table. Also, two cells are merged in the first column, so "Book" is in its own cell.

To merge cells, you use the two attributes of the th and td elements that are summarized in this figure. To merge cells so a cell in a row spans two or more columns, you use the colspan attribute. To merge cells so a cell in a column spans two or more rows, you use the rowspan attribute. The value you use for these attributes indicates the number of cells that will be merged.

The example in this figure illustrates how these attributes work. Here, you can see a table header that consists of two rows and five columns. However, the first header cell spans two rows. As a result, the second row doesn't include a th element for the first column.

Now, take a look at the second header cell in the first row of the header. This cell spans the remaining four columns of the row. As a result, this row includes only two th elements: the one that defines the cell that contains the "Book" heading, and the one that defines the cell that contains the "Sales" heading.

In the CSS for the merged cells, you can see how the CSS structural pseudo-classes are used in the selectors. First, the first-child class is used to bottom align "Book" in the merged cell that spans two rows. Second, the nth-child class is used to center "Sales" in the merged cell that spans four columns. Third, the nth-child class is used to right align the th cells within the second row of the table.

Attributes of the <th> and <td> tags for merging cells

Attribute	Description
colspan	Identifies the number of columns that a cell will span. The default is 1.
rowspan	Identifies the number of rows that a cell will span. The default is 1.

A table with merged cells

Book	Sales			
	North	South	West	Total
PHP and MySQL	$55,174	$73,566	$177,784	$306,524
JavaScript and jQuery	$28,775	$39,995	$239,968	$308,738
Python Programming	$27,688	$24,349	$168,228	$220,265
Python Data Analysis	$23,082	$24,858	$129,619	$177,559
Sales Totals	$140,775	$165,550	$762,794	$1,069,119

The HTML for the table

```
<table>
    <thead>
        <tr>
            <th rowspan="2">Book</th>
            <th colspan="4">Sales</th>
        </tr>
        <tr>
            <th>North</th>
            <th>South</th>
            <th>West</th>
            <th>Total</th>
        </tr>
    </thead>
    <tbody>
        ...

    </tbody>
    <tfoot>
        <tr>
            <th>Sales Totals</th>
            <td>$140,775</td>
            <td>$165,550</td>
            <td>$762,794</td>
            <td>$1,069,119</td>
        </tr>
    </tfoot>
</table>
```

The CSS for the merged cells

```
th:first-child {  vertical-align: bottom; } /* bottom aligns "Book" */
th:nth-child(2) { text-align: center; }    /* centers "Sales" */
tr:nth-child(2) th { text-align: right; }  /* right aligns 2nd row hdgs */
```

Figure 12-7   How to merge cells in a column or row

How to provide for accessibility

Because tables are difficult for visually-impaired users to decipher, HTML provides a few attributes that can improve accessibility. These attributes are summarized in figure 12-8, and they can be read by screen readers.

First, it's important to provide a caption for each table that summarizes what the table contains. To do that, you can use the caption element as shown in this figure or the figure and figcaption elements as shown in figure 12-6.

Second, you can code the headers attribute on a td or th element to identify one or more header cells that the cell is associated with. To identify a header cell, you code the value of the cell's id attribute. In the example in this figure, you can see that an id attribute is coded for each of the three th elements in the table header as well as the th element in the table footer. Then, each of the td elements includes a headers attribute that names the associated th element or elements.

For instance, the headers attribute for the first td element in each row of the body names the header cell that contains the header "Book" because the content of these cells are book names. Similarly, the td element in the footer includes a headers attribute that names two th elements. The first one is for the header cell in the third column of the first row (the one with the heading "Sales"), and the second one is for the header cell in the first column of the last row (the one with the heading "Total Sales").

The last attribute for accessibility is scope. Although you can code this attribute on either a td or th element, it's used most often with the th element. The scope attribute indicates whether a cell is associated with a column, a row, or a group of merged cells in a column. In this figure, for example, this attribute indicates that each of the three th elements in the header row is associated with a column.

Even if you use these attributes, a table can be difficult for a visually-impaired person to interpret. So besides coding these attributes, try to keep your tables simple. That is not only good for the visually-impaired, but also for all the users of your website.

Attributes that can be used for accessibility

Attribute	Description
caption	Describes the contents of the table. The other alternative is to treat the table as a figure and use the figcaption element to describe the table.
headers	Identifies one or more header cells that describe the content of the cell.
scope	A keyword that tells if a cell is associated with a column or row. Common keywords are col and row. You can also use the keyword rowgroup to refer to merged cells.

The HTML for a table that provides for accessibility

```
<table>
<caption>Total sales for books published from 2012 to 2017</caption>
<thead>
    <tr>
        <th id="hdr_book" scope="col">Book</th>
        <th id="hdr_year" scope="col">Year Published</th>
        <th id="hdr_sales" scope="col">Sales</th>
    </tr>
</thead>
<tbody>
    <tr>
        <td headers="hdr_book">PHP and MySQL</td>
        <td headers="hdr_year">2017</td>
        <td headers="hdr_sales">$372,381</td>
    </tr>
    <tr>
        <td headers="hdr_book">JavaScript and jQuery</td>
        <td headers="hdr_year">2020</td>
        <td headers="hdr_sales">$305,447</td>
    </tr>
</tbody>
<tfoot>
    <tr>
        <th id="hdr_total" scope="row">Total Sales</th>
        <td></td>
        <td headers="hdr_sales hdr_total">$2,054,786</td>
    </tr>
</tfoot>
</table>
```

Accessibility guideline

- Use the attributes listed above to make a table more accessible to visually-impaired users who use screen readers.

Figure 12-8   How to provide for accessibility

How to make a table responsive

As you develop responsive websites, you may need to modify your tables so they're appropriate for smaller screen sizes. To do that, you can start by making the width of each table and its columns fluid. That way, the tables and columns will get narrower as the screen gets narrower.

In addition to making a table fluid, you may want to change how it's formatted for smaller screen sizes. Figure 12-9 shows one of the ways you could do that. Here, you can see the table in figure 12-4 after it has been reformatted by a media query for screens with widths that are 479 pixels or less.

To reformat this table, the first style rule in the media query sets the display property of the th and td elements to block. That way, each cell in the table will be displayed on a separate line. Then, the second style rule sets the display property for the header to none so it isn't displayed.

The next style rule formats the first td element within each tr element. These are the cells in the body that contain the book titles. As you can see, these cells are formatted so they identify each group of cells.

The next style rule removes the bottom border from all of the td elements in the body of the table. Because these cells are defined with a one-pixel border on each side, removing the bottom border will cause the cells to have just one border between them (the top border).

The style rule for the footer changes the background color to white, removes the border from around the footer, and then adds a border only to the top. Since the cell above the footer has a bottom border, this creates a wider border above the footer.

The last style rule formats the th element in the footer, which contains the text "Total Sales," as well as the first td element in the footer, which contains no content. Here, the display property of these elements is set to none so they aren't displayed.

In this example, most of the style rules in the media query are used to format the cells of the table after they're displayed in a single column. Remember, though, that this is just one way you could reformat the table for a smaller screen. It is just intended to give you some idea of what can be done.

The first table in figure 12-4 in desktop and mobile widths

Book		Year Published	Sales
PHP and MySQL		2017	$372,381
JavaScript and jQuery		2020	$305,447
Python Programming			
Python Data Analysis			
Total Sales			

PHP and MySQL
2017
$372,381
JavaScript and jQuery
2020
$305,447
Python Programming
2021
$292,444
Python Data Analysis
2021
$328,992
$1,399,264

The media query for the table

```
@media only screen and (max-width: 479px) {
    th, td { display: block; }
    thead { display: none; }
    tr td:first-child {
        font-weight: bold;
        font-size: 110%;
        background-color: lightgreen;
    }
    tbody td { border-bottom-style: none; }
    tfoot {
        background-color: white;
        border: none;
        border-top: 1px solid black;
    }
    tfoot th, tfoot td:nth-of-type(1) { display: none; }
}
```

Description

- To make a table responsive, you can make the table and column widths fluid, and you can reformat the table so it fits on smaller screens.

- One way to reformat a table is to change the display property of all the th and td elements for the table to block so each table cell starts on a new line. Then, you can hide elements that you don't want to be displayed, and you can change the formatting of other elements.

Figure 12-9   How to make a table responsive

Perspective

As you've seen in this chapter, it's relatively easy to create and format simple tables. Remember, though, that you should only use tables when you're presenting tabular data. You should be using CSS, not tables, for page layout.

Terms

table	header
row	footer
column	body
cell	structural pseudo-classes
data cell	merged cells
header cell	

Summary

- A *table* consists of *rows* and *columns* that intersect at *cells*. *Data cells* contain the data of a table. *Header cells* identify the data in a column or row.

- The rows in a table can be grouped into a *header*, a *body*, and a *footer*.

- To define a table in HTML, you use the table, tr, th, and td elements. Then, you can use CSS to apply borders, spacing, fonts, and background colors to these elements.

- If you use the thead, tfoot, and tbody elements to group the rows in a table, it's easier to style the table with CSS.

- You can use the CSS *structural pseudo-classes* to format the rows or columns of a table without using id or class selectors.

- The HTML figure element can be used to treat a table as a figure. The HTML figcaption element can be used within a figure element to provide a caption for the figure.

- To make a table easier to read, you can *merge* two or more cells in a header or footer column or row.

- To make tables more accessible to visually-impaired users, you can use the HTML attributes that can be read by screen readers.

- To make a table responsive, you can make the table and column widths fluid. You can also use media queries for smaller devices that use the display property to display each table cell on a new line.

Exercise 12-1   Add a table to the luncheons page

In this exercise, you'll enhance the luncheons page by adding a table to it so it looks like the one that follows.

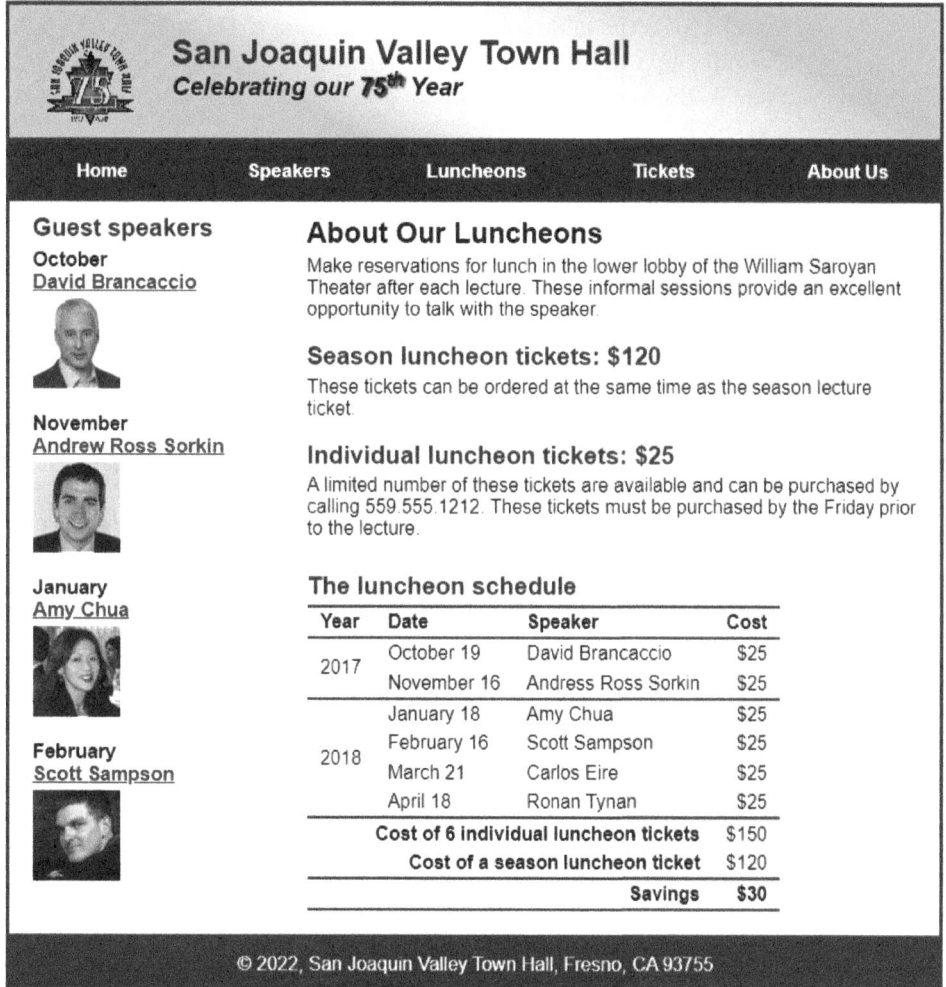

Enter the table into the luncheons.html file

1. Use your text editor to open the luncheons.html page in the town_hall_3 folder. Then, run the page to see that everything but the table is already in the file.

2. Add the table shown above to the page. To start the table, you may want to copy the HTML for one of the tables in the book examples into the file. Then, you can modify that code and add the data for the new table. To quickly add new rows to the table, you can copy and paste earlier rows.

3. Test the page to make sure the contents are all there, even though the table won't be formatted right.

Add the CSS for the table to the main.css file

4. Use your text editor to open the c12_main.css file in the styles folder. To start the code for the table, copy the CSS for one of the tables in the book examples into the file. Then, test to see how the table looks.

5. Modify the CSS so the table looks like the one above. Here, all of the borders and the text in the heading above the table should have #800000 as their color. To do some of the alignment and to add borders to some of the rows, you should use classes.

6. Test and adjust until the table looks the way you want it to.

Treat the table as a figure, provide for accessibility, and experiment

7. Enclose the table within a figure element, and code a figcaption element above the table, but within the figure element. Then, copy the h2 element that says: "The luncheon schedule" into the figcaption element.

8. Test this change. The page should look the same as it did in step 6, except the table will now be centered.

9. Using figure 12-8 as a guide, add the attributes for user accessibility.

10. Experiment with the CSS structural pseudo-classes to see whether you can replace some of your class selectors with pseudo-class selectors.

Chapter 13

How to work with forms

To create dynamic web pages, you use HTML to create forms that let the user enter data. Then, the user can click on a button to submit the data to a web server for processing. In this chapter, you'll learn how to code forms and the controls they contain.

How to use forms and controls

A *form* contains one or more *controls* such as text boxes and buttons. In the topics that follow, you'll learn how to create a form and how to add the controls to a form.

How to create a form

Figure 13-1 shows how to code a form that contains two controls: a text box and a button. To start, you code the form element. On the opening tag for this element, you code the action and method attributes. The action attribute specifies the file on the web server that should be used to process the data when the form is submitted. The method attribute specifies the HTTP method that should be used for sending the form to the web server.

In the example in this figure, the form will be submitted to the server using the HTTP "post" method when the user clicks the Subscribe button. Then, the data in the form will be processed by the code that's stored in the file named subscribe.php.

When you use the post method, the form data is packaged as part of an HTTP request and isn't visible in the browser. Because of that, the submission is more secure than it is when you use the "get" method.

When you use the get method, the form data is sent as part of the URL for the HTTP request. That means that the data is visible and the page can be bookmarked. This is illustrated by the URL in this figure. Here, the URL is followed by a question mark and name/value pairs separated by ampersands. In this case, two values are submitted: the email address that has been entered, and the value of the Submit button.

Between the opening and closing tags of the form element, you code the controls for the form. In this example, the first input element is for the text box that will receive the user's email address. The second input element displays a button. You'll learn how to code these controls in the next two figures.

But first, this figure summarizes the five attributes that are common to most controls. Here, the type attribute specifies the type of control you want to use, like the button and text types in this example. The id attribute specifies a unique id that can be referred to by JavaScript. And the name attribute must be coded if the form is going to be submitted to the server.

In contrast to the type, id, and name attributes, the disabled and readonly attributes are Boolean attributes that you'll use infrequently. The disabled attribute disables a control so the data in the control isn't submitted with the form. And the readonly attribute provides a value that can't be changed but is submitted with the form.

Attributes of the form element

Attribute	Description
id	A unique id that can be referred to by client-side code.
action	The URL of the file that will process the data in the form.
method	The HTTP method for submitting the form data. It can be set to either "get" or "post". The default value is "get".

Attributes common to most input elements

Attribute	Description
type	The type of control like "button", "text", or "checkbox".
id	A unique id that can be referred to by client-side code.
name	A name that can be referred to by client-side or server-side code.
disabled	A Boolean attribute that disables and grays out the control. Then, the control can't receive the focus, the user can't tab to it, and the value isn't submitted with the form.
readonly	A Boolean attribute that means a user can't change the control's value. But the control can receive the focus, the user can tab to it, and the value is submitted with the form.

The HTML for a form

```html
<form id="email_form" action="subscribe.php" method="post">
    <p>Please enter your e-mail address to subscribe to our newsletter.</p>
    <p>E-Mail: <input type="text" id="email"></p>
    <p><input type="submit" id="submit" value="Subscribe"></p>
</form>
```

The form in a web browser

Please enter your e-mail address to subscribe to our newsletter.

E-Mail: [   ]

[Subscribe   ]

The URL when the form is submitted with the get method

```
subscribe.php?email=zak%40modulemedia.com&submit=Subscribe
```

Description

- A *form* contains one or more *controls* like text boxes that can receive data.
- When a form is submitted to the server for processing, the data in the controls is sent along with the HTTP request.
- For the get method, the URL is followed by a question mark and name/value pairs that are separated by ampersands. For the post method, the data is hidden.

Figure 13-1   How to create a form

How to use buttons

Figure 13-2 shows five different types of *buttons*. To code the first four, you use the input element as shown in the HTML in this figure.

In the examples, the first button is a generic button, defined by setting the type attribute to "button". When the user clicks this type of button, client-side code is usually run. For instance, JavaScript can be used to validate the data on the form. Then, if the data is valid, the script can submit the form to the server.

The second button is a *submit button*. When it is clicked, the form and its data is submitted to the server for processing. Unlike a generic button, a submit button sends the data to the server automatically without using client-side code.

The third button is a *reset button*. When it is clicked, the values in all of the controls on the form are reset to their default values.

The fourth button is an *image button*. It works like a submit button. The difference is that an image button displays an image rather than text. To specify the URL for the image, you use the src attribute. To specify text if the image can't be displayed, you use the alt attribute. And if you want to size the image, you can set the width and height attributes.

If you don't specify a value attribute for the first three types of buttons, the web browser supplies a default value depending on the button type. For example, the default text for a submit button is usually "Submit", the default text for a reset button is usually "Reset", and the default text for a generic button is usually "Button."

To code the fifth type of button, you use the button element instead of the input element. When you use the button element, you can format the text that's displayed on the button, and you can include elements other than text. In the example in this figure, the img element has been used to add a shopping cart image in front of the "Add to Cart" text for the button. However, you still need to set the type attribute so the browser knows how to treat the button when it is clicked by the user.

Attributes of the input element for buttons and for the button element

Attribute	Description
type	The type of button. Valid values include "submit", "reset", "button", or "image".
value	The text that's displayed on the button and submitted to the server when the button is clicked.
src	The relative or absolute URL of the image to display.
alt	Alternate text to display in place of the image.
height	The height of the button in either pixels or a percent.
width	The width of the button in either pixels or a percent.

Four buttons that are created by the input element

```
<input type="button" id="message" value="Alert Me">
<input type="submit" id="checkout" value="Checkout">
<input type="reset" id="resetform" value="Reset">
<input type="image" src="images/submit.jpg" alt="Submit button"
       width="114" height="42">
```

A button that is created by the button element

```
<button type="submit">
    <img src="images/addtocart.png" width="30" height="23"
        alt="Add to Cart">Add to Cart</button>
```

The buttons in a web browser

Description

- You can use the input element to create four different types of *buttons*.

- You can also use the button element to create a button. The main difference between the input and button elements is that the button element can contain formatted text as well as other HTML elements such as images.

- When you click on a *submit button* for a form (type is "submit"), the form data is sent to the server as part of an HTTP request. When you click on a *reset button* (type is "reset"), the data in all of the fields is reset to the default values.

- You can use the button type to run a client-side script that validates the form data. Then, if the data is valid, the script can submit the form to the server.

Figure 13-2   How to use buttons

How to use text fields and text areas

The first example in figure 13-3 shows how to use the input element to create three types of *text fields*, also referred to as *text boxes*. Here, the first input element displays a text field that accepts input from a user. To do that, the type attribute for this element is set to "text".

Then, the second input element creates a *password field*. This works like the first input element, but when you enter a value, it is displayed as bullets or asterisks. This improves the security of an application by preventing others from reading a password as a user enters it.

The third input element creates a *hidden field*, which is a field that isn't displayed by the browser so the user can't enter data into it. Instead, its value is set by the value attribute. Then, you can use client-side or server-side code to work with that value.

In these examples, the username and password fields are displayed at their default widths. But as you will soon learn, you can use CSS to change that as well as to align the controls.

The second example in this figure shows how to code a text area. This is like a text field, but a text area can receive multiple lines of text. And if the user enters more lines than can be displayed at one time, the browser adds a scroll bar to the text area.

To create a text area control, you code a textarea element. Within that element, you can use the value attribute to code a default value. Or, you can code a placeholder attribute that displays text that disappears when the text area receives the focus, as shown in this example.

Attributes of the input element for text fields

Attribute	Description
type	The type of text field. Valid values include "text", "password", and "hidden".
value	The default value for the field, but the user can change this value.
maxlength	The maximum number of characters that the user can enter in the field.
autofocus	A Boolean attribute that tells the browser to set the focus on the field.
placeholder	A default value or hint in the field that is removed when the user's cursor enters the control.

The HTML for text fields

```
Username:<input type="text" id="username" autofocus><br><br>
Password:<input type="password" id="password" maxlength="6"
                placeholder="Enter your password"><br><br>
Hidden:<input type="hidden" id="productid" value="widget">
```

The text fields in a web browser

```
Username: [                    ]

Password: [Enter your password ]

Hidden:
```

The HTML for a text area with default text

```
Comments:<br>
<textarea id="comments"
    placeholder="If you have any comments, please enter them here.">
</textarea>
```

The CSS for the text area

```
textarea { height: 5em; width: 25em; }
```

The text area in a web browser

```
Comments:
[If you have any comments, please enter them here.]
```

Description

- The three most common types of *text fields* are text, password, and hidden.
- A *textarea field* (or just *text area*) can be used to get multi-line text entries.

Figure 13-3   How to use text fields and text areas

How to use radio buttons, check boxes, and labels

Figure 13-4 shows how to use label and input elements to code *checkbox fields* and *radio fields*, commonly referred to as *check boxes* and *radio buttons*. Although check boxes work independently of each other, radio buttons are typically set up so the user can select only one radio button from a group of buttons. In the example in this figure, for instance, you can select only one of the three radio buttons. However, you can select or deselect any combination of check boxes.

To create a radio button, you set the type attribute of the input element to "radio". Then, to create a group, you set the name attribute for all of the radio buttons in the group to the same value. In this figure, all three radio buttons have "crust" as their name attribute. That way, the user will only be able to select one of these radio buttons at a time. Note, however, that each of these buttons has a different value attribute. That way, the client-side or server-side code can get the value of the selected button.

To create a check box, you set the type attribute of the input element to "checkbox". Then, you set the name attribute so you can access the control from your client-side and server-side code. When you submit the form to the server, a name/value pair for the check box is submitted but only if it's selected.

If you want a check box or radio button to be selected by default, you can code the checked attribute. In this figure, for example, the first radio button has been selected by default.

Note, however, that the text for the radio buttons and text boxes is provided by the label elements that follow them. For instance, the first label element provides the text for the first radio button. To do that, the for attribute of the label is set to the id attribute of the radio button. As a result, the text for the first radio button is "Thin Crust".

When radio buttons and check boxes are coded this way, the user can click on the label text to turn a button or check box on or off. This makes the buttons and check boxes more accessible to users who lack the motor skills to click on the smaller button or box.

This also makes it easier for assistive devices such as screen readers to read the text associated with a control and tell it to the user. If you don't use labels in this way, the assistive devices have to scan the text around a control and guess which snippet of text is associated with the control.

Attributes of the input element for radio buttons and check boxes

Attribute	Description
type	The type of control, either "radio" or "checkbox".
name	A name that can be referred to by client-side or server-side code.
value	The value to submit to the server when the control is checked and the form is submitted.
checked	A Boolean attribute that causes the control to be checked when the page is loaded.

The HTML for a form with label elements

```
Crust:<br>
<input type="radio" name="crust" id="crust1" value="thin" checked>
<label for="crust1">Thin Crust</label><br>
<input type="radio" name="crust" id="crust2" value="deep">
<label for="crust2">Deep Dish</label><br>
<input type="radio" name="crust" id="crust3" value="hand">
<label for="crust3">Hand Tossed</label><br><br>

Toppings:<br>
<input type="checkbox" name="topping1" id="topping1" value="pepperoni">
<label for="topping1">Pepperoni</label><br>
<input type="checkbox" name="topping2" id="topping2" value="mushrooms">
<label for="topping2">Mushrooms</label><br>
<input type="checkbox" name="topping3" id="topping3" value="Black Olives">
<label for="topping3">Black Olives</label><br><br>
```

The HTML in a browser

Crust:
- ◉ Thin Crust
- ○ Deep Dish
- ○ Hand Tossed

Toppings:
- ☐ Pepperoni
- ☐ Mushrooms
- ☐ Black Olives

Accessibility guideline

- Use labels with radio buttons and check boxes so the user can click on the label to select the control that the label is associated with. This also helps assistive devices.

Description

- Only one *radio button* in a group can be selected at one time, but *check boxes* are unrelated, so more than one check box can be checked at the same time.
- *Labels* are related to input elements by the for attribute.

Figure 13-4   How to use radio buttons, check boxes, and labels

How to use drop-down lists and list boxes

The first example in figure 13-5 shows how to code a *drop-down list*. To display the list of options, the user can move the cursor into the control or click the arrow at the right side of the control.

To code a drop-down list, you use a select element with an id atribute. Then, between the opening and closing tags, you code two or more option elements with value attributes that provide the values that will be sent to the server. You also code the text that's displayed for each list item as the content of the element. This text is often the same or similar to the value for the option.

If you want to group the options in a drop-down list, you can code one or more optgroup elements. In this figure, for example, two optgroup elements are used to divide the options that are available into two groups: The New Yorker and The Chicago. To do that, the label attribute specifies the label for each group. Note, however, that the user can't select a group, only the options it contains.

When a drop-down list is first displayed, the first option in the list is selected by default. If that's not what you want, you can code the selected attribute for the option you want to be selected.

The second example in this figure shows how to code a *list box*. A list box differs from a drop-down list in that two or more of its options are always displayed. You can also define a list box so two or more options can be selected at the same time.

To code a list box, you use a select element with an id attribute. You also code the size attribute to indicate the number of options that are displayed at one time. In this example, the size attribute is set to 4, but the list contains seven options, so the browser adds a scroll bar to the list.

By default, the user can select only one option from a list box. But you can change that by coding the multiple attribute. Then, to select multiple options, the user can hold down the Ctrl key in Windows or the Command key in macOS and click on the options.

Attributes of the select element

Attribute	Description
size	The number of items to display in the control. The default value is 1.
multiple	A Boolean attribute that determines whether multiple items can be selected.

Attributes of the optgroup and option elements

Element	Attribute	Description
optgroup	label	The text that's used to identify a group of options.
option	value	The value of the selected option that will be sent to the server for processing.
option	selected	A Boolean attribute that causes the option to be selected when the page is loaded.

The HTML for a drop-down list

```
Style:<br>
<select id="style_and_size">
    <optgroup label="The New Yorker">
        <option value="ny10">10"</option>
        <option value="ny12">12"</option>
        <option value="ny16">16"</option>
    </optgroup>
    <optgroup label="The Chicago">
        <option value="chi10">10"</option>
        <option value="chi12">12"</option>
        <option value="chi16">16"</option>
    </optgroup>
</select>
```

The list in a browser

The HTML for a list box

```
<select id="toppings" size="4" multiple>
    <option value="pepperoni">Pepperoni</option>
    <option value="sausage" selected>Sausage</option>
    <option value="mushrooms">Mushrooms</option>
    <option value="olives">Black olives</option>
    ...
</select>
```

The list box in a browser

Description

- *Drop-down lists* and *list boxes* let the user select items.
- If a list box contains more options than can be displayed at one time, a scroll bar is added to the list box.
- You use the option element to define the options in a drop-down list or list box, and you can use the optgroup element to define option groups.
- To select multiple items, the user can hold down the Ctrl or Command key.

Figure 13-5   How to use drop-down lists and list boxes

How to use the number, email, url, and tel controls

Figure 13-6 shows how to use the number, email, url, and tel controls. These controls are good for semantics because they indicate the type of entry that should be made. The example in this figure shows how to code these controls.

Here, the number control has 100 as its minimum value, 1000 as its maximum value, 100 as the step value, and 300 as its starting value. Then, when the cursor enters the control, up and down arrows appear on the right side of the control so the user can move the number up or down by clicking on the arrows.

This control is followed by the email, url, and tel controls. As you will soon see, the email and url controls provide for automatic data validation. However, validation isn't done for tel fields because the format of telephone numbers varies so much from one country to another.

As you use these controls, keep in mind that mobile browsers also provide some support for these controls. When you move the focus to an email control, for example, a keyboard that is optimized for entering email addresses may be displayed.

The number, email, url, and tel controls

Control	Description
number	A control for receiving a number with min, max, and step attributes.
email	A control for receiving an email address. This implies that the entry will be validated by the browser when the form is submitted.
url	A control for receiving a URL. This implies that the entry will be validated by the browser when the form is submitted.
tel	A control for receiving a telephone number, but this doesn't imply validation because the formats vary from one country to another.

HTML code that uses the number, email, url, and tel controls

```
<form id="email_form" action="survey.php" method="post">
    <label for="investment">Monthly investment: </label>
    <input type="number" id="investment"
           min="100" max="1000" step="100" value="300"><br><br>
    <label for="email">Your email address:</label>
    <input type="email" id="email" required><br>
    <label for="link">Your website:</label>
    <input type="url" id="link" list="links"><br>
    <label for="phone">Your phone number:</label>
    <input type="tel" id="phone" required><br><br>
    <input type="submit" id="submit" value="Submit Survey">
</form>
```

The form in Chrome

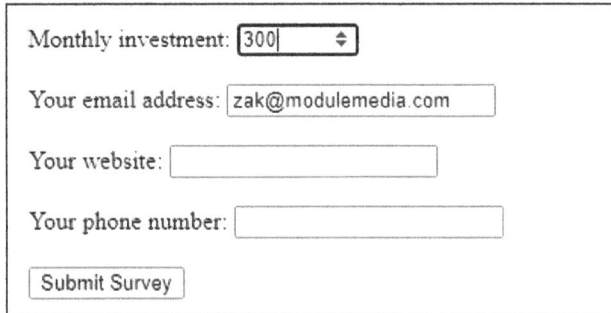

Description

- Because the number, email, url, and tel controls indicate the type of data that they accept, these controls are good for semantics.
- The entries in email and url controls are validated by the browser when the form is submitted, but numbers and phone numbers aren't validated.

Figure 13-6   How to use the number, email, url, and tel controls

How to use the date and time controls

Figure 13-7 shows how to use the date and time controls. When the user clicks on the symbol at the right of one of these controls, a panel drops down that makes is easy to select an entry. This is illustrated by the calendar for the last control in this figure

If you study the examples, you can see how to code the input elements for these controls. The only difference between the datetime and the datetime-local types is that datetime is formatted in Coordinated Universal Time, or UTC. This is the time by which the world sets its clocks. In contrast, datetime-local is based on the date and time used by your system's clock.

At this writing, not all browsers render these controls in the same way. But the worst case is that these controls get rendered as text boxes. And even then, it's good to use these controls for semantic reasons.

Attributes for the date and time controls

Attribute	Description
max	The maximum value that may be entered within a date or time field.
min	The minimum value that may be entered within a date or time field.

HTML that uses the date and time controls

```
Date and time:  
    <input type="datetime" name="datetime"><br><br>
Local date and time:  
    <input type="datetime-local" id="datetimelocal"><br><br>
Month:  
    <input type="month" id="month"><br><br>
Week:  
    <input type="week" id="week"><br><br>
Time:  
    <input type="time" id="time"><br><br>
Date:  
    <input type="date" id="date">
```

The controls in Chrome

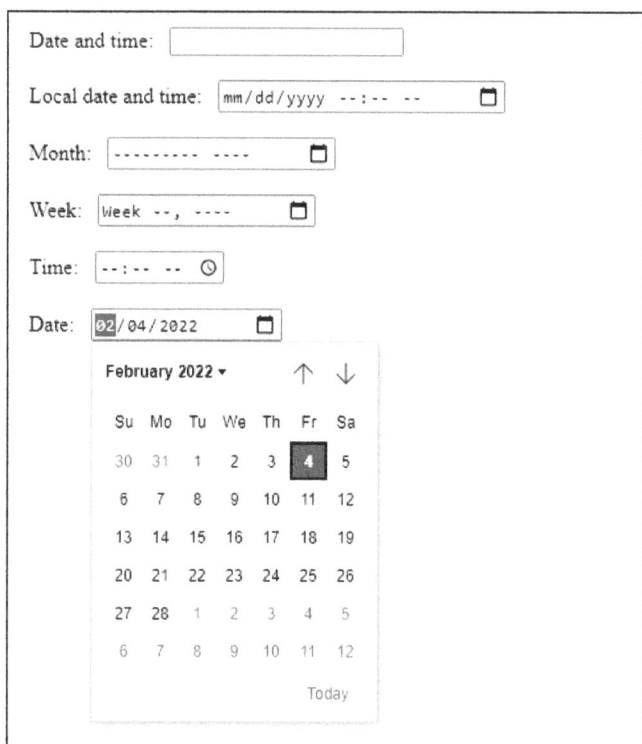

Description

- The HTML datetime, datetime-local, month, week, time, and date controls are designed for date and time entries. Here again, it's good to use these controls for semantic reasons.

Figure 13-7   How to use the date and time controls

Other skills for working with forms

Now that you know how to code a form and the basic controls, you're ready to learn some other skills for working with forms and controls. That includes aligning and grouping controls as well us setting the tab order and assigning access keys.

How to align controls

The best way to align controls is to use the technique shown in figure 13-8. Here, the style rule for the labels starts by floating the labels to the left. That causes the labels to be treated like block elements. Then, the style rule sets the width property so all the labels are the same width, and it sets the text-align property so the labels are aligned at the right. This makes the form more readable.

After the style rule for labels, a style rule is coded for the input controls. Here, the margin-left property increases the space between the labels and text boxes to 1 em. Then, the margin-bottom property sets the space after the text boxes to .5 ems.

The last style rule aligns the buttons on the form by adjusting the left margin of just the Register button to 7 ems. To do that, it uses the Register button's id as the selector. This aligns that button with the text boxes above it. Then, the Reset button is 1 em to the right of the Register button because the left margin for all input controls is set to 1 em.

Label, text box, and button controls aligned on a form

First name: [ ]
Last name: [ ]
Address: [ ]
City: [ ]
State: [ ]
Zip code: [ ]

[Register] [Reset]

The HTML for the form

```
<label for="firstname">First name:</label>
<input type="text" id="firstname" autofocus><br>
<label for="lastname">Last name:</label>
<input type="text" id="lastname"><br>
<label for="address">Address:</label>
<input type="text" id="address"><br>
<label for="city">City:</label>
<input type="text" id="city"><br>
<label for="state">State:</label>
<input type="text" id="state"><br>
<label for="zip">Zip code:</label>
<input type="text" id="zip"><br>
<input type="submit" id="button" value="Register">
<input type="reset" name="reset" id="reset">
```

The CSS for the controls

```
label {
    float: left;
    width: 5em;
    text-align: right;}
input {
    margin-left: 1em;
    margin-bottom: .5em;}
#button {
    margin-left: 7em;}
```

Description

- If a form includes a series of controls and labels that identify them, you can align the labels by floating them to the left of the controls and setting a width that provides enough space for all the labels. Then, you can set a left margin for the controls to add space between the labels and the controls.

- A series of labels is typically more readable if the labels are aligned at the right.

Figure 13-8 How to align controls

How to group controls

In many cases, you'll want to group related controls on a form to make it easy for users to see that they're related. To group controls, you use the fieldset and legend elements as shown in figure 13-9.

To start, you code the fieldset element. Then, you code the legend element right after the opening tag of the fieldset element. The content of this legend element determines the text that's displayed for the group. Then, the controls in the group follow the legend element.

The example in this figure illustrates how this works. Here, two groups are defined: one that contains radio buttons and one that contains check boxes. By default, this code places a thin gray border around the groups, as shown in this figure. To change the appearance of this border, though, you can use CSS.

HTML that uses fieldset and legend elements

```html
<form id="order" action="order.php" method="post">
<fieldset>
    <legend>Crust</legend>
    <input type="radio" name="crust" id="crust1" value="thin">
    <label for="crust1">Thin Crust</label><br>
    <input type="radio" name="crust" id="crust2" value="deep">
    <label for="crust2">Deep Dish</label><br>
    <input type="radio" name="crust" id="crust3" value="hand">
    <label for="crust3">Hand Tossed</label>
</fieldset>
<br>
<fieldset>
    <legend>Toppings</legend>
    <input type="checkbox" name="topping1" id="topping1" value="pepperoni">
    <label for="topping1">Pepperoni</label><br>
    <input type="checkbox" name="topping2" id="topping2" value="mushrooms">
    <label for="topping2">Mushrooms</label><br>
    <input type="checkbox" name="topping3" id="topping3" value="olives">
    <label for="topping3">Black Olives</label>
</fieldset>
</form>
```

The elements in a web browser

Description

- The fieldset element is used to group controls.
- The legend element can be coded within a fieldset element to label the group of controls.
- If you want to disable all of the controls within a fieldset element, you can code the disabled attribute for the fieldset element.

Figure 13-9   How to group controls

How to set the tab order and assign access keys

Figure 13-10 shows how to set the tab order of the controls and how to assign access keys to controls. By default, when the user presses the Tab key on a web page, the focus moves from one control to another in the sequence that the controls appear in the HTML, not including labels. This sequence is referred to as the *tab order* of the controls, and it includes the links created by <a> elements.

To change this default tab order, you can code tabindex attributes. To remove a control from the tab order, for example, you assign a negative number to its tabindex attribute. To include a control in the order, you start the tabindex attribute at zero or any positive number and then increment the index by any amount as you add more controls. You can also code the same tabindex value for more than one control. Then, within those controls, the tab order will be the sequence that the controls appear in the HTML.

Controls that aren't assigned a tabindex value will also receive the focus in the sequence that the controls appear in the HTML. These controls will receive the focus after all the controls that are assigned tabindex values. As a result, you usually assign tabindex values to all of the controls on a form if you assign values to any of the controls.

You can also use the autofocus attribute to put the focus in the control that you want the user to start with. This is often all you need to do to get the tab order the way you want it. This also gets around any browser variations that affect where the tab order starts.

When you provide an *access key* for a control, the user can press that key in combination with one or more other keys to move the focus to a control. If the page is displayed in Edge or Chrome on a Windows system, for example, the user can press Alt+Shift and the access key.

To define an access key, you code the accesskey attribute as shown in the first example. The value of this attribute is the keyboard key that the user should use to move the focus to the control. Here, the access key for the First name text box is "F", the access key for the Last name text box is "L", and the access key for the Email text box is "E". Here, the letters that are used for the access keys are underlined in the labels that are associated with the controls. This is a common way to identify the access key for a control.

The second example shows another way to code access keys for controls that have labels associated with them. Here, the accesskey attribute is coded for each of the labels instead of for the text boxes. Then, when the user activates one of these access keys, the focus is moved to the associated text box (the one specified by the for attribute) because labels can't receive the focus.

The attributes for setting the tab order and access keys

Attribute	Description
tabindex	To set the tab order for a control, use a value of 0 or more. To take a control out of the tab order, use a negative value like -1.
accesskey	A keyboard key that can be pressed in combination with a control key to move the focus to the control.

Three labels with access keys

First name: [_____]

Last name: [_____]

Email: [_____]

The HTML with the access keys defined for the input elements

```
<label for="firstname"><u>F</u>irst name:</label>
<input type="text" id="firstname" accesskey="F"><br>
<label for="lastname"><u>L</u>ast name:</label>
<input type="text" id="lastname" accesskey="L"><br>
<label for="email"><u>E</u>mail:</label>
<input type="text" id="email" accesskey="E">
```

The HTML with the access keys for the label elements

```
<label for="firstname" accesskey="F"><u>F</u>irst name:</label>
<input type="text" id="firstname"><br>
<label for="lastname" accesskey="L"><u>L</u>ast name:</label>
<input type="text" id="lastname"><br>
<label for="email" accesskey="E"><u>E</u>mail:</label>
<input type="text" id="email">
```

Accessibility guideline

- Setting a proper tab order and providing access keys improves the accessibility for users who can't use a mouse.

Description

- The *tab order* for a form is the sequence in which the controls receive the focus when the Tab key is pressed. By default, the tab order is the order of the controls in the HTML, not including labels, but most browsers also include links in the default tab order.

- *Access keys* are shortcut keys that the user can press to move the focus to specific controls on a form. If you assign an access key to a label, the focus is moved to the control that's associated with the label since labels can't receive the focus.

- To use an access key, you press a control key plus the access key. On a Windows system, use Alt+Shift for all browsers. On a Mac, use Ctrl+Option.

Figure 13-10　How to set the tab order and assign access keys

How to use the HTML features for data validation

Now, it's on to the HTML features for *data validation*. These features let you validate some of the data that the user enters into a form without using client-side or server-side scripting languages!

The HTML attributes and CSS selectors for data validation

As figure 13-11 shows, HTML provides three attributes for data validation. The autocomplete attribute is on by default in all modern browsers, which means that a browser will use its *auto-completion feature* to display a list of entry options when the user starts the entry for a field. These options will be based on the entries the user has previously made for fields with similar names or ids.

If you don't want the browser to use this feature, you can use the autocomplete attribute to turn it off for an entire form or for one or more fields. For instance, you may want to turn this off for fields that accept credit card numbers. In the example in this figure, this attribute is turned off for the phone field. Note, however, that this doesn't currently work for Chrome. This is a documented bug that should be fixed in the future.

In contrast, the required attribute causes the browser to check whether a field is empty before it submits the form for processing. If the field is empty, it displays a message like the one in this figure. The browser also highlights all of the other required fields that are empty when the submit button is clicked. Note, however, that the message, how it's displayed, and how the other empty fields are highlighted may vary from one browser to another.

If you would like to stop the controls on a form from being validated, you can code the novalidate attribute for the form. Alternatively, you can code the formnovalidate attribute on a submit button for the form. Then, none of the controls on the form are validated when the form is submitted using that button. You can use these attributes when you don't want some or all fields validated by the browser.

To format required, valid, and invalid fields, you can use the CSS pseudo-classes that are listed in this figure. For instance, you can use the :required pseudo-class to format all required fields. You'll see these pseudo-classes in action in the web page in figure 13-13.

The HTML attributes for data validation

Attribute	Description
autocomplete	Set this attribute to off to tell the browser to disable auto-completion. This can be coded for a form or a control.
required	This Boolean attribute indicates that a value is required for a field. If the form is submitted and the field is empty, the browser displays its default error message.
novalidate	This Boolean attribute tells the browser that it shouldn't validate the controls on the form that it is coded for.
formnovalidate	This Boolean attribute tells the browser that it shouldn't validate the controls on the form when the submit button that it is coded for is used to submit the form.

HTML that uses some of the validation attributes

```
Name:    <input type="text" name="name" required><br>
Address: <input type="text" name="address"><br>
Zip:     <input type="text" name="zip" required><br>
Phone:   <input type="text" name="phone" required autocomplete="off"><br>
<input type="submit" name="submit" value="Submit Survey">
```

The highlighting and error message used by Chrome

The CSS pseudo-classes for required, valid, and invalid fields

```
:required
:valid
:invalid
```

Description

- By default, the *auto-completion feature* is on in all modern browsers. That means that the browser will display entry options when the user starts an entry. These options will be based on previous entries for fields with similar names or ids.

Figure 13-11   The HTML attributes and CSS selectors for data validation

How to use regular expressions for data validation

A *regular expression* provides a way to match a user entry against a *pattern* of characters. As a result, regular expressions can be used for validating user entries that have a standard pattern, such as credit card numbers, zip codes, dates, phone numbers, URLs, and more. Regular expressions are supported by many programming languages including JavaScript and PHP, and now regular expressions are supported by HTML.

As figure 13-12 shows, HTML provides a pattern attribute that is used for the regular expression that will be used to validate the entry for the field. In the example, regular expressions are used for the zip code and phone fields. As a result, the user must enter a zip code that has either 5 digits or 5 digits, a hyphen, and 4 more digits. And the phone number must be 3 digits, a hyphen, 3 more digits, another hyphen, and 4 more digits. If these fields don't match those patterns when the user clicks the submit button, an error message is displayed by the browser and the form isn't submitted.

If you code a title attribute for a field that is validated by a regular expression, the value of that attribute is displayed when the mouse hovers over the field. It is also displayed at the end of the browser's standard error message for a field that doesn't match the regular expression. In the example, the browser's standard message is: "Please match the requested format.", which is followed by the value of the title attribute. But here again, the message that's displayed and how it's displayed are browser-dependent.

The trick of course is coding the regular expressions that you need, and that can be difficult. For more information or to find the expressions that you need, you can search the web. Or, you can refer to *Murach's JavaScript and jQuery*.

Attributes for using regular expressions

Attribute	Description
pattern	The regular expression that is used to validate the entry.
title	Text that is displayed in the tooltip when the mouse hovers over a field. This text is also displayed after the browser's error message.

Regular expressions for common entries

Used for	Expression
Password (6+ alphanumeric)	[a-zA-Z0-9]{6,}
Zip code (99999 or 99999-9999)	\d{5}([\-]\d{4})?
Phone number (999-999-9999)	\d{3}[\-]\d{3}[\-]\d{4}
Date (MM/DD/YYYY)	[01]?\d\/[0-3]\d\/\d{4}
URL (starting with http:// or https://)	https?://.+
Credit card (9999-9999-9999-9999)	^\d{4}-\d{4}-\d{4}-\d{4}$

HTML that uses regular expressions

```
Name: <input type="text" id="name" required autofocus><br>
Zip: <input type="text" id="zip" required
     pattern="\d{5}([\-]\d{4})?"
     title="Must be 99999 or 99999-9999"><br>
Phone: <input type="text" id="phone" required
     pattern="\d{3}[\-]\d{3}[\-]\d{4}"
     title="Must be 999-999-9999"><br>
<input type="submit" id="submit" value="Submit Survey">
```

The form in Chrome

Description

- To use *regular expressions* to validate entries in text fields, you code the expression in the pattern attribute of the control. Then, the user's entry must have the *pattern* that's defined by the regular expression.

- To learn how to code regular expressions, you can search the web or refer to our JavaScript and jQuery book.

Figure 13-12   How to use regular expressions for data validation

A web page with a form

The web page, HTML, and CSS that follow show how the skills that you just learned can be used in a complete web page.

The page layout

Figure 13-13 presents a web page that contains a form that uses some of the HTML controls that you just learned about. This includes an email control for the email address entry, a date control for the starting date entry, and a number control for the tickets for guests entry.

The CSS for this form puts a 3-pixel, red border around the required fields and a 1-pixel, black border around the fields that have valid entries. In this case, the address field, the phone number field, the membership type, and the tickets for guests entries are considered valid.

Because the autofocus attribute is used for the email field, you don't need to change the tab order for this form. But otherwise, the tab order would start with the five links in the navigation menu and continue with the six links in the navigation list in the right sidebar before the focus got to the first field in the form.

A web page in Chrome with a form that uses HTML validation

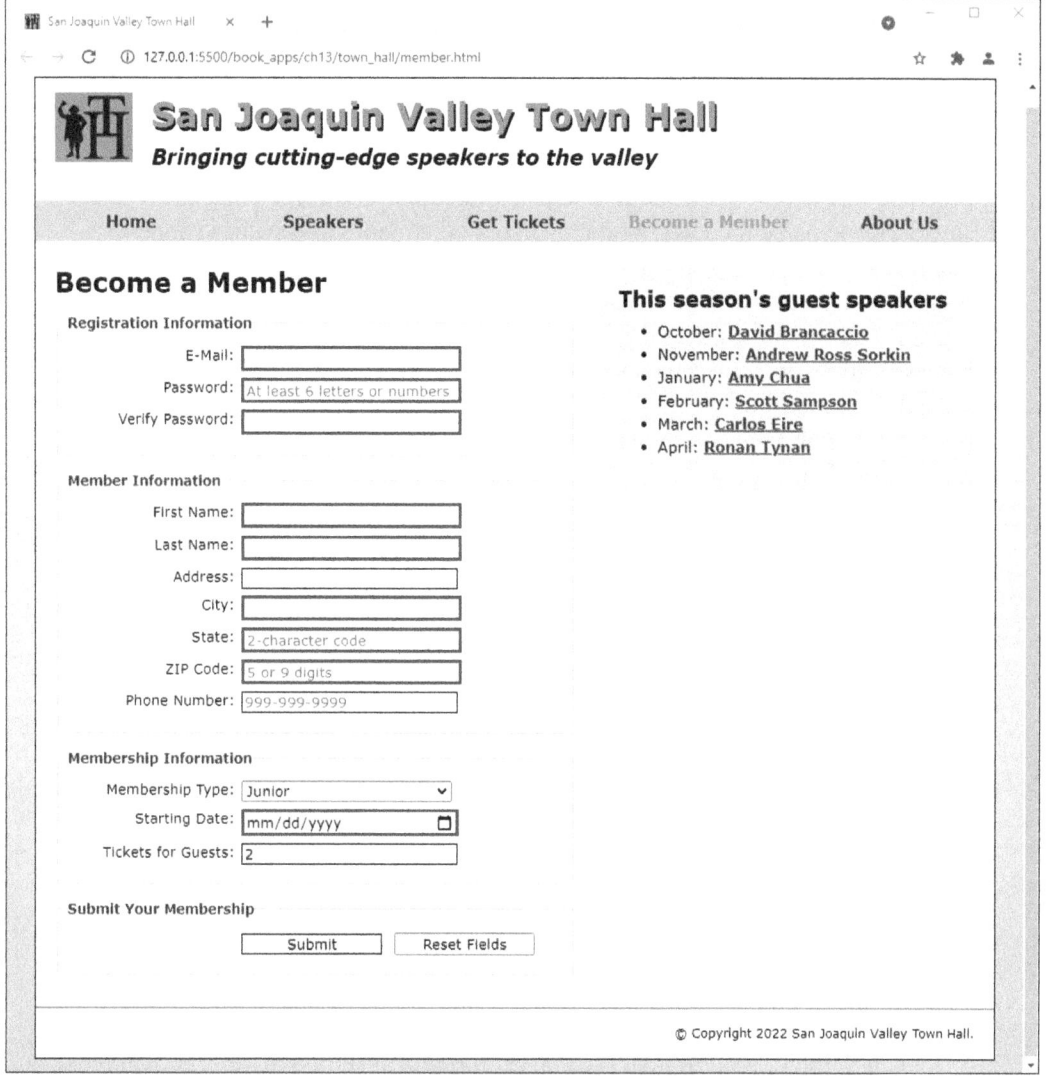

Description

- The form in this web page uses many of the HTML controls that you just learned about. These controls are formatted and aligned with CSS, and the CSS pseudo-classes are used to format the required, valid, and invalid fields.

- Form validation is done by using required attributes, regular expressions, and the email control.

- The autofocus attribute is used for the first control in the form so the tab order doesn't need to be changed. Otherwise, the navigation links and sidebar links would come before the form controls in the tab order.

- The placeholder attribute is used in some fields to indicate how the user should enter the data. When the focus moves to the field, the placeholder text is removed.

Figure 13-13   A web page with a form that uses HTML validation

The HTML

Figure 13-14 presents most of the HTML for the form within this web page. The rest of the code for this page is like the code that you've seen for this website in earlier chapters.

The first thing you should notice here is that when the Submit button is clicked, the get method is used to send the form to the server. Then, it's processed by another page named register_account.html. This page uses JavaScript to parse the URL so it can display the names and values of the controls on the form. Because of that, the name attribute is included on each control that accepts an entry. You should realize, however, that you would typically use the post method to send a form like this to the server and the page would be processed by server-side code. In that case, the name attributes wouldn't be required.

To help you focus on the HTML elements for a form, most of them are highlighted in this figure. For instance, the type attributes for the email, tel, date, and number controls are highlighted. Also, the autofocus and required attributes are highlighted. Last, the pattern and title attributes are highlighted for those fields that use regular expressions for data validation.

If you study this code, you'll see that it doesn't do a complete job of data validation. For instance, there's no way to verify that the second entry of the password is the same as the first entry when you use HTML.

Similarly, the state field uses the maxlength attribute to limit the entry to two characters, but those characters won't necessarily be a valid state code. In fact, they may not even be letters. You could fix this by using a regular expression that requires two letters, but even then the code may not be valid.

This illustrates some of the limitations of HTML data validation. That's why JavaScript is commonly used to do client-side data validation. For instance, JavaScript could check that the second password entry is the same as the first entry. And JavaScript could look up the state entry in a table that contains the valid state codes. Then, any entry that isn't in the table would be considered invalid.

Keep in mind, though, that the entries for a form should always be validated by the server-side code too. Like JavaScript, that code can validate data more thoroughly than the HTML features. As a result, the data validation on the client doesn't have to be thorough. In fact, the main point of client-side validation is to save some of the round trips that would be required if the validation was only done by the server. And if you use the HTML features for data validation, you will certainly save many round trips.

The HTML for the form

```
<form action="register_account.html" method="get" id="registration_form">
<fieldset>
    <legend>Registration Information</legend>
    <label for="email">E-Mail:</label>
    <input type="email" name="email" id="email" autofocus required><br>
    <label for="password">Password:</label>
    <input type="password" name="password" id="password" required
           placeholder="At least 6 letters or numbers"
           pattern="[a-zA-Z0-9]{6,}"
           title="Must be at least 6 alphanumeric characters"><br>
    <label for="verify">Verify Password:</label>
    <input type="password" name="verify" id="verify" required><br>
</fieldset>
<fieldset>
    <legend>Member Information</legend>
    <label for="first_name">First Name:</label>
    <input type="text" name="first_name" id="first_name" required><br>
    ...
    ...
    ...
    <label for="state">State:</label>
    <input type="text" name="state" id="state" required maxlength="2"
           placeholder="2-character code"><br>
    <label for="zip">ZIP Code:</label>
    <input type="text" name="zip" id="zip" required
           placeholder="5 or 9 digits"
           pattern="^\d{5}(-\d{4})?$" title="Either 5 or 9 digits"><br>
    <label for="phone">Phone Number:</label>
    <input type="tel" name="phone" id="phone" placeholder="999-999-9999"
           pattern="\d{3}[\-]\d{3}[\-]\d{4}"
           title="Must be 999-999-999 format"><br>
</fieldset>
<fieldset>
    <legend>Membership Information</legend>
    <label for="membership_type">Membership Type:</label>
    <select name="membership_type" id="membership_type">
        <option value="j">Junior</option>
        <option value="r">Regular</option>
        <option value="c">Charter</option>
    </select><br>
    <label for="starting_date">Starting Date:</label>
    <input type="date" name="starting_date" id="starting_date" required><br>
    <label for="tickets">Tickets for Guests:</label>
    <input type="number" name="tickets" id="tickets"
           value="2" min="1" max="4" placeholder="from 1 to 4"><br>
</fieldset>
<fieldset id="buttons">
    <legend>Submit Your Membership</legend>
    <label> </label>
    <input type="submit" id="submit" value="Submit">
    <input type="reset" id="reset" value="Reset Fields"><br>
</fieldset>
</form>
```

Figure 13-14   The HTML for the form

The CSS

Figure 13-15 presents the CSS for the form that's used in the web page. Of most interest is the use of the CSS selectors that include a pseudo-class. For instance, the input:required selector is used to put a 3-pixel, red border around required fields.

You can also see how the :valid and :invalid pseudo-classes are used to format the valid and invalid fields. First, a black border is applied to valid fields. Then, the box shadow is removed from invalid fields. This is done specifically for the Firefox browser because it's the only one that applies a box shadow to those fields.

The CSS for the form

```
fieldset {
    margin-top: 1em;
    margin-bottom: 1em;
    padding-top: .5em;
}

legend {
    color: #931420;
    font-weight: bold;
    font-size: 85%;
    margin-bottom: .5em;
}

label, input, select {
    font-size: 90%;
}

label {
    float: left;
    width: 12em;
    text-align: right;
}

input, select {
    width: 15em;
    margin-left: .5em;
    margin-bottom: .5em;
}

input:required {
    border: 3px solid red;
}

input:valid {
    border: 1px solid black;
}

input:invalid {
    box-shadow: none;
}

br {
    clear: both;
}

#buttons input {
    width: 10em;
}
```

Figure 13-15   The CSS for the form

How to use other HTML controls

This chapter ends by presenting six more controls that are useful for some websites. You can read these topics quickly and come back to them when you need them.

How to use the search control

Figure 13-16 shows how to add a search function to a website. To do that, you use the search control along with two hidden fields to create a form that submits the search data to a search engine.

At the top of this figure, you can see the two controls that are needed for a search function: a search element for the search entry and a Search button that submits the search entry to the search engine. This is the standard way to set up the controls for a search function, and this mimics the way Google uses these controls. If you want to vary from this at all, you can use a Go button instead of a Search button, but users expect all search functions to look this way. You should also make the text box large enough for a typical entry.

If you look at the HTML code for the search form, you will see that the form is submitted to www.google.com/search, which is the Google search engine. That's why the results of the search are displayed on the standard Google results page.

In the code for this search form, the first input element is for the search control. Then, to limit the search to www.murach.com, this HTML uses two hidden fields that pass the required data to the Google search engine. To use this HTML for a Google search of your site, you just need to change the value attributes in the two hidden fields to the URL for your website.

Note that the input elements for the search control and the two hidden fields use the name attribute instead of the id attribute. That's because these are the attributes that the Google search engine requires. It also requires the specific name values shown here.

The trouble with the standard Google search engine is that sponsored links will be displayed on the results page. That's why it's better to use a search engine that can be customized so it returns results that are appropriate for users of your site. To find a search engine like this, you can search the web for "add search function to website." Some of these search engines are free, and some like Google Site Search charge a nominal fee like $100 a year for a small site.

A search control in the Chrome browser

| sql server | Search |

The results of the search

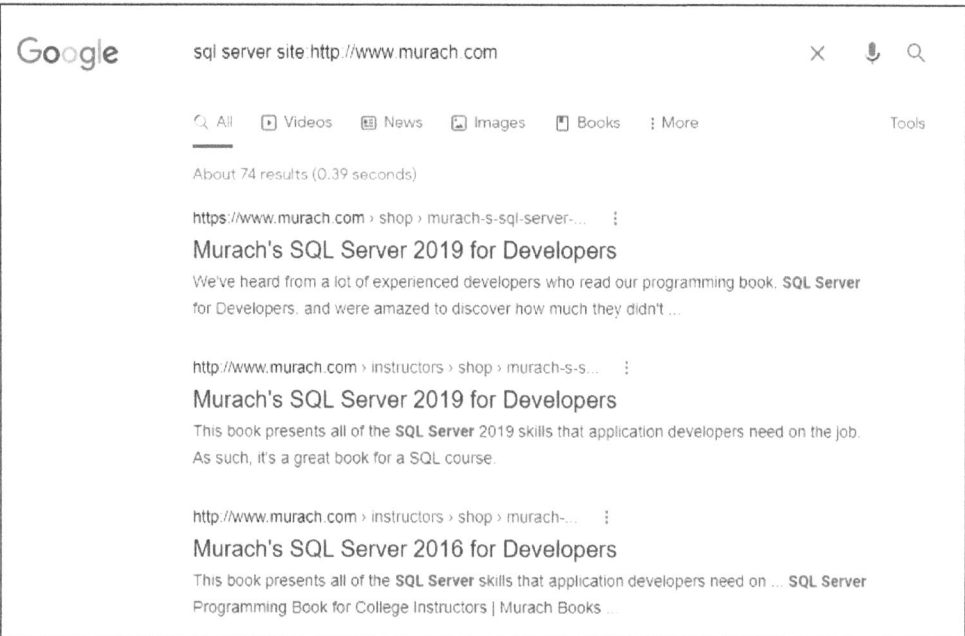

The HTML for the Google search engine

```
<form method="get" action="http://www.google.com/search">
    <input type="search" name="q" size="30" maxlength="255">
    <input type="hidden" name="domains" value="http://www.murach.com">
    <input type="hidden" name="sitesearch" value="http://www.murach.com">
    <input type="submit" id="search" value="Search">
</form>
```

Description

- To implement a search function, you use an HTML form to submit the search text and other required data to the search engine.

- Within the form for the search function, you can use an input element of the "search" type for the text that's entered. This is good for semantic reasons.

- This *search control* should be followed by a submit button that says Search or Go. The form must also include one hidden field to specify the domain for the search and another one to specify that only that domain should be searched.

- If you use a search engine like Google, you have no control over the search results. If you want to customize the results, you can use a search engine like Google Site Search.

Figure 13-16   How to use the search control for a search function

How to use the file upload control

Figure 13-17 shows how to use the *file upload control*. This control lets users upload one or more files to your web server. Typically, you'll use this control with a server-side programming language such as PHP, which transfers the file or files from the user's computer to the web server. When you code a file upload control, you set the type attribute to "file".

You can also code the accept attribute for a file upload control. This attribute lets you specify the types of files that will be accepted. In this example, the JPEG and GIF types are specified so the control will only display those types of files when the Browse button is clicked and the files are displayed. If you omit this attribute, all types of files will be displayed.

When using the file upload control, the method attribute of the form should be set to "post". In addition, the enctype attribute of the form should be set to multipart/form-data. This is typically the only time this attribute will be modified within the form element.

Attributes of the input element for a file upload control

Attribute	Description
accept	The types of files that are accepted for upload. When the operating system's open dialog box opens, only files of those types will be shown.
multiple	A Boolean attribute that lets the user upload more than one file.

The HTML for a file upload control that accepts JPEG and GIF images

```
<form id="upload_form" action="sendemail.php" method="post"
    enctype="multipart/form-data">
    Attach an image:<br>
    <input type="file" id="fileupload" accept="image/jpeg, image/gif">
</form>
```

The file upload control in the Chrome browser

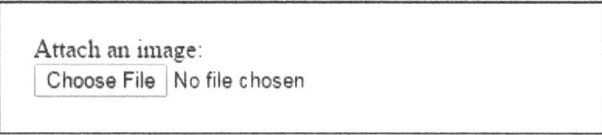

The Windows dialog box that's displayed when Choose File is clicked

Description

- To create a *file upload control*, code the input element with "file" as the type attribute. This control lets your users select the files they want to upload to your web server.

- In the form element that contains the file upload control, the method attribute must be "post", and you must code the enctype attribute as shown above.

- How the file upload control is implemented varies by browser.

Figure 13-17   How to use the file upload control

How to use the color, range, progress, and meter controls

Figure 13-18 demonstrates the use of the color, range, progress, and meter controls. All of these elements are good semantically.

The first example in this figure shows how to use the color control. It is rendered as a box that contains a color. This color is black by default, but you can set it to any color by coding the value attribute. Then, if the user clicks on this box, the color palette for the user's operating system is displayed so the users can click on the colors that they want. And when the color selection is submitted to the browser, it is sent as a hexadecimal code.

The second example shows how to use the range control. Here, the range control is rendered as a slider that the user can use to increase or decrease the initial value. When you code this control, you usually include the min, max, and step attributes. Those attributes set the minimum and maximum values that the control will accept, as well as the amount to increase or decrease the value when the slider is moved.

The third example shows how to use the progress and meter elements. These are designed to present output data that's delivered by JavaScript. To use these elements, you code an id attribute that can be referred to by the JavaScript code. Then, you can code some of the other attributes.

For instance, the min and max attributes can be used to define the lower and upper limits of the elements. Similarly, the high and low attributes can be used to define the points at which the progress or meter element's value is considered a high or low point, and at those points the color of the bar or meter will change from the default to another color.

The HTML for a color control

```
<label for="firstcolor">Choose your first background color:</label>
<input type="color" id="firstcolor" value="#facd8a">
```

The color control in Chrome

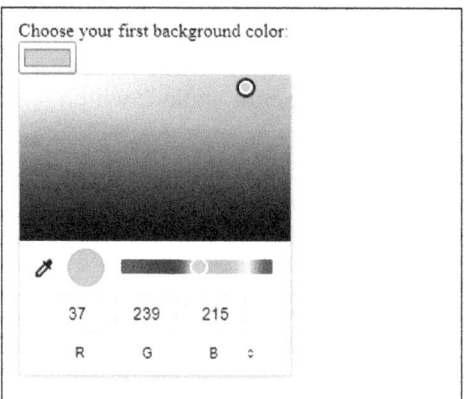

The HTML for a range control

```
<label for="book">Rate the book from 1 to 5: </label>
<input type="range" id="book"
       min="1" max="5" step="1"><br><br>
```

The range control in Chrome

Rate the book from 1 to 5: ◖━━━━━●━━━━━◗

The HTML for progress and meter controls

```
<body onload="setProgressAndMeter()">
    <p>Progress bar set by JavaScript on page load:
    <progress id="progressBar" max="100" value="0"></progress></p>
    <p>Meter set by JavaScript on page load:
    <meter id="meterBar" max="100" value="0"></meter></p>
</body>
```

The progress and meter controls in Chrome

Progress bar set by JavaScript on page load: ▬▬▬▬

Meter set by JavaScript on page load: ▬▬

Description

- The color control lets the user select a color in a variety of ways.
- The range control lets the user enter a number by using a slide.
- The progress and meter controls show the progress of a client- or server-side script.
- All of these controls are good semantically.

Figure 13-18   How to use the color, range, progress, and meter controls

How to use a data list and an output control

Figure 13-19 shows how to use a data list and how to use an output control. Let's start with the data list.

A data list is a list of the items that a user can select from. For instance, the first example in this figure shows a data list with two URLs that drop down from a URL element. Then, the user can select the URL that will be used for the entry. To make that work, the list attribute for the URL control is set to "links", which is the same as the id value for the datalist element.

To provide the items for a data list, you code option elements that consist of value and label attributes. Each value attribute should contain the value you want to be submitted to the server, and each the label attribute should be a short, text-based description of the option.

The second example in this figure shows how to use the output element. Unlike the other controls that you've seen in this chapter, the output element is used to display output data, not to accept input data. To create the output, though, you need to use client-side code like JavaScript or server-side code like PHP.

In the example in this figure, JavaScript is used to add the values in the number controls and display the output in the output element. In this case, I used CSS to add a border to the output element so it's easy to spot. Otherwise, this element wouldn't have a border. Although you could use a label or text box to display the output, using the output element is good for semantic reasons.

To show which fields the output element is associated with, you can code the for attribute. In this example, this attribute is used to show that the result is derived from the input fields with the ids x and y. In this case, the result is calculated by the Javascript that's coded for the onclick attribute of the Calculate button.

The HTML for a control with a datalist

```
<label for="link">What is your preferred search engine:</label>
<input type="url" name="link" id="link" list="links"><br><br>
<datalist id="links">
    <option value="http://www.google.com/" label="Google"></option>
    <option value="http://www.yahoo.com/" label="Yahoo"></option>
</datalist>
```

A url control with a datalist in Chrome

The HTML for an output control

```
<p>Enter numbers in both fields and click the Calculate button.</p>
<form onsubmit="return false">
    <input name="x" type="number" min="100" step="5" value="100"> +
    <input name="y" type="number" min="100" step="5" value="100"><br><br>
    <input type="button" value="Calculate"
        onclick="result.value = parseInt(x.value) + parseInt(y.value)">
    <br><br>
    Total: <output name="result" for="x y"></output>
</form>
```

The output control in Chrome

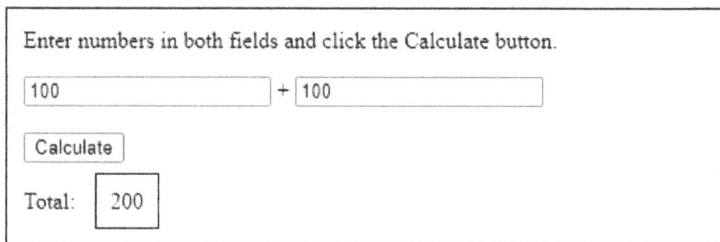

Description

- When the user clicks in a control that has a *data list*, the items in the list are displayed below the control so the user can select one of them.
- The output control is good semantically because it can be used to display output data that is returned by a client-side or server-side script.

Figure 13-19   How to use a data list and an output control

Perspective

Now that you've completed this chapter, you should have all the skills you need for creating forms. You should also be able to use the HTML features for data validation. Remember, though, that you can do a better job of data validation by using JavaScript, as shown in chapter 18. Also remember that data validation should always be done on the server too, so the client-side data validation doesn't have to be foolproof.

Terms

form
control
button
submit button
reset button
image button
text field
textarea field
password field
hidden field
radio button
check box
label
drop-down list
list box
tab order
access key
data validation
auto-completion feature
regular expression
pattern
search control
file upload control
data list

Summary

- A *form* contains one or more *controls* like text boxes, radio buttons, or check boxes that can receive data. When a form is submitted to the server for processing, the data in the controls is sent along with the HTTP request.

- When the get method is used to submit a form, the data is sent as part of the URL for the next web page. When the post method is used, the data is hidden.

- A *submit button* submits the form data to the server when the button is clicked. A *reset button* resets all the data in the form when it is clicked. Buttons can also be used to start client-side scripts when they are clicked.

- The controls that are commonly used within a form are *labels*, *text fields*, *radio buttons*, *check boxes*, *drop-down lists*, *list boxes*, and *text areas*.

- A *text field* is used to get data from a user. A *password field* also gets data from the user, but its data is obscured by bullets or asterisks. A *hidden field* contains data that is sent to the server, but the field isn't displayed on the form.

- A *label* is commonly used to identify a related control. To associate a label with a control, you use the for attribute of the label to specify the id value of the control.

- HTML also has input controls including the email, url, tel, number, range, date, time, search, and color controls that are good semantically.

- You can use CSS to align controls by floating the labels to the left of the controls. You can also use CSS to format the controls.

- The *tab order* of a form is the order in which the controls receive the focus when the Tab key is pressed. By default, this is the sequence in which the controls are coded in the HTML. To change that, you can use tabindex attributes.

- *Access keys* are shortcut keys that the user can press to move the focus to specific controls on a form. To assign an access key to a control, you use its accesskey attribute. To let the user know that an access key is available, you can underline the access key in the label for the control.

- HTML has some attributes for *data validation*, and CSS has some pseudo-classes for formatting required, valid, and invalid fields.

- The HTML attributes for data validation include the pattern attribute that provides for *regular expressions*.

- You can use a *search control* to provide a search function for your website.

- You can use a *file upload control* to upload a file from the user's system. Then, server-side code is used to store the file on the web server.

Exercise 13-1   Create a form for getting tickets

In this exercise, you'll create a form like the one that follows. To do that, you'll start from the HTML and CSS code that is used for the form in the chapter application.

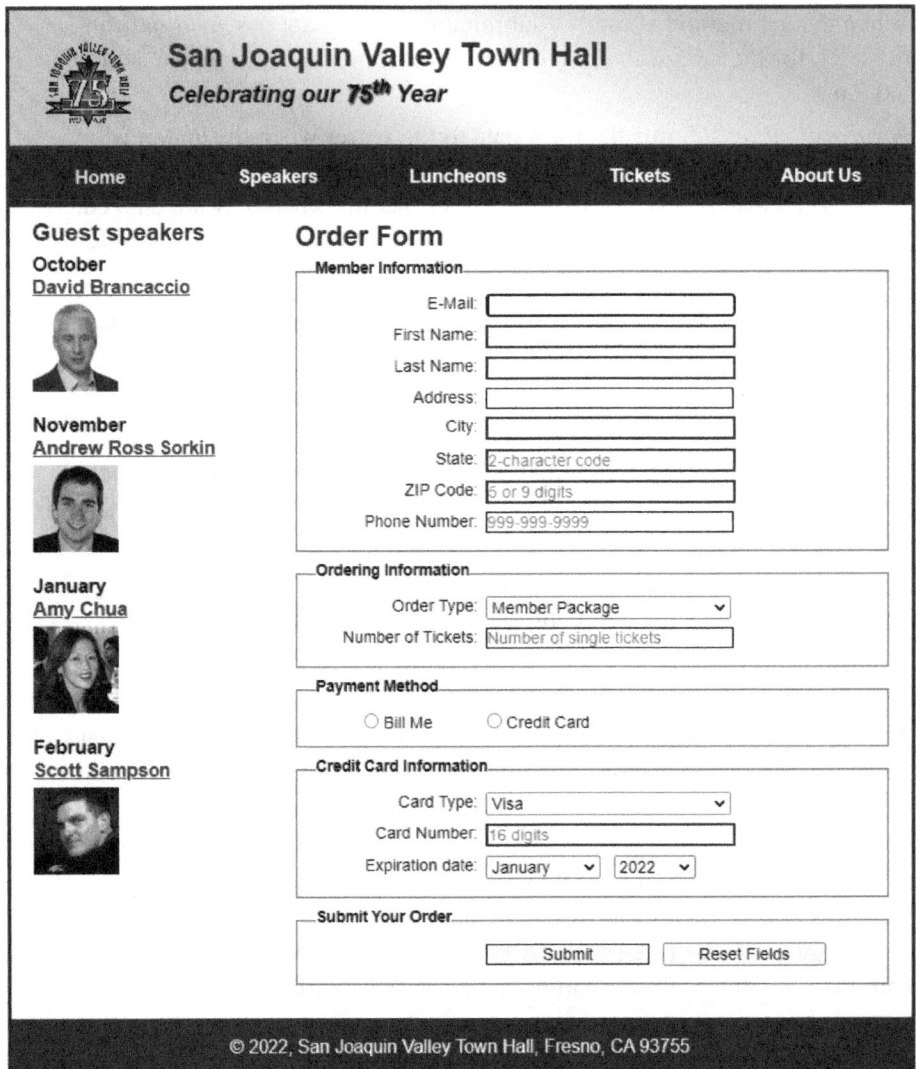

Open the HTML and CSS files

1. Use your text editor to open the HTML and CSS files for the Tickets page:

   `\html_CSS_5\exercises\town_hall_3\tickets.html`

   `\html_CSS_5\exercises\town_hall_3\styles\tickets.css`

2. Run the HTML file in Chrome to see that this page contains the form and the formatting that is used in the application at the end of the chapter. Your job is to modify the form and its CSS so the page looks like the one above.

Fix the formatting of the form and test after each change

3. Change the fieldset margins and padding so there is no top margin, the bottom margin is .5em, the top and bottom padding is .5em, and the right and left padding is 1em.

4. Change the legend formatting so the color is black.

5. Change the formatting so the required and the invalid fields have a 2-pixel border with #800000 as the font color, and the valid fields have a 1-pixel black border.

Fix the HTML one fieldset at a time and test after each change

6. In the HTML, change the heading before the form to "Order Form". Then, combine the first two fieldsets, change the legend to "Member Information", and delete the password fields so the first fieldset looks like the one above.

7. In the Membership Information fieldset, change the legend to "Ordering Information" and modify the HTML for the fields. Here, the Order Type list should have these choices: Member Package, Donor Package, and Single Tickets. Also, the Number of Tickets field should be a text field with the placeholder shown above.

8. Add the Payment Method fieldset with two radio buttons, and use the coding method in figure 13-4 so the user can activate the buttons by clicking on the labels. Then, adjust the CSS so the buttons are side by side as shown above.

   One way to do that is to code an id for the fieldset, and then use an id selector to turn off the float for the labels, to set the width of the buttons to "auto", and to set the left margin for the buttons to 3 ems.

9. Add the Credit Card Information fieldset. Here, the Card Type list should have these choices: Visa, MasterCard, and Discover. The Card Number field should have the placeholder shown. The month list should have values from January through December. And the year list should have values from the current year through four years in the future.

   To format these lists, you can use id selectors and set the width of the month to 7 ems and the width of the year to 5 ems. To check the validity of the card number, you can use this pattern: \d{16}.

10. For the Submit Your Order fieldset, you just need to change the legend.

Test the validation

11. Use Chrome to test the validation that's done by entering combinations of invalid data. Then, enter valid data for all the fields and click the Submit button. This should display a page (register_account.html) that shows the data that has been submitted.

12. To see the differences, test the validation again in Edge or Safari.

Chapter 14

How to add audio and video to a web page

In this chapter, you'll learn how easy it is to add audio and video to your website. But you'll start with a brief introduction to the media types.

An introduction to media on the web

Before you learn how to include media files in your web pages, you need to be familiar with the media types that are used for audio and video.

Common media types for audio and video

When most of us think about *media types*, a short list comes to mind: MPEG, MP3, and maybe even AAC. The reality, though, is that there are dozens of media types for both video and audio. A few of them are summarized in the first two tables in figure 14-1.

These media types are nothing more than containers of information that are used by *media players* to play the content that the types contain. For example, an MPEG file contains a video track, which is what the users see, and one or more audio tracks, which is what the users hear.

To keep the video coordinated with the audio, a media type contains markers that help the audio sync up with the video. In addition, a media type can contain metadata, such as the title of the video, any still imagery related to the video (cover art), the length of the video, and digital rights management information.

How to convert a file from one media type to another

Occasionally, you may need to convert a media file from one type to another. For instance, you may need to convert a raw, uncompressed video or audio file that you've captured on a digital recording device into a compressed format.

To do that type of conversion, you can use one of the many free or commercial software packages that are available. For instance, Miro Video Converter is a free product that lets you convert a file from just about any media type into the type that you need. But as you will see, you will rarely need to do that because modern browsers can recognize most media types and treat them as MP3 or MP4 files.

Common media types for audio

Type	Description
MP3	MPEG-1 Audio Layer 3, which is commonly known as MP3, is one of the most widely-used media types for audio.
AAC	Advanced Audio Coding is the format that Apple uses to deliver audio for its iTunes store. AAC was designed to deliver better quality audio than MP3.
Ogg	The audio stream of an ogg media type is technically referred to as Vorbis.
WebM	A file format that usually has the .webm extension. It is currently supported by all modern browsers except Safari.

Common media types for video

Type	Description
MPEG-4	Commonly found with either an .mp4 or .m4v extension. The MPEG-4 media type is loosely based on Apple's QuickTime (.mov) media type.
Ogg	Ogg is an open-source, open-standard media type. The video stream of the ogg media type is technically referred to as Theora.
WebM	A file format that usually has the .webm extension. It is currently supported by all modern browsers except Safari.

How to convert a file from one media type to another

- You can use a free converter like Miro Video Converter to convert an audio file to MP3 or a video file to MP4.
- However, you rarely need to convert an audio or video file from one media type to another because modern media players can identify the media types and treat them as MP3 or MP4 files.

Description

- A *media type* is a container for several components, including an encoded video track, one or more encoded audio tracks, and metadata.
- To play a media type, a browser requires a *media player* for that type.

Figure 14-1   Common media types for audio and video

How to use the HTML audio and video elements

Figure 14-2 shows how to add video and audio to your web pages. In simplest form, you just add the video and audio elements to a page and code the src attributes that point to the media files to be played. This is illustrated by the first example in this figure.

If you want to set some of the options that these elements support, you can code the other attributes that are summarized in this figure. This is illustrated by the second and third examples.

The second example is for an audio file. It includes the controls attribute so a toolbar will be displayed that includes play, pause, volume, and progress controls.

The third example is for a video file. Its width and height attributes set the dimensions of the media player in the browser. Its poster attribute displays an image that is displayed until the video is played. Its preload attribute loads the video file with the page so there won't be a delay when the user starts playing it. And its controls attribute displays the controls for the video.

In the accessibility and usability guidelines, you can see that you need to remember that some users won't be able to hear or see the audio or video. So if it presents essential content, you also need to provide a text version of it. You also need to remember that most web users like to control their web experiences. So, they don't want audio or video to play automatically.

Common attributes for the audio and video elements

Attribute	Description
src	The URL of the file to be played.
width	The width of the media file in the browser.
height	The height of the media file in the browser.
preload	One of three possible values that tell the browser whether to preload any data: none (the default), metadata (only preload metadata like dimensions and track list), or auto (preload the entire media file).
controls	Displays controls for playing the file.
poster	Provides the path to an image that will be displayed until a video file starts playing.
loop	Causes the media to repeat playing when it reaches the end.
muted	Supported only by the video element, this attribute causes the video to begin playing with the volume muted...but only if autoplay is also coded.
autoplay	Starts playing the media as soon as the web page is loaded in the browser.

Video and audio elements with just a src attribute

```
<video src="media/sjv_speakers_sampson.mp4"></video>
<audio src="media/sjv_welcome.mp3"></audio>
```

An audio element with two attributes

```
<audio src="media/sjv_welcome.mp3"
       controls>
</audio>
```

A video element with six attributes

```
<video src="media/sjv_speakers_sampson.mp4"
       width="480" height="270"
       poster="images/poster.png">
       preload
       controls
</video>
```

Accessibility and usability guidelines

- If the audio or video presents essential content, you need to provide a text version of it for those who can't hear or see.
- Don't use the autoplay attribute because users like to control their web experiences.

Description

- The HTML video and audio elements play the various media types within a browser.
- To play an audio file, all you need to do is code a src attribute that refers to an MP3 file.
- To play a video file, all you need to do is code a src attribute that refers to an MP4 file.

Figure 14-2   How to use the HTML audio and video elements

A web page with audio and video

Now that you've seen how the video and audio elements work, it's time to see them in a simple web page.

The page layout

The web page in figure 14-3 starts with a short audio message that welcomes the visitor to the site. But the user has to use the controls to start it.

Then, this page offers a video of one of the speakers who's scheduled to speak. In the area for the video, you can see an image of the speaker that will disappear when the user starts the video.

A web page in Chrome that offers both audio and video

Welcome to the San Joaquin Valley Town Hall

▶ 0:00 / 0:21 ━━●━━━━━ 🔊 ⋮

San Joaquin Valley Town Hall welcomes Dr. Scott Sampson

In February, Dr. Scott Sampson will present a lecture titled 'Fossil Threads in the Web of Life.' In the meantime, you can see a video of Dr. Sampson below.

Description

- This web page offers both audio and video. The audio is a brief introduction to the speakers. The video is a video of the speaker.
- The poster attribute of the video element is used to display an image in place of the media type when the page is displayed. The poster will be replaced by the video when the user clicks on the play button.
- The controls for the video are displayed when the page is loaded. But once the video starts playing, the controls are hidden if you move the cursor off the video and they reappear if you move the cursor over the video.

Figure 14-3   A web page with audio and video

The HTML

Figure 14-4 presents the HTML file for the web page. Here, the audio element is used to play an MP3 file and the video element is used to play an MP4 file. You shouldn't have any trouble following this code because it has become so simple in recent years.

In the code for the audio element, you might notice the absence of the autoplay attribute. This prevents the browser from automatically playing the sound when the page loads.

In the code for the video element, you might notice the poster attribute. This displays a static image in place of the video until the user starts the video.

The HTML for a page that uses both audio and video elements

```
<!DOCTYPE HTML>
<html lang="en">
<head>
    <meta charset="utf-8">
    <meta name="viewport" content="width=device-width, initial-scale=1.0">
    <title>Upcoming San Joaquin Valley Town Hall Lectures</title>
</head>

<body>
    <main>
        <h1>Welcome to the San Joaquin Valley Town Hall</h1>

        <audio id="audioplayer"
               src="media/sjv_welcome.mp3"
               controls>
        </audio>

        <h2>San Joaquin Valley Town Hall welcomes Dr. Scott Sampson</h2>
        <p>
            In February, Dr. Scott Sampson will present a lecture titled
            &lsquo;Fossil Threads in the Web of Life.&rsquo; In the
            meantime, you can see a video of Dr. Sampson below.
        </p>

        <video id="videoplayer"
               src="media/sjv_speakers_sampson.mp4"
               controls
               width="480" height="270"
               poster="images/poster.png"
               preload="auto">
        </video>
    </main>
</body>
</html>
```

Figure 14-4   The HTML for the web page

Perspective

Now that you know how to add audio and video to your web pages, please remember that users who can't hear or see won't benefit from audio or video. So, if the audio and video are essential, you should also provide text versions that deliver the same content.

Terms

media type
media player

Summary

- A browser uses a *media player* to play an audio or video *media type* that's embedded in a web page.
- Audio and video files come in a variety of media types, but MP3 and MP4 are the most common types for audio and video.

Exercise 14-1   Add video to a speaker's page

In this exercise, you'll add video to the speaker's page for Scott Sampson.
When you're through, the page should look like this:

Open the page and add the HTML for running a video

1. Use your text editor to open this page:

    `\html_css_5\exercises\town_hall_3\speakers\c14_sampson.html`

2. Add the code for running the video with a poster in place until the video
    starts. To do that, you need to use a document-relative path that goes up one
    level, and you need to use the right file names. For instance, the reference in
    the source attribute should be:

    `../media/sampson.mp4`

    and the reference in the poster attribute should be:

    `../images/poster.png`

3. Now, test this page.

Chapter 15

How to use CSS transitions, transforms, animations, and filters

This chapter introduces you to the CSS features for transitions, transforms, animations, and filters. Although you probably won't use these features often, you should at least be aware of what they can do and how you might use them in your web pages.

How to use CSS transitions

Transitions let you gradually change one or more of the CSS properties for an element over a specified period of time. As you'll see, transitions let you provide features with CSS alone that would otherwise require JavaScript.

How to code transitions

Figure 15-1 summarizes the five properties that can be used for transitions. Note, however, that the transition property is the shorthand property for the other four properties. Because using this shorthand property is the easiest way to code most transitions, that's what you'll see in the examples in this chapter.

The first example in this figure uses a transition for the change in two properties that are applied to an h1 element: font-size and color. In the CSS for this transition, the style rule for the h1 selector sets the font-size to 120% and the color to blue. Then, the shorthand transition property provides two sets of values that are separated by a comma.

The first set of values is for the font-size property. It says that the transition should take 2 seconds, use the ease-out *timing function* (or *speed curve*), and wait 1 second before starting. The second set is for the color property. It's the same as the set for the font-size property except it uses the ease-in timing function. This timing function causes the transition to start slowly and end quickly. In contrast, the ease-out timing function causes the transition to start quickly and end slowly.

This style rule is followed by one for the hover pseudo-class for the h1 element. It changes the cursor to the pointer, the font-size to 180%, and the color to red. This means that when the user hovers the mouse over the h1 heading, the two values in the transition are changed. As a result, the transition takes place. You can see this in the before and during views of the heading. When the user stops hovering, the transition returns to the original font-size and color settings.

Please note that the heading would change when the mouse hovers over it, even if a transition weren't applied to it. However, the changes would be immediate. What the transition does is provide a gradual change from one set of properties to another that gives the appearance of animation.

The second example in this figure shows the code for a transition with just one property. Note here that if you omit one of the values for the transition property, the default is assumed. In this case, the delay value is omitted so the transition will start right away. If you omit the timing function value, "ease" is assumed. And if you omit the duration function, 0 is assumed, which means that no transition will take place.

CSS properties for working with transitions

Property	Description
transition	The shorthand property for setting the properties that follow.
transition-property	The property or properties that the transition is for. Use commas to separate multiple properties.
transition-duration	The seconds or milliseconds that the transition will take.
transition-timing-function	The speed curve of the transition. Values include: ease, linear, ease-in, ease-out, ease-in-out, and cubic-bezier.
transition-delay	The seconds or milliseconds before the transition starts.

The syntax for the shorthand transition property

```
transition: [property] [duration] [timing-function] [delay];
```

A transition that occurs when the mouse hovers over a heading

Before the transition

Hover over this heading to see its transition

During the transition

Hover over this heading to see its transition

The HTML for the element that will be transitioned

```
<h1>Hover over this heading to see its transition</h1>
```

The CSS for this two-property transition

```
h1 { font-size: 120%;
    color: blue;
    transition: font-size 2s ease-out 1s,
                color 2s ease-in 1s; }
h1:hover {
    cursor: pointer;
    font-size: 180%;
    color: red; }
```

A transition for one property when the mouse hovers over the heading

```
h1 { font-size: 120%;
    transition: font-size 2s ease-out; }
h1:hover { font-size: 180%; }
```

Description

- A *transition* provides a smooth change from one set of properties to another.

Figure 15-1   How to code transitions

How to create an accordion using transitions

Figure 15-2 shows some of the power of CSS transitions. Here, transitions are used to create an accordion with three headings and three panels that contain the contents for those headings. When the user clicks on a heading, the related panel gradually opens and any other open panel gradually closes.

The HTML for this accordion consists of h3 elements for the accordion headings and div elements for the contents of the panels. Note, however, that the headings contain <a> elements that point to the placeholders in the div elements. For example, the href attribute of the first <a> element (#Q1) points to the id of the div element that follows (Q1).

The CSS that makes this accordion work starts with a style rule for the div elements. There, the height property is set to zero, and the transition property takes effect when the height property is changed. It will take 1 second for the transition and the transition will use the ease-in-out speed curve, which starts and ends slowly but progresses more quickly in between. Because the delay value is omitted, the transition will start right away.

The next style rule, however, is the one that makes this accordion work. It uses the target pseudo-class for the div elements in the accordion. This pseudo-class is activated when the user clicks on an <a> element that refers to a div element. Then, the height of the div element is changed from 0 to 120 pixels. And that starts the transition.

Here again, please note that the panel will be displayed whether or not a transition is applied to the change in height. The transition just makes the change gradual instead of immediate and adds an effect to the opening and closing of the panels.

An accordion created with CSS transitions

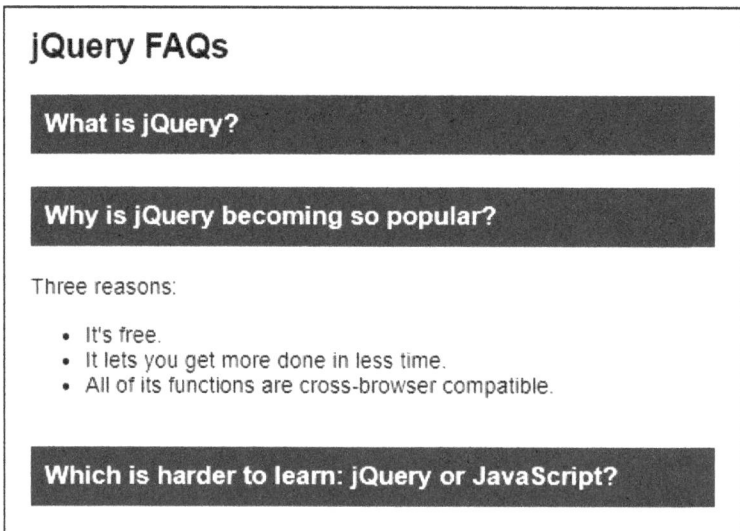

The HTML for the accordion

```
<h1>jQuery FAQs</h1>
<div id="accordion">
    <h3><a href="#Q1">What is jQuery?</a></h3>
    <div id="Q1">Contents for first panel</div>
    <h3><a href="#Q2">Why is jQuery becoming so popular?</a></h3>
    <div id="Q2">Contents for second panel</div>
    <h3><a href="#Q3">Which is harder to learn: ...?</a></h3>
    <div id="Q3">Contents for third panel</div>
</div>
```

The CSS for the transitions

```
#accordion div {
    overflow: hidden;
    height: 0;
    transition: height 1s ease-in-out;
}
#accordion div:target {
    height: 120px;
}
```

Description

- The transition for this accordion occurs when the user clicks on an <a> element. The transition is applied to the change in the height property of the div element.

- To change the height property for the div element, the CSS uses the target pseudo-class. This pseudo-class selects the div element that is the target of the <a> element that has been clicked.

- The style rule for the target selector changes the height property from 0 to 120 pixels. That opens the panel to a size that is large enough for the contents of the panel.

Figure 15-2   How to create an accordion using transitions

How to use CSS transforms

Transforms let you rotate, scale, skew, and position HTML elements using CSS alone. When you combine transforms with transitions, you can create some interesting animations for your HTML elements.

Although CSS supports both 2D and 3D transforms, this chapter only introduces 2D transforms. For an introduction to 3D transforms, we recommend David DeSandro's GitHub post at http://desandro.github.io/3dtransforms.

How to code 2D transforms

Figure 15-3 summarizes the properties and methods for working with 2D transforms. The transform property lets you apply one or more transforms to an HTML element. The transform-origin property lets you change the origin point for the transform.

This is illustrated by the example in this figure. Here, two copies of the same image are displayed side by side. Then, when the user hovers the mouse over the image on the right, it is rotated 180 degrees. As a result, it looks like a mirror image of the image on the left. In addition, the origin point has been changed so the rotation takes place from the right side of the second image. That's why there's an empty image space between the first image and the transformed image.

The HTML for this example is just a <p> element that contains two img elements for the same image, but the second one has a class attribute of "image1". Then, the first style rule in the CSS provides a two-second transition for all changes (the default) to the elements in the image1 class. This is followed by a style rule for the hover pseudo-class for the image1 class. It uses the transform property to rotate the image 180 degrees on its Y- axis. But it also uses the transform-origin property to change the origin point for the rotation to the right edge of the image.

Normally, though, the origin point is in the middle of the element that is being transformed. That's 50% or center on the X-axis and 50% or center on the Y-axis. Then, if you use the rotateX or rotateY method with a 360 degree value, the image will rotate in place horizontally or vertically and end up the way it started.

Properties for working with 2D transforms

Property	Description
transform	Applies one or more transform methods to the element.
transform-origin	Changes the default origin point. The parameters can be percents or keywords like left, center, right and top, center, bottom.

Methods for 2D transforms

Method	Description
rotate(angle)	Rotates an element by a specified angle.
rotateX(angle)	Rotates an element horizontally.
rotateY(angle)	Rotates an element vertically.
scaleX(value)	Changes the element's width by scaling horizontally.
scaleY(value)	Changes the element's height by scaling vertically.
scale(x-value,y-value)	Changes the element's width and height by scaling.
skewX(angle)	Skews an element along the X axis.
skewY(angle)	Skews an element along the Y axis.
skew(x-angle,y-angle)	Skews an element along the X and Y axis.
translateX(value)	Moves an element to the right or left.
translateY(value)	Moves an element up or down.
translate(x-value,y-value)	Moves an element right or left and up or down.
matrix(a,b,c,d,e,f)	The 6 parameters are values in a matrix that let you rotate, scale, translate, and skew elements with a single method.

The image on the right rotated to the right when the cursor moved over it

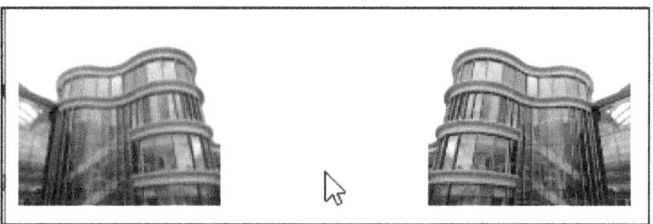

The HTML for the images

```
<p><img src="images/01.jpg" ><img src="images/01.jpg" class="image1"></p>
```

The CSS for the transform

```
.image1 {
    transition: 2s; }
.image1:hover {
    transform: rotateY(180deg);
    transform-origin: right; }
```

Description

- *Transforms* are often combined with transitions as shown by this example.

Figure 15-3   How to code 2D transforms

A gallery of images with 2D transforms

Figure 15-4 shows how 8 images will look after various transforms have been applied to them, all with the default origin point. Each of these transitions will be done when the user hovers over the image. The best way to understand what these transforms do is to experiment with them on your own.

The one method that isn't explained is the matrix method. It lets you rotate, scale, translate, and skew elements with a single method by setting the values in a matrix. If you're mathematically inclined and are familiar with matrixes, you can learn more about this method by searching the web.

Images that have 8 different transforms applied to them

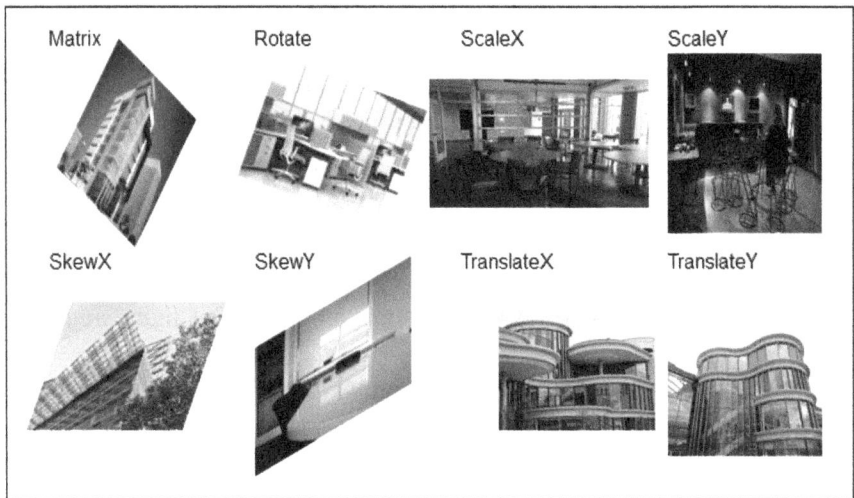

The HTML for the images

```
<ul>
    <li><p>Matrix</p><img src="images/01.jpg" class="image1"></li>
    <li><p>Rotate</p><img src="images/02.jpg" class="image2"></li>
    <li><p>ScaleX</p><img src="images/03.jpg" class="image3"></li>
    <li><p>ScaleY</p><img src="images/04.jpg" class="image4"></li>
    <li><p>SkewX</p><img src="images/05.jpg" class="image5"></li>
    <li><p>SkewY</p><img src="images/06.jpg" class="image6"></li>
    <li><p>TranslateX</p><img src="images/07.jpg" class="image7"></li>
    <li><p>TranslateY</p><img src="images/08.jpg" class="image8"></li>
</ul>
```

The CSS for the 2D transforms

```
.image1:hover { transform: matrix(0.5, 0.5, -0.5, 1, 0, 0); }
.image2:hover { transform: rotate(20deg); }
.image3:hover { transform: scaleX(1.4); }
.image4:hover { transform: scaleY(1.4); }
.image5:hover { transform: skewX(-20deg); }
.image6:hover { transform: skewY(-30deg); }
.image7:hover { transform: translateX(30px); }
.image8:hover { transform: translateY(20px); }
```

Description

- If you want the transforms applied when the mouse hovers over an image, you can use the hover pseudo-class as shown above.
- For an excellent resource on working with 3D transforms, please visit David DeSandro's GitHub post: http://desandro.github.io/3dtransforms.

Figure 15-4   A gallery of images with 2D transforms

How to use CSS animations

CSS *animations* allow HTML elements to be animated without the need for JavaScript code or third-party plugins. As you will see, animations can be simple or complex and can animate more than one CSS property at the same time.

How to code simple animations

Figure 15-5 summarizes the primary properties for working with animations. Here, the animation property is the shorthand property for the other six properties, and the animation property is used in the examples in this figure and the next figure.

Of the six values that the animation property can include, the values for the duration, delay, and timing function work as they do for a transition. The value for iteration count is the number of times the animation will run. And the value for direction is the direction in which the animation will run.

The other value for the animation property is the name you provide for the *@keyframes selector* rule. It's within this rule that you define the *keyframes* for the *animation sequence*. When those keyframes are played, they give the impression of motion.

The example in this figure shows how this works. Here, the left margin for a heading is changed from 20% to 60% and the color is changed from blue to red. As a result, the animation moves the heading from left to right and at the same time changes the color of the heading from blue to red.

In the CSS for this animation, the animation property for the h1 element points to the @keyframes selector named "moveright". It also says that each repetition should take 3 seconds, the start of the animation should be delayed 2 seconds, the animation should keep repeating, and the ease-in-out speed curve should be used. The animation property also says that the direction should alternate, which means the first animation will move from left to right, the second one from right to left, and so on.

The @keyframes selector rule that follows illustrates one way that the keyframes can be defined. Here, the from group sets the properties for the first frame and the to group sets the properties for the last frame. Then, the browser recognizes that it needs to fill the "in-between" frames for you. This is known as *tweening*.

Properties for working with animations

Property	Description
animation	The shorthand property for setting the properties that follow.
animation-name	The name of the @keyframes rule for the keyframe sequence.
animation-duration	The seconds or milliseconds that the animation will take.
animation-delay	The seconds or milliseconds before the animation starts.
animation-iteration-count	The number of times the animation should repeat or infinite.
animation-timing-function	The speed curve of the animation.
animation-direction	The direction of the animation: normal, reverse, or alternate.

The syntax for the shorthand animation property

```
animation: [name] [duration] [timing-function] [delay] [iteration-count]
           [direction];
```

A simple animation that moves a heading and changes its color

Starting in blue with a left margin of 20%

> This text will animate.

Ending in red with a left margin of 60%

> This text will animate.

The HTML for the heading

```
<h1>This text will animate.</h1>
```

The CSS for the animation

```
h1 {animation: moveright 3s ease-in-out 2s infinite alternate; }
@keyframes moveright {
    from { margin-left: 20%;
           color: blue; }
    to {   margin-left: 60%;
           color: red; }
}
```

Description

- The animation-name property points to an *@keyframes selector* rule that defines the *keyframes* for a CSS *animation*.
- For a simple animation, the keyframes are set automatically, as shown above, but you can define them yourself as shown in the next figure.

Figure 15-5   How to code simple animations

How to set the keyframes for a slide show

Figure 15-6 shows how you can set more of the keyframes for an animation and then let the browser do the tweening. This example creates a slide show for five images and captions without the need for JavaScript or jQuery.

The HTML for this slide show is just an unordered list, but each list item contains an h2 element for the caption and an img element for the image. Not shown is the CSS for the formatting of all the elements, but when that formatting is done, all five images are in a row with four of them hidden to the right of the one shown when the page is rendered in the browser.

This figure does show some of the formatting for the ul and li elements. Here, relative positioning is used for the ul element. That way, the keyframes for the animation sequence for that element can also use relative positioning. In addition, the width of the ul element is set to 500% of its containing block so it can accommodate all five images. Finally, the width of each list item is set to 20% of the ul element, or 100% of the ul element's containing block (20% of 500%).

The CSS for the animation is applied to the ul element. This animation uses the @keyframes rule named "slideshow". Unlike the @keyframes rule in the previous figure, this one sets the keyframes for eleven different points in the animation: 0%, 10%, 20%, and so on up to 100%. Here, the starting keyframe sets the left property for relative positioning to 0. This means that the first list item in the unordered list is shown. Then, at the 20% point in the animation, the left property is changed to -100%, which is the width of one list item. This means that the second image slides into place from the right and the first one is hidden. This animation continues until the left property is changed to -400% in the keyframe at the 80% point in the animation, which means that the last image slides into place and stays there until the animation is finished.

Then, because the animation property specifies "alternate" for the direction, the next repetition of the animation reverses the order of the slides so they go from the last to the first. If "normal" had been specified for the direction, the slides would restart from the first keyframe for the next repetition.

To get a better idea of how this works, you can review all of the CSS in the downloaded example for this figure. You can also experiment with the animation property and the keyframe settings.

A slide show animation with captions above the images

The HTML for an unordered list that contains the images and captions

```
<ul>
    <li>
        <h2>Front of Building</h2>
        <img src="images/01.jpg" alt="">
    </li>
    ...
</ul>
```

The CSS for the ul and li elements

```
ul { list-style: none;
    width: 500%;
    position: relative; }
ul li { width: 20%;
        float: left; }
```

The CSS for the animation

```
ul { animation: slideshow 15s infinite alternate; }
@keyframes slideshow {
    0%      {left:     0%;}
    10%     {left:     0%;}
    20%     {left: -100%;}
    30%     {left: -100%;}
    40%     {left: -200%;}
    50%     {left: -200%;}
    60%     {left: -300%;}
    70%     {left: -300%;}
    80%     {left: -400%;}
    90%     {left: -400%;}
    100%    {left: -400%;}
}
```

Description

- This animation works like a jQuery slide show. However, it is done with CSS alone.

Figure 15-6   How to set the keyframes for a slide show

How to use CSS filters

Filters let you change the appearance of images after they have been loaded into the browser without changing the image files. For instance, you can use filters to convert an image to grayscale or to blur an image.

How to code filters

Figure 15-7 summarizes the filter property and the ten filter methods that it supports. Most of these filter methods accept percent values that can either be expressed as a percent like 50% or a decimal value like .5. But some require degree values, and the drop-shadow method requires a series of values like the box-shadow property does.

The example in this figure shows how to invert an image. Here, the same image is displayed side by side, but the one on the right inverts the colors of the original image when the user hovers the mouse over it. In this case, an 80% inversion is used, but that can range from 0 (no inversion) to 100% (full inversion).

The syntax for adding a filter to an element

```
filter: filtermethod(value);
```

The filter methods

Method	Description
blur(value)	Applies a Gaussian blur. The value is in pixels.
brightness(value)	Adjusts the brightness, from 0% (black) to 100% (unchanged). Numbers higher than 100% result in a brighter image.
contrast(value)	Adjusts the contrast, from 0% (black) to 100% (unchanged).
drop-shadow(values)	Adds a drop shadow just as the box-shadow property does.
grayscale(value)	Converts the image to grayscale. 100% is completely grayscale, while 0% leaves the image unchanged.
hue-rotate(angle)	Adjusts the hue rotation of the image. The angle value is the number of degrees around the color circle that the image will be adjusted.
invert(value)	Inverts the colors of the image. 100% is completely inverted, while 0% leaves the image unchanged.
opacity(value)	Applies transparency to the image. 0 results in an image that is completely transparent while 1 leaves the image unchanged.
saturate(value)	Saturates the image. 0% results in an image that is completely saturated while 100% leaves the image unchanged.
sepia(value)	Converts the image to sepia. 100% is completely sepia, while 0% leaves the image unchanged.

An image before and after its colors are inverted

The HTML for the images

```
<li>Original<br><img src="images/01.jpg" alt=""></li>
<li>Inverted<br><img src="images/01.jpg" class="image1" alt=""></li>
```

The CSS for the filter

```
.image1:hover { filter: invert(.80); }
```

Description

- You can use *filters* to change the appearance of an image in the browser.
- Percentage values like 50% can also be expressed as decimal fractions like .5.

Figure 15-7   How to use filters

The ten filter methods applied to the same image

Figure 15-8 gives you an example of what an image will look like when each of the ten filters is applied to it. If you're reading this in black and white, of course, it's hard to evaluate some of the differences. So the best way to see what these filters can do is to experiment with them on your own.

The last example shows how you can apply two filters to the same image. To do that, you code one method after the other without using commas to separate them.

A web page in Chrome with different filters applied to an image

The HTML for the images that will have filters applied

```
<ul>
   <li>Blur<br>        <img src="images/01.jpg" class="image1" alt=""></li>
   <li>Brightness<br>  <img src="images/01.jpg" class="image2" alt=""></li>
   <li>Contrast<br>    <img src="images/01.jpg" class="image3" alt=""></li>
   <li>Drop Shadow<br> <img src="images/01.jpg" class="image4" alt=""></li>
   <li>Grayscale<br>   <img src="images/01.jpg" class="image5" alt=""></li>
   <li>Hue Rotate<br>  <img src="images/01.jpg" class="image6" alt=""></li>
   <li>Invert<br>      <img src="images/01.jpg" class="image7" alt=""></li>
   <li>Opacity<br>     <img src="images/01.jpg" class="image8" alt=""></li>
   <li>Saturate<br>    <img src="images/01.jpg" class="image9" alt=""></li>
   <li>Sepia/blur<br>  <img src="images/01.jpg" class="image10" alt=""></li>
</ul>
```

The CSS for the filters

```
.image1 { filter: blur(2px); }
.image2 { filter: brightness(50%); }
.image3 { filter: contrast(50%);}
.image4 { filter: drop-shadow(2px 2px 5px #333); }
.image5 { filter: grayscale(50%); }
.image6 { filter: hue-rotate(90deg); }
.image7 { filter: invert(.8); }
.image8 { filter: opacity(.50); }
.image9 { filter: saturate(30%); }
.image10{ filter: sepia(100%) blur(1px); }
```

Description

- This example shows how the 10 filter methods look when they're applied to the same image.
- The filters in this example are applied when the page is loaded, but you can use the hover pseudo-class to apply them when the mouse hovers over an image.
- Note, however, that you can't use transitions with filters.

Figure 15-8   The ten filter methods applied to the same image

Perspective

Now that you've been introduced to CSS transitions, transforms, animations, and filters, you should be able to use them in your own web pages. But what should you do with them? If you're looking for ideas, just search the web for examples. For instance, you can find lots of examples of transitions and animations that include slide shows, carousels, accordions, and some incredible animations. You can also find plenty of examples for transforms and filters.

But the other question you should ask is whether you need these CSS features. For example, as you'll learn in chapter 18, you can use a JavaScript library called jQuery UI to provide features like accordions, and you can use jQuery plugins to provide features like slide shows and carousels. Often, this is an easier way to provide these features, and they are likely to work even better than those you can create with CSS transitions and animations.

Of course, the benefit of using the CSS features is that they don't require JavaScript or jQuery. They are also relatively easy to use.

Terms

transition
timing function
speed curve
transform
animation
@keyframes selector
keyframe
animation sequence
tweening
filter

Summary

- When the CSS properties for an HTML element are changed, a CSS *transition* provides a smooth change over a specified period of time.
- CSS *transforms* let you rotate, scale, skew, and position HTML elements.
- CSS *animations* let you create frame-based animations.
- The CSS animation property always points to an *@keyframes selector* rule that defines the *keyframes* that are used in the *animation sequence*. When those keyframes are played, they give the impression of motion.
- CSS *filters* let you provide effects like blurring or grayscale to HTML elements like images and backgrounds.

Exercise 15-1   Use transitions, transforms, and animation

In this exercise, you'll have some fun with the CSS features that you learned about in this chapter. For instance, you'll animate the four images in the aside when the page is loaded, and you'll rotate the speaker image in the article when the user hovers the mouse over it. When both of those features are in progress, the page will look something like this:

Use a transition

1. Use your text editor to open these files:

   ```
   \html_css_5\exercises\town_hall_3\index.html
   \html_css_5\exercises\town_hall_3\styles\c15_main.css
   ```

2. With figure 15-1 as a guide, add a transition to the page that moves any of the images in the aside 100 pixels to the right and 20 pixels down when the user hovers the mouse over one of them. The duration of the transition should be 2 seconds. Then, test this change in Chrome and test each of the changes that follow using that browser.

3. Comment out the transition and test this again to see that the movement still works, but there isn't a gradual transition to the new location. Then, uncomment the transition.

Use a transition with a transform

4. With figure 15-3 as a guide, add a transition and a transform that rotates the image in the article by 720 degrees when the user hovers the mouse over the image. The duration of this transition should be 3 seconds.

5. Change the origin of this transform so it is at the upper left of the image. Then, test this change and note the difference.

Use animation with a transform

6. With figure 15-5 as a guide, animate the four images in the aside so they move to the right 100 pixels and down 20 pixels when the page is loaded into the browser. The animation should be delayed 2 seconds, last 3 seconds, be run 2 times, and alternate directions.

7. Add a transform to this animation that increases the size of the image 1.4 times. You can do that with the scale method.

Section 4

Web design, deployment, and JavaScript

In the three chapters in this section, you'll learn more about web design, deployment, and JavaScript. You can read these chapters any time after you complete the chapters in section 1, and you can read these chapters in whichever sequence you prefer.

In chapter 16, you'll learn some basic guidelines for designing a website that will help you develop effective web pages. In chapter 17, you'll learn how to deploy your website from your local computer or server to a web server that has Internet access. And in chapter 18, you'll learn how to use JavaScript for client-side processing.

Chapter 16

Users, usability, and web design

If you've read section 1, you know how to use HTML and CSS to develop web pages. Now, in this chapter, you'll learn about users and usability, and you'll learn some basic guidelines for designing a website.

Users and usability

Before you design a website, you need to think about who your users are going to be and what they are going to expect. After all, it is your users who are going to determine the success of your website.

What web users want is usability

What do users want when they reach a website? They want to find what they're looking for as quickly and easily as possible. And when they find it, they want to extract the information or do the task as quickly and easily as possible.

How do users use a web page? They don't read it in an orderly way, and they don't like to scroll. Instead, they scan the page to see if they can find what they're looking for or a link to what they're looking for. Often, they click on a link to see if it gives them what they want, and if it doesn't, they click on the Back button to return to where they were. In fact, users click on the Back button more than 30% of the time when they reach a new page.

If the users can't find what they're looking for or get too frustrated, they leave the site. It's that simple. For some websites, more than 50% of first-time visitors to the home page leave without ever going to another page.

In web development terms, what the users want is *usability*. This term refers to how easy it is to use a website, and usability is one of the key factors that determines the effectiveness of a website. If a site is easy to use, it has a chance to be effective. If it isn't easy to use, it probably won't be effective.

Figure 16-1 presents one page of a website that has a high degree of usability, and it presents three guidelines for improving usability. First, you should try to present the critical information for a page "above the fold." This term refers to what's shown on the screen when a new page is displayed, which is analogous to the top half of a newspaper. This reduces the need for scrolling, and it gives the page a better chance for success.

Second, you should try to group related items into separate components, and limit the number of components on each page. That will make the page look more manageable and will help people find what they're looking for.

Third, you should adhere to the current conventions for website usability. For instance, clickable links should look like they're clickable and items that aren't clickable shouldn't fool users by looking like they are clickable.

If you look at the website in this figure, you can see that it has implemented these guidelines. All of the critical information is presented above the fold. The page is divided into a header and nine other well-defined components. It's also easy to tell where to click.

Of course, it's relatively easy to build a website like this because it has a small number of products. In contrast, building usability into a large website with dozens of product categories and hundreds of products is a serious challenge.

A small website that is easy to use

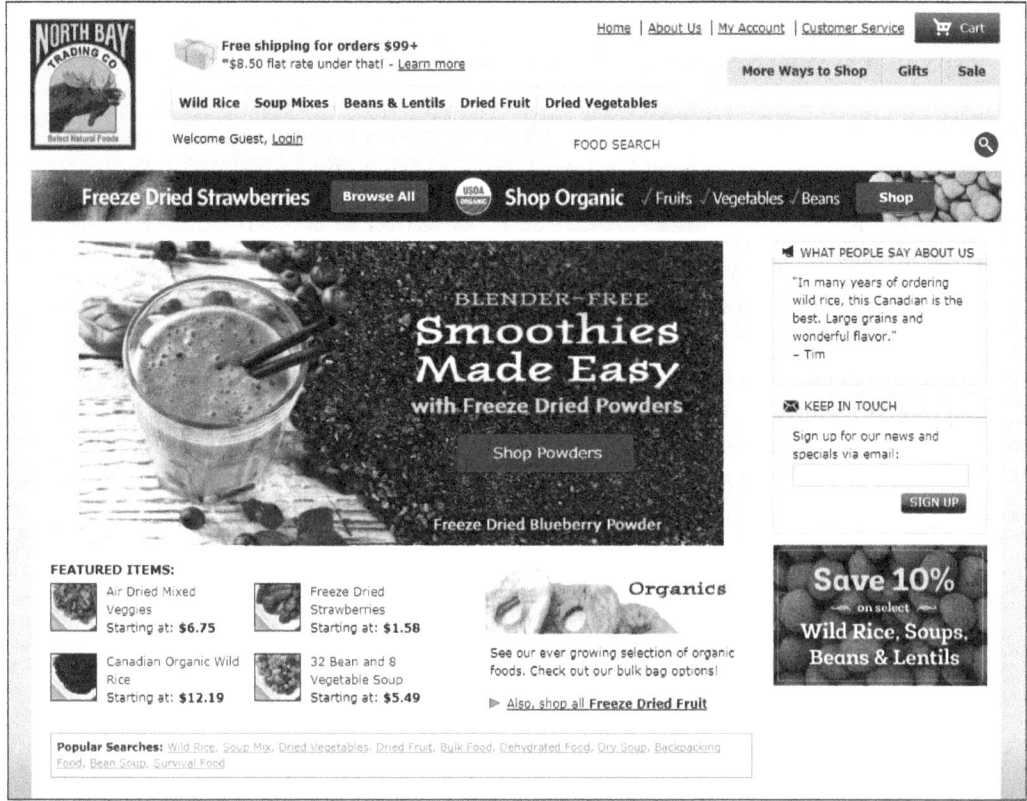

What website users want

- To find what they're looking for as quickly and easily as possible.
- To get the information or do the task that they want to do as quickly and easily as possible.

How website users use a web page

- They scan the page to find what they're looking for or a link to what they're looking for, and they don't like to scroll. If they get frustrated, they leave.
- They often click on links and buttons with the hope of finding what they're looking for, and they frequently click on the Back button when they don't find it.

Three guidelines for improving usability

- Present all of the critical information "above the fold" so the user doesn't have to scroll.
- Group related items into separate components, and limit the number of components on each page.
- Adhere to the current conventions for website usability (see the next figure).

Description

- *Usability* refers to how easy it is to use a website, and usability is a critical requirement for an effective website.

Figure 16-1   What web users want is usability

The current conventions for usability

If you've been using websites for a while, you know that you expect certain aspects of each website to work the same way. For example, you expect underlined text to be a link to another web page, and you expect that something will happen if you click on a button. These are website conventions that make a website easier to use because they work the same on almost all sites.

Figure 16-2 summarizes some of the other conventions that lead to improved usability. By following these conventions, you give the users what they expect, and that makes your website easier to use.

To start, a header usually contains a logo, a search function, and a navigation bar that provides links to the sections of the website. In addition, a header usually provides links to one or more *utilities*, like creating an account, signing in, or getting customer service. Some headers also include a *tag line* that identifies what's unique about the website, especially the headers for websites that need to sell themselves.

The navigation conventions are also critical to the usability of a website. In brief, a search function should consist of a text box and a search button, clickable items should look like they're clickable, items that aren't clickable shouldn't look like they're clickable, and clicking on the logo in the header of a page should take you back to the home page.

If you implement all of these conventions on your site, you will be on your way to web usability. But that's just a start. In the rest of this chapter, you'll learn other ways to improve the usability of a site.

A web page that illustrates some of the website conventions

Header conventions

- The header consists of a logo, an optional tag line, utilities, and a navigation bar.
- If there's a tag line, it identifies what's unique about the website.
- The navigation bar provides links that divide the site into sections.
- The utilities consist of links to useful but not primary information.
- If your site requires a search function, it should be in the header, and it should consist of a large text box for the entry followed by a search button.

Navigation conventions

- Underlined text is always a link.
- Images that are close to short text phrases are clickable.
- Short text phrases in columns are clickable.
- If you click on a cart symbol, you go to your shopping cart.
- If you click on the logo in the header, you go to the home page.

Description

- If your website implements the current website conventions, your users will be able to use the same techniques on your site that they use on other sites.

Figure 16-2   The current conventions for usability

Design guidelines

Did you ever think about what makes a good website? Well, a lot of experts have. What follows, then, is a distillation of some of the best thinking on the subject.

Use mobile-first design

Today, more than half of the visitors to a website are likely to be using mobile devices. As a result, you can no longer design your web pages for computer browsers and then deal with mobile devices as an afterthought.

Instead, the current development standard is to first design your web pages for mobile devices, and then expand the design for larger devices like tablets and computers. This can be referred to as *mobile-first design*.

The other approach to web design is to design for the browsers of desktop computers, and then redesign the pages for mobile devices. This can be referred to as *desktop-first design*.

Frankly, both approaches make sense. In figure 16-3, for example, you can see the relationship between a desktop home page and a mobile home page. Here, the contents of both pages are pretty much the same. They are just arranged differently. And that of course is what you try to do whether you use mobile-first or desktop-first design. That is, deliver all the content, but arrange it in the way that's works the best for the device.

The Lands' End home page
on a desktop computer and a mobile phone

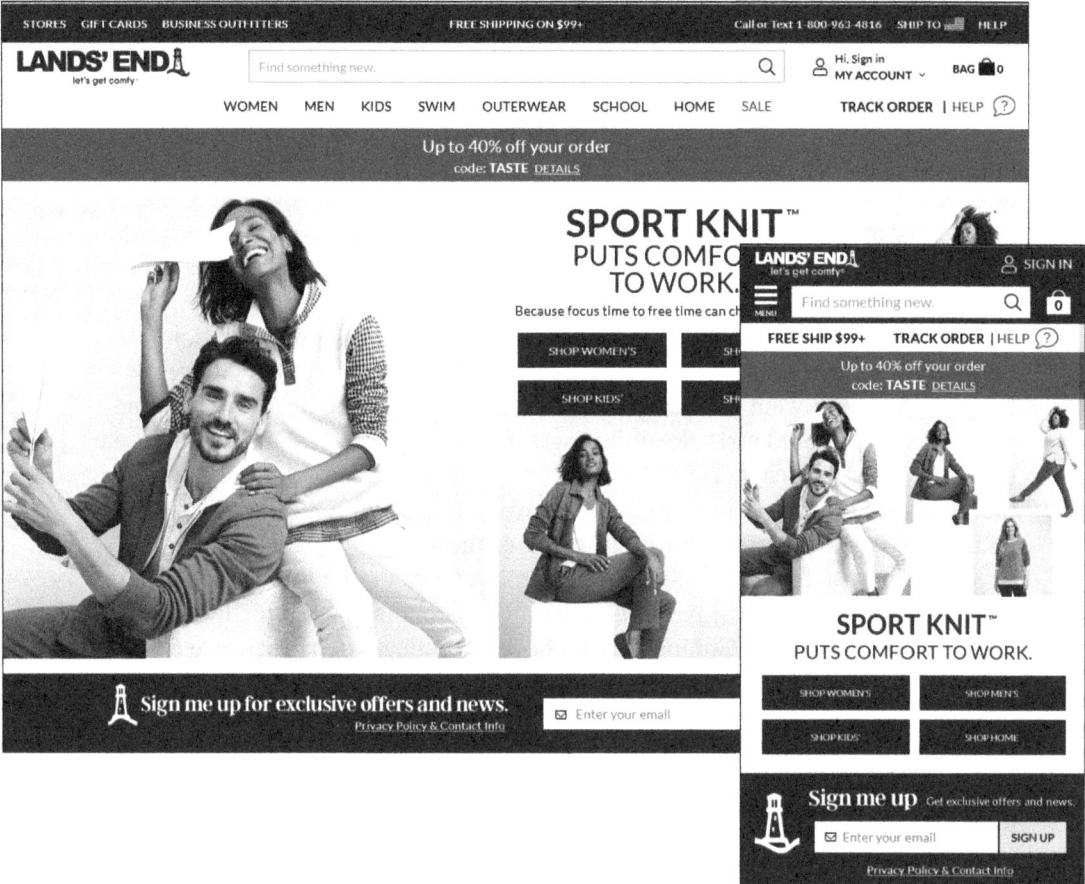

The essence of mobile-first design

- Design the mobile pages first.
- Expand those designs for larger browsers.

Description

- Because so much web activity is done on mobile devices, the current development standard is to use *mobile-first design*. In other words, you start by designing your pages so they work for mobile users and then expand them for desktop computer users.
- The other way to design web pages is to design for desktop computer browsers first, and then reduce them for mobile users. That can be referred to as *desktop-first design*.

Figure 16-3   Use mobile-first design

Use the home page to sell the site

Figure 16-4 presents 9 guidelines for the design of a home page. Most important is the first one, which says to emphasize what's different about your site and why it's valuable from the user's point of view. In other words, sell your site to your visitors.

If you're a well-known company with a successful site, this isn't as important. That's why the home pages for the websites of most large companies don't make any special efforts to sell their sites. But if you're developing the website for a small company that still needs to develop a customer base, by all means use the home page to sell the site. That may determine whether or not your site is successful.

The other guidelines should be self-explanatory. For instance, you don't need to welcome users to your site because that space should be used to sell the site. You don't want to include an active link to the home page on the home page because it would just reload the page. You do want to limit the length of the title element for the page to 8 words and 64 characters because it's displayed in the results for search engines. And you do want to use a different design for the home page to set it off from the other pages of the site.

If you look at the home page in this figure, you can see that it tries to sell the site. Its tag line says: "love what you buy." Then, the copy in the top block adds: "We Simplify The Complex" and shows their three-step procedure for doing that. That encourages me to at least try one of their recommendations for a product category.

If you're competing with a known brand like *Consumers Digest*, and most of us are, you obviously need to let people know what you do better, and you need to start that on the home page. If you don't do that, it is likely to limit the success of your site.

A home page that tries to sell the site

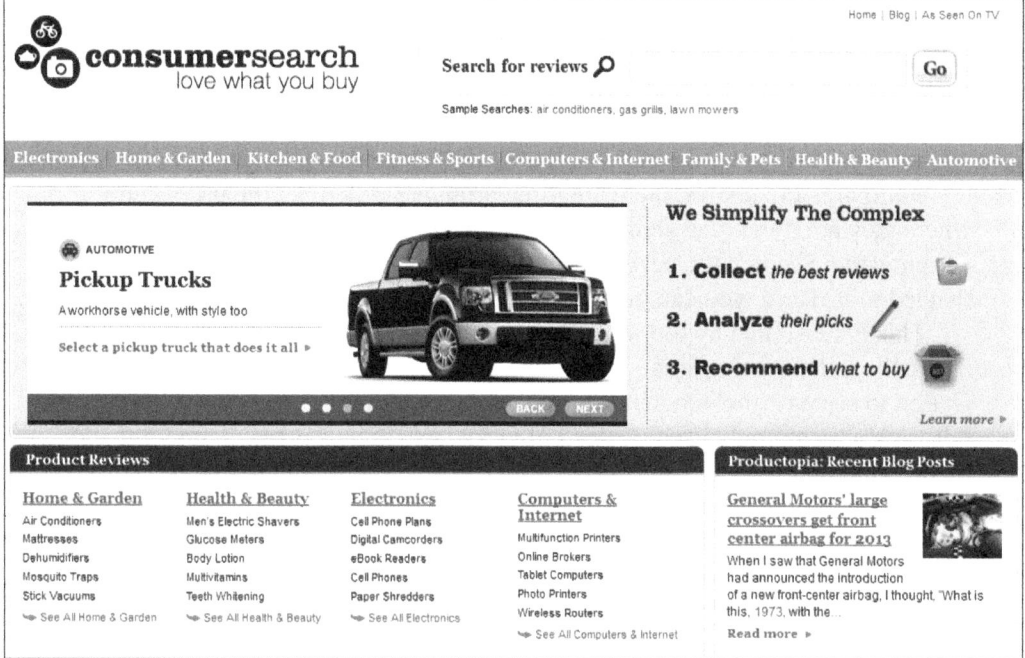

9 guidelines for developing an effective home page

1. Emphasize what your site offers that's valuable and how your site differs from competing sites.
2. Emphasize the highest priority tasks of your site so users have a clear idea of what they can do.
3. Don't welcome users to your site because that's a waste of space.
4. Group items in the navigation areas so similar items are next to each other.
5. Only use icons for navigation if the users will readily recognize them.
6. Design the home page so it is different from the other pages of the site.
7. Don't include an active link to the home page on the home page.
8. Code the title element for the home page as the organization name, followed by a short description, and limit the title to 8 or fewer words and 64 or fewer characters.
9. If your site provides shopping, include a link to the shopping cart on your home page.

Description

- To a large extent, the home page of your website will determine whether or not it gets the results that you want.

Figure 16-4   Use the home page to sell the site

Let the users know where they are

As users navigate a site, they like to know where they are. That's why letting the users know where they are is one of the current conventions for website usability. Remember too that many users will reach your site via search engines so they won't arrive at the home page. They have a special need to find out where they are.

As figure 16-5 shows, there are three primary ways to let the users know where they are. First, you should highlight the links that led the user to the current page. Second, the heading for the page should be the same as the link that led to it. Third, you can provide *breadcrumbs* that show the path to the page.

This is illustrated by the web page in this figure. Here, the breadcrumbs start above the left sidebar: Orvis / Dogs / Traveling with Dogs. In this case, the slash is used to separate the items in the path, but separators like greater than signs (>) are also commonly used. Instead of Orvis, which in this case represents the home page, you can just use Home for that page, as shown in figure 16-2.

Farther down the sidebar, you can see that the link that led to the page (Traveling with Dogs) is boldfaced. You can also see that the heading for the page is TRAVELING WITH DOGS, which is the same as the link that led to the page. On some sites, you will also see the link in the navigation bar highlighted, which in this case would be DOGS.

A product page with breadcrumbs and highlighted links

How to let the users know where they are

- Highlight the active links.
- Make the heading for the page the same as the link that led to the page.
- Provide breadcrumbs in this general format: Homepage > Dogs > Traveling with Dogs.

Description

- As your site gets more complex, the users are likely to lose track of where they are in the site. But even simple sites should let the users know where they are.

Figure 16-5   Let the users know where they are

Make the best use of web page space

As you design a web page, remember that the part of the page that's above the fold is the most valuable space. As a result, you want to put the most important components of the page in that space. That's why many of the most successful websites have relatively small headers. That way, they have more space for the components that make each page effective.

To emphasize this point, figure 16-6 presents an extreme example of a web page that doesn't get the most out of the space above the fold. In fact, none of the text of the page can be seen above the fold. You have to scroll down for all of the information. Granted that the photos are beautiful (if you're a fly fisher), but does the fish have to show on every page that relates to Bob Cusack's Alaska Lodge? This is a case where the graphics, as beautiful as they may be, probably diminish the usability of the page.

As you design your pages, then, remember the three guidelines in this figure. Keep your header relatively small. Prioritize the components that are going to go on the page. And then give the best space to the most important components.

Wasted space on a primary page

Guidelines for the effective use of space

- Keep the header relatively small.
- Prioritize the components for each page.
- Give the most important components the primary locations.

Description

- The most valuable space on each web page is the space above the fold. To get the most from it, you need to prioritize the components on each page and give the best locations to the highest-priority components.

Figure 16-6   Make the best use of web page space

Divide long pages into shorter chunks

Remember that website users don't like to scroll. So a general guideline for web page design is to limit the amount of scrolling to one-and-one-half or two times the height of the browser window. But what if you need to present more information than that?

The best solution is to use *chunking* to divide the content into logical pieces or topics. This is illustrated by the example in figure 16-7. Here, what could be a long page of copy is chunked into smaller topics like "What makes Murach books the best". Then, if the users are interested in the topic, they can click on the MORE button to expand that copy. Below the two topics with MORE buttons is an accordion that presents "Five more reasons why our customers love our books." So in all, the copy for this page has been broken down into seven topics.

This approach lets the users select the topics that they're interested in so they have more control over their website experience. This makes it easier for the users to find what they're looking for. And this reduces the need for scrolling. How much better this is than forcing the users to scroll through a long page of text trying to find what they're looking for.

Incidentally, you use JavaScript to reveal and hide portions of text as in this example. You also use JavaScript for common features like tabs and accordions that reveal and hide text. As a result, JavaScript is an integral part of effective chunking. That's why we recommend *Murach's JavaScript and jQuery* as the perfect companion for this HTML and CSS book.

Chunking on our home page

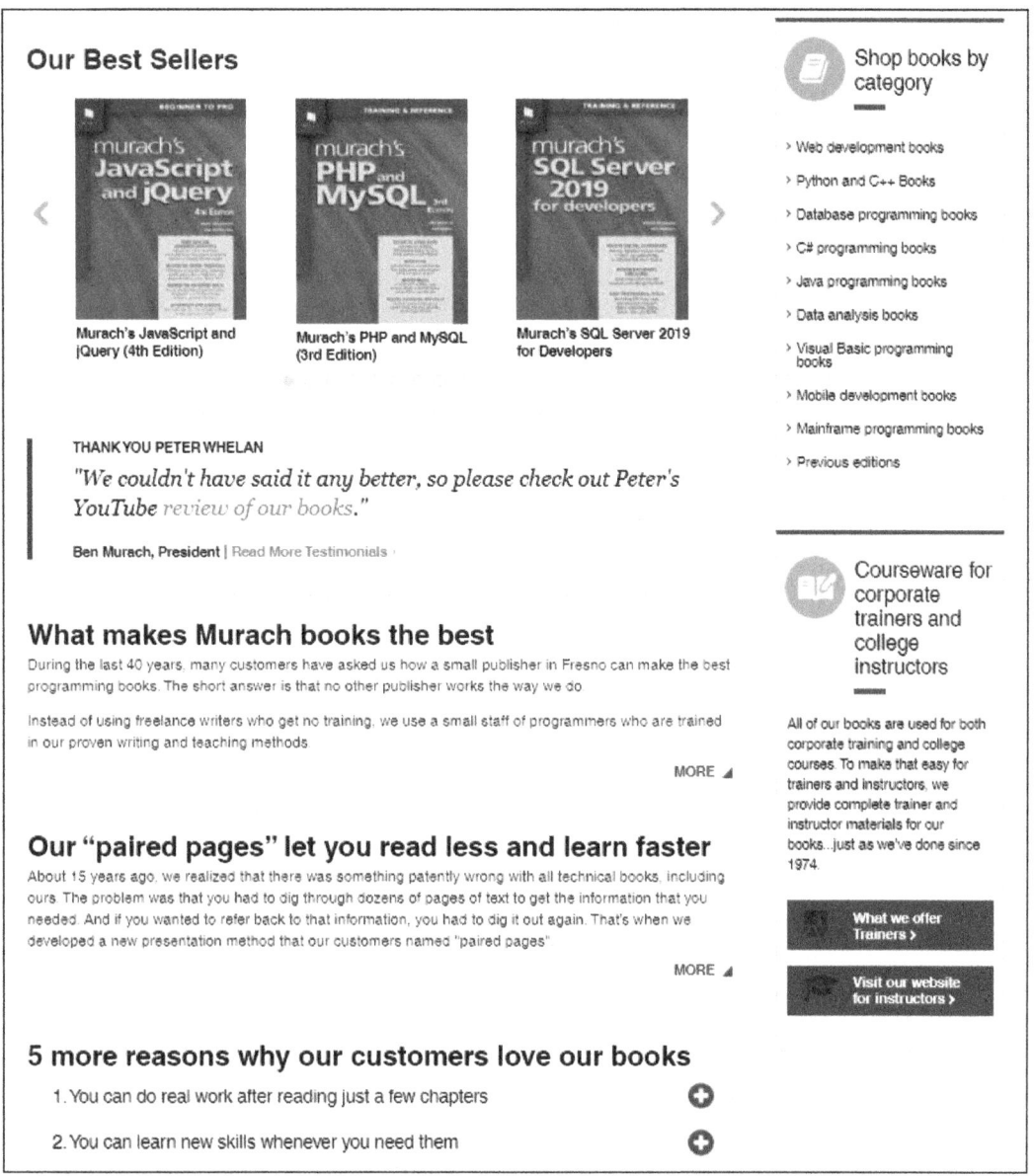

Description

- *Chunking* refers to the division of content into smaller chunks that can be presented on separate web pages or in separate components on the same page. This lets the users select the chunks of information that they're interested in.

- JavaScript is commonly used to implement chunking with features like accordions (see chapter 18), but you can also use CSS to implement some features (see chapter 15).

Figure 16-7   Divide long pages into shorter chunks

Know the principles of graphics design

If you aren't a graphics designer and you're developing a website, you should at least know the four basic principles of graphics design that are presented in figure 16-8. These principles are in common use on all of the best websites, so it's easy to find examples of their use.

For instance, *alignment* means that aligning related items gives a sense of order to a web page, and all of the examples to this point in this chapter make extensive use of alignment. Similarly, *proximity* means that related items should be close to each other, and all of those examples illustrate this principle too. When proximity is applied to headings, it means that a heading should be closer to the text that follows it than the text that precedes it.

The principle of *repetition* means that you repeat some elements from page to page to give the pages continuity. This is natural for web pages, starting with the header, which is usually the same on all pages. But it's the principle of *contrast* that draws your eye to a component. For instance, a component with a large heading or a yellow background will draw attention because it stands out from the other components of the page.

The home page in this figure illustrates some of these principle with the four images carefully aligned and the description of each image right below it. But like most websites, there is always room for improvement. For instance, the principle of proximity says that the Adventure Trips heading should be closer to the text below it. In other words, there shouldn't be such a large gap between the heading and the related text.

Besides adhering to the design principles, you need to get the typography right if you want your users to read the text on your website. That's why this figure presents six guidelines for doing that.

One common problem is text lines that are longer than 65 characters. You can see that in the text under the Adventure Trips heading in this figure. You can also see it in the first example in the next figure. Another common problem is using a background image or a background color that makes the text hard to read. And a third problem is the use of reverse type (white type on a darker background), especially for text, because that can make it much harder to read.

A website that adheres to the principles of graphics design

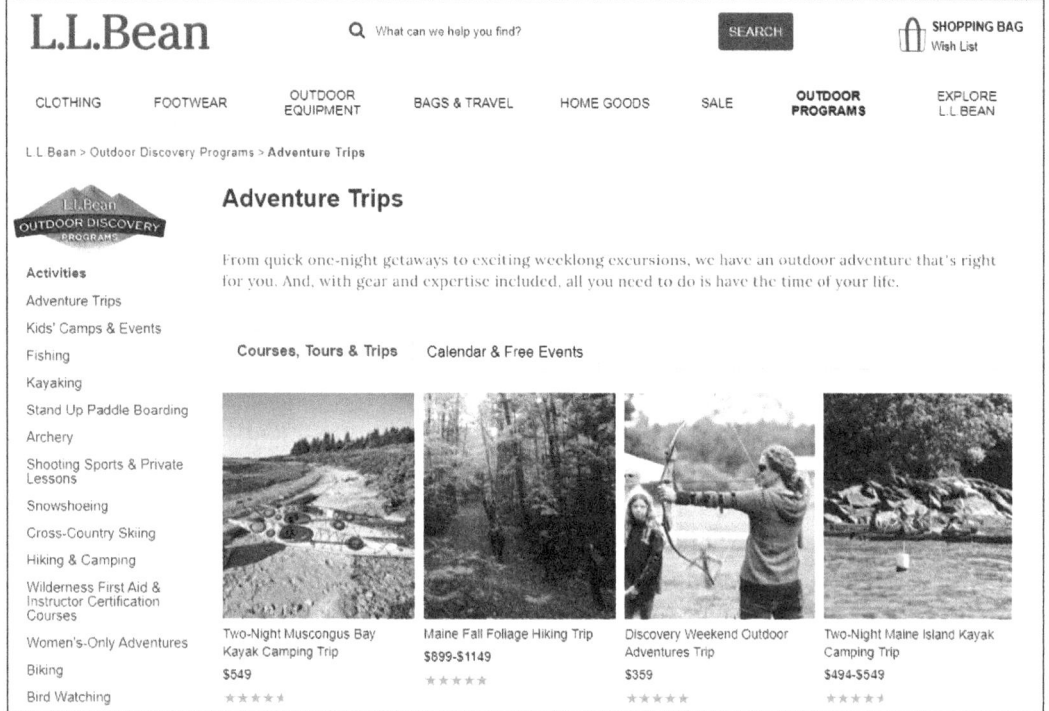

Four principles of graphics design

- *Alignment* means that related items on the page should line up with each other.
- *Proximity* means that related items should be close together.
- *Repetition* means that you should repeat some elements from page to page to give the pages continuity.
- *Contrast* is what draws your eye to some of the components on a web page.

Typographical guidelines

- Use a sans serif font in a size that's large enough for easy reading.
- Limit the line length of text to 65 characters.
- Use dark text on a light background, and don't use an image for the background.
- Don't center text and don't justify text.
- Don't use reverse type (white type on a colored background) for text.
- Avoid the use all caps (all capital letters) for headings because all caps are hard to read.

Description

- If you aren't a graphics designer, you can at least implement the principles of graphics design and get the typography right.

Figure 16-8   Know the principles of graphics design

Write for the web

Remember how web users use a website. Instead of reading, they skim and scan. They want to get the information that they're looking for as quickly as possible, and they don't want to have to dig through several paragraphs of text for it. That's why writing for a website is so different from writing for the printed page.

In figure 16-9, you can see a block of copy that isn't written for the web, followed by one that is. To present the same information in a way that is more accessible, the second example uses fewer words (135 to 177), which is the quickest way to improve your web writing. It also uses a numbered list to make it easy to find the flight information without having to dig through the text.

If you look through the other web writing guidelines, you'll see that they recommend what we implement in the figures of our books: an inverted pyramid style so the most important items are presented first; headings and subheadings to identify portions of the text; bulleted and numbered lists; tables for tabular information; and no headings with all caps. We do that so you don't have to read all of the text to review the information that you're looking for, and that's also the way web writing should work.

The last guideline is to make the text for all links as explicit as possible. For instance, "Find a job with us" is better than "Jobs", and "Apply for unemployment compensation" is better than "Unemployment". Remember that 30 to 40 percent of your users' clicks are likely to be on the Back button because a link didn't take them where they wanted. The more explicit your links are, the less that will happen.

Incidentally, the first example in this figure also illustrates poor typography. Above all, the text lines are 90 characters long, which makes the text unappealing and difficult to read. To fix that problem, you can increase the font size and shorten the line width, as shown in the second example. In addition, three different font sizes are used in the first four lines of the first example, but the font sizes don't reflect the relative importance of the text.

Writing that isn't for the web (177 words and 1041 characters)

The progressive air services you'll use to reach Cusack's Alaska Lodge are a wonderful reflection of your journey into the wilderness. First, you will fly a major jet service from near your home to Anchorage, Alaska; arriving here, most itineraries will mandate an overnight stay. The next morning you will board a small plane piloted by one of the fine bush pilots of Iliamna Air Taxi (often one of their Pilatus aircraft, a high-flying, very comfortable aircraft), for the transfer between Anchorage and the little village of Iliamna. Upon arriving, Iliamna Air Taxi's Iliamna crew will switch your gear from the mid-sized plane to a smaller, float-equipped Cessna or Beaver, and after a short wait, you will be on the final leg of your adventure, touching down on the lake's surface in front of Bob's lodge a short thirty minutes later. For the remainder of your week, Bob will be your pilot, flying you into amazingly beautiful country in his two small airplanes, giving you a peek into the enormity and grandeur of his corner of Alaska.

The same copy, but written for the web (135 words and 717 characters)

The three-part flight to Bob Cusack's Alaska Lodge is a fascinating journey into the Alaskan wilderness

1. You take a major jet service from your home to Anchorage, Alaska.
2. From Anchorage, you take the Iliamna Air Taxi to the little village of Iliamna. This flight will be piloted by one of the Air Taxi's fine bush pilots in a comfortable plane like the Pilatus.
3. In Iliamna, the Air Taxi's crew will switch your bags to a smaller, float plane like a Cessna or a Beaver. Then, after a short wait and a 30 minute flight, you will touch down on beautiful Lake Iliamna in front of Bob's lodge.

For the remainder of your week, Bob will be your pilot as he takes you into the beauty and grandeur of his corner of Alaska.

Web writing guidelines

- Use fewer words.
- Write in inverted pyramid style with the most important information first.
- Use headings and subheadings to identify portions of the text.
- Use bulleted lists and numbered lists to make information more accessible.
- Use tables for tabular information.
- Make the text for all links as explicit as possible.

Description

- Web users skim and scan; they don't read like book readers do. So when you write for the web, you need to change the way you think about writing.
- The writing in the first example above is bad enough, and the typography makes it worse.

Figure 16-9   Write for the web

Perspective

If you apply what you've learned in this chapter, you should be able to design simple websites of your own. But you should also realize that designing and developing a website is a challenging process that requires a wide range of skills. That includes graphics design, HTML and CSS, JavaScript and jQuery, writing for the web, and more. In short, the more you learn about web design and development, the better your websites will be.

Terms

usability	chunking
utility	alignment
tag line	proximity
mobile-first design	repetition
desktop-first design	contrast
breadcrumbs	

Summary

- When you design a website, *usability* is the primary issue. That refers to how easy a website is to use, and to a large extent that determines the success of the website. To achieve usability, a website needs to implement the current conventions for website use.

- The header of a web page usually consists of a logo, links to *utilities*, a search function, and a navigation bar. The header may also include a short *tag line* that tries to identify what's unique about the website.

- When you design a responsive website, you should use *mobile-first design*, even though the traditional approach has been *desktop-first design*.

- The home page of a website should be used to sell the site by emphasizing what's different about the site and why users should want to use it.

- To let the users know where they are as they navigate through a site, you can highlight the active links on the page, match the heading on the page to the link that led to it, and use *breadcrumbs*.

- *Chunking* refers to the division of information into topics (chunks) that can be presented on separate web pages or in separate components on a page.

- If you aren't a graphics designer, you should at least know the principles of *alignment*, *proximity*, *repetition*, and *contrast*. You should also know how to make the typography easy to read.

- Writing for the web isn't like writing for print. Instead, web writing should be in inverted pyramid style, and it should use headings and subheadings as well as bulleted and numbered lists.

Chapter 17

How to deploy a website

Once you've developed and tested your web pages on your computer or local server, you're just a few steps away from making those pages available to anyone in the world who is connected to the Internet. To do that, you just need to upload the files to a web server that's connected to the Internet. This chapter shows one way to do that.

Next, this chapter gives you some ideas for starting your own website. That includes getting a web host and a domain name, and then getting your site into search engines like Google and Bing. However, because there are so many ways to do what you need to do, you have to take the ideas in this chapter and then figure out how best to implement them for your own website.

How to transfer files to and from an Internet server

After you've developed and tested a web page or website on your own computer or local network, you are ready to *deploy* (or *publish*) it to a web server on the Internet. To do that, you can use *File Transfer Protocol* (or *FTP*) with an an *FTP client* like FileZilla, an IDE that includes an FTP client, or a tool for uploading files that's provided by your web host.

To give you some idea of how FTP clients work, figure 17-1 shows how FileZilla Client works. But keep in mind that if you're working with a development group, you may not have the authority to deploy the web pages that you develop or update. So after you've tested your pages on your computer or local server, you present them to the web master who will see that they get deployed properly.

How to connect to a website on the Internet

To connect to an existing website for the first time with FileZilla, you use the Site Manager dialog box to provide the site name, host name, server type, user name, and password for the site. Then, you click on the Connect button.

If the connection is successful, FileZilla displays a window like the one in this figure. Otherwise, it displays an error message that you can use to troubleshoot the problem.

After you connect to a site for the first time, you can easily connect to it again. To do that, you just select the site name in the Site Manager dialog box and click the Connect button.

How to upload and download files

After the connection has been made to a remote website, the left pane in FileZilla's main window shows the folder tree for the local site, and the right pane shows the folder tree for the remote site. You can see these panes in this figure. At that point, you can use the standard techniques for navigating and for opening and closing folders. And you can use the techniques in this figure to *upload* and *download* files.

FileZilla when it is connected to a web host

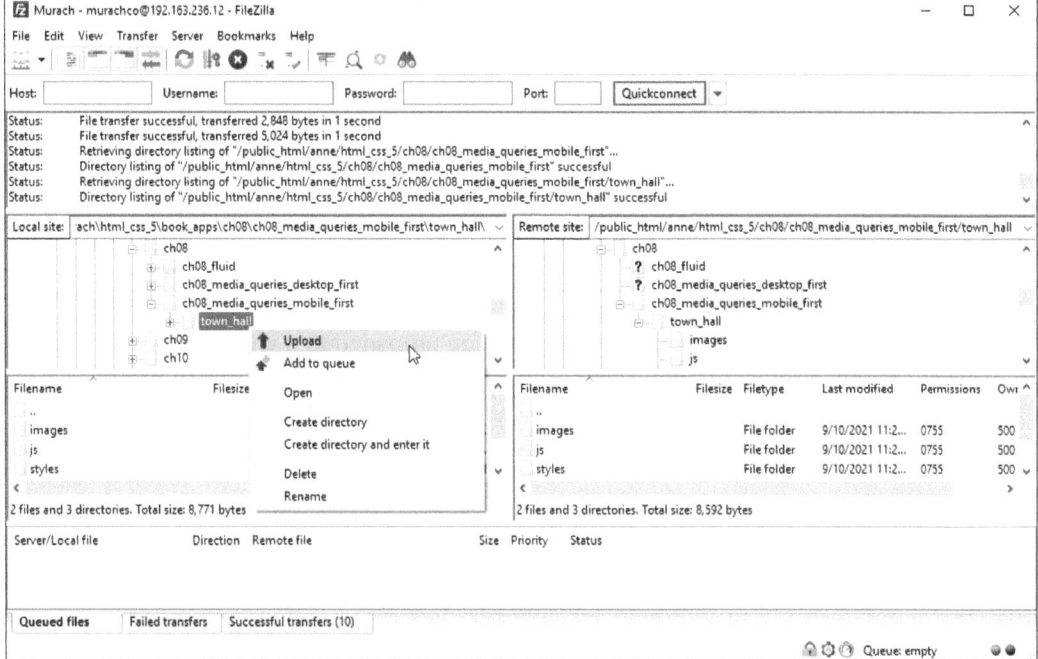

How to connect to an Internet website the first time

- Use File➜Site Manager to open the Site Manager dialog box. Then, click the New Site button, and enter the site name, host name, server type, user name, and password.

How to connect to an Internet website after it has been set up

- Open the Site Manager dialog box, click on the site name, and click the Connect button.

How to upload and download files

- To *upload* a file or folder from the local site to the remote site, display the folder on the remote site where you want the file or folder uploaded. Then, right-click on the file or folder in the local site and select the Upload command from the resulting menu.

- To *download* a file or folder from the remote site to the local site, display the folder on the local site where you want the file or folder downloaded. Then, right-click on the file or folder in the remote site and select the Download command.

- You can also upload or download files and folders by dragging them from the local site to the remote site, and vice versa.

Figure 17-1   How to transfer files to and from an Internet server

How to test a web page that has been uploaded to the Internet server

Figure 17-2 gives you some ideas for testing web pages that you have just uploaded to a web server on the Internet. To start, you need to make sure that all of the content is there. Then, you need to check all the links that go to and from the web page.

For instance, a web page often links to one or more HTML files, CSS files, and image files. Then, if you forget to upload a supporting file, one of the links won't work correctly. In that case, you can solve the problem by uploading the supporting file.

To test an entire website that has just been uploaded to a web server, you need to methodically review each of the pages on the site, including all of the links to and from each page. The larger the site, the more difficult this is, and the more methodical you need to be.

A web page on the Internet (www.murach.com)

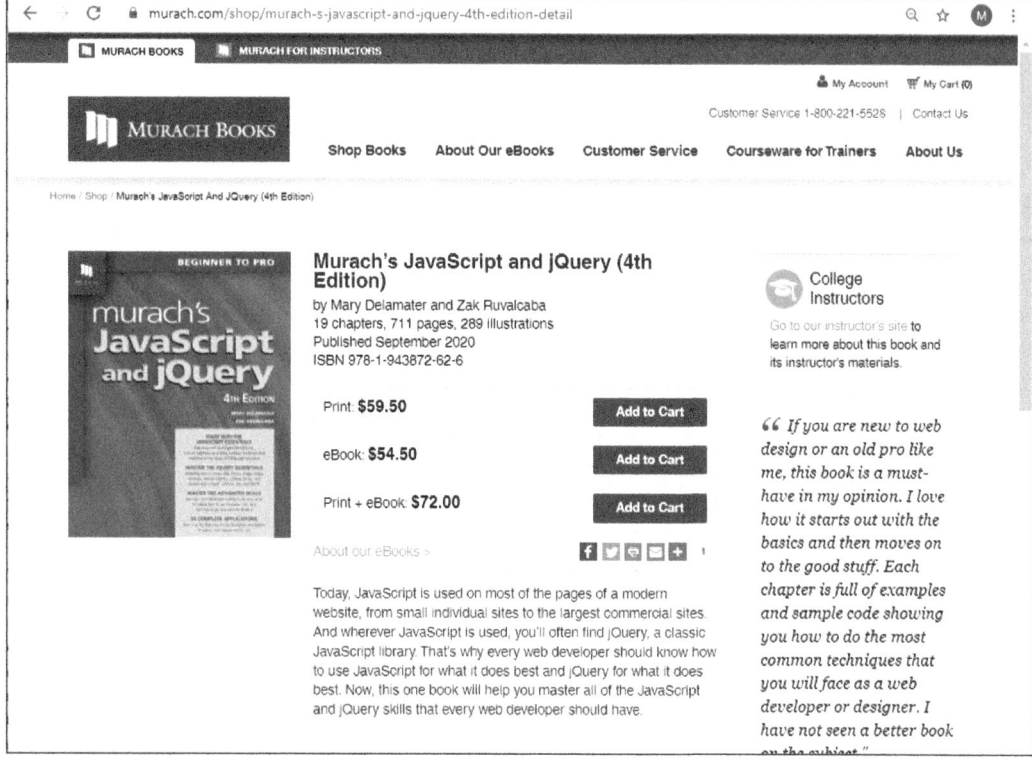

How to test a web page that you've just uploaded

- Use Chrome to go to your home page, and navigate to the new page using every route that your site has for getting there.
- Review the contents for the page, and make sure it's all there and it all works.
- Test all the links on the page to make sure they work correctly.
- Test the page in other browsers including tablet and mobile browsers.

How to test a new website

- Use Chrome to review all of the pages and test all of the links, one page at a time.
- Do the same for other browsers including tablet and mobile browsers.

Description

- Before you upload files to a web server, you should test them on your own computer or local server.
- Then, when you test your pages on your Internet server, what's most important is to make sure that all files have been uploaded to the right folders, including HTML, CSS, image, and JavaScript files.

Figure 17-2   How to test a web page that has been uploaded to the Internet server

How to start your own website

If you're developing a new website on your own, you need to get a web host that provides access to the Internet. You also need to get a domain name for your website. And after you get your website running on the Internet, you need to get its pages into the major search engines so people will go to them.

How to get a web host

Figure 17-3 shows the web page for one of the many sites that provides *web hosting services*. For small websites, you only need a small amount of disk space. For larger websites, you may need more disk space, access to a database server, and a server-side programming language such as PHP.

If you search the Internet, you'll find a wide range of services and prices for *web hosts*. For a small website, the price may be as little as a few dollars a month. And if you already pay an *Internet Service Provider* (*ISP*) to connect to the Internet, the ISP may provide free web hosting as part of its monthly fees.

How to get a domain name

When you use a web host, you can often use its *domain name* to access your website. If, for example, your web host has a domain name of

    bluehost.com

you may be able to access your website with a subdomain like

    murach.bluehost.com

For a professional website, though, you'll want to get your own domain name. And you can often get one from the same site that provides your web hosting. Otherwise, you can search for other sites that provide domain names.

Before you select your domain name, though, you need to decide what extension you want to use. The .com extension was originally intended for commercial websites, .net was intended for networking websites, and .org was intended for other organizations. Today, however, many other extensions are available, such as those for military (.mil), government (.gov), and business (.biz) websites.

When you use a site that provides domain names, you typically enter one or more domain names. Then, the site searches the *domain name registry* to see which of the names is available. You can then purchase any available name for a specific amount of time.

A website for web hosting (networksolutions.com)

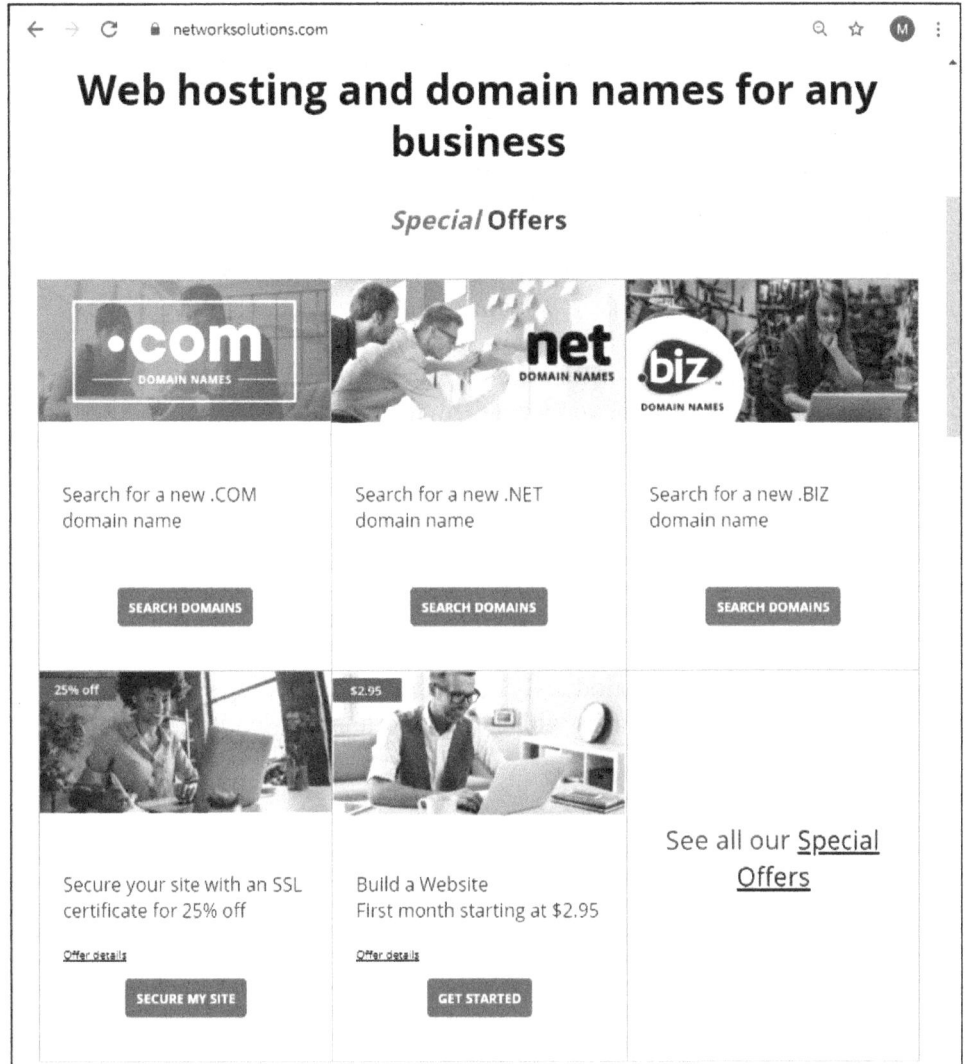

Description

- A *web host*, or *web hosting service*, provides space on a server computer that's connected to the Internet, usually for a monthly fee.
- A *domain name* is a user-friendly name that's used to locate a resource that's connected to the Internet.
- The .com, .net, and .org extensions are popular endings for domain names. These extensions were originally intended to be used for commercial websites (.com), networking infrastructure websites (.net), and other types of organizations (.org).
- The *domain name registry* is a database of all registered domain names.

Figure 17-3   How to get a web host and a domain name

How to get your website into search engines

After you deploy and test your website, you will want to get your pages into the major search engines so they will deliver visitors to your site. To start, you can go to the Google and Microsoft Bing sites that are listed in the table at the top of figure 17-4. These sites not only present the information that you need for getting into their search engines, but also all sorts of other information that will help you improve the search engine optimization for your pages.

When you get to the page for submitting your website for indexing to Google or Bing, you only need to submit the URL of your home page. Then, if your site is linked properly, the search engine's *robot* will "crawl" through the rest of your pages by following the links in your site. As it crawls, the robot will score your pages. Those scores will later determine how high your pages come up in the searches, and of course you want them to come up as high as possible.

The trouble is that the search engines use different algorithms for determining the scores of your pages. For instance, some search engines improve the score of a page if it has links to other sites. Some improve the score if the pages of other websites link to the page. To complicate the process, the search engines change their algorithms from time to time without any notice.

Once you've submitted your website for indexing, you don't have to do it again, even if you've made significant enhancements to the site. That's because the robot for a search engine periodically crawls through all of the sites and indexes the pages again, sometimes with a new algorithm for scoring.

The major search engines

Site name	Web address
Google	developers.google.com/search/
Bing	bing.com/webmasters/

The page for Google Search Central

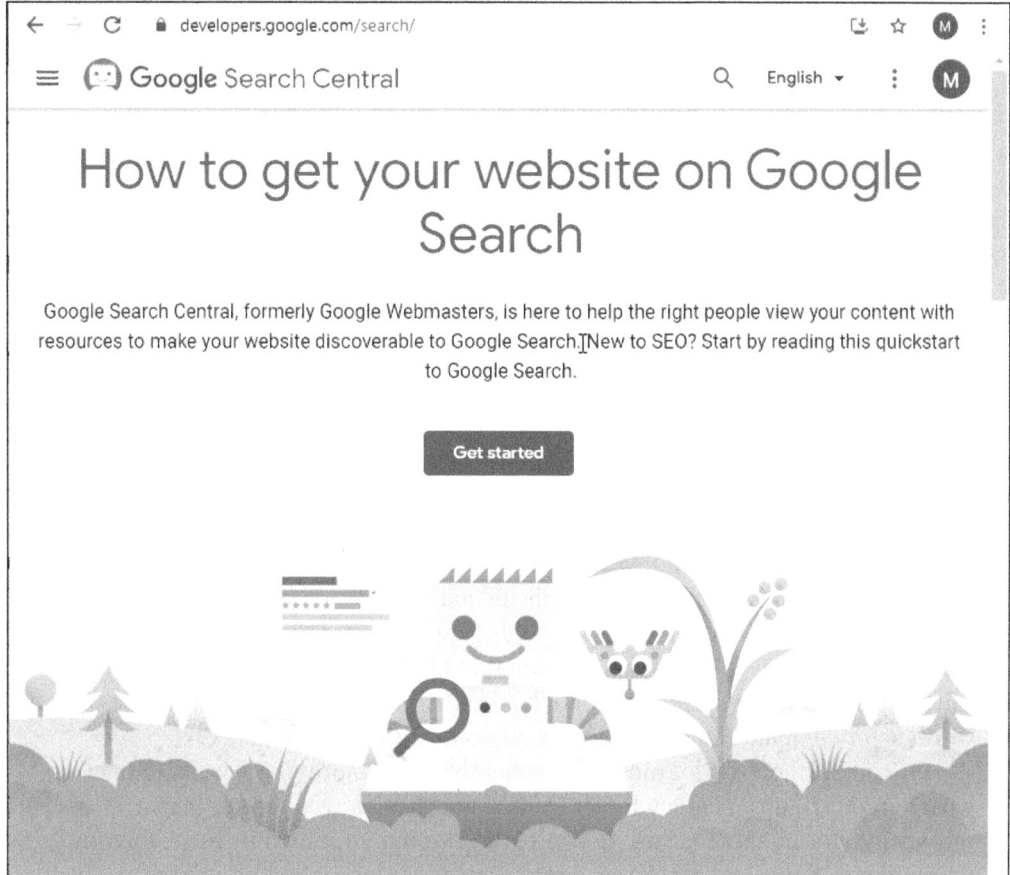

Description

- To submit your site to the two major search engines, go to the websites above and dig through the instructions.

- When you submit your site to a search engine, you provide the URL for your home page. Then, the *robot* (or *spider*) for that engine "crawls" through the pages of your site and indexes them.

- After your site has been indexed the first time, the robot will periodically crawl through your site again to update the index based on the changes that you've made to your site.

- At the site for each search engine, you can get all sorts of other information that will help you improve the SEO for your pages.

Figure 17-4   How to get your website into search engines

How to set up, maintain, and improve a website

For many websites, there are pages and maybe even folders of pages that you don't want indexed. For instance, you usually don't want your shopping cart pages indexed. So even before you submit your website to the search engines, you can use one of the two methods shown in figure 17-5 to stop or *exclude* pages from being indexed.

First, you can code a robots meta tag with the content set to "noindex" and "nofollow". This means that the robot shouldn't index the page and shouldn't follow any of the links on the page as it crawls through the pages of the site.

Second, you can set up a robots.txt file in the root folder of your website. Here, the * for user-agent means that it applies to all search engines. As these examples show, you can use a robots.txt file to exclude one or more folders or files from being indexed.

In some cases, you may also want to set up a *site map* (a sitemap.xml file) that tells the search engines which pages to *include* in their index. For a small site, you can use a website like the one that's listed in this figure to create the map for you.

Once your site is in the search engines, you enter the maintenance and improvement phase. For instance, whenever you add new pages and delete old ones, you also need to update the robots.txt file and site map.

Then, to improve your pages, you need to focus on web accessibility, search engine optimization, and more. To help you do that, the two free tools that are listed in this figure will grade your website and provide ideas for improvements.

On a medium or large website, though, you will want to use a more powerful tool like SiteImprove. It is an application that reports broken links, misspellings, SEO and accessibility issues, and much more. Although it's costly, it can be well worth it for companies that depend heavily on their online presence.

Of course, there's a lot more to maintaining and improving a website than what's in this figure. That's why larger websites have a web master that is responsible for all these issues. If you're developing your own website, though, you're the web master, which means that you're the one who will need to master these skills. Then, a good place to start is with Google Search Central.

But it's also good to get your site graded by Website Grader or Nibbler. If you've adhered to all the best practices and guidelines in this book, you may be pleasantly surprised by some of the results.

How to exclude a page from being indexed or followed

Add a meta tag to the page

```
<meta http-equiv="robots" content="noindex, nofollow">
```

How to exclude folders and files from being indexed

- Add a robots.txt file to the root directory of the page.

A file that tells search engines not to index the files in a folder

```
User-agent: *
Disallow: /cart/
```

A file that tells search engines not to index the pages in two folders

```
User-agent: *
Disallow: /cart/
Disallow: /private/
```

A file that tells search engines not to index one folder and one file

```
User-agent: *
Disallow: /cart/
Disallow: /backlist/private.html
```

How to make sure web pages are included by search engines

- Add a sitemap.xml file to the root directory of the site. This *site map* tells search engines which URLs are available for indexing, how often these pages should be crawled, when the last time each page was modified, and more.

- To create a free site map for small websites, you can go to: www.xml-sitemaps.com

Two of the free tools for grading your website

Tool	Web URL
Hubspot's Website Grader	website.grader.com
Nibbler	nibbler.silktide.com

A commercial tool for grading and maintaining your website

- SiteImprove: www.siteimprove.com

Description

- Before you submit your website to the search engines, you can use a robots meta tag or a robots.txt file to *exclude* some of the folders and files from being indexed. You can also use a sitemap.xml file to *include* specific pages of your site in the search engines.

- Once your site is up and running, you need to maintain and monitor it so it stays up-to-date and does well in the search engines.

- Hubspot's Website Grader and Nibbler are two websites that will grade your website and give you ideas for improving it...for free. SiteImprove will take that to the enterprise level, but it will charge you for the services that it provides.

Figure 17-5   How to set up, maintain, and improve a website

Perspective

If you understand the first three sections of this book, you can write and test the HTML and CSS code for a website on a local computer or server. Then, you can deploy your web pages by implementing the ideas in this chapter.

But once you deploy your website and get it into the search engines, the job of maintenance and improvement begins. That's when you need to take the ideas in this chapter and figure out how best to implement them for your website. That in turn will probably mean that you'll have to do some research on your own, and that's when you'll discover how complicated this can be.

Terms

deploy	web hosting service
publish	Internet Service Provide (ISP)
FTP (File Transfer Protocol)	domain name
FTP client	domain name registry
upload a file	robot
download a file	spider
web host	site map

Summary

- To *deploy* (or *publish*) a website, you transfer its files from your computer or local network to an Internet web server.
- To transfer files to and from an Internet web server, you can use *File Transfer Protocol* (*FTP*) with an *FTP client*.
- To deploy web pages, you *upload* files from your computer or local server to your Internet web server. If necessary, you can also *download* files from your Internet server to your computer or local server.
- To test a web page that's on an Internet server, you navigate to the URL for the page and make sure that everything looks right and works right. That in turn will prove that all the files for the page have been uploaded correctly.
- A *web host* (or *web hosting service*) provides a server that you can use to deploy your website.
- To find a *domain name* for your website, you can go to a website that will search for the name that you want in the *domain name registry*, which is a database of all registered domain names.
- To get your website into a search engine, you can go to the search engine's website and submit the URL for your website. Then, the search engine's *robot* (or *spider*) will crawl through your pages and score them for later searches.
- To *exclude* pages from being indexed by a search engine, you can use a robots meta tag or a robots.txt file. To include web pages, you can use a *site map*.

Chapter 18

How to use JavaScript to enhance your web pages

In this chapter, you will learn how you can use JavaScript and jQuery to enhance your web pages. To start, you'll learn the concepts and terms that you need for understanding JavaScript. Then, you'll learn how to do some simple JavaScript coding.

Next, you'll learn how jQuery makes it easier to get the results that you want. Then, you'll learn how to use prewritten scripts that get the results that you want, even if you don't understand the JavaScript and jQuery code that the scripts contain.

Introduction to JavaScript

In this introduction, you'll learn how JavaScript and DOM scripting work. This will be an early demonstration of why JavaScript is used on most websites.

How JavaScript works

Figure 18-1 presents a diagram that shows how JavaScript fits into the client/server architecture. Here, you can see that the *JavaScript* code is executed in the web browser by the browser's *JavaScript engine*.

This is referred to as *client-side processing,* in contrast to the *server-side processing* that's done on the web server. This takes some of the processing burden off the server and makes the application run faster. Today, almost all web browsers have JavaScript enabled so JavaScript applications will run on them.

To illustrate the use of JavaScript code, the example in this figure gets the current date and the current year and inserts both into an HTML document. To do that, the JavaScript code is embedded within script elements in the body of the document. This code is executed when the page is loaded.

You can see the results in the web browser in this figure. In this case, the JavaScript code in the first script element writes the first line into the web page, which includes the current date. And the JavaScript code in the second script element writes the copyright line into the web page, which includes the current year.

How JavaScript fits into the client/server architecture

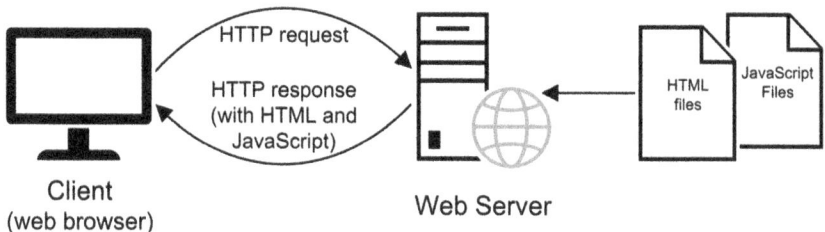

JavaScript in an HTML document that gets the current date and year

```
<p>
    <script>
        var today = new Date();
        document.write("Current date: ");
        document.write(today.toDateString());
    </script>
</p>
<p>
    <script>
        var today = new Date();
        document.write("&copy; ");
        document.write(today.getFullYear());
        document.write(", San Joaquin Valley Town Hall")
    </script>
</p>
```

The HTML in a web browser after the page is loaded

Current date: Wed Sep 08 2021

© 2021, San Joaquin Valley Town Hall

Description

- *JavaScript* is a scripting language that is run by the *JavaScript engine* of a browser. As a result, the work is done on the client, not the server.
- JavaScript can modify the contents of a web page when the page is loaded or in response to a user action.
- In this example, JavaScript inserts the text shown above into the two <p> elements on the page.

Figure 18-1   How JavaScript works

Three ways to include JavaScript in a web page

Figure 18-2 shows how to include JavaScript in an HTML document, or web page. To start, this figure describes two attributes that can be used with the script element. The src attribute specifies the location of the external JavaScript file that should be included in the document. The type attribute specifies that JavaScript is the client-side scripting language, but this attribute is no longer required. That's why the type attribute is omitted in the examples that follow.

These examples illustrate the three ways that you can include JavaScript in an HTML document. In the first example, the script element is coded in the head section of an HTML document, and the src attribute identifies an external JavaScript file named set_date.js. This assumes that the external file is in the same folder as the HTML page. If it isn't, you can code the path to the file along with the filename.

In the second example, the script element is again coded in the head section of an HTML document. In this case, though, the JavaScript is embedded in the script element.

In the third example, a script element that contains JavaScript is embedded in the body of an HTML document. As you saw in figure 18-1, a script element like this is replaced by the output of the JavaScript code when the page is loaded.

Two attributes of the script element

Attribute	Description
src	The location and name of an external JavaScript file.
type	No longer needed, but if coded it should be "text/javascript" for JavaScript code.

A script element in the head section that loads an external JavaScript file

```
<script src="set_date.js"></script>
```

A script element that embeds JavaScript in the head section

```
<head>
    ...
    <script>
        var $ = function (id) {
            return document.getElementById(id);
        }
        window.onload = function() {
            var today = new Date();
            $("date").firstChild.nodeValue =
                "Current date: " + today.toDateString();
        }
    </script>
</head>
```

A script element that embeds JavaScript in the body

```
<p>
    <script>
        var today = new Date();
        document.write("Current date: ");
        document.write(today.toDateString());
    </script>
</p>
```

Description

- If you have more than one script element in a web page, these elements are executed in the order that they appear in the document.
- If a script element in the head section includes an external JavaScript file, the JavaScript in the file runs as if it were coded in the script element.
- If a script element is coded in the body of a document, it is replaced by the output of the JavaScript code.
- The HTML document must be valid before and after all scripts have been executed.

Figure 18-2   Three ways to include JavaScript in a web page

How DOM scripting works

As an HTML page is loaded by the web browser, the *DOM (Document Object Model)* for that page is created in the browser's memory. This DOM is an internal representation of the HTML elements on a web page. In figure 18-3, you can see a simple HTML document and the structure of the DOM for that document.

Here, each element of the page is represented by a *node* in the DOM. The nodes in the DOM have a hierarchical structure based on how the HTML elements are nested inside each other. The DOM starts with the html element and follows the nesting of the elements down to the text that is in each element.

Within the DOM, several types of nodes are used to represent the contents of the web page. HTML elements are stored in *element nodes*, and text is stored in *text nodes*. In this figure, element nodes are shown as ovals, and text nodes are shown as rectangles. Other common node types are *attribute nodes* and *comment nodes*.

What's interesting about this is that JavaScript can be used to modify the nodes in the DOM. Furthermore, whenever a change is made to the DOM, the web browser updates the page in the browser window to reflect that change. This means that you can use JavaScript to modify the contents and appearance of a web page after it has been loaded. This is called *DOM scripting*, and this is what makes JavaScript so powerful.

In the HTML code in this figure, please note that a *span element* is used to display an asterisk (*) when the page is loaded. This is an inline element that has no special meaning. It just provides a way to identify a portion of text within a block element. Then, JavaScript can be used to modify the text in that element.

The code for a web page

```
<!DOCTYPE html>
<html>
<head>
    <title>Join Email List</title>
</head>
<body>
    <h1>Please join our email list</h1>
    <form id="email_form" name="email_form" action="join.html" method="get">
        <label for="email_address">Email Address:</label>
        <input type="text" id="email_address">
        <span id="email_error">*</span>
    </form>
</body>
</html>
```

The DOM for the web page

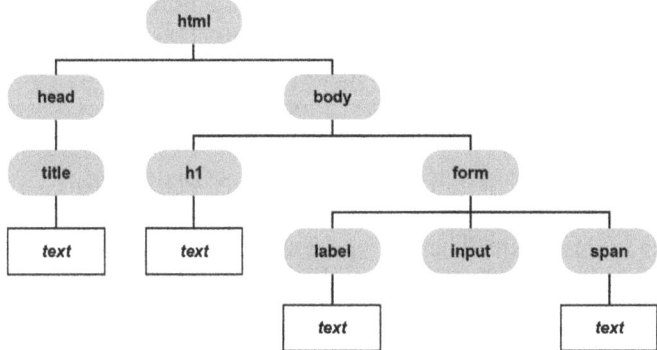

The DOM nodes that you commonly use in DOM scripting

Type	Description
Element	An element in the web page. It can have Element, Text, and Comment nodes as child nodes.
Attr	An attribute of an element. Although it is attached to an Element node, it isn't considered a child node. It can have a Text node as a child node.
Text	The text for an element or attribute. It can't have a child node.

About the span element

• The *span element* is an inline element with no specific meaning. It can be used within a block element to identify text that can be manipulated by JavaScript.

Description

• The *DOM* (*Document Object Model*) is a hierarchical collection of *nodes* in the web browser's memory that represents the current web page. The DOM is built as the page is loaded by the web browser.

• When you use JavaScript to modify the DOM, the web browser changes the web page to reflect the changes to the DOM. This is called *DOM scripting* or *scripting the DOM*.

Figure 18-3   How DOM scripting works

Methods and properties for DOM scripting

To give you some idea of how DOM scripting works, figure 18-4 presents a few of the methods and properties that you can use for DOM scripting. Here, the first table presents two *methods* of the *document object*, which is the object that lets you work with the DOM.

The first method is the getElementById() method. It gets the HTML element that's represented by the id attribute that's passed to it within the parentheses. In the first example after the table, you can see how this method is used to get the HTML element (or *object*) that has "rate" as its id attribute. In this case, that element (or the object that represents that element) is stored in a variable (var) named rateBox.

The second method in the first table is the write() method, which you've already seen in figures 18-1 and 18-2. It writes whatever is in the parentheses into the body of the document.

The third example after this table is the code for a standard function named $ that uses the getElementById() method to get an HTML element. This function can be called by coding just the $ sign followed by a set of parentheses that contains the id attribute of the element that the function should get. You'll see this used in just a moment.

To modify the DOM, though, you need to work with its nodes. To do that, you use the *properties* that are provided by the DOM. Three of these properties are shown in the second table in this figure. The first one gets or sets the value that's in an input element like a text box. The second one gets the Node object for the first child of an element. The third one gets or sets the text for a Text, Comment, or Attribute node.

The first example after this table shows how the value property can be used to get the value that has been entered into a text box. It uses the $ function to get the object for the text box with "email_address" as its id attribute, and it uses the value property to get the value that's in the text box. Then, this value is stored in a variable named emailAddress.

The second example shows how the firstChild and nodeValue properties can be used to set the value for an HTML span element with "email_error" as its id attribute. This example uses the $ function to get the HTML element, the firstChild property to get the text node for the element, and the nodeValue property to set the text in that node to "Entry is invalid."

If you're new to programming, this may seem complicated, and it is. But you don't need to worry about that right now. Just take away the concept that JavaScript can script the DOM by using its many methods and properties.

The code for a web page

```
<h1>Please join our email list</h1>
<form id="email_form" name="email_form" action="join.html" method="get">
    <label for="email_address">Email Address:</label>
    <input type="text" id="email_address">
    <span id="email_error">*</span>
</form>
```

Two methods of the document object

Method	Description
getElementById(id)	Returns the HTML element that has the id that's passed to it.
write(string)	Writes the string.

Examples of document methods

```
// returns the object for the HTML element
var rateBox = document.getElementById("rate");

// writes a string into the document
document.write("Today is " + today.toDateString());
```

A standard $ function that gets the object for an element by using its id

```
var $ = function (id) {
    return document.getElementById(id);
}
```

Three properties that can be used for scripting the DOM

Property	Description
value	For an input element like a text box, gets or sets the value in the element.
firstChild	Returns a Node object for the first child node of an element.
nodeValue	For a Text, Comment, or Attribute node, gets or sets the text that's stored in the node.

How to get the text of an HTML element with "email_address" as its id

```
var emailAddress = $("email_address").value;
```

How to set the text of an HTML element with "email_error" as its id

```
$("email_error").firstChild.nodeValue = "Entry is invalid.";
```

Description

- The *document object* is the object that lets you work with the Document Object Model (DOM) that represents all of the HTML elements on a page.
- When scripting the DOM, the $ sign is commonly used for a function that uses the getElementById() method of the document object to get the element that has the id that's coded in the parentheses.
- The second table above presents just three of the many properties that can be used for scripting the DOM.

Figure 18-4   Methods and properties for DOM scripting

How JavaScript handles events

One other concept that you should be aware of is the way JavaScript handles events. An *event* occurs when an action like loading a web page or clicking on a button occurs. Then, the JavaScript code can respond to the event with code that is called an *event handler*.

The diagram in figure 18-5 describes the event cycle that drives DOM scripting. First, the page is loaded and the event handlers are attached to the events that will be processed. Next, when an event occurs, the appropriate event handler is executed. Then, if the event handler modifies the DOM, the page is immediately updated.

The example in this figure illustrates the use of event handlers. In this case, JavaScript is used to print the page when a Print button is clicked. The JavaScript code in this example consists of the standard $ function, an event handler named printPage that is executed when the user clicks on the button, and an event handler for the onload event of the page.

When the page is loaded, the onload event handler for the onload event sets the onclick event of the button with "printButton" as its id so the printPage function will be called when the button is clicked. Then, when the button is clicked by the user, the printPage event handler is executed. Within that handler, the print() method of the window object is used to print the page.

It's worth noting that you don't have to understand this JavaScript code in order to use it. Since the JavaScript is stored in an external file named printPage.js, you start by coding a script element in the head section that includes the file. Then, you set the id attribute of the button that you want to use for printing to "printButton".

If you aren't a programmer, that's the approach you can take for adding other JavaScript features to your web pages. And that's the approach that's emphasized in the rest of this chapter.

A web page that prints the current page when the button is clicked

> Print the Page
>
> ### *Murach's JavaScript and jQuery*
>
> | Section 1 | **JavaScript essentials** | |
> |---|---|---|
> | Chapter 1 | Introduction to web development | 3 |
> | Chapter 2 | Getting started with JavaScript | 51 |
> | Chapter 3 | The essential JavaScript statements | 85 |
> | Chapter 4 | How to work with JavaScript objects, functions, and events | 111 |

The JavaScript in an external file named printPage.js

```javascript
var $ = function (id) {
    // this function returns the object for the HTML element
    return document.getElementById(id);
}
var printPage = function() {
    // this is the event handler for the click event of the button
    window.print();
}
window.onload = function() {
    // this is the event handler for the onload event
    $("printButton").onclick = printPage;
}
```

The HTML code for the external JavaScript file in the head section

```html
<script src="printPage.js"></script>
```

The HTML code for the button in the body section

```html
<input type="button" id="printButton" value="Print the Page">
```

The DOM event cycle

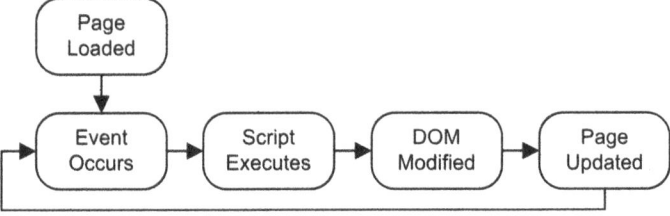

Description

- An *event* occurs when the page is loaded or the user performs an action like clicking on an HTML element.
- The JavaScript code that handles an event is called an *event handler*, and the event handler can script the DOM or use any of the methods of the objects in the DOM.
- In this example, the event handler for the onload event runs when the page is loaded. It sets up the button with "printButton" as its id so the printPage event handler is called when the button is clicked. Then, the printPage handler executes the print() method of the window object, which causes the page to print.

Figure 18-5   How JavaScript handles events

The Email List application in JavaScript

If you are interested in the programming side of JavaScript, the next two figures present a simple Email List application. It asks the user to make three entries and then click on the Join our List button. The asterisks to the right of the text boxes for the entries indicate that these entries are required.

When the user clicks on the button, JavaScript checks the entries to make sure they're valid. If they are, the entries are sent to the web server for server-side processing. If they aren't, messages are displayed so the user can correct the entries. This is a common use for JavaScript called *data validation* that saves a trip to the server when the entries are invalid.

The HTML

If you've read chapter 13, you should be familiar with the HTML in figure 18-6. Just note that each entry line on the form consists of a label, input, and span element. Also, each span element starts with an asterisk (*) in it, but DOM scripting will be used to replace that asterisk with an error message if the user makes an invalid entry or with nothing ("") if the entry is valid.

The HTML file in a browser after CSS has been applied to it

The code for the HTML file named index.html

```
<!DOCTYPE html>
<html>
<head>
    <meta charset="UTF-8">
    <title>Join Email List</title>
    <link rel="stylesheet" href="email_list.css">
    <script src="email_list.js"></script>
</head>
<body>
    <main>
        <h1>Please join our email list</h1>
        <form id="email_form" name="email_form"
                action="join.html" method="get">
            <label for="email_address1">Email Address:</label>
            <input type="text" id="email_address1" name="email_address1">
            <span id="email_address1_error">*</span><br>

            <label for="email_address2">Re-enter Email Address:</label>
            <input type="text" id="email_address2" name="email_address2">
            <span id="email_address2_error">*</span><br>

            <label for="first_name">First Name</label>
            <input type="text" id="first_name" name="first_name">
            <span id="first_name_error">*</span><br>

            <label> </label>
            <input type="button" id="join_list" value="Join our List">
        </form>
    </main>
</body>
</html>
```

Figure 18-6   The HTML for the Email List application

The JavaScript

Figure 18-7 shows how this application looks in a browser if the JavaScript finds any invalid data after the user clicks the Join our List button. Here, you can see that the asterisk after the first text box has been removed because the entry is valid, and error messages are displayed to the right of the entries for the second and third text boxes because the entries aren't valid. In other words, the JavaScript has actually changed the contents of the span elements.

After the browser display, this figure shows the JavaScript for this application. That should give you a better idea of how JavaScript is used. For this book, you don't have to understand this code. But if you're interested, here's a brief description of how it works.

To start, this code consists of three functions: a $ function, a joinList function that is executed when the user clicks on the button, and a function that is run when the page is loaded into the browser. Then, in the joinList function, you can see four if-else statements that provide most of the logic for this application.

Here, you can see that the if-else structures are similar to those in any modern programming language like Java, C#, or PHP. You can also see that declaring a variable (var) and assigning a variable is done in a way that's similar to the way that's done in other programming languages.

What's different about JavaScript are the methods and properties that let you modify the DOM. In this example, you can see how the value property is used to get the values from the text boxes and how the firstChild and nodeValue properties are used to set error messages in the span elements for invalid entries.

The web page in a browser with JavaScript used for data validation

```
🌐 Join Email List          ×    +                          ○   —   □   ×

←  →  C    ⓘ 127.0.0.1:5500/book_apps/ch18/email_list_javascript/index.html   ☆  📌  ▲  ⋮

┌──────────────────────────────────────────────────────────────────────┐
│                                                                        │
│  Please join our email list                                            │
│                                                                        │
│          Email Address:  ┌──────────────────┐                          │
│                          │ zak@yahoo.com     │                         │
│                          └──────────────────┘                          │
│   Re-enter Email Address: ┌──────────────────┐ This entry must equal first entry. │
│                           └──────────────────┘                         │
│             First Name  ┌──────────────────┐ This field is required.   │
│                         └──────────────────┘                           │
│                          ┌──────────────┐                              │
│                          │ Join our List│                              │
│                          └──────────────┘                              │
│                                                                        │
└──────────────────────────────────────────────────────────────────────┘
```

The script element in the HTML file that includes the JavaScript file

```html
<script src="email_list.js"></script>
```

The code for the JavaScript file named email_list.js

```javascript
var $ = function (id) {
    return document.getElementById(id);
}
var joinList = function () {
    var emailAddress1 = $("email_address1").value;
    var emailAddress2 = $("email_address2").value;
    var isValid = true;

    if (emailAddress1 == "") {
        $("email_address1_error").firstChild.nodeValue =
            "This field is required.";
        isValid = false;
    } else { $("email_address1_error").firstChild.nodeValue = ""; }

    if (emailAddress1 !== emailAddress2) {
        $("email_address2_error").firstChild.nodeValue =
            "This entry must equal first entry.";
        isValid = false;
    } else { $("email_address2_error").firstChild.nodeValue = ""; }

    if ($("first_name").value == "") {
        $("first_name_error").firstChild.nodeValue =
            "This field is required.";
        isValid = false;
    } else { $("first_name_error").firstChild.nodeValue = ""; }

    if (isValid) {
        // submit the form if all entries are valid
        $("email_form").submit(); }
}
window.onload = function () {
    $("join_list").onclick = joinList;
}
```

Figure 18-7   The JavaScript for the Email List application

Introduction to jQuery

jQuery is a free, open-source, JavaScript library that provides dozens of methods for common web features that make JavaScript programming easier. Beyond that, the jQuery functions are coded and tested for cross-browser compatibility, so they will work in all browsers.

Those are two of the reasons why jQuery is used by close to 80% of the top 100,000 websites today. And that's why jQuery is commonly used by professional web developers. In fact, you can think of jQuery as one of the four technologies that every web developer should know how to use: HTML, CSS, JavaScript, and jQuery. But don't forget that jQuery is actually JavaScript.

In this introduction, you'll learn how to include jQuery in your applications and how to use its selectors, methods, and event methods. Here again, the goal isn't to teach you how to program with jQuery. It's to give you a better idea of what you can do with jQuery and why you may want to master it.

How to include jQuery in your web pages

If you go to the website that's shown in figure 18-8 and go to the download page, you'll find links that let you download the file for the jQuery library in either of two forms: compressed or uncompressed. The compressed version loads quickly into browsers, which is another reason why developers like jQuery. The uncompressed version is for developers who want to study the JavaScript code in the download.

Once you've downloaded the compressed version of jQuery, you can include it in a web page by coding a script element like the first one in this figure. Then, if you store the file on your own computer or a local web server, you'll be able to develop jQuery applications without being connected to the Internet. For production applications, though, you'll need to deploy the file to your Internet web server.

In this script element, the filename includes the version number, but you can use whatever filename you want. However, if the filename doesn't include the version number, it's easy to lose track of which version you're using.

The other way to include the jQuery library in your web applications and the one we recommend is to get the file from a *Content Delivery Network* (*CDN*). A CDN is a web server that hosts open-source software, and the Google, Microsoft, and jQuery websites are CDNs for getting the jQuery libraries. In the second example in this figure, the script element uses the jQuery CDN with a URL that gets version 3.6.0 of jQuery. The benefit to using a CDN is that you don't have to download the jQuery file and you don't have to provide it from your own server.

The jQuery website at jQuery.com

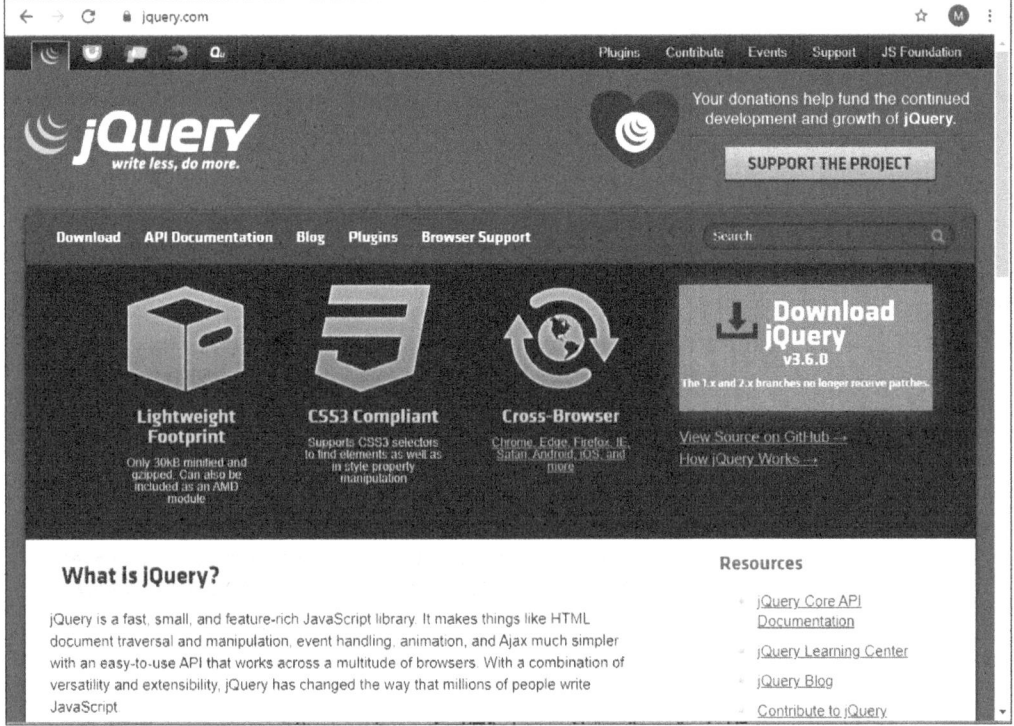

What jQuery offers

- Dozens of methods that make it easier to add JavaScript features to your web pages
- Methods that are tested for cross-browser compatibility

How to include the jQuery file after you've downloaded it to your computer

```
<script src="jquery-3.6.0.js"></script>
```

How to include the jQuery file from a Content Delivery Network (CDN)

```
<script src="http://code.jquery.com/jquery-3.6.0.min.js"></script>
```

Description

- *jQuery* is a free, open-source, JavaScript library that provides methods that make JavaScript programming easier. Today, jQuery is used by close to 80% of the top 100,000 websites.
- The jQuery download comes in two versions. One version (min) is a compressed version that is relatively small and loads fast. The other version is uncompressed so you can use it to study the JavaScript code in the library.
- If you include the jQuery file from a *Content Delivery Network* (*CDN*), you don't have to provide it from your own server.
- If you download the jQuery file to your system, you can change the filename so it's simpler, but then you may lose track of what version you're using.

Figure 18-8   What jQuery is and how to include it in a web page

How to code jQuery selectors, methods, and event methods

To give you some idea of how jQuery works, figure 18-9 introduces the selectors, methods, and event methods that you can use in your jQuery code. To start, you should know that the $ sign always refers to the jQuery library. Then, in the parentheses after the dollar sign, you code a selector that identifies the HTML element or elements that the jQuery will be applied to.

This is illustrated by the first set of examples in this figure. Here, the first *selector* is a type selector that applies to all h2 elements. The second selector is an id selector that applies to the HTML element with "email_address" as its id. And the third selector is a class selector that applies to all of the elements with "warning" as their class name. This shows how closely the jQuery selectors relate to the CSS selectors, which is another reason why developers like jQuery.

After the selector, you can use the dot syntax to run a jQuery *method* on the HTML element that's referred to by the selector. This is illustrated by the second set of examples in this figure. Here, the first statement uses the val() method to get the value in the text box with "email_address" as its id attribute. The second statement uses the text() method to set the text that's in an HTML element with "email_address_error" as its id. And the third statement uses the next() and text() methods to set the text for the sibling element that follows the element with "email_address" as its id. This is a nice simplification over comparable JavaScript code.

The third group of examples shows how to use *event methods*. The first example in this group uses the ready() event method. It is executed when the DOM for the entire page has been built. In this example, the alert() method of the window object is executed when the ready event occurs.

The ready() method is important because some applications that use the DOM can't be run until the entire DOM has been built. As a result, this event method is a nice improvement over the JavaScript onload event, which occurs while the page is being loaded and the DOM is being built.

The second example in this group shows how the click() method can be used to provide an event handler for the click event of all h2 elements. Here again, an alert() method is executed when an h2 element is clicked.

The third example combines the ready() and click() methods. In this case, the click() method isn't prepared until the ready event has occurred. As a result, the click() method will apply to all of the h2 elements in the DOM.

How to code jQuery selectors

By element type
```
$("h2")
```

By id
```
$("#email_address")
```

By class attribute
```
$(".warning")
```

How to call jQuery methods

How to get the value from a text box
```
var emailAddress = $("#email_address").val();
```

How to set the text in an element
```
$("#email_address_error").text("Email address is required");
```

How to set the text for the next sibling
```
$("#email_address").next().text("Email address is required");
```

How to code jQuery event methods

How to code the ready() event method
```
$(document).ready(function() {
    alert("The DOM is ready");
});
```

How to code the click() event method for all h2 elements
```
$("h2").click(function() {
    alert("This heading has been clicked");
});
```

How to use the click() event method within the ready() event method
```
$(document).ready(function() {
    $("h2").click(function() {
        alert("This heading has been clicked");
    }); // end of click event handler
}); // end of ready event handler
```

Description

- When you use jQuery, the dollar sign ($) is used to refer to the jQuery library. Then, you can code jQuery *selectors* by using the CSS syntax within quotation marks within parentheses.

- To call a jQuery *method*, you code a selector, the dot operator, the method name, and any parameters within parentheses. Then, that method is applied to the element or elements that are selected by the selector.

- To code a jQuery event handler, you code a selector, the dot operator, the name of the jQuery *event method*, and a function that handles the event within parentheses.

- The event handler for the ready() event method will run any methods that it contains as soon as the DOM is ready, even if the browser is loading images and other content for the page.

Figure 18-9   How to use jQuery selectors, methods, and event methods

The Email List application in jQuery

If you are interested in the programming side of jQuery, you're ready to see how jQuery can be used in the Email List application that you studied in figures 18-6 and 18-7. That will show you how jQuery can simplify coding.

To refresh your memory, figure 18-10 presents the user interface and HTML for the Email List application. To use the application, the user enters text into the first three text boxes and clicks on the Join our List button. Then, the JavaScript validates the entries and displays appropriate error messages if errors are found. If no errors are found, the data in the form is submitted to the web server for processing.

The HTML

In the HTML in this figure, note first the script element that loads jQuery. It is followed by the script element that identifies the file that holds the JavaScript for this application. That sequence is essential because the JavaScript file is going to use the jQuery file.

In the HTML for the form, note that the span elements are adjacent siblings to the input elements for the text boxes. The starting text for each of these span elements is an asterisk that indicates that the text box entry is required. Later, if the JavaScript finds errors in the entries, it displays error messages in these span elements.

Note also that the span elements don't require id attributes as they did for the JavaScript version of this application in figure 18-6. That's because jQuery can change the text in those elements without referring to them by id. In other words, the use of jQuery has simplified the HTML requirements for this application.

The user interface for the Email List application

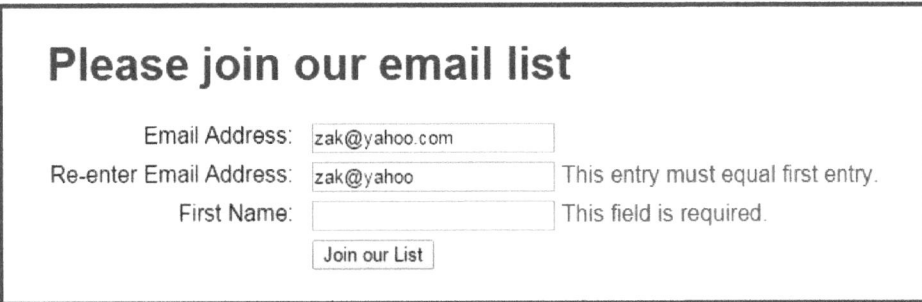

The HTML

```
<!DOCTYPE html>
<html>
<head>
    <meta charset="UTF-8">
    <title>Join Email List</title>
    <link rel="stylesheet" href="email_list.css">
    <script src="http://code.jquery.com/jquery-3.6.0.min.js"></script>
    <script src="email_list.js"></script>
</head>
<body>
    <main>
        <h1>Please join our email list</h1>
        <form id="email_form" name="email_form"
              action="join.html" method="get">
            <label for="email_address1">Email Address:</label>
            <input type="text" id="email_address1" name="email_address1">
            <span>*</span><br>

            <label for="email_address2">Re-enter Email Address:</label>
            <input type="text" id="email_address2" name="email_address2">
            <span>*</span><br>

            <label for="first_name">First Name:</label>
            <input type="text" id="first_name" name="first_name">
            <span>*</span><br>

            <label> </label>
            <input type="button" id="join_list" value="Join our List">
        </form>
    </main>
</body>
</html>
```

Figure 18-10 The HTML for the Email List application

The jQuery

Figure 18-11 presents the jQuery for this application. This is the code in the email_list.js file that's included by the HTML. Here, all of the jQuery is highlighted. The rest of the code is JavaScript code.

To start, you can see that an event handler for the click event of the Join our List button is coded within the event handler for the ready event. Within the click event handler, the first two statements show how jQuery selectors and the val() method can be used to get the values from text boxes.

In the first if statement, you can see how an error message is displayed if the user doesn't enter an email address in the first text box. Here, the next() method gets the adjacent sibling for the text box, which is a span element, and then the text() method puts an error message in that span element. This changes the DOM, and as soon as it is changed, the error message is displayed in the browser.

The next() and text() methods are used in similar ways in the next two if statements. Note here that the first if statement starts by checking if no entry was made for the second email address. This is different from the JavaScript code shown in figure 18-7, which just checked if the entry was the same as the first entry. This provides more complete data validation.

Finally, the fourth if statement tests to see whether the isValid variable is still true. If it is, the submit() method of the form is issued, which sends the data to the web server.

If you compare this jQuery code to the JavaScript code in figure 18-7, you can see that the jQuery provides some nice simplifications. That's another reason why programmers like jQuery, but this example doesn't begin to illustrate the power of jQuery.

The jQuery for the Email List application (email_list.js)

```javascript
$(document).ready(function() {
    $("#join_list").click(function() {
        var emailAddress1 = $("#email_address1").val();
        var emailAddress2 = $("#email_address2").val();
        var isValid = true;

        // validate the first email address
        if (emailAddress1 == "") {
            $("#email_address1").next().text("This field is required.");
            isValid = false;
        } else {
            $("#email_address1").next().text("");
        }

        // validate the second email address
        if (emailAddress2 == "") {
            $("#email_address2").next().text("This field is required.");
            isValid = false;
        } else if (emailAddress1 != emailAddress2) {
            $("#email_address2").next().text(
                "This entry must equal first entry.");
            isValid = false;
        } else {
            $("#email_address2").next().text("");
        }

        // validate the first name entry
        if ($("#first_name").val() == "") {
            $("#first_name").next().text("This field is required.");
            isValid = false;
        }
        else {
            $("#first_name").next().text("");
        }

        // submit the form if all entries are valid
        if (isValid) {
            $("#email_form").submit();
        }
    }); // end click
}); // end ready
```

Figure 18-11   The jQuery for the Email List application

How to use JavaScript as a non-programmer

Now that you have a general idea of how JavaScript and jQuery work, you'll learn how you can use jQuery as a non-programmer. To that end, you'll review two applications that are typically developed with jQuery. However, the jQuery for these applications isn't even shown. Instead, the focus is on how you can use jQuery code without knowing how it works.

The Image Swap application

Figure 18-12 presents a typical jQuery application that works like this: When the user clicks on one of the thumbnail images at the top of the browser window, the caption and image below the thumbnails are changed. This is called an *image swap*.

To use this application without knowing how the code works, you need to code the two script elements that are shown in this figure in the head section of your document. The first one is for the jQuery library. The second one is for a JavaScript file that uses jQuery to get the intended results. Then, in the body of the HTML, you need to code the HTML for the elements that are involved in the image swaps.

Here, img elements are used to display the six thumbnail images. However, these elements are coded within <a> elements so the images are clickable and they can receive the focus. In the <a> elements, the href attributes identify the images to be swapped when the links are clicked, and the title attributes provide the text for the related captions. In this case, both the <a> elements and the img elements are coded within a ul element.

After the ul element, you can see the h2 element for the caption and the img element for the main image on the page. The ids of these elements are highlighted because the jQuery will use those ids as it swaps captions and images into them.

For the motor-impaired, this HTML provides accessibility by coding the img elements for the thumbnails within <a> elements. That way, the user can access the thumbnail links by clicking on the Tab key, and the user can swap the image by pressing the Enter key when a thumbnail has the focus, which starts the click event.

Of note in the CSS for this page is the style rule for the li elements. Their display properties are set to inline so the images go from left to right instead of from top to bottom. Also, the padding on the right of each item is set to 10 pixels to provide space between the images.

The user interface for the Image Swap application

The script elements for the external files in the head section of the HTML

```
<script src="http://code.jquery.com/jquery-3.6.0.min.js"></script>
<script src="image_swaps.js"></script>
```

The HTML for the images

```
<main>
    <h1>Ram Tap Combined Test</h1>
    <ul id="image_list">
        <li><a href="images/h1.jpg" title="James Allison: 1-1">
            <img src="thumbnails/t1.jpg" alt=""></a></li>
        <li><a href="images/h2.jpg" title="James Allison: 1-2">
            <img src="thumbnails/t2.jpg" alt=""></a></li>
        ...
        ...
        <li><a href="images/h6.jpg" title="James Allison: 1-6">
            <img src="thumbnails/t6.jpg" alt=""></a></li>
    </ul>
    <h2 id="caption">James Allison 1-1</h2>
    <p><img src="images/h1.jpg" alt="" id="image"></p>
</main>
```

The CSS for the li elements

```
li {padding-right: 10px; display: inline; }
```

How to use the JavaScript for an image swap

1. Code the script elements as shown above.
2. Set up the HTML as shown above, with the id of the ul element set to "image_list", the id of the h2 element set to "caption", and the id of the main img element set to "image".
3. Set the href attribute for each <a> element in the unordered list to the large image, and the title attribute to its caption. Then, set the src attribute of each img element in the unordered list to the thumbnail image.

Figure 18-12   The Image Swap application in jQuery

The Slide Show application

Figure 18-13 presents another example of a jQuery application that you can use without understanding the code. This is a Slide Show application that fades the old slide out and the new one in. Also, the slide show stops when the user clicks on the current image and restarts when the user clicks on it again.

To use this application, you again code the script elements in the head section and then set up the HTML in the body as shown. In the div element in the HTML, you can see that five img elements provide the slides for the show, and each of these has an alt attribute that provides the caption that is shown above the slide. Note, however, that the slide show will work for as many images as you code in the div element.

Before the div element for the slides, an h2 element is used for the caption of each slide and an img element is used for the slide show. The id attributes for these elements should be "caption" and "slide", and these elements should contain the caption and slide for the first slide in the series. The id for the div element that follows should be "slides".

In the CSS that's shown for this application, the display property of all of the img elements in the div element named "slides" is set to "none". This means that those img elements will be loaded into the browser when the page is loaded, but they won't be displayed.

A Slide Show application with fading out and fading in

The script elements for the external files in the head section of the HTML

```
<script src="http://code.jquery.com/jquery-3.6.0.min.js"></script>
<script src="slide_show.js"></script>
```

The HTML for the slide show

```
<section>
    <h1>Fishing Slide Show</h1>
    <h2 id="caption">Casting on the Upper Kings</h2>
    <img id="slide" src="images/casting1.jpg" alt="">
    <div id="slides">
        <img src="images/casting1.jpg" alt="Casting on the Upper Kings">
        <img src="images/casting2.jpg" alt="Casting on the Lower Kings">
        <img src="images/catchrelease.jpg"
            alt="Catch and Release on the Big Horn">
        <img src="images/fish.jpg" alt="Catching on the South Fork">
        <img src="images/lures.jpg" alt="The Lures for Catching">
    </div>
</section>
```

The critical CSS for the slide show

```
#slides img {
    display: none;
}
```

How to use the JavaScript for a slide show

1. Code the script elements as shown above.

2. Set up the HTML as shown above, with the ids for the h2 element, the first img element, and the div element set to "caption", "slide", and "slides".

3. Put the images for the slide show in the "slides" div element, and set the alt attribute for each image to the caption that will be displayed in the slide show.

Figure 18-13   The Slide Show application in jQuery

Three sources for tested JavaScript and jQuery

Now that you have seen how easy it can be to use tested JavaScript and jQuery code, you should know about the three ways that you can get code for dozens of JavaScript applications. They are summarized in figure 18-14.

First, many websites provide JavaScript and jQuery code that you can use in your programs, and much of it is free. To find sites like this, you can search for "free javascript code" or "jquery code examples", and two of our favorite sites are listed at the top of this figure. Often, these sites provide JavaScript and jQuery for games and special effects that you can easily add to your site.

Another way that a non-programmer can add jQuery features to a website is to use jQuery plugins. A *jQuery plugin* is just a jQuery application that does one web task or set of related web tasks. A plugin makes use of the jQuery library, and most plugins can be used with limited knowledge of JavaScript and jQuery. Even better, most plugins are either free or available for a small price or donation.

To find jQuery plugins, you can search the web for "jQuery plugins". But be sure to include the word *jQuery* because there are other kinds of plugins. Some of the most popular plugins provide for slideshows, carousels, and galleries. In this figure, you can see the bxSlider plugin, which is a popular plugin for a carousel.

The third way that a non-programmer can add jQuery features to a website is to use jQuery UI. *jQuery UI (User Interface)* is a free, open-source, JavaScript library that extends the use of the jQuery library by providing higher-level features that you can use with a minimum of code. To provide those features, the jQuery UI library uses the jQuery library. In fact, you can think of jQuery UI as the official plugin library for jQuery.

Although jQuery UI provides features like themes, interactions, and effects, *widgets* are the feature that web designers use the most. Widgets provide common functions like tabs, accordions, and date pickers. In this figure, for example, you can see both tabs and accordion widgets.

This summary shows that you can add many JavaScript and jQuery features to a website without knowing much about JavaScript programming. But the problem is that you often need to do some coding to make the best use of these applications, plugins, and widgets. That's why it pays to learn how to program with JavaScript and jQuery. That will not only make it easier for you to use the applications that you get from these sources, but it will also let you write your own code if you can't find what you want.

Two of the many websites that provide JavaScript and jQuery code

- Dynamic Drive (<u>dynamicdrive.com</u>)
- The JavaScript Source (<u>javascriptsource.com</u>)

A jQuery plugin for a carousel called bxSlider

jQuery UI widgets for tabs and accordions

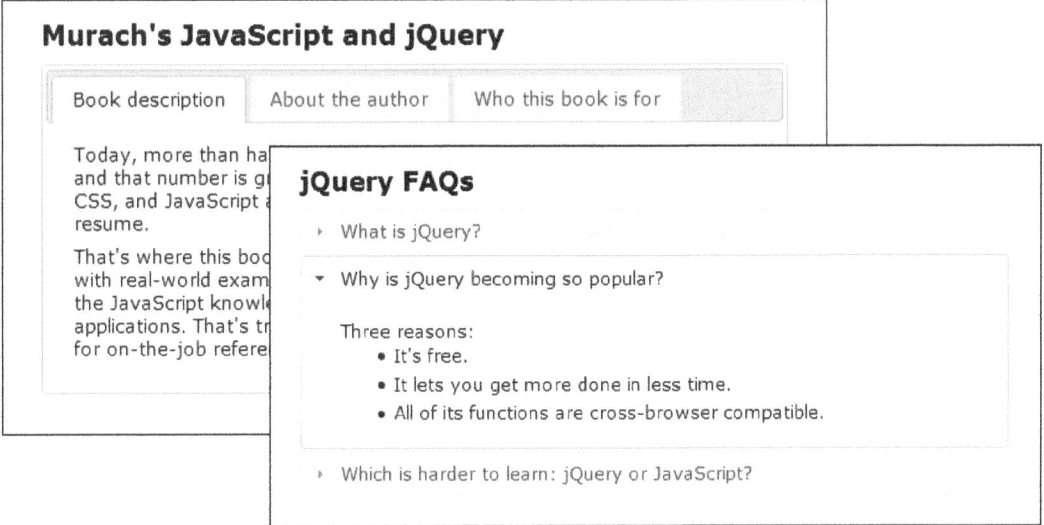

Three sources for tested JavaScript and jQuery

- Many websites provide JavaScript and jQuery code that you can download or cut-and-paste into your web pages.
- *jQuery plugins* are JavaScript applications that extend the functionality of jQuery by providing functions like carousels and slide shows.
- *jQuery UI* is a free, open-source, JavaScript library that extends the jQuery library by providing *widgets* for common features like tabs and accordions.

Figure 18-14   Three sources for tested JavaScript and jQuery

Perspective

At this point, you should understand how JavaScript and jQuery can be used to enhance web pages and how important these skills can be for web developers. Now, if you want to master these skills, including the use of jQuery and jQuery UI, please consider *Murach's JavaScript and jQuery*.

Terms

JavaScript	document object
JavaScript engine	event
client-side processing	event handler
server-side processing	jQuery
span element	CDN (Content Delivery Network)
DOM (Document Object Model)	jQuery selector
node	jQuery method
element node	jQuery event method
text node	image swap
attribute node	jQuery plugin
comment node	jQuery UI widget
DOM scripting	

Summary

- *JavaScript* is a scripting language that is run by the *JavaScript engine* of a browser. As a result, the work is done on the client, not the server.

- To embed JavaScript code or to include JavaScript files in an HTML document, you code a script element.

- The *DOM (Document Object Model)* is a hierarchical collection of *nodes* in the web browser's memory that represents the current web page. The DOM for each page is built as the page is loaded.

- *DOM scripting* is the process of changing the DOM by using JavaScript. When the DOM changes, the browser immediately displays the results of the change.

- An *event* is an action the user performs, like clicking on a button or image. When an event occurs, it can be handled by JavaScript code known as an *event handler*.

- *jQuery* is a JavaScript library that makes JavaScript programming easier. To use jQuery, you code a script element in the head section that either includes a downloaded jQuery file or accesses it through a *Content Delivery Network* (*CDN*).

- When you code statements that use jQuery, you use *selectors* that are like those for CSS. You also use jQuery *methods* and *event methods*.

- To add JavaScript and jQuery features to your website without writing the code yourself, you can search for tested JavaScript code as well as *jQuery plugins*. You can also install and use *jQuery UI widgets*.

Exercise 18-1   Use JavaScript to enhance a page

In this exercise, you'll enhance the page that follows. First, you'll use JavaScript to update the year in the footer. Then, you'll use jQuery to do image swaps.

Open the HTML file for this page
1. Use your text editor to open this HTML file:
   `\html_css_5\exercises\town_hall_4\image_swaps.html`
2. Look in the head section of the HTML file to see that it contains two script elements that load the jQuery library and the JavaScript file for this application. Then, test this page to see that it looks okay, but the image swaps don't work.

Automatically update the year in the footer
3. With figure 18-1 as a guide, use JavaScript to get the current year and put it into the copyright line in the footer. Then, test this change.

Modify the HTML so the image swaps work
4. Using figure 18-12 as a guide, modify the HTML so it should work. You can assume that the ul element is coded correctly, so the problem is elsewhere.
5. When the image swaps are working, try each one and note that the caption for Amy Chua is incorrect. That means that there's a problem somewhere within the ul element. Now, fix it.

Appendix A

How to set up your computer for this book

This appendix shows how to install the software that we recommend for editing and testing the web pages and applications for this book. That includes Visual Studio Code as the text editor and Chrome as the primary browser. To start, though, this appendix shows how to download and install the source code for this book.

How to install the source code for this book

Figure A-1 shows how to install the source code for this book. This includes the source code for the applications in this book, all of the significant examples, the starting files for the exercises, and the solutions for the exercises.

The Murach website

www.murach.com

The folder that contains the source code

\murach\html_css_5

The subfolders

Folder	Description
book_apps	The applications that are presented throughout this book.
book_examples	The examples that are presented throughout this book.
exercises	The starting points for the exercises at the end of each chapter.
solutions	The solutions to the exercises.

How to download and install the source code for this book

1. Go to www.murach.com.
2. Find the page for *Murach's HTML and CSS (5th Edition)*.
3. Scroll down to the "FREE Downloads" tab and click it.
4. Click on the DOWNLOAD NOW button for the the zip file. This should download a file named htm5_allfiles.zip.
5. Double-click on the zip file to extract the files for this book into a folder named html_css_5.
6. If necessary, use Explorer (Windows) or Finder (macOS) to create the murach folder directly on your hard disk. On macOS, you can do that by modifying the preferences for Finder so it includes your hard disk in its sidebar.
7. Use Explorer (Windows) or Finder (macOS) to move the html_css_5 folder into the murach folder.

Description

- We recommend that you store the files for this book in the folders shown above.

Figure A-1   How to install the source code for this book

How to install Visual Studio Code

Figure A-2 shows how to install Visual Studio Code (VS Code) on both Windows and macOS systems. This is the text editor that we recommend. It's free, it has many excellent features, and it runs on Windows, macOS, and Linux systems. And to help you get going with it, chapter 2 presents a short tutorial that will get you started right.

The first two procedures in this figure show how to install Visual Studio Code on Windows and macOS systems. Both procedures are straightforward so you shouldn't have any trouble with them.

The third procedure shows how to make sure Visual Studio Code and the source code for this book are installed correctly. To do that, you can use VS Code to open the book_apps folder that you've downloaded. Then, you can use the Explorer window in VS Code to expand and collapse the folders that contain the HTML and CSS files for this book.

The Visual Studio Code website

https://code.visualstudio.com

How to install Visual Studio Code on Windows

1. Go to the URL for Visual Studio Code (VS Code).
2. Click the button for downloading the Windows version and respond to any dialog boxes. This should download the exe file for the Setup program.
3. When the exe file finishes downloading, double-click on it to start the installation.
4. If you get a dialog box that indicates that this app isn't a verified app from the Microsoft Store, click the Install Anyway button.
5. If you're asked if you want to allow the program to make changes to your computer, click the Yes button.

How to install Visual Studio Code on macOS

1. Go to the URL for Visual Studio Code (VS Code).
2. Click the button for downloading the macOS version and respond to any dialog boxes. This should download the application file for Visual Studio Code.
3. Move the application file for Visual Studio Code from the Downloads folder to the Applications folder.

How to make sure your system is set up correctly

1. Start VS Code.
2. Select File→Open Folder from the menu system, and use the resulting dialog box to select this folder:
   \murach\html_css_5\book_apps
3. This should open the folder that contains all applications for this book in the Explorer window that's displayed on the left side of the main VS Code window. If this works, VS Code and the source code for this book are installed correctly.

Description

- *Visual Studio Code*, also known as *VS Code*, runs on the Windows, macOS, and Linux operating systems.
- Chapter 2 of this book presents a tutorial that will get you started with VS Code.

Figure A-2   How to install Visual Studio Code as your text editor

How to install Chrome and other browsers

If you're a Windows user, you already have the Edge browser on your computer. And if you're a macOS user, you already have the Safari browser on your computer. Chrome, however, is the most-used browser by far, so we recommend that you use it as the primary browser for testing your web pages and websites.

If you haven't already installed Chrome, figure A-3 shows how. As the last step in this procedure suggests, we recommend that you make Chrome your default browser.

You may also want to install Firefox and Opera so you can test with them too. To do that, you can use the website addresses in this figure. The procedures for installing all of these browsers are easier than ever before.

The URL for downloading Chrome

https://www.google.com/chrome

How to install Chrome

1. Go to the Chrome website and click on the link for downloading Chrome.

2. When the download finishes, run it.

3. As you step through the wizard that follows, you can accept all of the default settings.

4. When you're asked whether you want to make Chrome your default browser, we suggest that you do that.

The URL for downloading Firefox

http://www.mozilla.com

The URL for downloading Opera

http://www.opera.com

Description

- Because Chrome is the most popular browser today, we suggest that you test all the exercises for this book on that browser.

- If you have a Windows system, Edge will be on it so you can test with it too. And if you have a Mac, Safari will be on it so you can test with it.

- Because Firefox and Opera are also popular browsers, you may want to install and test with them too.

Figure A-3   How to install Chrome and other browsers

Index

F

G

H

What software you need for this book

- To enter and edit HTML and CSS, you can use any text editor, but we recommend VS Code. It is a free, runs on Windows, macOS, and Linux systems, and has many excellent features.
- To help you get started with VS Code, chapter 2 provides a short tutorial.
- To test the web pages that you develop on a Windows system, we recommend that you use Edge and Chrome. On a Mac OS system, we recommend that you use Safari and Chrome.
- Appendix A shows you how to install Chrome. It also provides the URLs for installing Firefox and Opera in case you want to use them for more testing.

The downloadable applications and files for this book

- All of the applications that are presented in this book
- All of the examples that are presented in this book
- The starting files for the exercises in this book
- The solutions for the exercises

How to download the applications and files

- Go to www.murach.com, and go to the page for Murach's HTML and CSS3 (5th Edition).
- Scroll down the page until you see the "FREE downloads" tab. Then, click on it and proceed from there.
- For more information, please see appendix A.